D1598203

REFORMING CATHOLICISM IN THE ENGLAND OF MARY TUDOR

Reforming Catholicism in the England of Mary Tudor

The Achievement of Friar Bartolomé Carranza

Edited by
JOHN EDWARDS
University of Oxford, UK

RONALD TRUMAN
Christ Church, Oxford, UK

ASHGATE

© John Edwards and Ronald Truman 2005

John Edwards and Ronald Truman have asserted their moral rights under the Copyright, Designs and Patents Act, 1988, to be identified as the editors of this work.

Published by
Ashgate Publishing Limited
Gower House
Croft Road
Aldershot
Hants GU11 3HR
England

Ashgate Publishing Company
Suite 420
101 Cherry Street
Burlington, VT 05401-4405
USA

Ashgate website: http://www.ashgate.com

British Library Cataloguing in Publication Data
Reforming Catholicism in the England of Mary Tudor : the achievement of Friar Bartolomé Carranza.—(Catholic Christendom, 1300–1700)
1. Carranza, Bartolomé, 1503–1576 —Congresses 2. Catholic Church—England—History—16th century—Congresses 3.England—Church history—16th century—Congresses 4.Great Britain—History—Mary I, 1553–1558
I.Edwards, John, 1949– II.Truman, R.W.
282.4'2'09031

Library of Congress Cataloging-in-Publication Data
Reforming Catholicism in the England of Mary Tudor : the achievement of Friar Bartolomé Carranza / edited by John Edwards and Ronald Truman.
    p. cm. — (Catholic Christendom, 1300–1700)
 Includes bibliographical references and index.
 ISBN 0-7546-5236-X (alk. paper)
1. Carranza, Bartolomé, 1503–1576. 2. Catholic Church—England—History—16th century. 3. England—Church history—16th century. 4. Great Britain—History—Mary I, 1553–1558. I. Edwards, John,
1949–II. Truman, R. W. III. Series.

BX4705.C316R44 2005
282'.42'09031—dc22

2004026334

ISBN 0 7546 5236 X

Printed and bound in Great Britain by MPG Books Ltd, Bodmin, Cornwall

Contents

Series Editor's Preface

The still-usual emphasis on medieval (or Catholic) and reformation (or Protestant) religious history has meant neglect of the middle ground, both chronological and ideological. As a result, continuities between the middle ages and early modern Europe have been overlooked in favor of emphasis on radical discontinuities. Further, especially in the later period, the identification of 'reformation' with various kinds of Protestantism means that the vitality and creativity of the established church, whether in its Roman or local manifestations, has been left out of account. In the last few years, an upsurge of interest in the history of traditional (or catholic) religion makes these inadequacies in received scholarship even more glaring and in need of systematic correction. The series will attempt this by covering all varieties of religious behavior, broadly interpreted, not just (or even especially) traditional institutional and doctrinal church history. It will to the maximum degree possible be interdisciplinary, comparative and global, as well as non-confessional. The goal is to understand religion, primarily of the 'Catholic' variety, as a broadly human phenomenon, rather than as a privileged mode of access to superhuman realms, even implicitly.

The period covered, 1300-1700, embraces the moment which saw an almost complete transformation of the place of religion in the life of Europeans, whether considered as a system of beliefs, as an institution, or as a set of social and cultural practices. In 1300, vast numbers of Europeans, from the pope down, fully expected Jesus's return and the beginning of His reign on earth. By 1700, very few Europeans, of whatever level of education, would have subscribed to such chiliastic beliefs. Pierre Bayle's notorious sarcasms about signs and portents are not idiosyncratic. Likewise, in 1300 the vast majority of Europeans probably regarded the pope as their spiritual head; the institution he headed was probably the most tightly integrated and effective bureaucracy in Europe. Most Europeans were at least nominally Christian, and the pope had at least nominal knowledge of that fact. The papacy, as an institution, played a central role in high politics, and the clergy in general formed an integral part of most governments, whether central or local. By 1700, Europe was divided into a myriad of different religious allegiances, and even those areas officially subordinate to the pope were both more nominally Catholic in belief (despite colossal efforts at imposing uniformity) and also in allegiance than they had been four hundred years earlier. The pope had become only one political factor, and not one of the first rank. The clergy, for its part, had virtually disappeared from secular governments as well as losing much of its local authority. The stage was set for the Enlightenment.

Thomas F. Mayer,
Augustana College

List of Contributors

John Edwards. Research Fellow in Spanish at the University of Oxford, and formerly Reader in Spanish History at the University of Birmingham, he is the author of several books and articles on the religious and social history of Spain in the fifteenth and sixteenth centuries, and a Corresponding Member of the Spanish Royal Academy of History.

Dermot Fenlon. Now a member of the Congregation of the Oratory in Birmingham, he taught early modern history in Cambridge and Church history at Oscott College. Author of *Heresy and obedience in Tridentine Italy: Cardinal Pole and the Counter-Reformation* (1972), he is a Fellow of the Institute for Advanced Research in the Humanities at the University of Birmingham.

Andrew Hegarty. Currently Assistant Editor of a new history of Magdalen College, Oxford, he is completing a biographical register of St John's College, Oxford, 1557–1660. His research focuses on the early modern universities of Oxford, Salamanca, and Paris.

David Loades. Director of the British Academy John Foxe Project, he is Professor Emeritus of the University of Wales and Honorary Research Professor of the University of Sheffield. His publications include *Mary Tudor: A life* (1989) and *The reign of Mary Tudor* (1991).

Thomas F. Mayer. Professor of History at Augustana College, Rock Island, Illinois and Director of the Center for the Study of the Christian Millennium, he is the author of *Reginald Pole: Prince and prophet* (2000) and editor of *The correspondence of Reginald Pole* (2002–).

Patrick Preston. Research Fellow in Church History in the Department of Theology and Ministry, University College, Chichester, he has published several articles on aspects of Italian history in the sixteenth century, and in particular on Ambrosius Catharinus.

José Ignacio Tellechea Idígoras. A native of the Basque provinces, where he was ordained priest, he is Emeritus Professor of Church History at the Pontifical University of Salamanca and a Corresponding Member of the Spanish Royal Academy of History. He has devoted much of his life to the study of Fray Bartolomé Carranza (see Preface).

Ronald Truman. Emeritus Fellow of Christ Church, Oxford, and formerly Tutorial Fellow and University Lecturer in Spanish at Oxford, he is the author of various studies of the intellectual and religious history of early modern Spain, among them an edition of Felipe de la Torre, *Institución de un rey christiano* (1979) and *Spanish treatises on government on religion and government in the time of Philip II: The 'de regimine principum' and associated traditions* (1999).

William Wizeman. A member of the Society of Jesus, he completed his University of Oxford doctoral thesis, 'Recalled to life: The theology and spirituality of Mary Tudor's Church', in 2002. He is Assistant Professor of Historical Theology at Fordham University, New York, and is currently preparing his thesis for publication by Ashgate.

Lucy Wooding. Lecturer in Early Modern History at King's College, London, she is the author of *Rethinking Catholicism in Reformation England* (2000).

Anthony Wright. Reader in Ecclesiastical History at the University of Leeds, he is the author of *The Counter-Reformation: Catholic Europe and the non-Christian world* (1982), *Catholicism and Spanish society under the reign of Philip II and Philip III* (1991), and *The early modern Papacy from the Council of Trent to the French Revolution* (2000).

Preface

The papers in this volume were first delivered at a Symposium entitled 'An Apostle of Reform: Fray Bartolomé Carranza in the England of Mary Tudor', held on 26–9 March 2001. Scholars from Spain, the United States, and Britain assembled at Christ Church, Oxford, to discuss Carranza's activities and achievements in England, and to place them in the religious and political context of Mary Tudor's joint reign with Philip of Spain. The keynote paper was given by Father José Ignacio Tellechea Idígoras, Emeritus Professor of Church History at the Pontifical University of Salamanca, and pioneer and originator of modern studies of the Navarrese friar.

Professor Tellechea was born in 1928 at San Sebastián, on the north coast of Spain, into a family with deep roots in the Basque Country. His first school was in the building where his sister and family still occupy an apartment. In 1934 the Tellecheas moved to Ituren, a village in northern Navarre where Don Ignacio attended the school and where, in later years, he would spend every August and September in his study in the family home, working on his most recent archival discoveries for publication. Already in 1940 he had decided to seek ordination and the following year he entered the Seminary at Vitoria, in those days full of ordinands, where he was to spend the next ten years—'ten years of total isolation from the world, without radios or newspapers', he recalls—but with access, exceptional in the seminaries of Spain of that time, to an abundance of books and European learned journals. It was here that he read, among so much else, the learned Prof. Dr Hans Lietzmann's four-volume manual of Church History… by special permission of the Rector, the work being by a Protestant author. Ordained priest on St Peter's Day 1951, he went on to spend five years in Rome at the Gregorian University, studying Theology and Church History, and exploring the great libraries around him. It was there that he began his investigation of hitherto unregarded archive material, and he recalls that it was on 6 March 1952 that he made his first discovery of the Carranza manuscripts that have so much occupied him over the following fifty years and more. His career as a university and seminary teacher began in 1956. For a decade he divided his time between seminaries in San Sebastián and Madrid, with a lengthy visit each summer to the libraries and archives of Rome. In 1966 he succeeded Professor Luis Sala Balust as a professor at the Pontifical University of Salamanca, whose resonant name disguised, both then and afterwards, its proverbial poverty and the exiguousness of its stipends. He continued in this post until his retirement in 1988, teaching one day a week in Vitoria, at the new Theology Faculty there.

Since his retirement he has extended his huge bibliography by well over two hundred further items, as the list of his 149 works connected with Carranza, published in 2002, bears testimony... and in which each volume of his great edition of the documents relating to Carranza's *proceso* is but a single entry.[1] Time and again a hitherto quite unknown document, brought to light by Professor Tellechea, has opened up wholly new perspectives and new possibilities for further investigation. A notable early example of this, for which many scholars have special reason to be grateful, is his 1963 article on 'Spaniards at Louvain, 1551–1558', centred on a long report that a Spanish Dominican wrote for the Inquisition about his former Spanish associates in the Low Countries.[2] The frequent references to a number of Professor Tellechea's studies in this present volume bear similar witness. The sheer scale of his output is astonishing—all the more so when one recalls his grave illness of the 1980s, when he received the Last Rites more than once. Upon his recovery, he rapidly completed his 400-page study of St Ignatius Loyola, published in 1986 and now translated into seven languages, including Hungarian, Japanese, and Basque.

He has himself pointed out that his work on Carranza amounts to no more than a quarter of his publications, but he would probably allow that, even when so much of the rest represents a contribution of the first order as regards the religious history of his country (this very much including his own native Basque Province of Guipúzcoa), his work on Carranza is of special importance, for the world of scholarship and for himself. It represents the remarkable achievement of one man working alone and betokens a personal commitment to the investigation of the facts and issues and significance of the Carranza *cause* that is quite out of the ordinary. It should be recalled that this dedicated investigation was pursued over many years when neither the secular nor the ecclesiastical powers in Spain were much disposed to look with favour

---

1   'Bibliografía de José Ignacio Tellechea sobre Carranza', in José Ignacio Tellechea Idígoras, *Fray Bartolomé Carranza de Miranda (investigaciones históricas)*, Historia 109 (Pamplona: Gobierno de Navarra, Departamento de Educación y Cultura, 2002), pp. 519–24; also id. (ed.), *Fray Bartolomé Carranza: Documentos históricos*, 7 vols, Archivo Documental Español 18 etc. (Madrid: Real Academia de la Historia, 1962–94), VII.

2   José Ignacio Tellechea Idígoras, 'Españoles en Lovaina en 1551–1558: Primeras noticias sobre el bayanismo', *Revista Española de Teología*, 23, pp. 21–45. See also id., 'Españoles en Lovaina en 1557', in *Encuentros en Flandes: Relaciones e intercambios hispanoflamencos a inicios de la Edad Moderna*, ed. Werner Tomas and Robert A. Verdonk, Avisos de Flandes 6 (Louvain/Leuven: Leuven University Press and Fundación Duques de Soria, 2000), pp. 133–55.

on the approach to Spain's religious history in that country's 'Golden Age' which Professor Tellechea's work embodied. It helped a good deal that, in time, he had the episcopal support of Mgr José María Setien, when that fellow student and friend of his became Bishop of San Sebastián. Fifty years on, in contrast with earlier difficult times, one of Tellechea's university pupils, Mgr Antonio Cañizares, holds Carranza's former post as Archbishop of Toledo and Primate of Spain, and, thanks to the intervention of the previous Archbishop, Cardinal Marcelo González, the remains of Fray Bartolomé now lie not in Rome, but in the primatial cathedral over which he so briefly presided in person.

Spanish scholarship has long since liberated itself from the antagonistic rigidities of outlook represented and long perpetuated by Marcelino Menéndez y Pelayo's *History of the heterodox of Spain*, whose opening volume went on bearing on its title-page (in successive editions published *'con censura eclesiástica'*), a Biblical text: 'They went out from us but were not of us' (I John 2:19). Professor Tellechea's work has contributed greatly to that evolution, by its sheer scale and scholarly distinction, of course, but also by its insistence on grounding the study and discussion of religious history on the tireless, open-minded investigation—and publication—of primary material. Thanks to his dedication, a vast amount of new documentary evidence has been brought within our reach, to extend our knowledge and deepen our sense of the complexities and challenges to interpretation that lie within it. Don Ignacio has never tired of the search or indeed lost his sense of excitement and delight in pursuing it. On his journey from Salamanca to Oxford for this Symposium, he found time to call in at the great archive of Simancas and reported, on his arrival here, that in those few hours he had come upon another *'precioso documento'*. He was reporting other finds as he stepped into the coach taking him back to Heathrow Airport. May he be granted many years yet to continue the quest, with undiminished enthusiasm, energy, and eyesight (he still has no need of glasses) and to enrich us still further with an erudition which, in its own ample field, is without equal.

Acknowledgements

The editors wish to express their gratitude to all those who helped to make the 2001 Carranza Symposium a success, and in particular to those who gave papers and those who chaired sessions and otherwise participated in the discussions. Thanks are due in the first place to the Governing Body of Christ Church for allowing the Symposium to take place in the college and to benefit from the privileged terms that it makes available for occasions of this kind. The Symposium had a particularly friendly and constructive atmosphere, and this was greatly encouraged by the care and service given by the Steward and staff of Christ Church. Thanks are also owed to Mr Robert Webb and the Oxford Cathedral Singers for changing their Evensong music at short notice to provide settings of special interest. The evening spent by participants in the Symposium in The Queen's College contained two highlights, and thus especial thanks go to the Organist and Praelector in Music at Queen's, Dr Owen Rees, for organizing a concert of relevant music, sung in Chapel by his choir, A Capella Portuguesa, and to the Provost of the College, Sir Alan Budd, for hosting a reception afterwards in his Lodgings.

Gratitude is also here expressed to those who supported the Oxford Carranza Symposium financially, particularly the Faculty of Medieval and Modern Languages, the Faculty of Modern History, and Professor Robert Evans, whose Regius Fund provided a reception in Christ Church. The editors wish to thank Professor Ian Michael for organizing support for this publication from Spanish Funds, and to the former Cultural Attaché at the Spanish Embassy in London, Señor Ramón Abaroa, himself a descendant of the Carranza family, for arranging further financial support.

The editors cannot adequately express their gratitude to Dr Nigel Griffin, who has selflessly and indefatigably worked to help them bring this book to publication, and they are deeply grateful to Mr John Smedley at Ashgate, for his enthusiasm and readiness to take on the project. The Ashgate staff have been helpful and efficient in producing this book, and the editors, of course, offer their appreciative thanks to them as well.

Oxford, 2 May 2004
being the Feast of St Athanasius and the 428th
anniversary of the death of Fray Bartolomé Carranza de Miranda

John Edwards
Ronald Truman

Abbreviations

ACDF	Archivio della Congregazione per la Dottrina della Fede, Vatican City
ASV	Archivio Segreto Vaticano, Vatican City
BAC	Biblioteca de Autores Cristianos
BAV	Biblioteca Apostolica Vaticana, Vatican City
BI	Borthwick Institute, University of York
BL	British Library, London
BNM	Biblioteca Nacional de España, Madrid
CPRPM	*Calendar of Patent Rolls, Philip and Mary*
CSPD	*Calendar of State Papers, Domestic*
CSPS	*Calendar of State Papers, Spanish*
CSPV	*Calendar of State Papers, Venetian*
LMA	London Metropolitan Archives, London
NA	The National Archives, London (formerly Public Record Office)
OB	Bodleian Library, Oxford
OUA	Oxford University Archives, Oxford

Fray Bartolomé Carranza de Miranda: A biographical outline

1503	Born, to noble (*hidalgo*) parents, Pedro de Carranza and María Musgo, in Miranda de Arga (Navarre).
1515	Matriculated at the Colegio de San Eugenio in the University of Alcalá de Henares.
1521	Professed, at the convent of Benalaque, as a member of the Order of Preachers (Dominicans).
by 1525	Member of the Dominican Colegio de San Gregorio, in the University of Valladolid.
1533	Regent of Studies at San Gregorio.
1539	Received his Order's degree of Master of Theology, in the Dominican church of Santa Maria sopra Minerva, Rome.
1540	Once more in San Gregorio, Valladolid; distributed relief during a famine.
1542	Declined Emperor Charles V's offer of the bishopric of Cuzco (Peru).
1545–8	Attended the First Period of the Council of Trent, as theologian for Charles V.
1548	Declined Charles's request to become bishop of the Canary Islands, or confessor to Prince Philip.
1550	Elected Dominican Provincial of Castile.
1551–3	Imperial theologian in the second period of the Council of Trent.
1553–4	Royal chaplain and Court preacher in Valladolid.
1554	Accompanied Prince Philip to England as an ecclesiastical adviser and as representative of the General of the Dominican Order.
1557	Left England for Flanders: at Philip's urging and, on his nomination, succeeded Juan Martínez de Silíceo as Archbishop of Toledo and Primate of Spain.
1558	Published in Antwerp his *Commentaries on the Christian Catechism*.
	Returned to Spain to take up his post in Toledo (October).
1559	Arrested by the Inquisition in Torrelaguna, north of Madrid (22 August).

1559–66 Investigated and tried by the Spanish Inquisition in Valladolid.

1566–76 Trial continued by the Papal Inquisition in Rome.

1576   On 14 April, abjured sixteen 'heretical' propositions and was released into the custody of the Dominicans at Santa Maria sopra Minerva in Rome, where he died on 2 May.

Carranza in England

John Edwards

Bartolomé Carranza de Miranda is still, despite the massive efforts, over more than five decades, of Professor José Ignacio Tellechea (see Preface), only beginning to be fully recognized as a historical figure, even in his native Spain. There, as elsewhere, if he is known at all, his place in history is still generally seen as being owed to the fact that he was the subject of what was described in 1972, on the publicity wrapper which surrounded the dust-jackets of Tellechea's two-volume edition of his *Catechism*, as 'the Spanish Inquisition's most famous trial'.[1] Certainly, it was not normal for inquisitors to arrest an archbishop, and Carranza's trial, over nearly seventeen years, between 1559 and 1576 (see below, Chapters 10 and 11), was not lacking in drama, from the time of his arrest on 22 August 1559, in Torrelaguna (thirty miles north of Madrid) under night-time curfew, through his contested transfer to Rome in 1566–7, to his final brief period of freedom there in April 1576, during which he celebrated the sacraments once more as a priest, after an enforced hiatus of nearly seventeen years. Yet if the archiepiscopal prisoner is only just becoming known as a rounded Christian personality in Spain in general and his native Navarre in particular, his role in England, as an adviser to Philip of Spain in the reign of Mary Tudor, is even more of a novelty to the many who interest themselves, professionally or more generally, in sixteenth-century English history. In the midst of that history, though, Carranza most certainly belongs.

When, in July 1553, Mary Tudor seized the throne of England from Lady Jane Grey, whom her half-brother Edward VI had designated as his successor, she was already thirty-seven years old, and marriage was clearly a high priority. Not only were her child-bearing years nearly over, but, as the first fully effective female ruler of England, she went against the prevailing values even of the most *avant-garde* Renaissance Humanists.[2] It was thus generally assumed

1 Bartolomé Carranza de Miranda, *Comentarios sobre el Catechismo christiano*, ed. José Ignacio Tellechea Idígoras, 2 vols, BAC 1 (Madrid: Editorial Católico, 1972).
2 David Loades, *The chronicles of the Tudor Queens* (Stroud: Sutton Publishing, 2002), pp. 22–4; Sharon L. Jansen, *The monstrous regiment of women: Female rulers in early modern Europe* (Basingstoke: Palgrave Macmillan, 2002).

that she would need a husband to carry out for her those duties and functions of government which were unfitting for a woman. In these circumstances, the only realistic options were an English subject or a foreign prince, but while the Court and Parliament were strongly in favour of the former, despite a fear of reviving internal political conflict of the kind that had been seen in the fifteenth-century 'Wars of the Roses', the Queen was known to be likely to look abroad. For twenty years, since her troubled childhood amidst the torments of her mother, Catherine of Aragon, she had regarded the Emperor Charles V as a source of emotional as well as political support, and her search for a husband coincided with his preoccupation with the Habsburg succession in general and his son Philip's future role in particular. Although Philip was eleven years younger than Mary, a marriage alliance between them had its attractions for Charles, if not for his son. Not only would England be restored ecclesiastically to the Roman obedience, but the Habsburgs would gain control of the vital central passage of the English Channel, between Calais and Dover, thus further hemming in the power of France. As Susan Brigden puts it, 'this would be Habsburg conquest of England by marriage'.[3]

Prince Philip had already been married once. In December 1542 he was betrothed to Princess Maria of Portugal and the couple were married in Salamanca on 12 November 1543. However, the unfortunate queen, who seems not to have got on well with her husband, suffered a haemorrhage while giving birth to their son, the ill-fated Don Carlos, and died on 12 July 1545. After that, Philip had remained a widower, with the reputation, hard to imagine in his later years, of having a taste for the ladies. However, when Mary Tudor unexpectedly ascended the English throne, negotiations were already under way for Philip to marry another Portuguese princess called Maria. Indeed, in a letter dated 9 September 1553, the Imperial ambassador in London, Simon Renard, wrote to the Imperial chancellor, Antoine Perrenot de Granvelle:

> It is said that the marriage negotiations of His Highness [Prince Philip, with the Infanta Maria of Portugal] are so far advanced that it will be impossible to withdraw, in which case to mention him might disincline the Queen [Mary] from following His Majesty's advice, which she is at present very anxious to know, desiring to hear what aspirant he will propose.

In other words, if Mary heard of Philip's Portuguese plans, she might frustrate the Emperor's design by marrying someone else, English or foreign. Nevertheless, the idea of Mary's marrying Philip had evidently already been broached, at least at Charles's Court, and apparently in the English Court as well. Renard had, probably rightly, gained the impression that many of the

---

3   Susan Brigden, *New worlds, lost worlds: The rule of the Tudors, 1485–1603*, Penguin History of Britain 5 (London: Allen Lane), p. 201.

Queen's Council were anxious to avoid an alliance with Philip, preferring, if a Habsburg marriage was to take place, that it should be with his brother Ferdinand, King of the Romans, or else with this future Emperor's son, also called Ferdinand. In a further despatch to Charles, dated 5 October 1553, Renard reaffirmed that 'the Queen would not marry without your Majesty's advice', but also that Lord William Paget, prominent in Mary's Council, was generally against Philip's candidacy, on the grounds that the Prince of Spain was too young—he was 26—and spoke no English.[4] Nevertheless, before October was out, an agreement had been made with the Emperor's agents that Philip and Mary should marry. Both parties were in need of the alliance. The Queen was getting no younger, and was anxious both to restore her kingdom as soon as possible to the Roman obedience and also to produce a male heir who would exclude her half-sister Elizabeth from the succession to the Crown. Despite her advanced age according to the conditions of the time, Mary still believed that she could bear a child, and she was also convinced that she needed a husband if she was fully to exercise the role of an English monarch. Charles, on the other hand, saw a marriage between Mary and Philip as the best way of reviving the fifteenth-century alliance between England and Burgundy. Such was his anxiety for this outcome that the ageing Emperor acted with unaccustomed speed—such speed, in fact, that he failed to inform Philip of the plan until negotiations were well advanced. Indeed, it was not until January 1554 that the Count of Egmont, who was representing Charles in London, wrote to enlighten the Prince as to his marital destiny.

Philip was furious, both at not being consulted and at the identity of his planned spouse. Mary was thirty-seven years of age, to his twenty-six, and not, at least by this time, noted for her good looks. Also, Renard had indeed been right to suppose, some months previously, that the Prince had nearly completed his own negotiations to marry the Infanta Maria of Portugal. His father's plan, however, envisaged that any child of Philip and Mary Tudor would inherit England and the Habsburg possessions in the Netherlands. If Philip's existing son, Don Carlos, failed to produce an heir, the child of the English marriage would also inherit the Crowns of Spain (Castile, Aragon, and Navarre) and the Spanish possessions overseas. In any case, once he had become Mary's husband, Philip himself would only be king-consort, without regal powers in England, all of which would remain with the Queen. A condition of the agreement was that England should not in future engage in warfare against Habsburg interests. Philip would much have preferred to marry the Infanta Maria, thus uniting Spain and Portugal (as would indeed happen under his rule in 1580), and the rebellion led by Sir Thomas Wyatt, which started in Kent late in January 1554, briefly, if inadvertently, offered him a possible way out.

4   *CSPS*, XI. 227–9, cited in Loades, *Chronicles of the Tudor Queens*, pp. 25–6.

News of this significant gentry rebellion, and news also that Wyatt was heading towards London, with about 4000 men and explicitly in order to prevent the 'Spanish marriage', seems to have reached Mary's Council at once, on 25 January. The extreme vulnerability of her regime was immediately exposed, with a number of suspects, including prominent subjects such as the Marquis of Northampton, being arrested, or else fleeing to avoid incarceration. The strategically vital Dover castle was in rebel hands from the start, and, the next day, news reached London that Wyatt's men had seized the crucial bridge over the Medway at Rochester. On Saturday 27 January, 500 'white-coats', or City levies, were assembled at Leadenhall to defend London, being despatched to Rochester the next day. According to the anonymous *Chronicle of Queen Jane*, even many of these supposed defenders of London shared the rebels' antipathy towards Philip and his countrymen; their commander, named Bret, made a speech to the troops before battle in which he expressed the evidently widely-shared view, so often repeated against enemies throughout history, that:

> yf we should be under their subjection they wolde, as slaves and villaynes, spoyle us of our goodes and landes, ravyshe our wyfes before our faces, and deflowre our daughters in our presence.[5]

Yet despite the defection of Bret's Londoners, Wyatt's rebellion, which was originally intended to be paralleled by uprisings in Leicestershire, Devon, and the Welsh Marches, began prematurely, and was soon crushed, after a conspicuous display of courage by Queen Mary, which was entirely worthy both of her mother Catherine facing Scottish invasion in 1513 and her grandmother Isabella during the Granada war of 1482–92. Her decisiveness at this stage saved her capital and, had her reign lasted longer, Mary's speech at the City Guildhall, delivered on 1 February, would probably be as legendary as her half-sister Elizabeth's Tilbury discourse, spoken against, not for, the Spanish in 1588, later became. At the time, it certainly stiffened the Londoners' resistance and, two days later, when Wyatt and his men reached Southwark, they found London Bridge blocked by a raised drawbridge and cannon. After a stand-off lasting three days, the rebel leader took his forces up-river to the next bridge, at Kingston, doubling back to attack Westminster and London from the west. Although some of his troops passed near her palace of White-hall, and given the feebleness of the guards might easily have captured it, Mary was saved. In Christopher Haigh's words, 'the Protestants had played the Spanish card, and lost', but it remained to be seen how severe Mary's retribution would be, and how the marriage project would proceed.[6] For many, in

---

5   Cited in Loades, *Chronicles of the Tudor Queens*, p. 35.
6   Christopher Haigh, *English Reformations: Religion, politics, and society under the Tudors* (Oxford: Clarendon Press, 1993), p. 222.

fact, feeling against the prospect of Philip as king seems to have been more important than matters of religion.

In the event, firstly, Wyatt himself was executed for treason, along with about two hundred of his followers, and Princess Elizabeth, who appears not to have taken any part in the rebellion but to have known about it, was imprisoned in the Tower of London on suspicion of treason.[7] Against this backdrop of violence, the Spanish marriage was nevertheless to go ahead, Philip having most reluctantly accepted his father's orders. By the beginning of April 1554 English ambassadors had gone to Spain with a view to escorting him to their kingdom. In return, Philip sent Mary a jewel, by the hand of the Marquis of Las Navas. The Prince, though, still viewed the voyage to England with the greatest foreboding, not only objecting strongly to the terms of the marriage agreement but also, not unreasonably in view of Wyatt's recent rebellion, fearing for his personal safety in the 'sceptred isle'. Thus, on the day after he had signed the marriage treaty, he also signed a further document, in which he declared his earlier signature to be null and void, on the grounds that he had never agreed to some of the terms included in it.[8] In addition, as a precaution, he proposed to take to England an immediate household of about 4000 people. In Henry Kamen's words, 'he apparently thought the proposed retinue was modest, but was later persuaded that it looked more like an invasion force'.[9] The Prince seems not to have realized that the English would provide him with a complete household as well. Having summoned his widowed sister Joanna (Juana) from Portugal to Valladolid to act as regent, and leaving the Castilian parliament (Cortes) in session there, he headed for Galicia to meet the fleet of 125 ships which had been assembled at A Coruña (Corunna), under the command of Álvaro de Bazán. It set sail for England on 12 July 1554, Philip being accompanied by a still considerable number of courtiers and nearly 4000 troops. At the rear of the convoy, as it headed north across the bay of Biscay, was an escort of thirty warships, completing a fairly awe-inspiring force. Some of the flower of the Spanish nobility went to England with Philip. In his own ship, for example, were Gómez Suárez de Figueroa, Count of Feria, who would later marry an Englishwoman from Buckinghamshire, Jane Dormer, and Ruy Gómez de Silva, who was then Count of Melito but is better known as Prince of Eboli, and as a result of his time with Philip in England, would become the King's most notable, and durable, favourite (*privado*).[10] Also among the courtiers in Philip's ship were

7   Loades, *Chronicles of the Tudor Queens*, pp. 39–41.
8   Patrick Williams, *Philip II*, European History in Perspective (Basingstoke: Palgrave, 2001), pp. 21–3.
9   Kamen, *Philip of Spain* (New Haven CT and London: Yale University Press, 1997), p. 56.
10 James M. Boyden, *The courtier and the king: Ruy Gómez de Silva, Philip II and the Court of Spain* (Berkeley and Los Angeles CA: University of California Press, 1995); id., '"Fortune

Antonio de Toledo, Prior of the Spanish Military Orders (by this time effectively Crown property), Juan de Benavides, Marquis of Cortes, Don Alonso de Aguilar, the royal secretary Pedro de Hoyo, the chief quartermaster (*aposentador mayor*) Luis Venegas, the chief steward (*mayordomo mayor*) Gutierre López de Padilla, and the chief almoner (*limosnero mayor*) Lupercio de Quiñones. However, the fleet also contained numerous churchmen, including Don Pedro de Castro, bishop of Cuenca, Don Fernando de Valdés, archbishop of Seville and Inquisitor General of Spain, Dr Bartolomé Torres, future bishop of the Canary Islands, and several friars. Among the latter were two Franciscans, Fray Alonso de Castro and Fray Bernardo Fresneda, and two Dominicans, Fray Juan de Villagarcía and his teacher (*maestro*), Fray Bartolomé Carranza de Miranda.[11]

Bartolomé Carranza, as he will generally be known in this volume, was born (see above, p. xix), probably in 1503, in the small town of Miranda de Arga, in the Pyrenean kingdom of Navarre, the southern part of which was to be annexed by Castile after 1512. His surname indicates origins in the Basque lordship (*señorío*) of Vizcaya, and he was the son of Pedro Carranza and María Musco. His family appears to have been part of the minor nobility (*hidalguía*), and also to have been 'Old Christian' (*cristiano viejo*), which meant that they had no acknowledged or then identifiable Jewish or Muslim ancestry. Bartolomé's mother died while he was still a child, and his father married again, but, as Andrew Hegarty notes below (p. 154), the beginning of the boy's career was the help which received from his uncle, Sancho Carranza de Miranda. Sancho, already a canon of Calahorra Cathedral, invited young Bartolomé to the University of Alcalá de Henares, near Madrid, which had been founded in 1499 by the Franciscan Cardinal Francisco Jiménez de Cisneros, and had begun to function in 1508. The younger Carranza matriculated at the College of San Eugenio, where he studied the undergraduate subjects of Grammar and the Arts. In that theologically-orientated university, he soon acquired a reputation for exceptional Christian devotion, and some of his contemporaries apparently mocked what they regarded as his exaggerated Lenten observances. Bartolomé completed his Arts course in 1520, and seemed to be heading for a cathedral or university career, but, in the following year, apparently surprised everyone by joining the Order of Preachers. His uncle Sancho was strongly opposed to this decision, and enlisted some of his fellow professors at Alcalá to put pressure on his nephew, but all was in vain, as the teenager was completely

---

has stripped you of your splendour": Favourites and their fates in fifteenth- and sixteenth-century Spain', in *The world of the favourite*, ed. John H. Elliott and Laurence W. B. Brockliss (New Haven CT and London: Yale University Press, 1999), pp. 26–37.

11 José Ignacio Tellechea Idígoras, *Fray Bartolomé Carranza y el cardenal Pole: Un navarro en la restauración católica de Inglaterra (1554–1558)* (Pamplona: Diputación Foral de Navarra, Institución Príncipe de Viana, and CSIC, 1977), pp. 27, 29.

determined to retain the Dominican habit, which he was to do until his dying day. He duly made his profession in that year, in the now-vanished convent of Benalaque. From this time until his appointment as archbishop of Toledo, he was generally known as Bartolomé de Miranda.

By 1525, Bartolomé was at San Gregorio in Valladolid, as an elected member of that prestigious Dominican university college.[12] He had professed in the Order of Preachers in the midst of the disturbances associated with the 'Comunero' rebellion in Castile, in which some major towns took on the government of Charles V, but there was also turmoil at that time in Castilian religious and academic life. Much of this controversy, though by no means all of it, centred round the work of the Christian Humanist from the Netherlands, Desiderius Erasmus (c. 1466–1536). As is well known, Erasmus's ideas quickly began to influence Spanish religious and intellectual life through his admirers and disciples at Charles V's Court. The Dutchman's views aroused hostility as well as enthusiasm, though, and one of his prominent Spanish opponents was Bartolomé's uncle Sancho. It was natural, in these circumstances, that Sancho Carranza should have been invited by the then Inquisitor General, Archbishop Alonso Manrique de Lara of Seville, to take part in the conference which was held in Valladolid, in June to August of 1527, to examine and judge Erasmus's works. During these proceedings, which were never completed, Sancho Carranza appeared to be less blankly hostile to Erasmus than he had formerly been. Nevertheless, and typically in the case of leading Spanish churchmen at that time, he managed to combine a relative theological openness at Valladolid with action, in the following year, as an inquisitor in the diocese of Calahorra, during which he became a notable persecutor of witches, believing that human pacts with the Devil really existed.[13] In the sphere of religious repression, his nephew Bartolomé, too, would need to be watched in the future.

---

12 Carranza, *Comentarios*, I. 10–11.

13 Marcel Bataillon, *Érasme et l'Espagne: Nouvelle édition en trois volumes*, ed. Daniel Devoto and Charles Amiel, Travaux d'Humanisme et Renaissance 250 (Geneva: Librairie Droz, 1991), esp. I. 253–7, 285, 295, 298–9; Miguel Avilés Fernández, *Erasmo y la Inquisición (El libelo de Valladolid y la Apologia de Erasmo contra los frailes españoles)*, Publicaciones de la FUE: Documentos Históricos 10 (Madrid: Fundación Universitaria Española 1980); id., 'Erasmo y los teólogos españoles', in *El erasmismo en España: Ponencias del coloquio celebrado en la Biblioteca de Menéndez Pelayo del 10 al 14 de junio de 1985*, ed. Manuel Revuelta Sañudo and Ciriaco Morón Arroyo, Estudios de Literatura y Pensamiento Hispánicos 5 (Santander: Sociedad Menéndez Pelayo, 1986), pp. 175–93; Erika Rummel, *Erasmus and his Catholic critics*, 2 vols, Biblioteca Humanistica et Reformatorica 45 (Nieuwkoop: De Graaf, 1989), II. 91, 149; Lu Ann Homza, *Religious authority in the Spanish Renaissance*, Johns Hopkins University Studies in Historical and Political Science, 118th s. 1 (Baltimore MD and London: The Johns Hopkins Press, 2000), pp. 49–76.

Tellechea notes that, in the years around 1530, the young Dominican immersed himself, apparently approvingly, in Erasmus's works, and particularly in his *Paraphrases of the New Testament*, which would soon be taken up by Cranmer and other English Reformers.[14] At this time, Bartolomé appeared to be pursuing an academic career, which must have pleased his uncle, even if his choice of the Dominican Order did not. In 1530, he was teaching Arts, but three years later he became Regent of Theology, soon afterwards being promoted to *Regente mayor* at San Gregorio. Basing himself on contemporary and later sources, Tellechea judges that Carranza was sympathetic to 'Erasmian' ideas at this time, though he regarded Holy Scripture, and the works of the Dominican Doctor, St Thomas Aquinas, as the twin pillars of his religious faith and practice. Significantly for the future, Carranza also devoted much study at this time to the Fathers of the Church, and was evidently enthused by the then current search, in circles that would subsequently be divided into 'Catholic' and 'Protestant', for the true character of the 'Primitive Church' (*Ecclesia primaeva*). Also during the 1530s, Fray Bartolomé became a consultant (*consultor*), on possibly heretical books, to the Valladolid tribunal of the Spanish Inquisition. Thus he began his lengthy acquaintance with the religious controversies of that turbulent century, which were eventually to cost him so dearly.[15] At this time, though, the scholarly, austere, religiously and socially conscientious friar appeared to have immense and bright prospects ahead of him. In 1539, he paid his first visit to Rome, to attend the General Chapter of his Order. There, in the Dominican church of Santa Maria sopra Minerva, he was granted by his brothers their Order's own, highly prestigious, degree of Master of Theology, in the presence of Cardinal Giampietro Carafa, the future Pope Paul IV, who was later to become his nemesis. The two adversaries would eventually lie in this same church.

On his return to the routine of San Gregorio in Valladolid, Carranza soon had an opportunity to display another of his governing characteristics, which was a practical social conscience. In 1540, famine afflicted the city, and Fray Bartolomé personally welcomed to his convent, and subsequently fed, forty poor people. San Gregorio joined forces with the neighbouring parish of Santiago to administer relief, and Carranza worked with its parish priest to care for the sick, obtaining doctors and medicines for them, but eventually falling ill himself. As a teacher at San Gregorio, he is said to have been so open to his pupils that he allowed them to consult his books and manuscripts

14 Basil Hall, 'Cranmer's relations with Erasmianism and Lutheranism', in *Thomas Cranmer: Churchman and scholar*, ed. Paul Ayris and David Selwyn (Woodbridge: The Boydell Press, 1993), pp. 3–37 (pp. 11–12).

15 On Carranza's reading see José Ignacio Tellechea Idígoras, 'La biblioteca del arzobispo Carranza', in *Miscelánea conmemorativa del Concilio de Trento (1563–1963): Estudios y documentos* (Madrid and Barcelona: CISC Instituto Enrique Flórez, 1963), pp. 458–99.

even in his absence—a generosity, as Tellechea notes, that would damage him when his activities later came under inquisitorial review. During the 1540s, Carranza became known at Court, as well as to his Dominican brothers and to the citizens of Valladolid, as a confessor and spiritual adviser, and also as a fine preacher, both within and outside San Gregorio. His ideas, and their expression, very much paralleled those of other Catholic reformers in Spain at that time, including 'Maestro' Juan de Ávila and his 'spiritual twin' (*alma gemela*), Fray Luis de Granada. The Bible was their inspiration, and on that basis, as well as that of some words of the Church Fathers, they preached a Pauline Christianity, with which Erasmus would, in many respects, have been very much at home. Carranza and his allies stressed the need for a Christian to have a personal faith, and an inner conversion that would manifest itself in Christian behaviour in the world. They also had practical advice to offer to clergy and laity of all social ranks.[16] At this stage of his career, Carranza seems to have seen no contradiction between this spiritual and social Gospel and his activities on behalf of the Inquisition. His success in advising the Valladolid tribunal led to his being appointed *consultor* to the Supreme Council of the General Inquisition (the 'Suprema') in Madrid. Evidently regarded by senior inquisitors as the very repository of orthodoxy, he took part in Inquisition trials, and preached at *autos de fe*. By this time, Fray Bartolomé had evidently come to the attention of Charles I and V. The King-Emperor, no doubt thinking that he had abilities suited to the mission field in the New World, for which members of religious orders were commonly preferred at this time, unsuccessfully offered Carranza the rich episcopal see of Cuzco, in Peru. Later, apparently in 1548, the friar was similarly to refuse both the bishopric of the Canary Islands and the post of confessor to Prince Philip. Not many years were to pass before Carranza would respond more positively to a request from the Prince of Spain to act as his spiritual counsellor, but, in the meantime, the long-awaited General Council of the Western Church, summoned in 1545 to the northern Italian town of Trent by Pope Paul III, was to provide him with new opportunities to shine.

In April of that year, Fray Bartolomé joined the Imperial delegation to the First Period of Trent, remaining there after the first group of sessions was concluded in 1548. He took part in general congregations (plenary sessions) and specialized sessions and committees on specific subjects, and worked closely with members of Charles' household. As well as voting on the theological matters discussed at Trent, he also exercised his Dominican vocation of preaching, for example giving a notable reformist sermon to the whole Council,

16 For a fuller discussion of this Spanish version of 'evangelical' Christianity see John Edwards, 'Spanish religious influence in Marian England', in *The Church of Mary Tudor*, ed. Eamon Duffy and David Loades (Aldershot: Ashgate, 2005).

in the Cathedral of San Vigilio, and in 1546 he addressed a sermon on the vexed question of Justification by Faith to the Spanish delegation. In the same year, he published, in Venice, a set of four *Controversiae*, or debates, which concerned, respectively, the authority of Scripture, Church tradition, the relationship between Popes and General Councils, and the need for bishops to reside in their dioceses. This last was a particular cause of controversy, not least between Carranza and his fellow Dominican Catharinus (see below, Chapter 6). Having evidently made his mark at Trent, in 1548 Fray Bartolomé returned to Spain, and was elected Prior of the Dominican house in Palencia, where he remained for two years. There he taught the Cathedral clergy as well as his fellow friars, and finally agreed to become Prince Philip's confessor. In 1550, he was elected Dominican Provincial for Castile, in which capacity he began a more public ministry to his Order, travelling extensively, preaching, and reforming convents of both men and women. However, in May 1551, he answered Charles V's call to return to Trent, for the second group of sessions of the Council, which lasted until the Spring of 1552. During this period, he was accorded the signal honour of giving the concluding oration in the Council's debate about the Sacrifice of the Mass, on this occasion speaking for three hours. He also continued his work as a censor of books, by his own account consigning many of them to the flames, before returning to Spain in January 1553, no longer as Castilian Provincial but once again as a member of the College of San Gregorio in Valladolid. During that year, Carranza began to preach regularly to the Court, in the Chapel of his penitent, Prince Philip, and, in these circumstances, it is natural that he should have been chosen to join the Spanish party on its voyage to England in 1554.[17]

The papers in this volume focus primarily on Carranza's activity and significance in England's brief return to the Roman obedience under Mary Tudor, also placing them in the context of the wider Church, especially in Spain and Italy. It is clear throughout that knowledge and understanding of the life and achievements of Bartolomé Carranza depend overwhelmingly on the scholarly labour and skill of Father Ignacio Tellechea, and the Preface to the volume outlines this scholar's biography and continuing career. Chapter 1 is a version of Fr Tellechea's keynote address to the Christ Church Symposium, which indicates his own connections with England as well as those of his subject. The chapter summarizes Carranza's work in England, and focuses particularly on Papal intervention at this time in the affairs of the English Church, on the basis of documentation in the Vatican archive that Tellechea has edited and published.[18]

17 Carranza, *Comentarios*, I. 11–15.
18 José Ignacio Tellechea Idígoras, *El papado y Felipe II: Colección de Breves pontificios*, 3 vols, Publicaciones de la FUE: Monografías 73 (Madrid: Fundación Universitaria Española, 1999–2002), I.

Many of the questions he raises in his overview are addressed by other contributors. David Loades, in Chapter 2, provides a general discussion of another kind, surveying the character of the English Church which met Carranza and his companions in July 1554, and concentrates especially on the repression of Protestantism by the English government and bishops. In Chapter 3, Lucy Wooding focuses on the theological and ecclesiological ideas that were current in the Marian Church, and stresses the extent to which both Catholic and Protestant thinkers and writers in England derived their ideas from a common Humanistic heritage, which influenced the Queen herself. It was into this intellectual and religious context that the Spanish churchmen came, bringing their own notions of reformed, and reforming, Christianity. The close personal bond between Carranza and the Cardinal Legate to England, Reginald Pole, has long been established by Tellechea, and in Chapter 4 Thomas Mayer explores further the reformed Catholic Christianity which Pole attempted to implement during what turned out to be the last few years of his life. The Continental context, and in particular that of Rome, is further emphasized in Chapter 5, where Dermot Fenlon takes up the question of how to preach the Christian faith, which had been a vital issue at Trent, and was evidently highly relevant to the restoration of Roman Catholicism in Mary's England. Another Tridentine issue, on which both Pole and Carranza had strong views, was the residence of clergy in the benefices which supported them. Patrick Preston, in Chapter 6, goes back to the relevant debates at Trent, and describes how Carranza forged his vehement views on the subject in controversy with his Italian Dominican colleague, Ambrosius Catharinus. In Chapter 7, William Wizeman, in contrast to Wooding, though using much of the same evidence, links these Continental ideas on Catholic Reform, as reflected in the Catechism that Carranza wrote primarily for the English Church, with the native English ideas that are studied here by Wooding. Unlike the latter, Wizeman highlights the stress on the importance of the Papacy which may be found in at least some English writing of the period. Central to the conflict between Catholic and Reformed Christianity, in England as elsewhere, was the nature and meaning of the Sacrament of the Body and Blood of Christ, which Jesus, in the New Testament, instructed his disciples to re-enact. As Loades demonstrates in Chapter 2, the Eucharist became a touchstone of orthodoxy in Marian England, and John Edwards, in Chapter 8, highlights Carranza's important part in the restoration of devotion to this Sacrament, by means of public processions on and about the Feast of Corpus Christi. Another aspect of Carranza's work in England was his involvement in the restoration and reform of the two English universities, a subject which was evidently important to the Queen. Up to now, it has been hard to discern more than a marginal role for Spaniards in the Legatine Visitations of Oxford and Cambridge, but, in Chapter 9, Andrew Hegarty gives a detailed account of what can be known of the activities in this connection of Carranza and his fellow friars.

The deaths of Queen Mary and Cardinal Pole, on 17 November 1558, ended the attempt to make England a Roman Catholic country once more. By that time, not only had English and Spanish churchmen, including those old friends, Pole and Carranza, become highly unpopular with English Protestants, but the Cardinal had lost the favour of Rome. Spain, too, was in conflict with the Papacy, and Carranza, despite the initial support of the new King, Philip II, was soon to reap the whirlwind. The last two chapters of the book thus look forward. In them, Anthony Wright, in Chapter 10, and Ronald Truman, in Chapter 11, explore the subsequent reputation of Bartolomé Carranza, and obtain some surprising results. Although Father Tellechea has, at times, had to struggle to 'rehabilitate' the subject of his lifetime's devotion, such was evidently not always the case during the centuries which have passed between Carranza's death, in Rome on 2 May 1576, and the pontificate of Pius XII, during which, also in the 'Eternal City', he began his researches into the career of the unfortunate Archbishop.

Various contributors to this volume address the still vexed question of the nature of the English Church which met Carranza and his companions when they landed in Mary's kingdom in July 1554. As a background to the controversies which surfaced at the Oxford Symposium in 2001, it is worth noting that there have traditionally been, both in England and abroad (notably in Spain), two conflicting and denominationally based 'stories' of the country's religious history in the mid-sixteenth century. The 'Reformed' or 'Protestant' story, which retains considerable influence in the present day, tells how the late medieval 'Catholic' Church, in England as elsewhere in Europe, fell into ignorance, corruption, and superstition, even, or above all, among its leaders. Ill-educated and venal clergy systematically robbed the misguided faithful, by extracting from them tithes and money in return for papal Bulls which falsely claimed to guarantee them a reduction of their time in a non-existent 'purgatory', which the medieval Church had placed as an unbiblical testing-ground before admission to heaven. The people were also required to pay other taxes, notably 'Peter's Pence', which were sent to support the bloated apparatus of the Papal Curia in Rome. Nevertheless, in this version of events, the light of the true Gospel had begun to shine through once again, in the teachings of the late fourteenth-century Oxford reformer John Wycliffe, and his 'Lollard' followers. They cut away the false claims of the Bishop of Rome, and the unscriptural teaching which had come to surround the main focus of late medieval Christian devotion, the Eucharist or 'Mass'. They also restored to the people the text of the Bible and the liturgy in English, instead of the largely unintelligible Latin then used in church. In the sixteenth century, Martin Luther renewed this 'true' religion on the Continent. His ideas began to be accepted in the partial 'reformation' of Henry VIII, which was extended under Edward VI, and was to be violently halted and persecuted under Mary.[19] Many English people at the time of Carranza's visit, apart from the Protestant martyrologist John Foxe, would have devoutly subscribed to all these views, adding accusations against the Spaniards of the kind that Captain Bret expressed so forcefully to his fellow-Londoners during Wyatt's rebellion. Evidence was already reaching England, from the Continent and the Americas, of Spanish atrocities which would constitute what was eventually to be named, in the twentieth century and by a Spaniard, Julián Juderías, a 'Black Legend' (*leyenda negra*).

But, on the other hand, the Queen's Spanish husband and his entourage had a 'Spanish' and 'Catholic' tale to tell. In this, as an anonymous Spaniard in Philip's overblown household wrote home, the English were seen as 'a barbarous and heretical race, with no fear of God or his saints'.[20] Another described Mary's subjects as 'white, pink, and quarrelsome', adding that 'they have a lot of beer, and drink more of it than there is water in the river at Valladolid'.[21] This view developed not only out of the mutual hostility between Spanish and English, especially in London and Westminster, where the former mainly lodged, but also from events in the two preceding reigns—Henry VIII's ill-treatment of Philip's great-aunt, Catherine of Aragon, the destruction on government orders of monasteries and shrines, and the judicial murder, as most on the Continent saw it, of defenders of the Catholic Faith such as Sir Thomas More and Bishop John Fisher. Yet the Spanish story of England, which Philip and his entourage brought with them in their minds, also had much more positive characteristics. Two days after the wedding in Winchester cathedral, some of the Spaniards paid their respects to the supposed 'Round Table' of King Arthur, in the castle there. This piece of tourism did not happen by chance, as the visitors' minds were filled with the stories of Arthur and Amadis of Gaul, the latter being the hero of one of the most popular chivalric romances in Spain, who performed many of his supposed deeds in Wales (then, as so often, regarded as part of England). The fertile landscape which they saw seemed to these Spanish enthusiasts to leap straight from the pages of these familiar romances, thus increasing their shock at the curmudgeonly behaviour of so many of their hosts.[22] In any case, they had wandered into an

19 Such views are vividly summarized, though certainly not endorsed, in, for example, Norman Jones, *The English Reformation: Religion and cultural adaptation* (Oxford: Blackwell, 2002), p. 1, and Peter Marshall and Alec Ryrie, 'Introduction: Protestantisms and their beginnings', in *The beginnings of English Protestantism*, ed. Marshall and Ryrie (Cambridge: Cambridge University Press, 2002), pp. 1–13 (pp. 1–2).
20 Loades, *Chronicles*, p. 46.
21 Kamen, *Philip of Spain*, p. 58.
22 Kamen, *Philip of Spain*, p. 58; Martin Biddle *et al.*, *King Arthur's Round Table: An archaeological investigation* (Woodbridge: The Boydell Press, 2001), pp. 484–7.

ideological battleground, which involved official England's entire perception of its historical identity, in which its 'true' religion was central.

Clear signs of this were visible when London welcomed the newly-married Philip and Mary, by way of a Garter ceremony at Windsor. The customary pageant was devoted not just to proper courtesies, such as a comparison between Philip and his namesake of Macedon, the father of another hero of medieval and 'early modern' romance, Alexander the Great, and also with the new King's own grandfather, Philip 'the Fair' of Castile, but also to semi-dramatized genealogy. This was directed at demonstrating to the English public that their rulers, whom they supposed to be a 'Spanish' King and a 'half-Spanish' (and half-Welsh) Queen were in fact as 'English' as could be, thanks to their common descent from the French-speaking Plantagenet Edward III's younger brother John 'of Gaunt', or 'of Ghent', as Philip's own father, Charles V, had been known in his youth. Both Philip and Mary were descended from two of John of Gaunt's daughters, Philippa and Catherine, the respective wives of John I of Portugal and Henry III of Castile. Mary was additionally descended from John of Gaunt through her father, Henry VIII, though in this case via Gaunt's liaison with Catherine Swinford. One of the London pageants was devoted to counteracting the natural tendency in England to see Mary as 'half-Spanish' and Philip as 'wholly Spanish', a view carefully fomented by the French embassy and apparently believed in by most of the couple's English subjects. Thus, during the performance, some verses were displayed, written in gold on a silver background:

> England, if thou delight in ancient men
> Whose glorious acts thy fame abroad did blaze,
> Both Mary and Philip their offspring ought thou then
> With all thy heart to love and to embrace,
> Which both descended of one ancient line
> It hath pleased God by marriage to combine.

Of course, accurate genealogical study would have treated both the 'Spanish' and the 'English' interpretations harshly, given the 'mongrel' nature of the whole of European royalty, but that was not the point. What was at issue was the very identity of Mary's people and kingdom. The aim was to replace the Tudor myth of the reconciliation of the houses of York and Lancaster, after the Wars of the Roses, with one of a Lancastrian restoration which would also reconcile Spain and England.

The new story inevitably had religious implications too. Another of the 1554 London pageants included a painting of Henry VIII, who had been, as it were, the ghost at the Winchester wedding feast, holding in his hand a book which bore the legend, '*Verbum Dei*', the 'Word of God'. This image was derived from Henry's English 'Great Bible' of 1539, the frontispiece of which showed him distributing it to his grateful subjects. In the new climate of Mary's reign, however, the English Scriptures were not to be trusted, and certainly not to be thus celebrated. So the Lord Chancellor and Bishop of Winchester, Stephen Gardiner, ordered the artist to paint out the Bible and replace it with a pair of gloves.[23] On 2 December 1554, the Sunday after England was restored to the Roman obedience, Gardiner preached an open-air Advent sermon at Paul's Cross, in which, as well as urging the English to awake from the 'sleep' of heresy and schism, he attempted to demonstrate that they were not a 'peculiar' Protestant people, but a 'chosen' Catholic one. As Starkey puts it:

> And who were the heroes of England? Were they King Arthur, King John and King Henry [II], who had fought for England against Rome? Or were they the saints and martyrs and kings, who had risked death, exile and imprisonment for the Catholic faith: from Edmund and Edward [the Confessor] under the Anglo-Saxons to Mary, Pole and Gardiner in their own time?[24]

Having been a royal councillor throughout, Gardiner was well aware that, from 1530 onwards, Henry VIII had set scholars to work with the aim of demonstrating, from Church history, that England had always been independent of the Papacy. His 'Empire' was thus ecclesiastical as well as secular.[25] Henry's research committee had treated as an authority the largely mythological work of the twelfth-century Welsh historian Geoffrey of Monmouth, the source of many stories which were much beloved of Spaniards as well as the British. Bartolomé Carranza, on the other hand, came to England as an experienced researcher into the Synods and Councils of the Catholic Church, who had published a book on the subject in Venice in 1546.[26]

The Navarrese Dominican and his Spanish ecclesiastical companions arrived with well-developed views on the proper nature and conduct of Church and Society, and they found a kingdom riven by controversy, in both these tightly interlocking areas. In 1554, both Spanish and English generally assumed that monarchy was the only proper form of human government, and that the Church, however it was constituted and whatever doctrine it taught, should be one, as Christ had commanded (John 10:16). Thus, as far as the Church was concerned, both Spanish and English leaders were preoccupied, from whatever doctrinal and ecclesiological point of view, with the same problems: the ability and conduct of the clergy (especially in the parishes), the religious orders, the relationship between 'national' churches and the Papacy, the possessions and funding of the Church, and its doctrine. In social terms—and it was held

---

23 David Starkey, *Elizabeth: Apprenticeship* (London: Chatto and Windus, 2000), pp. 168–70.
24 ibid., p. 175.
25 Diarmaid MacCulloch, *Thomas Cranmer: A life* (New Haven CT and London: Yale University Press, 1996), pp. 54–5.
26 Bartolomé Carranza de Miranda, *Summa conciliorum* (Venice: Ad Signum Spei, 1546); also id., *Comentarios*, I. 17–18.

to be axiomatic, certainly in England and increasingly, in this period, in Spain, that Church and Society should in principle be one—these Spanish and English churchmen, as well as those in Rome, had strong views on the right ordering of 'Society', and an acute sense of the need to confront problems within it.[27]

Almost since the events themselves took place, historians of the English Reformation have commonly adduced 'anticlericalism' as a 'cause' of the overthrow of the traditional structure of the Church during the reigns of Henry VIII and Edward VI. The hostility of many lay people towards the clergy, both non-monastic ('secular') and monastic ('religious'), for which there is considerable evidence dating from both before and after Mary's accession to the throne, has commonly been ascribed to economic and social abuses on the part of greedy, and frequently ignorant and/or absentee, clergy.[28] This was the unsavoury underside of Eamon Duffy's 'traditional religion'.[29] As Preston (Chapter 6) demonstrates, the question of 'residence' by clergy in their benefices had been a preoccupation of Carranza since at least the 1540s. There is some evidence, though it is not uncontroversial, that, in alliance with Pole and very probably with the Queen, progress was made, between 1553 and 1558, in securing more regular residence of English bishops in their dioceses.[30] At the very least it is certain that Carranza, both before and after his departure from England, upbraided his old friend Pole for not setting a better example in this respect. It is clear, though, that most of the idealistic (and Gospel-based) schemes of Marian Catholic reformers with Continental experience, just like those of their Protestant predecessors in Edward's reign, foundered on the rock of lay impropriation.[31] At that time and for centuries to come, the ability of lay people and private corporations, such as Oxford and Cambridge colleges, to appoint parish clergy would act, for better or worse, as a check on zealous bishops and their advisers. Tellechea has long since demonstrated that both Carranza and Pole were preoccupied with this question, which was also much debated in Spain and Rome. Those English people who had profited from the legal or illegal looting of ecclesiastical property, in which monasteries and

---

27 Carranza's Thomist social views are effectively illustrated in Bartolomé Carranza de Miranda, *Tratado sobre la virtud de la justicia (1540)*, ed. and tr. Teodoro López *et al.* (Pamplona: Ediciones Universidad de Navarra, 2003).

28 Ethan H. Shagan, *Popular politics and the English Reformation*, Cambridge Studies in Early Modern History (Cambridge: Cambridge University Press, 2003), pp. 131–61.

29 Eamon Duffy, *The stripping of the altars: Traditional religion in England, c. 1400–c. 1580* (New Haven CT and London: Yale University Press, 1992).

30 Stephen Thompson, 'The pastoral work of the English and Welsh bishops, 1500–1558', unpubl. doctoral dissertation, University of Oxford (1984), pp. 1–9 and appendices ; cited in Felicity Heal, *Reformation in Britain and Ireland*, Oxford History of the Christian Church (Oxford: Clarendon Press, 2003), p. 183.

31 Jones, *English Reformation*, pp. 58–70.

chantries, in particular, seem to have provided domestic building materials such as nowadays are more commonly offered by urban and out-of-town 'do-it-yourself' stores, resisted the repossession of their 'property' with a tenacity quite independent of any doctrinal stance.[32] In respect of this disappointment, Latimer and Carranza might well have wept together.

The largely frustrated desire to see Church property used for good public causes was not the only common ground between Catholic and Protestant reformers, as seen from the distance of four-and-a-half centuries. 'Evangelical' Christians, in England as on the Continent, put a large premium on 'conversion', seen largely as a 'blinding' single experience, modelled on the recorded sudden transformation of Paul the Apostle, St Augustine, and Martin Luther.[33] Of course, Carranza and his Spanish companions in England came from a country which had experienced, during the previous century or so, the 'conversion' of tens of thousands of Jews into baptized Christians and, since 1502, the beginnings of a similar process among Spanish Muslims. In most cases, between 1390 and 1554, Jews and Muslims were baptized in family groups, and it is interesting to note that John Knox, no less, advocated a similar process in the case of converts from Catholicism to the 'Evangelical' faith.[34] Behind the thinking of Carranza and his companions, though, lay medieval monastic notions of 'conversion' as a lifelong and frequently painful process, in which relapses were both likely and rightfully to be punished, even by death.[35]

---

32 Fine, detailed accounts of the illegal pillaging of monasteries and chantries, under Henry VIII and Edward VI, may be found in Shagan, *Popular politics*, pp. 162–96, 235–69, and in Jones, *English Reformation*, pp. 70–94.

33 See Peter Marshall, *Beliefs and the dead in Reformation England* (Oxford: Oxford University Press, 2002).

34 For example, in 1413–14, at Tortosa in eastern Spain, a conversionist 'disputation' was held between Jewish and Christian religious leaders, under the auspices of the anti-Pope Benedict XIII. The contemporary Christian account characteristically records, concerning the fourteenth session, that 'on the said day, eleven Jews were converted to the [Christian] Faith, *together with their wives and families*': Hyam Maccoby, *Judaism on trial: Jewish-Christian disputations in the Middle Ages* (London and Toronto: Associated University Presses, 1982), p. 191 (emphasis added). John Knox appears to have had a similar expectation to that of the Spanish Catholic authorities, no doubt based on the same Pauline texts: 'Brethren, you are ordained by God to rule your own houses in His true fear, and according to His Word. Within your houses, I say, in some cases, you are bishops and kings; your wife, children, servants, and family are your bishopric and charge' (cited in Jones, *English Reformation*, p. 37).

35 On older notions of conversion, and its association with pain, see: Arthur D. Nock, *Conversion: The old and the new in religion from Alexander the Great to Augustine of Hippo* (Baltimore MD and London: The Johns Hopkins University Press, 1998); Karl F. Morrison, *Understanding conversion*, Page-Barbour Lectures 1991 (Charlottesville VA and London: University Press of Virginia, 1992); and Ariel Glucklich, *Sacred pain: Hurting the body for the sake of the soul* (Oxford: Oxford University Press, 2001).

Here seems to have lain the reason for the willingness of Philip's Spanish ecclesiastical advisers, and in particular Carranza, who had considerable inquisitorial experience behind him (see Chapter 1), to condone, or even advocate, the violent repression of English Protestants. For both sides, the 'true' Faith was literally a matter of life and death, and relativism was not an intellectual or practical option, this being a characteristic of the sixteenth century throughout the former 'Catholic' Europe.

Finally, in terms of 'common ground' between the Catholic Spaniards and their Evangelical English opponents, there was an acceptance of the Crown as a main agent of Church reform. Although the events of Mary's reign were predicated on the restoration of England to obedience to the Roman See, she, like her father and half-brother, used her royal prerogative to full effect. This is well known, but it is often forgotten that Carranza's own sovereigns, both Trastamaran and Habsburg, had similarly used their monarchical power to pursue the cause of Church reform, and in Philip II's reign would continue to do so, though without a definitive break with Rome.[36] With inevitable hindsight, it may appear that, in principle at least, there was much in common between the aims, not only of Spanish and English Catholic leaders, but also of their 'Evangelical' equivalents.

In the event, of course, the deaths of both Queen Mary and Cardinal Pole on 17 November 1558, followed by the undisputed accession of Elizabeth, caused what has been, to date, a definitive parting of the ways. By stages, in 1557 and the following year, Philip and his Spanish courtiers and advisers, including Carranza, left the country, first for the Low Countries and then for Spain itself. Philip supported and fomented the repression of Protestantism in his Iberian kingdoms, and allowed his faithful counsellor, though Primate of Spain by his choice, to fall into the clutches of the Inquisition. In England, meanwhile, the new Queen devoted herself, as many had hoped or feared, to the demolition of her half-sister's religious and political settlement, returning to the 'Island Story' that their father had largely created. Successive events, from the 'Spanish Armada' of 1588 to the 'miraculous' retreat of the British Army from Dunkirk in 1940, and now to the plans of some to remove 'England' from a European Union, have been held by many to validate it. Yet, ever since the reign of 'Good Queen Bess', both interpretations of England's history,

---

36 On the relationship between Church and State in Castile, particularly in the areas of ideology, patronage, and reform, see: José Manuel Nieto Soria, *Iglesia y génesis del estado moderno en Castilla (1369–1480)*, Colección Historia (Madrid: Editorial Complutense, 1993); Tarsicio de Azcona, *Isabel la Católica: Estudio crítico de su vida y su reinado*, BAC 237 (Madrid: Editorial Católico, 1993), pp. 543–631; id., 'El hecho episcopal hispánico en tiempo de Carlos V (1516–1558)', in *Erasmismo*, ed. Revuelta and Morón, pp. 265–88; and John Edwards, *The Spain of the Catholic Monarchs, 1474–1516*, History of Spain (Oxford: Blackwell, 2000), pp. 194–223.

'Catholic' and 'Protestant', have in fact had a long life, and still influence accounts of Mary's reign, and of Spanish involvement in it, up to the present day.[37] It was not expected, let alone required, that the contributors to the Oxford Symposium of 2001, whose work is included in this volume, would resolve this fundamental conflict of interpretation, but the outcome undoubtedly contributes to the continuing historical and ecclesiastical debate. Obviously, no one can know what the English Church would have been like if Mary had lived longer, and her kingdom had remained within the Habsburg sphere of influence, as a small but significant part of a world power. Nevertheless, the papers delivered at the 2001 Oxford Symposium on Carranza, here duly revised and updated by their authors in consultation with the editors, open the way to a fuller understanding, in the English as well as the Spanish-speaking world, of the complex cross-currents of developments within the Christian Church, in England and on the Continent, which produced such turmoil in the mid-sixteenth century, and still have their consequences today. It should be added that, since then, the work begun in Oxford in 2001 has been continued and expanded at the international conference held in the University of Navarre at Pamplona, in December 2003, to commemorate the 500th anniversary of Carranza's birth in nearby Miranda de Arga. In Miranda, a public library bearing his name is under construction—a project of which he would surely have approved.

In a paper delivered in Santander in 1985, Fr Tellechea expressed the view that 'the ideological frontiers between Protestantism and Catholicism were quite clear, as much in Europe as in Spain, in 1558–9'.[38] This collection of studies tests his statement in both English and Continental contexts, and points the way to future exploration of this still vital question. On the Spanish side, the historian and anthropologist Julio Caro Baroja remarked, many years ago, with particular reference to Bishop Diego de Simancas (who in his auto-biography prided himself on having pursued Carranza to his death, as Philip II's representative in Rome between 1567 and 1576) on the mutually destructive urge of so many Spanish intellectual and religious leaders in that period, and its international consequences:

> It is clear that the figure of [Diego de] Simancas must not be studied in isolation, but within its social context; and thus it is added to, and included in, a mass of Spaniards who, beginning with the king [Philip II] himself, produced extraordinary anxiety in [the rest of] Europe, while, within Spain, they acted in full

37 See John Edwards, 'Carranza y la Iglesia en Inglaterra', in *Carranza y su tiempo: Actas del Congreso Internacional V Centenario del nacimiento del arzobispo Bartolomé Carranza de Miranda (Universidad de Navarra, Pamplona, 11–13 diciembre 2003)* (at press).
38 José Ignacio Tellechea Idígoras, 'El protestantismo castellano (1558–1559): Un *topos* (M. Bataillon) convertido en *tópico* historiográfico', in *Erasmismo en España*, ed. Revuelta and Morón, pp. 306–21 (p. 321).

consciousness, not just of their uprightness but of their perfection, in a world in which heresy was triumphant, [and] in which the English, Germans, Dutch, and even French, lived with a 'liberty of conscience' which was represented [in Spain] as scandalous.[39]

More than forty years ago, in his short illustrated history of what, happily circumventing much recent debate, he immediately accepted as *both* a 'Counter-' and a 'Catholic' reformation, A.G. Dickens rightly placed Bartolomé Carranza with St Ignatius of Loyola, St Teresa of Ávila, St John of the Cross, St Juan de Ávila, Luis de Granada, and Luis de León, as distinguished Spanish Christians who were suspected and persecuted for their beliefs. In the English context, and in an essay of tribute to Dickens, Andrew Pettegree has recently asked:

> What was the nature of the Catholicism that was to be restored—or rebuilt—or crafted from those elements of traditional religion that had survived, or could be resuscitated ?...Was this...an opportunity to create a new sort of Catholic Church—leaner, fitter, attuned to modern Continental thinking, a beacon of reform Catholicism as the Edwardian Church had been to Protestants?[40]

This volume is offered to all who are concerned with these questions, and in memory of Fray Bartolomé Carranza de Miranda.

39 Julio Caro Baroja, 'El señor Inquisidor', in *El señor Inquisidor y otras vidas por oficio* (Madrid: Alianza Editorial, 1997), p. 37.
40 Arthur G. Dickens, *The Counter Reformation* (London: Thames and Hudson, 1968), p. 161; Andrew Pettegree, 'A.G. Dickens and his critics: A new narrative of the English Reformation', *Historical Research*, 77 (2004), pp. 39–58 (p. 56).

CHAPTER 1

Fray Bartolomé Carranza: A Spanish Dominican in the England of Mary Tudor

José Ignacio Tellechea Idígoras

In 1964 I published, in the Rome journal *Anthologica Annua*, a long article entitled 'Bartolomé Carranza and the English Catholic Restoration (1554–1558)'. Two years later I brought out an important document in my article 'Pole and Paul IV: A Celebrated "Apologia" of the English Cardinal (1557)'. Subsequently, and again on the theme of the English religious climate of those years, appeared my 'Pole, Carranza, and Fresneda: The reverse sides of a friendship and a hatred'. Then, in 1975, I published a series of letters which Carranza wrote from the Low Countries to England in the years 1557–8. All these, plus the text of four sermons given by Carranza in England, were brought together in 1977 in a volume entitled *Fray Bartolomé Carranza and Cardinal Pole: A Navarrese in the English Catholic Restoration (1554–1558).*[1] That book brought me a first invitation to Oxford, where I gave a lecture at which Sir Peter Russell and my friend Ronald Truman were present. I never thought that, a quarter of a century later, the theme of my book could become that of a Symposium on 'Bartolomé Carranza and the England of Mary Tudor', in Oxford itself, under the auspices of Christ Church, and that I should be invited to open it. I should like to express my warmest thanks for this invitation, one of the greatest satisfactions of my life, proving again that research is not in vain.

It will soon be fifty years since I first set about the task of discovering and getting closer to this figure—Fray Bartolomé Carranza—forgotten and ill-treated by History, and unfortunately little remembered except for having

---

[1] José Ignacio Tellechea Idígoras, 'Bartolomé Carranza y la restauración católica inglesa (1554–1558)', *Anthologica Annua*, 12 (1964), pp. 159–282; id., 'Pole y Paulo IV: Un célebre "Apologia" del cardenal inglés (1557)', *Archivum Historiae Pontificiae*, 4 (1966), pp. 105–54; id., 'Pole, Carranza y Fresneda: Cruz y cara de una amistad y de una enemistad', *Diálogo Ecuménico*, 8 (1974), pp. 287–393; id., 'Inglaterra, Flandes y España (1557–1559) en cartas inéditas de Carranza y otros', in *Miscelánea José Zunzunegui, 1911–1974: Estudios históricos*, 5 vols (Vitoria: Seminario de Vitoria, 1975), I. 375–421; id., *Fray Bartolomé Carranza y el cardenal Pole: Un navarro en la restauración católica de Inglaterra (1554–1558)* (Pamplona: Diputación Foral de Navarra, Institución Príncipe de Viana, and CSIC, 1977).

suffered an inquisitorial investigation that lasted more than seventeen years. Born of modest origins in the old Kingdom of Navarre, when it was still independent, he entered the Dominican Order when very young, distinguished himself as a student and later as a professor in the Colegio de San Gregorio at Valladolid, became a famous preacher, a consultant of the Holy Office, Dominican Provincial of Castile, and twice Imperial theologian at the Council of Trent, where he distinguished himself by his reforming zeal. Twice Charles V wanted to nominate him for a bishopric; he also wished to appoint him confessor to Prince Philip; but Carranza declined these proposals. On the other hand, he accepted the invitation to accompany Prince Philip on his journey to England to marry Mary Tudor and remained in England from July 1554 until July 1557, when he went to the Low Countries and very soon found himself becoming Archbishop of Toledo on the nomination of Philip II. Having arrived in Spain in the summer of 1558, he would be made prisoner by the Inquisition a year later and subjected to an inordinately long trial (*proceso*). Despite having such misfortunes visited upon him, we owe some thanks to the Inquisition for giving us the possibility of getting to know in extensive detail about Carranza's time in England.

Among the various stages of his *proceso*, one consisted of the 'abonos', that is, the presentation of the positive facts of his life. Carranza presented these in the form of a hundred questions to be answered by witnesses brought in for the purpose. Now, in that retrospective survey of his life, no fewer than twenty-three questions (running from number forty-two to number sixty-four) are concerned with his stay in England and with his activities during that time. And to substantiate the factual basis of those questions nearly twenty Spanish witnesses were called, people who were present with him in England and close to the Court. It comes as a surprise to find that among the witnesses called was Philip II himself. His statement was given in Madrid on 14 October 1562. In addition to the King, statements were made by the royal secretaries Gonzalo Pérez, Gabriel de Zayas, and Pedro de Hoyo; the royal 'Aposentador Mayor' (Quartermaster General), Luis de Venegas; Gómez Suárez de Figueroa, Count of Feria; Ruy Gómez de Silva, Prince of Eboli; Francisco de Castilla, 'Alcalde de Corte'; Juan de Silva, Marquis of Montemayor; Juan de Benavides, Marquis of Cortes; and others.[2]

With all this first-hand material I was able to piece together Carranza's activities in England, an important chapter in his life-story and at the same time an important chapter in the religious history of England, long wholly unknown to English historiography.

2   José Ignacio Tellechea Idígoras (ed.), *Fray Bartolomé Carranza: Documentos históricos*, 7 vols, Archivo Documental Español 18 etc. (Madrid : Real Academia de la Historia, 1962–94), III. 53–287.

Fray Bartolomé Carranza, taken to England by Philip II, appears as a highly-placed figure in Court circles, enjoying particular esteem on the part of the King and Queen and the Papal Legate, Cardinal Reginald Pole. Carranza had an active role in preparing the way for the arrival of Pole in England and would recall that the King personally gave him the news of the Cardinal's imminent arrival in Whitehall. After he arrived, the difficulties relating to the Kingdom's return to the Roman obedience had to be faced. In this Carranza played a particular part, in association with the King and Pole. We know that, as regards the restitution of property—monasteries and convents—that formerly belonged to the Church, Carranza favoured a gentle approach, and by persuasion rather than by force he achieved the return of three Dominican houses, a Carthusian one, a Benedictine one (Westminster), and a further one belonging to the Knights Hospitallers. Furthermore, he had been given the title of Commissary for his own Order in England. In the Royal Council he was a regular consultant on religious matters. How far will English historians, I wonder, be able to follow the course of his activity in such high places?

Among his activities at a lower level we encounter his preaching. In 1555 he preached in the King's Chapel (the Spanish Capilla Real which Philip brought with him to England) and, during Lent of that year, he gave a sermon which he was asked to have published. Thus came into being his little book entitled 'How to hear the Mass', printed at London, Antwerp, and Salamanca. We know that he preached at Hampton Court, defending the primacy of the Pope, on St Peter's Day, in that same year of 1555. In each case, I have published the text.[3] He re-established Corpus Christi processions, specifically at Kingston upon Thames (see below, Chapter 8), and preached there before a great concourse of people. In 1556 he accompanied the Bishop of London, Edmund Bonner, in a Corpus Christi procession at Fulham, and, the following Sunday, himself celebrated Mass and preached at Whitehall. The King and Queen provided liturgical ornaments, silver, and wax candles for the occasion, and many attended, especially Spaniards, Italians, Portuguese, and the households of Pole and the ambassadors of Venice and Portugal, as well as English people.

When Philip crossed to the Low Countries, in September 1555, he ordered Carranza to remain in England and busy himself with religious matters. Here a matter of outstanding importance was the English Synod that began on 1 November of that year. In this Carranza took an active part. The Synod's decrees were drawn up with his advice and agreement as instructed by Pole as Legate. In Lent the following year the Synod was suspended so as to allow bishops to visit their dioceses, to permit the visitation of Oxford and Cambridge Universities (see below, Chapter 9), and to assist the work of the

---

3   Tellechea, *Carranza y Pole*, pp. 379–84; id., 'Un tratadito de Bartolomé Carranza sobre la Misa', *Archivio Italiano per la Storia della Pietà*, 11 (1998), pp. 145–79.

Synod, when it began again, with the information thus gathered. It should not be forgotten that, among the decrees of this Synod, there is one relating to the creation of seminaries. This was some years ahead of the decrees that would be issued in the closing stages of the Council of Trent. In line with the aims of the Synod, it fell to Carranza in person to take part in the visitation of Oxford and its thirteen colleges. He was able to satisfy himself that the doctrine taught there was indeed Catholic. Among others teaching there were the Spaniards Fray Pedro de Soto, former confessor to Emperor Charles V, and Fray Juan de Villagarcía, a great friend of Carranza.

Strangely, in questions that Carranza presented in the course of his *proceso* to be answered by witnesses, he was silent about something regarding the Synod that he would many times repeat in other documents. In view of the ignorance of the English clergy and the disarray brought about by three profound religious changes within a few years, the Synod decided to draw up a set of homilies and an extensive catechism expounding Christian doctrine. The second of these tasks fell to Fray Bartolomé Carranza, who composed his *Commentaries on the Christian Catechism* in England and for England. He wrote it in Spanish, but its translation into Latin and English was immediately set in hand. Does any manuscript of these translations survive, I wonder? The work itself was published at Antwerp in 1558. It comes as a surprise that a work devised to counteract Protestant propaganda reaching England should itself, in the hands of the Spanish Inquisition, become an object warranting the accusation of Protestantism.

The Synod of London (or Westminster, as it is sometimes known), with its two sessions planned for 1555–6, represents the most positive factor in the great attempt to restore Roman Catholicism—a project officially endorsed by Parliament. The Synod's decrees, which we have now published, invite study, as does the make-up of the Catholic hierarchy involved in the Synod. Did the latter reassemble in 1556? Did it contribute new information on the state of the dioceses? Did it approve new synodal initiatives? What was on balance the overall outcome of this synodal activity? Did the latter perhaps fall away because things began to move in a new direction?

Among Carranza's activities in England are some that relate to the repression that marked the second period of Mary's reign. After an initial period in which a certain spirit of understanding and willingness to proceed by persuasion seems to have prevailed, there followed another where severity took over, extending as far as the persecution of dissidents. It would be interesting to establish the moment of this change and the motivations that brought it about. Was it prompted by intolerance strictly speaking, or does it rather represent an inevitable reaction against certain forms of provocation and challenge? How far is it possible to know who those were who suffered punishment and repression, and what the reason for their condemnation was?

The cases in which Carranza intervened throw some light on this delicate question. He recalls the case of a 'heretic sacramentarian'. Was this a Wycliffite, a Calvinist, an Anabaptist? This heretic set upon a Dominican, dressed in clerical (not Dominican) attire, with a knife, when he was distributing communion in the parish church of St Margaret, Westminster. The atrocious nature of the crime, rather than the fact of religious dissidence, merited exemplary punishment. Carranza was in favour of this and gave his approval to the cutting off of the man's right hand and his subsequent condemnation to the flames; nevertheless, Carranza gave help to the victim of the attack, and assisted his return to the Order in which he had professed. How far is it possible for us to know about the trials of those condemned to death at the end of Mary Tudor's reign and the reasons for their condemnation?

Other episodes of a repressive character recalled by Carranza and in which he played some part include the following. On his visit to Oxford he found that, buried in the Cathedral, close to the body of St Frideswide, was the wife of Peter Martyr Vermigli, the Italian apostate who became Regius Professor of Theology at Oxford. Considering her burial in such a place to be a profanation, he ordered her remains to be disinterred and burnt. Another condemnation was of a different order of importance: that of Archbishop Thomas Cranmer. Carranza recalls Cranmer's condemnation by the Pope and the College of Cardinals in Rome. In the face of the difficulty of carrying out their sentence, Carranza persisted, as he stresses, even though Cranmer's supporters were placing obstacles in the way. In a sermon which he preached in the Observant Franciscan church at Greenwich, he had emphasized royal responsibility for ensuring that exemplary punishment was carried out; at the same time he condemned Cranmer's past conduct. He thereby earned the hostility of those of the Archbishop's supporters who were present, and who declared that a black-clad friar was waging war on them at Court. The Papal sentence passed on Cranmer dates from 4 December 1555. Right here in Christ Church Cathedral he was disgraded from his episcopal order, on 14 February 1556, by the Bishop of London, Bonner, by Thomas Thirlby, Bishop of Ely, and John Harpsfield, Archdeacon of London.

Along with this celebrated case, Carranza collaborated in lesser cases where judgement was given by bishops, especially the Bishop of London, and contributed his vote or advice as regards the sentences passed. He recalled in particular the case of Sir John Cheke, who was captured in the Low Countries, condemned, and later reconciled after the opportune recantation that he made before the Queen in St James's Palace.

Another aspect to be noted of this repressive attitude on Carranza's part is his effort against the diffusion of heretical books or the vernacular Bibles that had been withdrawn from churches, and his part in the promulgation of an edict against booksellers offering such books for sale.

Indicative of the same spirit is the impulse that he gave to the appointment of Catholics to major posts in government. Carranza says that it was at his request that a Catholic was appointed Chancellor of the Kingdom, against the wishes of certain others. Philip II himself would recall years later that Carranza and Don Juan de Figueroa wrote to him on the matter, and he wrote to Queen Mary, recommending Nicholas Heath for the post of Archbishop of York, and Heath was in fact appointed. Finally, Carranza states that he approved of the exhumation and burning, in Cambridge in December 1557, of the remains of the Continental Protestant preacher Martin Bucer, who had been buried in Great St Mary's Church. It is not at all surprising, in view of his manifest belligerence in such matters, that Carranza should have acknowledged that his antagonists wanted to kill him and one night broke down the door of his room. Such, in outline, is the story of Fray Bartolomé's activities in England.

So far I have only touched on his closeness to the King, the Queen, and to Cardinal Pole, the weight he carried in religious questions, the frequent visits he made to one place and another, and the friends with whom he conversed. More needs to be said on this. Between Cardinal Pole and Carranza there was great friendship, which began in their days at the Council of Trent and grew in their time of common endeavour after they had met again in England, the one as Papal Legate and the other as 'consultant'. The letters between them bear witness to the warmth of their feelings for each other, their shared aspirations, the pastoral demands that they faced. These letters deserve to be read and re-read. To them I would add a remarkable document, Cardinal Pole's 'Apologia', written by him as he faced the hidden persecution that he suffered from Pope Paul IV after he had been suspended from his Legate's functions and summoned to Rome, where trial and imprisonment would have awaited him, as it did Cardinal Morone.[4] It was, of course, the intervention of the Queen that prevented Pole's departure from England and thus saved him from what would have been a most painful chapter in his life.

When Carranza, summoned by Philip II, left England for the Low Countries, he left behind him three years of intense labour and a network of friends and acquaintances. His letters are for the most part addressed to Fray Juan de Villagarcía at Oxford, some of them sent from London or Westminster, the majority from Brussels.[5] In one of them he speaks of the recovery of the Dominican convent at Oxford. These letters offer abundant information about Spain and France, the victory of St Quentin, the moment when King Philip II announced to him that he was going to propose him to the Pope for the archbishopric of Toledo, the difficulties with Paul IV. There are many greetings to his English friends, John Rastell, Nicholas Sanders, Fuller, and others, and

4   Tellechea, 'Pole y Paulo IV'.
5   id., *Carranza y Pole*, pp. 258–73.

espccially those in Oxford, 'whom I carry not just written on my soul but imprisoned there'. These are letters that I came upon years ago in the archives of the Holy Office in Rome, to consult which I received special permission from Pope John XXIII. In the same set of documents I found two extremely important letters from the Count of Feria, one of them to Fray Juan de Villagarcía, written four days after Mary's death, the second sent to Philip II in April 1559, when the new Queen Elizabeth had given a fresh turn to her religious policy. All this material is important not only for the personal history of Carranza but for the religious history of England during those years.

There is a further contribution to this period of English religious history that I have been able to offer. This is the text of four sermons Carranza preached during his stay here, as I have already mentioned.[6] One of them gives its place and year of composition: London, 1555. The other three were acknowledged by him, during his inquisitorial *proceso*, as having been 'preached in the Chapel of the King our Lord in England', one on the Feast of the Conception of Our Lady (8 December 1554), another on the Seventh Sunday after Trinity, a third on the Feast of St Peter (29 June). In the development of their themes one finds ideas that can readily be linked to the situation he found himself in during those years. In this fashion such sermons became means of conveying the dominant message that he set before English Catholics who were in the process of recovering their own existence and identity.

My interest in this chapter of the spiritual history of England is not limited to these studies of mine already published. Drawn by the figure of Cardinal Pole, I have already transcribed the series of letters that he sent to Rome from the moment when he was appointed Papal Legate to England. Much time passed before Pole was able to set foot on English soil. Probably what kept him on the Continent was the attitude of Charles V, who feared that Pole would oppose Philip's marriage to Mary. Numerous letters date from those months of waiting, many of them sent from Brussels. Some were written when he had arrived in England. The correspondence stops precisely on the day on which the English Parliament, presided over by the Queen and the Cardinal, was reconciled to Rome and received the Legate's absolution. This collection of letters represents a privileged source of information concerning an event that could have changed the history of England, had not unexpected circumstances intervened: the lack of a direct successor to the throne, the absence of the King, the wholly unforeseeable death of the Queen and the Cardinal within twenty-four hours of each other, and the consequent succession of Elizabeth to the throne.[7] Pole's correspondence is currently being edited by a contributor to this volume, Professor Thomas Mayer.

6   Tellechea, 'Inglaterra, Flandes y España'.
7   Thomas F. Mayer, *Reginald Pole: Prince and prophet* (Cambridge : Cambridge University Press, 2000), pp. 203–20; also Chapter 4, below.

I myself have undertaken the systematic publication of Papal Briefs to Philip II, of which three volumes have appeared with the title *The Papacy and Philip II*.[8] In these I present documentation, little known so far, that bears on the period of English history which is of interest to us now. The relevant documents are considerable in number and merit some comment. The first series is from Pope Julius III. In a Brief of 1 January 1554 he grants the dispensation regarding consanguinity and affinity necessary for the marriage of the Spanish prince with the Queen of England, and seven days later sends congratulations, openly hoping for the Kingdom's return 'to the unity of Holy Church and its ancient devotion and reverence towards the Holy See'.[9]

There is an episode relating to that marriage which is perhaps not sufficiently well known in detail. This is the ceding of the kingdom of Naples by Charles V to Philip, with the intention that it should be with the rank of sovereign King of Naples that his son and heir, Prince Philip, should contract marriage with the Queen of England. This cession on the part of Charles V involved certain diplomatic complications. Naples was a vassal kingdom of the Holy See and its transfer to the Crown of Aragon, which the Emperor's plan required, involved certain contractual undertakings that had to be duly observed. Charles had to request that his son be invested with that kingdom—a request repeated by Philip himself following the appointment of the Marquis of Pescara and Don Juan Manrique de Lara to be his representatives at the ceremony, where they would swear vassalage and obedience in the name of the new King of Naples. It was the Marquis of Pescara, Don Fernando de Ávalos, who discharged this distinguished mission. The investiture, authorized by a *motu proprio* of Julius III, finally took place on 19 October 1554, and the event was communicated to Charles V on the 29th. It was on the 23rd, and at a public Consistory, that the official transfer of power to Philip took place—to Philip 'Angliae et Siciliae citra Pharum Regi illustri'.[10]

On 7 November, in a new Brief addressed to 'Philippo et Mariae, Angliae regibus illustribus', more extensive powers were granted to Cardinal Pole for resolving the thorny problem of the property previously confiscated from the Church, and on 30 November 1554 there took place in Parliament the ceremony of the reconciliation of England to the Holy See. That same day Philip wrote in Spanish to the Pope a letter giving a precious account of the great event. 'This afternoon, on this St Andrew's Day, this whole kingdom, its representatives being unanimous and at one, and with deep repentance for the

---

8   Thomas F. Mayer, *The correspondence of Reginald Pole*, 2 vols (to date) (Aldershot: Ashgate, 2002–); José Ignacio Tellechea Idígoras, *El papado y Felipe II: Colección de Breves pontificios*, 3 vols, Publicaciones de la FUE: Monografías 73 (Madrid: Fundación Universitaria Española, 1999–2002).

9   Tellechea, *El papado*, I. 7–11.

10 ibid., I. 12–25.

past and joy at what they had come to enact, have yielded obedience to Your Holiness and the Holy See, and, at the request of the Queen and myself, received absolution from the Legate... The Queen and I, as true and devoted children of Your Holiness, have received from all this the greatest satisfaction that words can express.'

This eloquent letter was answered by Julius III with a lengthy Brief, dated 27 January 1555, in which the Pope shows himself exultant at England's return and proclaims a jubilee to celebrate so great an event. At the same time he sent an eminent Spaniard to England as nuncio, Antonio Agustín, auditor of the Rota. There is a detail in this Papal reply that deserves to be pointed out. At the head of the document one reads, 'Charissimis in Christo Filiis nostris Philippo Regi et Mariae Reginae Angliae illustribus, Fidei defensoribus'. The Papal title—'Fidei defensor'—bestowed on Henry VIII for his work against Luther is recognized here as applicable to his successor and heir, Queen Mary, and also her consort. Furthermore, in another Brief of the same date, announcing to each of them separately the sending of a sword of honour to Philip and a golden rose to the Queen, one reads, in the first case, 'Philippo, Angliae Regi illustri, Fidei defensori'. Such forms of distinction bestowed on the King and Queen were intended to signify the Pope's gratitude regarding the extraordinary event that had taken place and his hopes for further success. There is express mention of the bringing back of England to the right way, 'in viam rectam', the re-establishment of Papal authority, the liberty of the Roman Church, unity within orthodox faith—all of this confirmed and increased by the support of Philip and Mary. Especially eulogistic terms are addressed to the Queen in the Brief announcing the sending of a golden rose.[11]

No sooner had Julius III tasted the honey of events in England than he died, on 7 February 1555. Marcellus II, elected Pope on 9 April that same year, wrote the following day to the King and Queen of England, informing them of his election and of his hope that both would help bring about a stable peace between the Emperor and France.[12] Scarcely was the month out when Marcellus died, on 1 May.

On 23 May, Giampietro Carafa became Pope Paul IV. The following day he sent word of his election to 'Philippo Regi et Mariae Reginae Angliae, illustribus defensoribus fidei'. It would fall to Paul IV to reap the fruit of the previous pontificates. The English embassy which set out in the time of Julius III to render obedience in person now arrived in Rome, after Paul had been elected. The embassy consisted of Lord Montague, Sir Edward Carne, and Thomas Thirlby, Bishop of Ely. These were received in Consistory, and admitted to the Kiss of Peace in the presence of the cardinals. Bishop Thirlby

---

11 ibid., I. 27–34.
12 ibid., I. 39–40.

made a speech and presented a document guaranteeing the return of the Kingdom to the Roman obedience, and the abolition of earlier laws that had been passed and were contrary to Catholicism. There followed embraces, tears of emotion, and great celebrations in Rome. All this is related at length in the Brief of Paul IV of 30 June, which ends with the Pope's recognition of his immense debt to the English Monarchs.[13]

There being a new Pope, Philip had to renew the oath of vassalage and fidelity which he owed to him as King of Sicily. He did so in a document dated Brussels, 1 October 1555, in which he bears the title 'Philippus, Dei gratia Angliae, Franciae, Citerioris Siciliae, Hierusalem et Hiberniae Rex, Fidei defensor, Princeps Hispaniarum, Archidux Austriae, Dux Burgundiae, Medio-lani, Brabantiae'. Attached to this document is a pendant seal of solid gold, 803 grammes in weight, and the finest of all those to be found in the Vatican Archive collection. On this seal too one finds the titles already mentioned: 'Angliae, Franciae, Citerioris Siciliae...'

On 28 November 1555, in Briefs sent to them separately, Paul IV exhorted the King and Queen of England to collaborate in promoting the peace of Europe. On 22 April 1556, the same exhortation went to Philip, 'Hispaniarum Regi Catholico', as he is addressed here, after Charles V's renunciation of power; this exhortation went simultaneously in another Brief to the Queen of England.[14]

Even while still united in matrimony, their paths and concerns were begin-ning to move apart, and before long the Queen's death would untie the conjugal knot. The 'Hispaniarum Rex' was now Philip II, who would continue to follow closely the course of events in England under Elizabeth I. The religious change of direction quickly brought about by Elizabeth prompted in the irascible Paul IV the intention to excommunicate her, but—intriguingly—his hand was stayed by Philip II. The latter worked for a possible marriage with Elizabeth, but the proposal was rejected.

On 6 May 1559, three months before his death, Paul IV sent a new Brief to Philip in which he mentioned the recent visit of the King's envoy, Ascanio Caracciolo, with letters from his sovereign. Here the Pope expressed his concern for the Catholic religion, and mentioned the efforts he had made in the past and would make in the future to ensure that the restored Catholic religion of England would be preserved.[15] History would take a different course. Already in the spring of 1559 the new religious forms would be imposed with severe sanctions. The Count of Feria, Gómez Suárez de Figueroa, married to Jane Dormer, would leave England, but before doing so,

13 ibid., I. 6–9, 44–5.
14 ibid., I. 6–7, 52–3, 62–5.
15 ibid., I. 85–6.

obtained leave from the Queen to take with him all members of religious orders (Franciscans, Dominicans, etc.) who wished to go, rather than find themselves obliged to follow the new norms.

The long reigns of Elizabeth I and Philip II were beginning on their parallel tracks. The image, long predominant in the historical field, of a continuous confrontation between them is open to correction. Over many years, Philip II kept his distance, but also maintained his respect, as regards Elizabeth I, and was not in favour of the excommunication that Pius V issued against her in 1570. It was only well into the 1580s that he decided to undertake the so-called 'Enterprise of England', which ended in disaster rather than mere defeat. Before that date, and at the behest of Popes, Philip would constitute himself the protector of English, Scottish, and Irish exiles on the Continent and would favour the establishment of seminaries for them in Seville, Valladolid, Salamanca, Douai, and Rome. At the same time Elizabeth would make herself the ally of the rebels in the Low Countries against Philip II, or the protector— in what were officially times of peace—of those who committed acts of piracy in the New World or along the Spanish and Portuguese coasts.

The overall outcome of these tensions and confrontations led on into the seventeenth century with decisive results that were to endure for several centuries, marking definitively the religious history of both Spain and England. Seen from the dominant English situation, the very brief period of Mary Tudor's reign can be considered a parenthesis or interruption of the English tradition and an unsuccessful reaction against the developments of the preceding years. Seen from another point of view, the failed attempts of Mary Tudor were an attempt to take England back to an age-long tradition, profoundly shaken by political decisions of great economic and social reach. The task for us as historians is to establish with maximum objectivity and honesty *what happened*, proceeding then to the further question, *why?*

CHAPTER 2

The English Church during the reign of Mary

David Loades

The Church with which Bartolomé Carranza was in contact during his stay in England was a curious hybrid. Traditional Protestant historiography has represented it as highly reactionary, full of the grossest superstition, as it was depicted by John Foxe.[1] A generation ago Geoffrey Dickens declared that Mary 'never discovered the Counter Reformation', implying thereby that her Church lacked spiritual fervour and evangelical zeal. I have myself expressed the view that it was too negative; too concerned with discipline and administration, and insufficiently concerned to rebuild the traditional faith.[2] On the other hand, revisionists of various kinds have pointed out that Mary had very little time, and have drawn repeated attention to the evidence of the great popularity of her 'proceedings' (see below, note 13). Jennifer Loach described, a number of years ago, the quantity of pastoral writing which was published during the reign, refuting the notion that the Catholics were outgunned at the printing press, and declaring that the Marian hierarchy had a different priority, which it discharged effectively.[3] Rex Pogson was prepared to concede that the Church probably spent too much time and effort recovering its financial position, but

---

1   To Foxe, the gross superstition of the Roman Catholic Church consisted partly in the adoration of the consecrated elements, which was 'plain idolatry', and partly in diluting the unique intercessory function of Christ, particularly in attributing a similar function to the Virgin Mary. See especially his marginal comments on the Canon of the Mass in John Foxe, *Acts and monuments of these late and perilous days* (London: John Day, 1563), pp. 1397–1405, 1598–1601. There are later editions of his *Acts and monuments* from the same publisher (see note 53, below).
2   David Loades, *The reign of Mary Tudor: Politics, government, and religion in England, 1553–58*, 2nd edn (London and New York: Longman, 1991), a view slightly modified in id., 'The spirituality of the restored Catholic Church (1553–1558) in the context of the Counter Reformation', in *The reckoned expense: Edmund Campion and the early English Jesuits: Essays in celebration of the first centenary of Campion Hall, Oxford (1896–1996)*, ed. Thomas M. McCoog SJ (Woodbridge: Boydell Press, 1996), pp. 3–20.
3   Jennifer Loach, 'The Marian establishment and the printing press', *English Historical Review*, 101 (1986), pp. 135–48.

pointed out that this was not only necessary but required by the priorities which the restored Papal jurisdiction imposed. More recently, Eamon Duffy has emphasized that the Marian Church was 'Reformed Catholic', but with its roots in the Christian Humanism of the 1530s, rather than in the fervour of the Council of Trent, thereby agreeing with Geoffrey Dickens, but for different reasons. More recently still, Lucy Wooding has analysed a wide range of pastoral and theological writings from the period, broadly agreeing with Duffy, but going further in suggesting a subtle and enlightened school of theology which endeavoured to utilize all the best thinking of the previous thirty years, including that of Protestants, while remaining firmly insular and detached from contemporary movements on the Continent. To her, the insularity of Marian Catholicism, which Cardinal Pole rather surprisingly endorsed, was a great source of potential strength; it failed eventually for purely political reasons, unconnected with any internal defects.[4]

This argument for 'concordance' in Marian theology, harking back to the reign of Henry VIII, is persuasive, even convincing, but if accepted it raises questions of a different kind. However enlightened its thinking, and however broad its base of support, Mary's Church conducted one of the fiercest and most concentrated persecutions in Christian history, and ended by having the effect of demonizing Catholicism, in Protestant circles, for centuries. The impact of these events should not be underestimated. The majority of Christians of all shades of opinion believed that the death penalty was appropriate for obstinate heretics.[5] Henry VIII had burned dozens in the course of a thirty-eight year reign, and the Inquisition or its equivalent executed significant numbers in Spain, France, and the Low Countries. Even Calvin burned a few when he could get his hands on them. However, no other jurisdiction appears to have matched Mary's tally over a comparable period of time. Some six or seven hundred English Protestants were driven into exile abroad, an unknown number were displaced from their homes, and dozens died in prison. However, the Queen's crowning achievement was to burn about 280 in three-and-a-half years; probably more than the Spanish Inquisition and the French *Chambre ardente* put together, in an equivalent period.[6] John Foxe may have

---

4   Rex Pogson, 'Reginald Pole and the priorities of government in Mary Tudor's Church', *Historical Journal*, 18 (1975), pp. 3–21; Eamon Duffy, *The stripping of the altars: Traditional religion in England, c. 1400–c. 1580* (New Haven CT and London: Yale University Press, 1992), pp. 524–64; Lucy E. C. Wooding, *Rethinking Catholicism in Marian England*, Oxford Historical Monographs (Oxford: Clarendon, 2000), pp. 115–51. Also below, pp. 49–64.

5   For a full discussion of this opinion and its implications, see Brad S. Gregory, *Salvation at stake: Christian martyrdom in early modern Europe*, Harvard Historical Studies 134 (Cambridge MA and London: Harvard University Press, 1999), esp. pp. 74–138. John Foxe was unusual in strongly dissenting from this consensus.

6   Gregory, *Salvation*, p. 80. The *Chambre ardente*, for example, burned fifty-seven between

invented or distorted the doctrinal inquisitions which so often accompanied these burnings, but he did not invent the executions themselves.[7] Even his fiercest polemical critic, Robert Persons, did not claim that Foxe lied about that. Nor did he invent the hostile public reactions which often, and particularly after 1555, accompanied these *autos de fe*. Spanish, French, and Venetian observers all confirm that the burnings were unpopular, and provoked demonstrations against the authorities.[8] So how can we explain this apparently schizophrenic Church, in which enlightened and eirenic theology was apparently mixed with such cruel and brutal repression?

The answer of Catholic polemicists, both at the time and afterwards, has been that the Protestants wilfully brought their fate upon themselves. They were obstinate criminals, offenders against both ecclesiastical and temporal law, who out of sheer arrogance and vainglory refused to accept the truth when it was mercifully offered to them, casting themselves into the flames with the perverse enthusiasm of the criminally insane.[9] Foxe indeed identifies a few who were clearly mentally deficient, but he then observes bitterly that such poor lunatics were more suited to Bedlam than to a fiery pyre.[10] Unless one is disposed to classify all deeply held religious convictions as a form of insanity, Mary's Protestant victims were not insane; and the same Catholic polemicists who dismissed their pretensions to martyrdom went on to make identical claims for those Catholics who died as alleged traitors under both Henry VIII and Elizabeth. The question of martyrdom is not at issue here, because of course it is the cause which makes the martyr and not the death. William Campion was no more, and no less, a martyr than Thomas Cranmer.

1547 and 1550, its period of maximum activity. As with the Spanish Inquisition in this period, the English headcount is somewhat uncertain. Foxe counted 284, exclusive of those who died in prison. He missed a few, and may have counted some twice. A minimum of 280 is probably safe.

7   Ceri Sullivan, '"Oppressed by the force of truth": Robert Persons edits John Foxe', in *John Foxe: An historical perspective*, ed. David Loades (Aldershot: Ashgate, 1999), pp. 154–66.

8   See, for example, the comment of Giovanni Michieli on 1 June 1555: 'Two days ago, to the displeasure as usual of the population here, two Londoners were burned alive, one of them having been Public Lecturer in Scripture, a person sixty years of age, who was held in great esteem. In a few days the like will be done to four or five more; and thus from time to time to many others, who are in prison for this cause, and will not recant, although such sudden severity is odious to many people' (*CSPV*, VI. 93–4).

9   See esp. Robert Persons SJ, *A treatise of three conuersions of England from paganisme to Christian religion*, 3 vols (St-Omer: François Bellet, 1603–4); and Miles Hogarde (Huggarde), *The displaying of the Protestantes, and sondry their practices, with a description of diuers their abuses of late frequented* (London: Robert Caly, 1556).

10 On the case of William Nichols, he comments: 'And the more simplicity or feebleness of wit appeared in him, the more beastly and wretched doth it declare theyr cruell & tyrannicall act therein' (Foxe, *Acts and monuments*, 1563, p. 570).

The problem for us is not, as it was for Foxe, whether those who died in the Marian persecution were martyrs for the True Church, but, rather, why did they die? Parliament restored the heresy laws in 1555, reinforcing the responsibility of the secular authorities to carry out executions, but those laws were no more insistent than they had been over the century-and-a-half during which they had been in force before their repeal by Edward VI.[11] It was frequently hinted at the time that the real issue was sedition. In a period when confessional orthodoxy was seen as an inextricable part of a state's identity, dissidence meant at least disloyalty, and at most an active conspiratorial intent. Mary's proclamations made it perfectly clear that heresy and sedition were linked in her mind, and in the minds of her councillors.[12] Moreover, the Protestants were assiduously blamed for every disorder, whether great or small, and the strenuous denials of any such intent that they always made were never believed, any more than similar Catholic disclaimers were believed after 1570.[13] No Protestant power threatened war on Catholic England after 1553, so such suspects were not traitors in the same sense as Reginald Pole had been in the 1540s, or William Allen would be in the 1580s, but they could plausibly be accused of plotting a domestic revolution and the restoration of something like the Edwardian regime. However, when a clear opportunity arose to execute a Protestant leader for treason, it was passed over. Thomas Cranmer was actually convicted for his involvement in the Duke of Northumberland's abortive coup in July 1553, but the sentence was never carried out because the Queen decided that he should die for heresy.[14] As far as I am aware, the only person executed for treason who could have been convicted of heresy was the eccentric Essex preacher, George Eagles.[15]

11 The three statutes were 5 Richard II, c.5 (1382), 2 Henry IV, c.15 (1401), and 2 Henry V, c.7 (1414). They had been repealed in 1547, and were reinstated by 1 & 2 Philip and Mary, c. 6. See *Statutes of the Realm, printed by command of His Majesty King George the Third* (London: George Eyre and Andrew Strahan, 1810–32), IV/i. 244.

12 See, for example, the proclamation enforcing the statutes for public order of 26 May 1555, in James F. Hughes and Paul L. Larkin, *Tudor royal proclamations*, 3 vols (New Haven CT and London: Yale University Press, 1964–9), II. 53, n° 420.

13 Cranmer's *Homily of obedience*, and numerous sermons by Latimer during Edward VI's reign, had emphasized the duty of temporal allegiance without reservations. Cranmer made the same point at his trial in 1555, when he said: 'There is no subject but to a king. I am a subject, I owe my fidelity to the Crown' (Foxe, *Acta and monuments*, 1583, p. 1880). Catholics constantly referred to 'the Queen's proceedings' after 1553, in order to emphasize that the heretic was disobeying the sovereign.

14 Foxe was mistaken in claiming that Cranmer's treason was pardoned: Diarmaid MacCulloch, *Thomas Cranmer: A life* (New Haven CT and London: Yale University Press, 1996), p. 555.

15 Foxe, *Acts and monuments*, 1583, pp. 2009–10. He was convicted under the statute against seditious assemblies.

The Protestants themselves were aware of their vulnerability to such charges, and went out of their way repeatedly to emphasize their willingness to obey the Queen in all matters which did not touch their consciences—just as the Catholics were to do later under Elizabeth. It was only from the relative safety of exile that writers such as John Ponet, and more obviously Christopher Goodman, urged resistance against an ungodly ruler.[16] If Mary's Council was indeed using the heresy laws to eliminate political opponents, then it chose some very odd victims. Good cases could have been made against several noblemen, and a number of substantial gentry, but exile was the worst that befell any of them.[17] The overwhelming majority of the victims, both men and women, were artisans or husbandmen, who posed not the slightest threat to the security of the realm, even if their professions of temporal obedience were not honest.

There are, I think, three possible explanations why the Council acted as it did. It may have been the more or less willing instrument of an aggressive and vengeful Church, which was concerned to reimpose its damaged authority and its even more ruffled dignity. That is what Foxe wanted to believe, because it fitted his model of a 'False Church'.[18] So he demonized the clergy, and particularly Bishops Gardiner and Bonner, with constant emphasis upon their cruelty. It also enabled him to represent the Queen as the almost innocent victim of clerical machinations, her own misfortunes becoming the measure of the extent to which she had been deluded. If the bishops were indeed driving the persecution, then it makes our present perception of the spirituality of the restored Church even more paradoxical, but there are other good reasons for not accepting such a view. The second explanation is that the persecution represented a failure of policy. Stephen Gardiner, who was the most active protagonist of terror at the beginning, did not take Protestantism seriously as a religious movement. His own experience had persuaded him that the so-called 'Reformed Faith' was no more than an ideological smoke-screen, behind which ambitious politicians manoeuvred to plunder the Church and secure control of the government.[19] He believed that the mere thought of death would

---

16 John Ponet, *A shorte treatise of politicke power and of the obedience which subiectes owe to kynges and other ciuile gouernours* (Strasburg: W. Köpfel, 1556); Christopher Goodman, *How superior powres oght to be obeyd of their subiects* (Geneva: John Crispin, 1558).

17 For example Francis Russell, second Earl of Bedford; see Christina H. Garrett, *The Marian exiles: A study in the origins of Elizabethan Puritanism* (Cambridge: Cambridge University Press, 1938).

18 In his general thesis, Foxe followed John Bale, *The image of bothe Churches* (Amsterdam: S. Mierdman?, 1548); see David Loades, *John Foxe and the English Reformation*, St Andrew's Studies in Reformation History (Aldershot: Scolar Press, 1997), pp. 1–11.

19 See Lacey B. Smith, *Tudor prelates and politics*, Princeton Studies in History 8 (Princeton NJ: Princeton University Press, 1953), p. 99; Glyn Redworth, *In defence of the Church*

38   Reforming Catholicism

send them all running for cover, exposing their so-called 'convictions' for the
sham they were. 'Thou wilt not burn in this gear when it cometh to the point,'
as one of the early victims was told.[20] He tried to frighten as many as possible
into leaving the country, but was forced to put his policy to the test when
some leading preachers refused to be intimidated. After the first half-dozen
burnings, it was clear that his gamble had failed; indeed it had had the
opposite of the intended effect. Foxe's acknowledgment that Gardiner had
'given over' as utterly discouraged by the summer of 1555 seems to be
accurate.[21] The third possibility is that it was not an ecclesiastical policy at all
but was driven by secular authority. The coincidence of an unprecedented
persecution with the unprecedented experience of a foreign king was too
obvious to miss. Some Catholic historians, notably Philip Hughes, anxious to
exonerate the Church from charges of having acted cruelly, have been inclined
to blame Philip's influence, and that of his theologians.[22] However, all the
contemporary evidence is against such an explanation. Philip avoided any
direct involvement, and although there is no means of knowing what he said
in private to his wife, he appears to have been alarmed by the developing
political implications. He could hardly have urged a policy of toleration, even
if he had been inclined to it, but he was also uneasily aware that the burnings
were being used by some (not necessarily Protestants) who were anxious to
increase his unpopularity. In so far as the Spanish theologians became involved
at all, it was on the side of moderation. Juan de Villagarcía did his honest best
to rescue Cranmer, and it was not his fault that the English government was
cynically determined to burn the ex-archbishop, no matter what he said. Nevertheless, there has to be an explanation of why the persecution continued to be
driven on remorselessly, even after its original instigator, Gardiner, had drawn
back, and the sad fact is that Mary considered it to be her duty.[23]

Heresy, she believed, had ruined her mother's marriage and her own early
life. When it took hold, it destroyed the immortal souls of those whom it
afflicted, and the most extreme steps were justified in eliminating it, and thus

Catholic: The life of Stephen Gardiner (Oxford: Blackwell, 1990), pp. 285–310.

20 Examination of John Bradford, in Foxe, Acts and monuments, 1583, pp. 1603 ff.

21 Redworth, Defence, p. 331; Foxe, Acts and monuments, 1583, p. 1786.

22 Hughes did not blame Philip directly for the persecution, but believed that Mary was
    generally too subservient to her husband's influence: Philip Hughes, The Reformation in
    England, 3 vols (London: Hollis and Carter, 1952–4), II. 254–304.

23 Mary's only recorded explanation of her position is measured but implacable:
    'Touching punishment of heretics, methinketh it ought to be done without rashness,
    not leaving in the meanwhile to do justice to such as by learning would seem to
    deceive the simple, and the rest to be so used that the people might well perceive them
    not to be condemned without just occasion, whereby they shall both understand the
    truth and beware to do the like' (BL, Harleian MS 444, fol. 27).

protecting the realm. Like Gardiner, she did not believe that the Edwardian Reformers had been sincere, and the fulsome recantation of the Duke of Northumberland before his death had confirmed her in that conviction.[24] They were merely ambitious and time-serving hypocrites. When it became clear that this was not the case, the Queen's reaction was the opposite of Gardiner's. Sincere heretics, however deluded, were much more dangerous than bogus ones. This was not because they threatened rebellion (although they might), but because they were the Devil's agents, threatening the salvation of God's people. So it did not matter to Mary whether a heretic was rich or poor, male or female, influential or totally obscure.[25] If he and she would not recant, then they had to be burned like an infected animal, to protect the rest of the flock.

So although Foxe would not admit it, the persecution was driven by the Queen. Gardiner was certainly a willing agent at first, but most of the other front-line bishops were visibly distressed by what they were called upon to do. Edmund Bonner was a rough diamond, but even he preferred to flog his victims into submission if he could thereby avoid burning them.[26] As Bishop of London he was constantly in the firing-line, but, as Gina Alexander demonstrated some time ago, there is plenty of evidence to suggest that he was being driven by the Council—and the Council was driven by Mary, who always showed the greatest resolve when her conscience was involved.[27] Pole was in an invidious position. In principle he agreed that heresy was a dangerous virus, and he could hardly disagree with his Queen in public; but he was much less sure that he knew what heresy was, or rather where the boundary between acceptable and unacceptable doctrine should be drawn. Such uncertainty was unacceptable in a persecutor, so although it was his Legatine Commissions which provided the jurisdictional apparatus for heresy trials, there is very little sign that he was proactive, and even Foxe admitted that he was 'no great bloody persecutor'. As in the case of King Philip, what he may have said in private, we do not know. He is unlikely to have urged Mary to greater efforts, but he would have known Tudor obstinacy when he saw it, and may not have been sufficiently sure of his ground to do the opposite.

Consequently, I think we have a Church whose leadership was seriously at odds with a very important part of the agenda which it was compelled to

---

24 See *The saying of John late duke of Northumberland upon the scaffold* (1553) in *The chronicle of Queen Jane and of two years of Queen Mary, and especially of the rebellion of Sir Thomas Wyat, written by a resident in the Tower of London*, ed. John G. Nichols, Camden Society, 1st s. 48 (London: Printed for the Camden Society, 1850), pp. 18–19.

25 BL, Harleian MS 444, fol. 27.

26 A case in point is the scourging of Thomas Hinshaw and John Milles in Bonner's orchard, famously illustrated in Foxe, *Acts and monuments*, 1570, pp. 2242–3.

27 For a discussion of this aspect of her personality see David Loades, *Mary Tudor: A life*, (Oxford: Blackwell, 1989), pp. 327–8.

follow. The connecting link is Mary's personal faith, and although her proclamation of 18 August 1553 declared that this was well known, in fact it was
not, and is not.[28] She never set down the salient points of her beliefs in
writing, and they can only be reconstructed from what she did, or is reported
to have said. What was well known was that she had defended the Mass from
its Protestant detractors, and insisted on continuing the elaborate ceremonies
and rituals of traditional worship after they had been abolished by public
authority.[29] Where she stood on such central issues as Justification, Free Will,
and Purgatory, no one now has any idea. It was generally assumed from her
public stance during her brother's reign that she accepted her father's settlement, but in one very important respect that soon turned out to be untrue.
Whether she had abandoned the Papacy under pressure in 1536, and only
returned to it now, or whether she had dissembled her true convictions for
nearly twenty years, we do not know. What we do know is that within weeks
(and possibly days) of her accession, she had told her Council of her intention
to restore the Roman obedience.[30] However, that should not be taken to mean
that she endorsed, or even knew about, the doctrinal definitions which had
already been made at two sessions of the Council of Trent. Mary insisted,
against all advice (including that of the Emperor), on having a Requiem Mass
said for the soul of her brother, and in her will she requested the restored
Benedictine monks of Westminster to pray for her own soul and that of her
husband.[31] Unlike her father, however, she did not endow large numbers of
Masses of special intention, and during her lifetime founded no perpetual
chantry. During the reign, a number of chantries were founded by pious noblemen, so the practice was regarded as perfectly acceptable, but the Queen did
not take advantage of it. Similarly, she seems to have had very little interest in
the revival of the monastic *opus Dei*. Virtually all the half-dozen or so religious
houses established during her reign were endowed by the Crown, and Mary
remembered most of them in her will; but only Westminster was endowed on
a significant scale.[32] Each house seems to have been created on the initiative

28 See David Loades, *The chronicles of the Tudor Queens* (Stroud: Sutton Publishing, 2002),
   pp. 17–19.
29 Loades, *Mary Tudor*, pp. 162–4.
30 The Imperial ambassador in England, Simon Renard, reported this as old news in
   September 1553 (*CSPS*, XI. 218).
31 See *Diary of Henry Machyn, citizen and merchant-taylor of London, 1550 to 1563*, ed. John G.
   Nichols, Camden Society, 1st s. 42 (London: Printed for the Camden Society, 1848),
   p. 49. Mary's will and codicil survive in a transcript (BL, Harleian MS 6949), printed in
   Loades, *Mary Tudor*, pp. 370–83. An extract appears in id., *Chronicles*, pp. 93–5.
32 Two legal instruments, of 7 September and 10 November 1556, gave Westminster
   Abbey restored legal existence as a monastic community, and an endowment of £1600
   per annum (*CPRPM*, III. 546, 354; NA, SP/12/64).

and petition of a group of ex-religious who wished to return to the cloister, and although the Queen was supportive of such moves, she seems to have done nothing to initiate them, and did not respond with any particular alacrity to such petitions. Although Mary was famously enthusiastic about the Mass, and attended at least one every day, she is not known to have had any favourite devotion, not even to her Virgin namesake. She loved solemn ceremonies and processions, and the music of the Chapel Royal flourished, but this was a matter of taste and had no particular doctrinal significance. Contemporaries several times commented upon her adoration of the consecrated Host, from which we may assume that she was strictly orthodox on Transubstantiation, but some of her other attitudes were less predictable. Unlike some of her more conservative clergy, she was an enthusiastic supporter of preaching, expressing a desire for 'good' sermons to remedy the harm done by so many 'bad' sermons in recent years.[33] Apart from the Host, however, holy objects interested her not at all. No attempts were made on her behalf to collect or restore the relics which had recently been scattered, although we know that many had been retrieved by pious individuals. The only shrine to have been restored was that of Edward the Confessor, rebuilt by the monks of Westminster, and Mary (as far as I can discover) never undertook a pilgrimage, or sent anyone on her behalf, even when she believed childbirth to be imminent.

So the Queen's piety was not quite what one would expect of a ruler of such zealous Catholic orthodoxy. It was in fact shaped by her Humanist upbringing between 1525 and 1533, and owed more to her tutors, and the scholars whose work she had read, than it did to the more conservative zeal of her mother, Catherine of Aragon. So it fitted comfortably with the piety of her Cardinal kinsman, Reginald Pole, which had been forged at the same time, but in the rather different climate of Renaissance Italy.[34] Although both believed that the Latin liturgy was necessary to preserve the unity of the Church, neither was specifically hostile to vernacular Scripture. Although some conservative clergy argued openly against it, and no new editions were produced during Mary's reign, the Great Bible of 1539 was never withdrawn, or officially denounced. Pole seems to have considered the English Bible a risk worth taking, because although it could be dangerous in the wrong (lay) hands, it was a necessary tool for orthodox preachers, and the Biblical education of the clergy was high on his list of priorities.[35] Pole was well aware that Catholic clergy had all too often allowed the initiative in Biblical exposition to fall into

---

33 In the document quoted above (BL, Harleian MS 444), the Queen is also reported to have said: 'Touching good preaching, I wish that may supply and overcome the evil preaching in time past.'

34 Thomas F. Mayer, *Reginald Pole: Prince and prophet* (Cambridge: Cambridge University Press, 2000), esp. pp. 251–61.

35 ibid., pp. 279–301.

the hands of their opponents, and was determined to remedy that defect. John Foxe constantly insisted, and sought to demonstrate, that ignorance of the Bible was damning proof that those who called themselves Catholics did not possess the Word of God.[36]

What, then, constituted heresy, for which the penalties were so frightful, and how did a Church which carried so much doctrinal ambivalence contrive to isolate it satisfactorily? We find, on reading the interrogatories which were issued to suspects, whether these are in the pages of Foxe or in the registers from which he drew many of them, that the same themes are endlessly repeated. They fall broadly into two categories: ecclesiastical and doctrinal. Apart from the preachers, who come into a rather distinct category, the majority of suspects were apprehended for failing, or refusing, to attend their parish churches. The reason commonly given was that the Latin liturgy was unedifying (because incomprehensible) and contrary to New Testament prescription. To this the normal official response was that the Universal Church had so decided, and that in being 'singular', the suspect was putting his or her private judgement above that of the Church, from which such people were cutting themselves off by so doing. Were they not aware that there could be no salvation outside the Church? The suspect usually accepted that point, and then claimed to be a member of the True Church of Christ, with which the Church of Rome had 'nought to do'.[37] In other words, the issue was one of discipline and jurisdiction rather than doctrine. It was an offence against the Canon Law to refuse obedience to the Church, but it was not strictly heresy, so the inquisitors normally went further, seeking an issue where true error could be identified. Some times this was Predestination, or good works, but usually it was the Sacraments. How many Sacraments were there? Two: Baptism and the Lord's Supper. This was good progress from the inquisitors' point of view, and a *prima facie* case of heresy had already been established. The crunch question then followed: 'How say you to the Sacrament of the Altar?' At that point the issue ceased to be disciplinary, and became doctrinal.

In almost every case this was used as the acid test of the heretic. The suspect would begin by denying that there was any such sacrament, sometimes

36 Foxe repeatedly sought to demonstrate that unlearned Protestants, particularly women, knew their Bible better than Catholic priests. The examination of Elizabeth Young is an example (*Acts and monuments*, 1583, pp. 2065–8). The official position was that it was the responsibility of the Church to interpret the Scriptures, rather than the individual's, and that the traditions of the Church (particularly the Church Fathers) were of equal importance.

37 See, for example, the examination of Richard Woodman in Foxe, *Acts and monuments*, 1583, pp. 1984–90. The identity of the True Church was a prime issue.

quibbling over what was meant by 'altar'.[38] Rejection was based on the alleged failure of the Mass to reflect the Dominical institution of the sacrament. The exchanges took a variety of forms, but the basic issue was always Transubstantiation. Foxe almost certainly tidied up a variety of opinions into specific statements of Edwardian orthodoxy, but that is not the point here. The characteristic position adopted by the suspects was 'receptionist', meaning that the elements of bread and wine remain unchanged after consecration.[39] According to this view, Christ's Body and Blood were spiritually, but not physically, present in the elements, but because this presence was induced by the faith of the recipient, and not by the words of the priest, Christ was not received in this way by the evil or faithless person.[40] So the crucial point was not whether Christ's presence was spiritual or corporeal, but how it came about. The protagonists of both sides were aware that the distinction between a spiritual presence and a corporeal presence without 'accidents' (in other words entities which inhere to a distinct essence, in this case Christ's 'Body' and 'Blood', rather than 'bread' and 'wine') was purely semantic. Indeed, this was often a dialogue of the deaf, because there is no bridging the gap between a person who can believe in a physical 'body' which cannot be detected by the senses, and one who cannot. It has recently been observed that 'Marian views of the sacrament were... both intricate and carefully nuanced', and that may have been true of sophisticated theologians, but it was not (and could not) be true of those whose job it was to detect heretics.[41]

Like Catholics, Protestants believed in Christ's humanity, but the latter went on to conclude that His body, even in its resurrected state, could only be in one place at a time, and after His Ascension that place was heaven. For them it was thus a conceptual absurdity to claim that Christ's body was materially present in the Eucharist. It was also absurd to suggest that the bread and wine which Our Lord had broken and distributed at the Last Supper could already, at that time, have been His physical flesh and blood, since his

38 Some Protestants argued that the Body of Christ could itself be regarded as an altar, but usually confined themselves to denying Transubstantiation. See the examination of Mathew Plaise in Foxe, *Acts and monuments*, 1583, p. 1982.

39 Although such a view of the Eucharist was common among Anglicans of the sixteenth and seventeenth centuries, the term 'receptionism' itself is first found only in 1867. See *Oxford dictionary of the Christian Church*, 3rd edn, ed. Frank L. Cross and Elizabeth A. Livingstone (Oxford: Oxford University Press, 1998), p. 1371.

40 See the examination of Richard Woodman in Foxe, *Acts and monuments*, 1583, p. 1996.

41 Wooding, *Rethinking Catholicism*, p. 167. Some orthodox Catholic writers were keenly aware that their position could not be defended by 'common reason', and were therefore anxious to emphasize the mystery. Thomas Watson wrote of 'our faith in this matter induced by hys onely authorytie, and not by our wytte, whose wordes require necessarily our fayth, and in no wise do admitte our reason' in his *Holsome and catholyke doctrine concerninge the seven sacramentes of Chrystes church* (London: Robert Caly, 1558), fol. 37v.

whole natural body was not only present, but also alive at the time. The words 'this is my Body...this is my Blood' could not therefore be understood materially but only symbolically. In support of this view it was usually urged that Christ had also described Himself as a 'vine' and a 'door', without meaning either thing literally. In so far as there was a 'Presence', which most of them acknowledged, it was spiritual and not corporeal, and therefore did not alter the fact that the Eucharistic elements remained fully bread and wine. There was some disagreement (which Foxe did not acknowledge) between those who believed that the Presence was evoked by the faith of the congregation as a whole, and those who believed in the 'receptionist' position outlined above. The then current Catholic position was not only rejected by all Protestants as incredible; it was also regarded with genuine horror. To treat any material objects (in this case bread and wine) as though they partook of the Divine Substance was to commit both idolatry and blasphemy.[42] Whatever subtle reservations they may have had about the formulation of the doctrine of Transubstantiation that was then current, Catholics had to take a robust stand against this radical, and often abusively expressed, incredulity. 'What seest thou yonder?', the inquisitor would demand, indicating the pyx; and on being told that it was a pretty pot, he would go on to demand to know the nature of the contents. If the answer was 'bread', the respondent was a heretic, and although the interrogation might then continue at tedious length, little more would be elicited. Orthodox clergy made a habit of emphasizing their devotion to the Host by removing their hats every time the Sacrament was mentioned, and their rejection of wholly materialistic human thought by insisting that the whole of Christ's 'body and members, bones and teeth' was present in the elements.

Various secondary disagreements sprang from this confrontation. Because they did not accept any priestly act of transformation, Protestants tended to reject all clerical authority except that conferred by public authority. Neither Orders nor Penance were Biblical sacraments, and auricular confession was unnecessary because it was widely held, in such circles, that priests had no power to absolve sins.[43] Similarly, by this interpretation, a sacrament derived

---

42 See Thomas Cranmer, *A defence of the true and catholike doctrine of the sacrament*, in Henry Jankyns, *The remains of Thomas Cranmer, D.D., Archbishop of Canterbury* (Oxford: Oxford University Press, 1882), II; also Peter N. Brooks, *Thomas Cranmer's doctrine of the Eucharist: An essay in historical development*, 2nd edn (London: Macmillan, 1992).

43 All those Protestants accused of heresy under Mary seem to have agreed that only God can forgive sin, and to have held that the claim of any human being to do so was mere *hubris*. Under questioning, several admitted that it was proper to consult a priest for advice about spiritual problems, and therefore that confession was not in itself unlawful. But it was not a sacrament because such a consultation could not be a channel of Divine Grace. [*Editorial note:* It should be observed that the Second [1552] Prayer Book of Edward VI stated in the most explicit terms that priests did indeed have the

its efficacy from the participation of the faithful; just as there was no Baptism if there was no one to be baptized (a point which orthodox Catholics conceded), so there was no Eucharist if there was no one to receive with the celebrant (which was strenuously denied).[44]

Responsibility for these confrontations rested with both sides, and the question remains why a Church which was in many respects so Humanist and flexible in its pastoral and theological ministry should have insisted on defining itself by a crude interpretation of Transubstantiation about which many of its own leaders had reservations. It may have been because the power of ordination (*potestas ordinis*), and all that this implied, depended upon such a doctrine, but such an argument was never used in these inquisitions, and the Marian Church in fact derived its authority from statute rather than from the truth of its faith, a point on which Gardiner at least was perfectly clear.[45] Orthodox Catholics' need to identify heretics seems to have sprung rather from a keen sense of the danger of heresy than from any clear perception of what it was; hence the desirability of a 'crunch issue' which could leave no doubt. On the Protestant side, the fact that the Mass was wicked and idolatrous was one of the few points upon which all could agree; and there was also an awareness that Protestants needed to redeem their spiritual credit, which had been compromised by the Edwardian establishment. To some the prospect of martyrdom may have been irresistible, but many who did not go so far felt an urgent need to stand up and be counted, and an urge to obey the Biblical injunction to 'come out from the midst of them' (II Corinthians 6:14–15). Although some Catholics were disposed to use the judgement of the Universal Church as a knockdown argument, very few appealed to the Papacy, and most laboured conscientiously to meet the challenge of Protestants that they should be convinced 'out of the Word of God'.

If Mary had not been so concerned to purge the land with fire, most of this need never have happened, but, as it was, 'prince-pleasers', both lay and clerical, hastened to oblige. Most of those who appeared before episcopal courts or legatine commissioners got there by being denounced either by their parish

power and authority to absolve sins. See, e.g., 'The Ordre for the Visitacion of the Sicke', in which the 'Priest' [not 'Minister', here] says: 'by his [Christ's] aucthoritie committed to me, *I absolue thee* [emphasis added] from all thy synnes', in *The first and second Prayer Books of Edward VI* (London: The Prayer Book Society, 1999), p. 419.]

44 See Foxe, *Acts and monuments*, 1583, p. 1994.

45 Mary implicitly accepted the validity both of her father's and her brother's statutes by repealing them. Papal jurisdiction was restored by the second Act of Repeal (1 & 2 Philip and Mary c. 8). This was contrary to Pole's advice, that all Acts against the Holy See were *ultra vires* and thus automatically null and void; see Jennifer Loach, *Parliament and Crown in the reign of Mary Tudor*, Oxford Historical Monographs (Oxford: Clarendon Press, 1986), pp. 108–9.

priests or by orthodox neighbours.[46] Some of the more conspicuous, such as
Cranmer and John Philpot, were referred by the Council itself, but the ordinary rank and file appear to have been the victims of purely local circumstances.
Some conservative clergy quickly welcomed the opportunity to rid themselves
of parishioners who had been thorns in their flesh for years, and some Protestants paraded their dissent in ways which virtually forced the authorities to act
against them. However, most appear to have been the victims of disputes which
had more to do with money, sex, or bad neighbourliness than with religion as
such. The classic example is that of Perrotine Massy, who, with her sister and
mother, was burned on Guernsey for no worse an offence, it would seem,
than falling out with the Dean of the island, Jacques Amy. The three women
had indeed been Protestants during Edward's reign, but now expressed a
complete willingness to submit to the jurisdiction of the Church. By all normal
standards this was a recantation, but the three women were executed anyway,
apparently because Amy simply decided not to accept their recantation—a
decision which he was not entitled to make.[47] Turning over the stones of persecution reveals some unpleasant wildlife. Richard Woodman was denounced
by his father after a row concerning inheritance; both men and women were
turned in by spouses who were clearly tired of them.[48] Occasionally, constables
and Justices endeavoured to curry favour with their superiors by displays of
zeal; and of course, some were persecutors by conviction. Bishops and
Chancellors struggled with a task which most of them would willingly have
avoided, and often displayed extraordinary vigilance and patience in their
efforts to avoid burning their victims. What they wanted was explicit recantations of explicit heresies; and although they were usually successful in finding
the heresies, they were often denied their recantations. Their anger and
frustration comes over clearly, even in Foxe's slanted narratives.

So how far were the Spanish theologians who came with Philip involved in
this tragedy? Juan de Villagarcía appears in at least two episodes; when he was
snubbed by Julius Palmer in Oxford, and when he laboured unavailingly with
Cranmer. Beyond the clerical and university élite he could do little, because he
spoke no English. It is also clear that he was not made privy to the Council's
policy, because he was under the impression that if Cranmer recanted, his
punishment would be commuted in accordance with Canon law. The Archbishop's last stand, which caused his confessor such genuine anguish, was thus
the direct result of Mary's refusal to play the game according to the rules: 'of
her purpose to burn him', as Foxe correctly observed, 'she would in no way

---

46 See the stories of Hugh Laverock, John Apprice, Katherine Hut, and Elizabeth
    Thackwell in Foxe, *Acts and monuments*, 1583, pp. 1909–11.
47 Foxe, *Acts and monuments*, 1583, p. 1943. For a full discussion of this case, see Darryl M.
    Ogier, *Reformation and society in Guernsey* (Woodbridge: The Boydell Press, 1996), pp. 55–8.
48 Foxe, *Acts and monuments*, 1583, p. 1985.

relent'.[49] Alonso de Castro also appears at least twice, most famously when he preached at Court against the persecution, allegedly at Philip's instigation. Carranza does not appear in the pages of Foxe, and much of his work in England was as a personal adviser to Pole. He preached at Court on a number of occasions, presumably in Latin, and took part in the legatine visitation of Oxford University.[50] In direct opposition to Villagarcía, although perhaps in ignorance of the fact, he seems to have urged both Pole and Philip to severity against Cranmer. Like Villagarcía ('Friar John' to Foxe), Pedro de Soto held an academic post in Oxford (see Chapter 9) and appears to have been one of the Spanish friars who 'laboured' with John Philpot, but we have no idea what he thought of what was going on under his nose. Such evidence as we have of Spanish and Imperial attitudes to Mary's ecclesiastical policy is ambiguous. Simon Renard was frankly horrified by the persecution, although it did not really start until after his influence in England had been eclipsed.[51] He had no sympathy with heresy, and was not squeamish, but he considered the policy of violent oppression to be a serious tactical mistake, and on the whole events were to prove him right. Several of Philip's courtiers denounced the English in general terms as barbarous heretics but did not stay in England long enough to comment on their fate. Apart from Castro's somewhat uncharacteristic sermon, the Spanish Religious seem to have accepted what was going on without comment, either because it was a familiar situation to them, or because they considered it to be none of their business. By a supreme irony, both Pole and Carranza came themselves to be suspected of heresy: Pole by Rome during the last two years of his life, and Carranza after his return to Spain, on account of his activities in England.[52]

Appropriately enough, the English persecution was brought to a halt by Mary's death in November 1558, although it was to be another six months before the religious settlement was changed. Although they were almost all dismissed, and some languished in prison for years, no Marian bishop (or any other priest) was sent to the scaffold or the stake. It was to be almost twenty years before the Recusant community would begin to gain for itself the credit of new martyrs to add to John Fisher and Thomas More, and to set them against their Protestant counterparts. Elizabeth effectively prevented her Protestant subjects from taking their revenge, and this was one of her most sensible and enlightened policies. It would have been so easy to let a fresh

---

49 Foxe, *Acts and monuments*, 1583, p. 1884.

50 Mayer, *Reginald Pole*, pp. 279–300; also below, Chapter 9.

51 See Renard's letters, to Philip on 5 February 1555 and to the Emperor on 25 March 1555 (*CSPS*, XIII. 138–9, 147).

52 José Ignacio Tellechea Idígoras, *Fray Bartolomé Carranza y el cardenal Pole: Un navarro en la restauración católica de Inglaterra (1554–1558)* (Pamplona: Diputación Foral de Navarra, Institución Príncipe de Viana, and CSIC, 1977).

bunch of fanatics turn upon their tormentors, and so destructive of the peace and order which she needed. The revenge which they did take was peaceful and totally effective; it was called the *Acts and monuments of the English martyrs*.[53] We now know that the Marian Church was not obscurantist or reactionary; nor was it ultramontane, except in the most formal sense. There can be argument about the effectiveness with which it discharged its pastoral mission, but there can be no doubt of the seriousness with which its leaders took their duties. Their doctrine was reformed, and their practice rooted in the English past. However, it was not only Mary's death which frustrated their constructive purposes. The Marian Church undoubtedly carried a baggage of unreformed attitudes, both among the clergy and the laity, and the persecution gave free rein to some base instincts. However, the Queen herself made three serious errors, each one understandable and defensible in itself, but together eventually fatal. She insisted on destroying her father's religious settlement, which had been long accepted and was popular, in addition to her brother's, which was neither. She married Philip, thereby linking a Church which should have had impeccable national qualifications with foreign interference. And she discharged her religious duty by burning scores of perfectly innocuous people who would not accept the doctrinal framework that was primarily represented by Transubstantiation.

Mary was undeniably unfortunate. She was childless, and her country was ravaged by harvest failure and disease. She lost England's last Continental possession, Calais, and she died when things were almost at their worst. However, it was her mistakes which made her death a turning point in English history. Had her Church not been linked to an unpopular Papacy, and an even more unpopular king, there would have been less incentive for Elizabeth to turn to the Protestant alternative. Had her policy of coercive uniformity been more politic and sensitive, there would have been less anger, and the cry that England was under judgement for murdering the saints of God would have had no resonance. Had she confined herself to restoring her father's settlement, her Church would have remained impeccably English, and its distinctive theology would have served such a settlement well. Without Elizabeth's Protestantism, John Foxe would probably have remained in Strasburg, and much subsequent English history would have been different. However...

---

53 The first edition was published in 1563, and the second, substantially modified, in 1570. It was to go through another five editions and two abridgements before 1641, and became one of the most influential books written in the English language. See James F. Mozley, *John Foxe and his book* (New York: Octagon, 1970); V. Norskov Olsen, *John Foxe and the Elizabethan Church* (Berkeley CA and London: University of California Press, 1973); Loades, *John Foxe*; and id. (ed.), *John Foxe: An historical perspective* (Aldershot: Ashgate, 1999).

CHAPTER 3

The Marian Restoration
and the language of Catholic Reform

Lucy Wooding

The reign of Mary Tudor was once easily classified: reactionary, repressive, misguided, unsuccessful. Nowhere was this description held to be more true than when applied to her religious policy.[1] But more recent research, which has brought a very welcome challenge to these views, has left us with a far more complicated task when trying to understand the assumptions, expectations, and motivations behind the religious policy of the Marian Restoration.[2] The present chapter will approach this hazardous undertaking through the medium of the religious literature published in the English vernacular during Mary's reign. It will argue that the language of much of this literature provides an important indication of some of the preoccupations of the reign. There were, of course, variations among the works published between 1553 and 1558, and yet a great many of them used what might be termed the 'language of Catholic reform'. The suggestion here is that such language had become an established aspect of English Catholic identity by the 1550s, and that it deployed a rhetoric which was firmly rooted in Scripture, open to the Augustinian and Pauline emphases beloved of Catholic as well as Protestant reformers, and fully aware of the need for religious regeneration within the Church.

---

1 For the classic exposition of this view see Arthur G. Dickens, *The English Reformation*, 2nd edn (London: Batsford, 1989), pp. 287–315.
2 For more recent interpretations of Mary's policies and the possible strengths of Marian Catholicism see: Jennifer Loach, 'The Marian establishment and the printing press', *English Historical Review*, 101 (1986), pp. 135–48; Elizabeth Russell, 'Mary Tudor and Mr Jorkins', *Bulletin of the Institute of Historical Research*, 63 (1990), pp. 263–76; Eamon Duffy, *The stripping of the altars: Traditional religion in England, c. 1400–c. 1580* (New Haven CT and London: Yale University Press, 1992), pp. 524–64; Christopher Haigh, *English Reformations: Religion, politics, and society under the Tudors* (Oxford: Clarendon Press, 1993), pp. 203–34; Lucy E. C. Wooding, *Rethinking Catholicism in Marian England*, Oxford Historical Monographs (Oxford: Clarendon Press, 2000), pp. 114–80. Also Loades, Chapter 2, above.

It will immediately become clear from comparison with other views expressed in this volume that this interpretation is a contentious one.[3] It should perhaps be seen as part of a wider debate concerning the onset of confession-alization in England. For some, Catholic identity is a given, to a large extent an immutable expression of a clearly defined tradition. Discussion of sixteenth-century Catholicism, it could therefore be claimed, has a reasonably unequivocal standard of Catholic orthodoxy against which religious statements of the time can be measured. Conversely, it could also be argued that such an approach is deeply misleading, imposing a false coherence on an age when religious belief and identity were subject to as much change as continuity.[4] This chapter propounds the view that the reforming influences of the sixteenth century had a profound effect upon English Catholicism, broadening the range of emphases possible within what might still be considered the boundaries of orthodoxy. The use of language both Catholic and reformed within the vernacular publi-cations of Mary Tudor's reign is just one indication of some of the ways in which English Catholicism was adapting to the era of Reformation. The chapter will outline a few of the characteristic themes in this literature, and will also attempt to address the question of why the Marian works might have pursued such themes, and what political considerations, as well as what religious convictions, may have guided their use of rhetoric.

One immediate reason for adopting the language of Catholic reform may have been the standpoint of the Queen herself. The reactionary and blood-thirsty queen of legend was in fact often associated, in her own time, with the educated Christian Humanist attitudes which had long pervaded the world of the intellectual élite. Although we have frustratingly little evidence of the Queen's own personal convictions, it is striking that the writers who published work during her reign frequently addressed her as someone who shared their Humanist background and education, and seemed to assume that she would approve of the way in which they were expounding and defending the Faith. The descriptions of Mary which appear in these works constantly refer to her reputation for learning: as John Standish wrote in 1554, 'surely the common voyce is that her grace is not onelye most noble, mooste vertuous, mooste wyttye, and moste studious, but also mooste excellent in learnyng'.[5] Mary's

3 See William L. Wizeman, 'Recalled to life: The theology and spirituality of Mary Tudor's Church', unpubl. doct. diss., University of Oxford (2002), pp. 1–25, and Chapter 7, below.
4 See Peter Marshall and Alec Ryrie, 'Introduction: Protestantisms and their beginnings', in *The beginnings of English Protestantism*, ed. Marshall and Ryrie (Cambridge: Cambridge University Press, 2002), pp. 1–13 (pp. 5–8); Ethan H. Shagan, *Popular politics and the English Reformation*, Cambridge Studies in Early Modern History (Cambridge: Cambridge University Press, 2003), pp. 1–25.
5 John Standish, *A discourse wherin is debated whether it be expedient that the scripture should be in English* (London: Robert Caly, 1554), sig. B1r.

Humanist education was frequently acknowledged, and one corollary of such learning was a commitment to Scripture. John Proctor, also writing in 1554, expressed the hope

> that where as heretofore... the trueth of Gods word, and the zeal of good workes have decaied: so hereafter, under Mary a lady of heavenly simplicitie, the lively sparke of godly love may eftsones kindle that was extinct; the bright sterre of Evangelike lighte maye shine, that was obscured: the right vaine of heavenlye doctrine maye appere, that was stopped up.[6]

Mary's 'evangelical' dimension may not have featured very much in the histories of her reign, but the use of such a description must tell us something about the changing currents in religious language of the time. And that twofold commitment to 'the trueth of Gods word, and the zeal of good workes' in many ways sums up the reformist rhetoric of her reign: progressive even while remaining Catholic.

It has recently been pointed out by both Diarmaid MacCulloch and Susan Doran how much Elizabeth I's religion owed to the Humanist influences of the royal household of Catherine Parr.[7] Her childhood influences left Elizabeth with tendencies which might be classed as both evangelical and conservative: on the one hand, a pious dedication to the Word of God, and a commitment to the defeat of superstition, but on the other, very moderate churchmanship, and a willingness to countenance what many of her more Puritan subjects saw as 'popish' survivals.[8] It is possible that some of the same influences might have had a similar impact on Mary, who had already been educated according to the precepts of the leading Spanish Humanist Juan Luis Vives, before her fall from favour. The work Vives wrote was translated into English by Richard Hyrde, one of Thomas More's circle, and became a popular text in England.[9] Discussing the fraught question of which books a woman should be encouraged to read, Vives concluded that:

> there are some on which everyone is agreed, as the Gospels of the Lord, the Acts of the Apostles and the Epistles, the historical and moral books of the Old Testament, Cyprian, Jerome, Augustine, Ambrose, Chrysostom, Hilary, Gregory,

---

6   St Vincent of Lerins, *The waie home to Christ and truth leadinge from Antichrist and errour*, tr. John Proctor (London: Robert Caly, 1554), sig. A2r.
7   Diarmaid MacCulloch, *Tudor Church Militant: Edward VI and the Protestant Reformation* (Allen Lane: London, 1999), pp. 186–9; Susan Doran, 'Elizabeth's religion: The evidence of her letters', *Journal of Ecclesiastical History*, 51 (2000), pp. 699–720 (p. 720).
8   Patrick Collinson, 'Windows in a woman's soul', in his *Elizabethan essays* (London: Hambledon Press, 1994), pp. 89–118 (pp. 109–15).
9   Juan Luis Vives, *The education of a Christian woman: A sixteenth-century manual*, ed. and tr. Charles Fantazzi, Other Voice in Early Modern Europe (Chicago IL and London: University of Chicago Press, 2000), pp. xxiii, 1, 8, 15, 16, 24, 30–41.

Boethius, Fulgentius, Tertullian, Plato, Cicero, Seneca, and other such [Patristic and Classical] authors.

How many of these authors Mary read we cannot be sure, but she seems to have obeyed another of Vives's injunctions, namely to 'learn from other learned women of her own age, either when they read to her or recount the things they have read'.[10] Certainly it was under Catherine Parr's tutelage that Mary translated some of Erasmus's *Paraphrases* on the New Testament.[11] The picture of Mary as the vengeful Catholic traditionalist is obviously incompatible with this impression of the learned princess who contributed to what ironically became one of the key texts of the Edwardian Reformation.[12] The preface to the Edwardian publication, perhaps gleefully aware of the propaganda advantage thus conferred, thanked her for 'the unestimable benefite of fertheryng both us and our posteritee in the knowelage of Goddes word, and to the more clere understandyng of Christes ghospell', and it asked of the reader 'what could bee a more plain declaracion of hir moste constaunt purpose to promote Goddes woorde, and the free grace of his ghospell?'.[13] Mary's plight in the 1530s had indeed been pitiful, but after 1543 she not only had her place in the succession restored, but she also had a place in the pious atmosphere of the royal household, where among other things she helped Queen Catherine Parr with her Latin.[14] Her time back in favour may have been as influential as her time out of favour is usually held to be: it can only have served to confirm her Humanist leanings.

Another suggestive indication is given by the work of 1550 called *The piththy and moost notable sayinges of al Scripture*. Thomas Paynell served as chaplain to Henry VIII and all three of his children, but his works consistently demonstrated his Catholic convictions alongside his obvious enthusiasm for Humanism; among many other works he translated Vives's *On the duties of a husband* into English in 1540.[15] The 1550 work is a collection of Scriptural texts translated into English and dedicated to Mary, with Paynell demanding

---

10 ibid., pp. 78, 72.

11 Jack J. Scarisbrick, *Henry VIII* (London: Eyre and Spottiswoode, 1968), p. 589. Mary translated some of the paraphrase on St John's Gospel, although ill health prevented her from completing the translation and it was finished by Dr Francis Malet.

12 The Edwardian Injunctions of July 1547 ordered that the *Paraphrases* be placed alongside the English Bible in every parish church. The Marian regime collected them up again (see Duffy, *Stripping of the altars*, pp. 485, 530).

13 Desiderius Erasmus, *The paraphrase of Erasmus upon the Newe Testamente*, 2 vols (London: Edward Whitchurch, 1548–9), I, sig. C2 r–v.

14 David Loades, *The reign of Mary Tudor: Politics, government, and religion in England, 1553–58*, 2nd edn (London and New York: Longman, 1991), p. 11; Scarisbrick, *Henry VIII*, pp. 589–90.

15 Wooding, *Rethinking Catholicism*, pp. 46–7, 117–19; Vives, *Education*, p. 16.

in the preface, 'For what is more excelent, or more precious then the word of god? what thyng maye be estemed equall unto it?' And he gave as his reason for dedicating it to Mary, 'youre liberal hand and fauour to those, whiche diligently do exercyse themselues in the spirituall and morall study of the sincere worde of god'.[16] His belief in Mary's Biblicism he maintained beyond Edward's reign into her own, after 1553, when in several publications he did good service to the Marian literary campaign.[17]

The upheavals in English Catholicism during Henry VIII's reign had made a lasting alteration to the parameters of Catholic loyalism. Whilst it was undoubtedly still possible to take a 'traditionalist' stance in the defence of Catholic doctrine, the language of Henrician Catholicism had become well enough established to provide an equally acceptable alternative. Many of the works published during Mary's reign showed clear signs of Henrician influences, suggesting that the more reformed approach to the Faith was the one favoured by the regime. Marian authors took the Mass, rather than the Papacy, as the centrepiece of their Catholic loyalties, and in imitation of the propaganda trend established under Henry VIII, made constant appeals to Scripture. Indeed, Catholic literature from Henry's reign could be easily adapted to the circumstances of that of his daughter. A collection of sermons by Roger Edgeworth, delivered in Henry VIII's time, was compiled and published in 1557. The sermons' assertion that 'the true rule of our beliefe is the whole booke of holye scripture', was entirely appropriate to the rhetoric of the new regime.[18] Thus the insistence on *Verbum Dei* was almost as marked in the literature of Mary's reign as it had been in her father's time. Thomas Watson, proving a point in 1558, insisted that 'our fayth in this thinge is grounded not in mans reason or sense, but in the almighty power of gods worde'.[19] And the Catholic propagandists of the time quoted Scripture with a degree of ease and reverence in every way the equal of that shown by their Protestant counterparts.[20] Also, they ordered their lists of authorities in a way which clearly reflected the influence of Humanist thinking about Scripture, the early Fathers, and the importance of Church Councils. Take, for example, Watson's defence of the Real Presence, which, he said,

---

16 Thomas Paynell, *The piththy and moost notable sayinges of al Scripture* (London: T. Gaultier for R. Toye, 1550), sig. [A2]r, [A1]v.

17 See, for example, *Twelve sermons of Saynt Augustine*, tr. John Paynell (London: John Cawood, 1553), and *Certaine sermons of sainte Augustines translated out of Latyn*, tr. Paynell (London: John Cawood, 1557).

18 Roger Edgeworth, *Sermons very fruitfull, godly and learned* (London: Robert Caly, 1557), fol. lxxiii r.

19 Thomas Watson, *Holsome and catholyke doctrine concerninge the seven sacramentes of Chrystes church* (London: Robert Caly, 1558), fol. xxxvii r.

20 Wooding, *Rethinking Catholicism*, pp. 119–25.

is set forth to us by the mouth of our savior Christ himself and the sacred bookes of al his holye Evangelistes, and is confirmed with the blood of his martirs, with the miracles of God and hys saintes shewed for that purpose, with the testimony of all catholyke wryters in every age, and with the aucthoritie and consente of the holle church of Christ throughout the worlde, as well in general counsels assembled in the name of oure Lord Jesus Christ.[21]

The primary emphasis upon Scripture, the appeal to Fathers and Councils, the omission of any mention of the Papacy, and the description of the Church in vague, universalist terms, all these were characteristic of the Marian approach.

Reforming impulses joined forces with traditional loyalties when this Biblicist approach was used in the defence of the Mass which formed the centrepiece of many of the Marian publications. These works reiterated emphatically that their belief in Christ's presence in the Eucharist was based on a literal interpretation of Scripture, a defence which they upheld as incontrovertible by any standards. Rather than emphasizing this belief as a badge of distinctively Catholic identity, they were often more keen to stress its true universalism. A translation of Erasmus's letter to Pelicanus defending the Real Presence, published in 1554, noted the words of Christ on the subject, and commented: 'whiche wordes of holy scripture did compell, yea Luther him selfe... to professe the same, which the universal church doth professe, although he is wont gladly to dissent from the same churche'.[22] To be able to appeal to the literal meaning of a Biblical text in this way was obviously seen as a guarantee of doctrinal truth. Bonner wrote 'And this is evidently proved fyrst by the vj of John, where oure Savioure Christ him selfe thus sayeth. *The bread that I wyl geve unto you is my fleshe*'.[23] Watson also used the opportunity to emphasize the power of God's word: 'In man the trueth of hys word dependeth of the trueth of the thyng. Contrarye in God, the trueth of the thynge dependeth upon the speaking of the woorde, as the Psalme sayeth: *Ipse dixit et facta sunt*'.[24]

The writings on the Mass epitomize the reformed Catholic approach which asserted orthodox doctrine in an emphatically Scriptural context, whilst taking tacit account of Protestant (or indeed Lollard) criticisms in their insistence that Christ's one sacrifice had been sufficient, that Masses on earth participated in that one sacrifice, that frequent communion was to be desired, and that

---

21 Watson, *Holsome doctrine*, fol. xiii v.
22 Desiderius Erasmus, *The epistle... unto Conradus Pelicanus* (London: John Cawood, 1554), sig. A5v.
23 Edmund Bonner, *A profytable and necessarye doctryne with certayne homilies adioyned thereunto* (London: John Cawood, 1555), sig. T2r.
24 Thomas Watson, *Twoo notable sermons made the thirde and fyfte Fridayes in Lent last past, before the quenes highnes, concernynge the reall presence of Christes body and bloude in the blessed sacrament* (London: John Cawood, 1554), sig. C2v.

superstitious beliefs were to be challenged. Bishop Bonner, in his book of homilies, was quick to deny the 'magical' role of the priest, explaining that at the moment of consecration 'it is not the visible preist that nowe worketh thys hyghe mysterye, by his owne power or strengthe, but it is Chryst himselfe, the invisible preist that doth worke it'. Bishop Watson, in another collection of homilies, also emphasized that 'it is not the power of the priest, being a man, that in the creatures which be set upon the aultare to be consecrate, causeth the body and bloud of oure Lorde to be made present, but it is Christ him-selfe, that was crucified for us'.[25] In implicit response to Protestant criticism, Watson wrote that 'this merveylous and hevenly doctrine is not invented by mans wytte, but reveled by Gods spirit in his holy scripture, and taught us by the mouth of our Saviour Christe'. He also countered the common Protestant argument that Christ could not be in more than one place at the same time: 'Christes bodie is but one, and although it be consecrate and offered in many places, yet there is but one Christ in every place, being both full Christe here, and full Christe there one bodye'.[26]

In all this there was a constant reiteration of how much Catholic teaching was directly inspired by Scripture. Paul Bushe, former bishop of Bristol, had been deposed from his see for marrying. Yet he wrote a work in defence of the Real Presence, and relied solely on Biblical quotations to prove his point, arguing that the Devil 'goeth alwaye about to shadowe the truth of gods most holy word, and the true understandynge of the same'. The Devil, he said, like a miller binding the eyes of his horse to make it walk in circles, 'goeth aboute to gryende the worde of god in his devyllyshe mylle of scismaticall and heretycall Doctryne'. The attempt was to portray the Bible as an ally of the Catholic cause, not a source of opposition to it. Indeed, in many cases, the authority of the Bible was held to be sufficient. As Bushe wrote, 'And as thys holye evan-gelyste hath here mooste truly declared the maner and fourme of this godlye institution and ordinaunce, even soo and no lesse do al the other three evan-gelistes and also the blessed Apostle Saynt Paule, whose sayinges at thys tyme I doo here omyt, because I truste in God, this frutefull declaratyon shalbe sufficiente unto you'.[27] The use of Biblical testimony must in part have been in response to Protestant attacks, but there was more to it than that. The Henrician insistence on Biblical authority, which had itself drawn on a pre-existing Erasmian tradition of Scriptural renewal, had undoubtedly added an extra dimension to Catholic thought in this context. Many of the Marian authors had been members of the Henrician Church establishment in their earlier years: their perpetuation of these reformist themes might suggest that

25 Bonner, *Profytable*, sig. U2r; Watson, *Holsome doctrine*, fol. xxviii r.
26 Watson, *Holsome doctrine*, fols xxxvi v, xl v.
27 Paul Bushe, *A brefe exhortation* (London: John Cawood, 1556), sigs A7r, B2v.

their compliance with the policies of Mary's father was more than mere time-serving.

This commitment to a Biblicist approach to doctrine surely lay behind the hesitancy and sensitivity of the Marian restoration when it came to vernacular Scripture. As Eamon Duffy has pointed out, although the Protestant translations of the Bible and the Erasmian paraphrases were collected up from parish churches during visitations, there was never any direct condemnation of Bible-reading or the possession of Bibles.[28] Although the literature of the restoration expressed caution at times on the subject of free access to Scripture, it was also accepted that the Bible lay at the heart of any hope of regeneration. Miles Hogarde, a relatively uneducated and populist writer, produced a vivid account of the assault upon Faith that he had witnessed under Edward, and its restitution under Mary. For him, it was *Verbum Dei*, the Word of God, that defended the true religion. He described Faith as a beautiful woman on a pedestal marked 'Christus', a Host in her hand, surrounded by the Evangelists and St Paul. He then described the attacks launched upon her by a succession of heretics, concluding with Cranmer.

> Then sawe I the cheife byshop of them all,
> Rushe to the doctours unreverently,
> And rent out of their bookes in gobetes small,
> Peices for his purpose, which perversly,
> He chewde with his teeth, and then spitefully,
> Shot them at lady faieth in pellet wyse
> And beastly did the sacrament despise.[29]

Even in more populist literature, then, the link between the evangelists and the defence of Catholic truth was established. And even the tract of the time which was most pessimistic about vernacular Scripture, in which John Standish gave fifty reasons why Scripture should not be freely available in English, nonetheless stopped short of complete disapproval:

> Neuerthelesse, to the entent none shoulde have occasion to misconstrue the trew meanyng herof, it is to be thought that if all men were good and catholike, then were it lawefull, yea, and verye profitable also, that the scripture shoulde be in Englishe, so that the translation were trew and faythfull.

He did, however, conclude gloomily 'But neither all the people be good and catholyke, nor the translations trewe and faythfull'.[30]

This kind of approach prioritized ideas of reform, clerical education, the correction of past abuses, and the furtherance of fervent devotion. It was not

---

28 Duffy, *Stripping of the altars*, p. 530.
29 Miles Hogarde (Huggarde), *The assault of the Sacrament of the Altar* (London: Robert Caly, 1554), sig. C2v.
30 Standish, *Discourse*, sig. A3r–v.

just reform in terms of institutional reform: it extended also to include doctrine. The literature of the Marian Restoration was capable of speaking with startling emphasis of the importance of salvation through faith. It stopped short of Protestant notions of salvation by faith *alone*, but none the less laid great weight on Augustinian notions of human degeneracy and Christocentric ideas of justification by the divine gift of grace. As Bonner argued, the process of salvation began with faith, but 'yf it do procede no farther, adioyning with it, hope and charitie, it is called in Scrypture, a dead faythe, because it is voyde and destitute of lyfe, and wanteth the helpe, and efficacie of charitie'.[31] He cited St Paul in support of this: 'fayth thus considered, is a lyvelye faythe, and worketh in manne a ready submission of hys wil to Goddes wyll. And thys is the effectuall faythe, which worketh by charitie, and which (as S. Paule testifieth unto the Galathians) is of value and strength in Christ Jesu.'

In the *Homelies* of 1555, a discussion of sin and salvation again sounded the Augustinian note:

> We have neither fayth, Charitie, hope, pacience, chastitie, nor anye thing els that good is, but of God, and therefore these vertues be called there the frutes of the holye ghost, and not the fruites of men. Let us therefore acknowledge ourselves before God: (as we be in dede) miserable and wretched sinners.[32]

The striking fact about this passage, written by John Harpsfield, was that it had in fact first been composed for the Edwardian homilies in 1547; it was then lifted almost word for word and made part of the book of homilies published under Bonner's auspices in 1555. The many similarities between the two collections have been discussed elsewhere, but it should be noted that two of the homilies were almost entirely the same—significantly enough, the one entitled 'Of the misery of all mankind', and a later one 'Of Christian love and charity'.[33] They stressed salvation that came primarily through faith, but a faith which was a living faith and which thus also produced good works. The emphasis on the unworthiness of mankind was a key feature of this approach. Both sets of homilies used this passage:

> Let us now learne to knowe our selves, our frailtie, and weakenes, wythoute anye ostentation, or boastyng of oure owne good dedes, and merytes. Let us also knowledge the exceadynge mercye of God, towarde us, and confesse, that as of our selves commeth all evyll and dampnation, so lykewyse of hym, commeth all goodnes, and salvation.[34]

31 Bonner, *Profytable*, sig. B1v–2r.
32 Edmund Bonner *et al.*, *Homelies sette forthe by the Righte Reuerende Father in God, Edmunde Byshop of London* (London: John Cawood, 1555), fol. 10v, from 'Of the misery of all mankind'.
33 Wooding, *Rethinking Catholicism*, pp. 161–6; Duffy, *Stripping of the altars*, p. 536.
34 Bonner *et al.*, *Homelies*, fol. 12v.

The notion of salvation by faith, if not by faith alone, had become an intrinsic part of the language of Catholic reform. After all, only eight or so years before these homilies were published, Mary herself had translated this passage of Erasmus:

> If we have grace in the meane whyle to behold any parte therof, it is more truely comprehended with pure fayth, then with the helpe of mannes wysedome. And in the meane tyme it is enough for to attaine eternall salvacion, to beleve those thynges of God, whiche he did openly set foorth of himself in holy scripture.[35]

The published works of the Marian Restoration revolved, then, around the Mass and the Bible. Manifestly, Papal supremacy was not capable of providing the same focus for Catholic loyalism. Fifty years of Humanist rhetoric and twenty years of the Royal Supremacy had shaped the way scholars, at least, now thought. The limited treatment of Papal supremacy in the works of Mary's reign is perhaps hardly surprising, given how many of the writers of the time had begun their careers under her father. Those who did discuss the Papacy seemed more keen to stress its functional value than its spiritual importance. Pole's enthusiasm for obedience to Papal authority found only a subdued echo in the literature of the reign (see Chapter 7, below). The most central argument used was that which built on recent experience and appealed to the practicalities of maintaining Church unity. Harpsfield tried to tie together the relief brought by the Marian restoration of Catholicism with the restoration of Papal authority: 'I shal not nede much to speak of the great evils that this realme is ryd from by this benefit,' he insisted. 'Euery man feleth in him self the great relife, that he hath by his reconciliation'. And he reminded his readers, again in an echo of Henrician propaganda, that 'it chaunced in the tyme of a parliament, and by the full consent and glad approbation of the whole realme, in that parliament represented'.[36] Parliament had dispensed with Papal authority, and only Parliament could bring it back.

The literature of the Marian Restoration, then, spoke a language which was peculiar to its context, shaped by the distinctive progression of Reformation in England. Yet as Professor Loades has illustrated (Chapter 2, above), the moderation and tolerance of the rhetoric sits ill-at-ease with the extraordinary rigour and apparent vengefulness of the persecution of Protestants, a persecution which clearly made many of Mary's closest allies uneasy and unhappy. How should this be understood? It is possible that both the gentleness of the language and the fierceness of the persecution may have had the same root. A hint is given in Mary's description of her father as *regem piissimae memoriae*, a phrase which Pole deplored, and which was used in the restoration of the

---

35 Erasmus, *Paraphrase*, I. sig. A1r.
36 John Harpsfield, *A notable and learned sermon or homilie, made vpon saint Andrewes daye last past 1556, in the cathedral churche of S. Paule in London* (London: Robert Caly, 1556), sig. B7r, B6v.

Mass by Parliamentary rather than Papal authority, something else that he found profoundly worrying.[37] Whereas many Continental observers viewed Henry VIII as a schismatic, or perhaps even a heretic, to Mary he was the pious Catholic prince, her father. His legacy was an important one in the shaping of her religious policy, and this influence was perhaps felt as much in the *implementation* of that policy as in its religious content.

It has been demonstrated elsewhere how much the Marian church owed to the reforms of Henry VIII.[38] The literature of the Marian restoration took many Henrician publications as a model. Bonner's *Profitable and necessary doctryne* was based upon the 'King's Book' of 1543, and Duffy has shown how the Wayland primers incorporated an extraordinary collection of prayers which ranged from traditional pre-Reformation prayers used at the reception of the Sacrament, through Scriptural paraphrases from the 1530s to the Protestant rewriting of the *Salve Regina* and prayers by Protestants like Thomas Becon.[39] Marian writers often dated the start of the attack upon true religion, not to 1533, but to 1547. Since they took the test of Catholic loyalty to be the Mass, and the Mass had not been banished until the reign of Edward VI, their position on this was only logical.

This resemblance between the two regimes, however, went beyond a certain number of shared Humanist assumptions and reformist religious language. It is important to realize that the religious ideas of this time cannot be separated from their political context. Mary's policies, like her father's, were at the same time both spiritual formulations and political initiatives. The emphases discussed here might indeed be regarded as Erasmian, and undoubtedly there is a Humanist heritage at work, but this may have been as much concerned with issues of authority as with questions of piety. As well as stressing the influence of Erasmian notions concerning Scripture, it might also be worth considering the way Erasmus dealt with princes. The Dutch reformer, for all his piety, pursued patronage with remorseless dedication. The famous quotation of 1517 in which he described the dawning of an 'age of gold' rejoiced in the rediscovery of Scripture and true learning. But it also employed the language of political clientage in its sycophantic praise of Leo X, the 'Cardinal of Toledo' (Francisco Jiménez de Cisneros), and Henry VIII.[40] Humanists not only knew how to extol the joys of Gospel study, they also knew how to get the right backers. The Humanist approach to religious reform was not just

---

37 Thomas F. Mayer, *Reginald Pole: Prince and prophet* (Cambridge: Cambridge University Press, 2000), p. 210; Russell, 'Mary Tudor', p. 272.
38 Wooding, *Rethinking Catholicism*.
39 Duffy, *Stripping of the altars*, pp. 537–43, 536.
40 Erasmus to Wolfgang Capito, 1517, in *The collected works of Erasmus*, ed. Richard J. Schoeck and Beatrice Corrigan, 84 vols (to date) (Toronto: Pontifical Institute for Medieval Studies, 1979–), IV. 263.

about pious aspirations, it was about a meaningful alliance between Church and Court. And for this alliance to be a workable one, it had to benefit princes as much as scholars and churchmen.

This alliance had solidified in England in the 1520s. Henry VIII had already been inclined towards the patronage of Humanism, but he became a particularly fervent admirer after Humanist scholarship not only helped to secure his Papal title of 'Defender of the Faith', in 1521, but, as Virginia Murphy has shown, also helped bring about the annulment of his marriage to Catherine, subsequently providing the Imperial rhetoric which justified the Royal Supremacy.[41] This had been a spectacular illustration of the usefulness of Humanism in securing royal authority, as Stephen Gardiner realized when he employed similar rhetoric in his *De vera obedientia* of 1535. But this same Humanism, as Gardiner also realized, whilst it had been used to defeat the Papacy, could also be used to defend the Catholic cause; indeed, after the Royal Supremacy had been established, it was Catholicism's only practical hope. If Henry could pose successfully as a pious, learned, and reforming Catholic prince, he had no need to venture further into Protestant experimentation. Moreover, it could be argued that Henry's personal inclinations in any case tended towards this kind of Catholicism.[42] So whilst he emphasized the godliness of his kingship, and posed as the Old Testament king purging his realm of idolatry, Catholic apologists strove to confirm him in this role, and describe what he was doing in phrases hastily culled from Erasmus and others. This portrayal of Henry as a reforming Catholic prince was therefore advantageous both to the king and to those of his Catholic subjects who were unwilling to be martyrs. For Henry, it preserved his Supremacy and kept it as free as possible from the taint of heresy; for Catholic apologists, it was perhaps the only workable way of preserving the Mass. The propaganda effort that accompanied these joint efforts was extremely successful, and its effects would seem to have been felt also in the reign of Mary.

So it was the Humanist notion of the 'godly prince', just as much as more high-minded notions of the rediscovery of Scripture, that shaped Henry's behaviour, and which left a powerful legacy to his daughter. Henry's Reformation promoted the Word of God, and attacked idolatry and superstition, but it

41 Virginia Murphy, 'The literature and propaganda of Henry VIII's first divorce', in *The Reign of Henry VIII: Politics, policy, and piety*, ed. Diarmaid MacCulloch, Problems in Focus, (Basingstoke: Macmillan, 1995), pp. 135–58; George Bernard, 'The piety of Henry VIII', in *The education of a Christian society: Humanism and the Reformation in Britain and the Netherlands: Papers delivered to the thirteenth Anglo-Dutch Historical Conference*, ed. Scott N. Amos, Andrew Pettegree, and Henk van Nierop, St Andrew's Studies in Reformation History (Aldershot: Ashgate, 1999), pp. 62–88.

42 George Bernard, 'The making of religious policy, 1533–1546: Henry VIII and the search for the middle way', *Historical Journal*, 41 (1998), pp. 321–49; Wooding, *Rethinking Catholicism*, pp. 49–81.

kept the Mass, and indeed defended it against all comers. In so doing, it placed enormous emphasis on the authority of the Crown, and the necessity of obedience.[43] The obvious consequence of such an emphasis was that it persecuted ruthlessly any who opposed it. Was it perhaps here that Mary took the inspiration for her own rigorous approach to the problem of heresy? It has been demonstrated how in many ways Mary's religious policies only make sense in the context of the Henrician Reformation from which they borrowed so extensively. Might this perhaps have been true, not just in terms of religious rhetoric, but also in terms of the authoritarian rhetoric of 'Imperial' kingship?

When Mary inherited the emphases of Henrician Catholicism, she also inherited its implied alliance with the Royal Supremacy, and her decision to seek reconciliation with Rome did not prevent her exercising her authority over the Church in forthright manner.[44] Under Henry, opposition to the Supremacy had been equated with opposition to true religion: heresy and treason, therefore, had become inextricably linked. The prolongation of this attitude might explain why, on the one hand, those who defended the Marian Church settlement could speak the language of Erasmian reform, whilst on the other hand, their government was persecuting religious dissidents with a vigour usually reserved for punishing treason. Both elements seem to have been inspired by the Henrician example. It is true that Henry VIII's total of fifty-eight people burned at the stake is not as massive as his daughter's, but then Protestantism had yet to spread as widely in the realm: it must also be acknowledged that Mary's policies became more desperate once her hopes of a Catholic heir had been disappointed.[45] But Mary's determination to purge the realm of heresy is undoubtedly reminiscent of her father's approach. In July 1540, Henry burned six people on the same day, three for upholding Papal supremacy and three for denying Transubstantiation.[46] The point was not the doctrinal questions as such, but opposition to a religious settlement which also impugned royal authority. The occasion in 1538, when Henry burned the Franciscan and Papal loyalist, John Forest, with great cruelty and mockery, is also a case in point.[47]

Moreover, for Mary, the uncertainty surrounding the exercise of authority by a woman must have made her father's example all the more compelling. It

---

43 Richard Rex, 'The crisis of obedience: God's Word and Henry's Reformation', *Historical Journal*, 39 (1996), pp. 863–94.

44 Gina Alexander, 'Bonner and the Marian persecutions', in *The English Reformation revised*, ed. Christopher Haigh (Cambridge: Cambridge University Press, 1987), pp. 157–75 (p. 162); Russell, 'Mary Tudor', pp. 266–7, 269.

45 Russell, 'Mary Tudor', p. 264.

46 Susan Brigden, *London and the Reformation* (Oxford: Clarendon Press, 1989), pp. 315–16.

47 Peter Marshall, 'Papist as heretic: The burning of John Forest, 1538', *Historical Journal*, 41 (1998), pp. 351–74.

has often been pointed out how Elizabeth's policies were made more extreme by the insecurity of her position as a female monarch, and how her religious antipathies were usually firmly rooted in her defence of the Royal Supremacy.[48] Mary was also in the unenviable position of trying to impose her authority despite her physical inadequacy. In such a situation, her father must have been an important role model. His use of reformist rhetoric to justify the Royal Supremacy had fused together notions of religious reform with the dignity of his imperial kingship. Significantly, Mary was to retain the 'Imperial' title and, arguably, much that went with it. Whilst fostering the use of the same religious rhetoric in the literature of the time, this inheritance also prompted an extraordinarily draconian approach to heresy. In this she was her father's daughter.

One other small illustration demonstrates the possible continuities between father and daughter. Richard Rex has shown how at the centre of the Supremacy lay the ideal of Old Testament kingship with which Henry made great play, and with which he justified so many of his reform initiatives.[49] His exploitation of this theme prompted the use of similar imagery by all of his children in turn. As Edward was Josiah, or Solomon to his father's David, and Elizabeth was Deborah, so Mary appeared as Judith. John Angel, defending the Faith in 1555, wrote of how Edward's reign had extinguished the light of Scripture, only for Mary to restore it. He began by relating how the Edwardian reforms had been based on the perversion of Scripture: 'false interpretinge of Scriptures, utterly denying of the holy doctours and fathers of Christes churche, but only such as made for their purpose.' He then described how Mary had rescued England from her plight:

> Tyll suche tyme that it pleased God of his infinite mercy, to sende us a newe Judith, by whose godlines the trewe light and knowledge of Goddes worde is nowe by her broughte agayne, whiche frome the death of that noble prince her father Henry ye VIII was here in this realme extuncte, and vtterly abolished.[50]

Leonard Stokes used the same theme in his *Ave Maria* for Mary:

> Marie the mirrour of mercifulnesse
> God of his goodness hath lent to this land
> Our Jewell oure joye, our Judith doubtless
> The great Holofernes of hell to withstand.[51]

---

48 Doran, 'Elizabeth's religion', pp. 702–3.
49 Richard Rex, *Henry VIII and the English Reformation*, British History in Perspective (Basingstoke: Macmillan, 1993), pp. 173–5.
50 John Angel (Aungell), *The agrement of the holye Fathers and Doctores of the Churche vpon the cheifest articles of Christian religion . . . very necessary for all curates* (London: William Harford for William Seres, 1555?), sig. A2v–3r.
51 *An Ave Maria in commendation of oure most vertuous Quene*, in Loades, *Reign*, p. 112.

One does wonder if these authors realized the delicate point they were scoring by alighting on a heroine from the Apocrypha. It is probable, however, that they were not being that precise in their choice of Old Testament figure, but choosing someone well established in popular legend as pious but valiant, who overcame her frailty as a woman to conquer the pagan invasion that threated both her nation and her religion.[52]

It is important to add some qualification here. This chapter has emphasized the reformist elements within the literature of Marian restoration, but it should be acknowledged that not all writers used exactly this rhetoric. There were works which dated the decay of true religion back to 1533, rather than 1547. This was true of John Standish who wrote defending Papal authority, in *The triall of the supremacy* in 1556, and dedicated the work to Pole. Standish's other treatise on the dangers of vernacular Scripture asked pardon in its preface for a work he had written during Henry VIII's reign, which had enthusiastically described Henry purging his realm of heresies in pursuit of Catholic truth. Standish hoped men would forgive him 'remembrynge well that his offense was neyther committed in a catholyke realme, nor yet wythout lawes, thoughe they were wicked'.[53] Richard Smyth, whose *Bouclier of the Catholyke fayth* was published in 1554, gave a much more vigorous assertion of the saving power of good works than many of his contemporaries. He also lamented the loss of the monasteries more explicitly than was usual. Yet his reasons for deploring the dissolution none the less had Humanist overtones, describing how it had caused 'a gret dammage and decay unto the honour and service of God, the godly bryngyng up of scholers in vertue and learning, and unto the common weale in worldly thynges'. There was also a personal reason here, since he described how the monasteries had educated poor children, adding 'emongst the which I was one, or els I should neuer have bene learned'.[54] And he seemed less concerned about vernacular Scripture than Standish, since he addressed his book to the 'unlearned' and included an anti-Scholastic dig, asking 'what profiteth the speakers, teachers or writers

---

52 Note how popular the story of Judith was in the Renaissance, and also how Protestant versions of the Bible were slow to reject the Apocrypha: no English version did so until 1599, and it formed part of the 'Authorized Version' of 1611. The Lollard Bible included the book of Judith, and readings from Apocryphal books were included in the Church of England lectionary from 1549. Carlstadt's treatise of 1520 identified them as outside the Hebrew canon, yet declared that some of them, including Judith, were still holy writings. The first Swiss-German Bible included them, although set apart. Trent declared them canonical in 1546. See *The new Oxford annotated Apocrypha* (Oxford: Oxford University Press, 1991), pp. vii–viii.

53 Standish, *Discourse*, sig. M2v.

54 Richard Smyth (Smith), *A bouclier of the Catholyke fayth of Christes Church, conteynyng diuers matiers now of late called into controuersy, by the newe gospellers* (London: R. Tottell, 1554), sig. C3r.

eloquence, yf it open not the doore, or locke off the holy Scriptures unto the people?' There were variations in approach, and there were different interpretations of the Henrician legacy. On the whole, however, the reformist language discussed here seems to have been more prevalent than any other, and of course, if the Queen adjudged her father a Catholic, who were her subjects to disagree?

The paradigm of reform established by Henry VIII had been influential not just in its 'via media' of moderate reform, enthusiastic Biblicism, and Catholic sacramental doctrine. It had also established an even closer synthesis of religious and royal authority. It has been pointed out before now that Mary was often as defensive of the royal prerogative against Papal interference as her father.[55] But when she retained *praemunire* in the face of Papal pressure to repeal it, or when she retained her father's 'Imperial' title, she signalled her retention of a lot more besides. It seems probable that she was accepting many of the religious expectations shaped in the earlier reign, as were her fellow-countrymen who tried to restore Catholicism in England. Henry VIII may have been more interested in the political potential of this alliance of kingship with godly rhetoric, but it could work the other way around. The Henrician Reformation was brutal, but it was effective, and Mary too was in need of effective policies.

The literature of the Marian restoration employed a language of reform which bore testimony to fifty years of Humanistic influence in England. The published works of Mary's reign, whilst defending what they saw as the key aspects of Catholic doctrine—which mostly meant the Mass—also appealed to Scripture, evoked Augustinian and Pauline notions of the unworthiness of man and the saving power of grace, and managed to strike a mild but convincing evangelical note. If Mary did not discover the Counter-Reformation, it was in large part because she was still pursuing the Henrician Reformation. But the appeal of her father's legacy was probably as much a matter of preserving her royal authority as preserving her faith. Unfortunately for Mary's reputation, that legacy proved to be a mixed blessing.

55 Conrad Russell, *The crisis of Parliaments: English history 1509–1660*, Short Oxford History of the Modern World (Oxford: Oxford University Press, 1971), p. 134.

CHAPTER 4

Cardinal Pole's concept of *Reformatio*: The *Reformatio Angliae* and Bartolomé Carranza*

Thomas F. Mayer

An old debate is currently heating up again: what to call the Counter-Reformation. The problem stems largely from the fact that all the good labels are already taken—plain 'Reformation', for example. When I first began to address this issue, intending to return to fundamentals and examine what sixteenth-century people meant by the term reformation (*reformatio*), I made a startling discovery. Apart from lexica, there is almost no work on the subject, the only large-scale studies being heavily or entirely Patristic and medieval.[1] I was therefore very glad to be invited to join a Symposium in part devoted to just this issue. My purpose now is to examine how one high-profile individual used the term *reformatio* and its cognates. Cardinal Reginald Pole was one of the most important figures in the European international arena during the first stages of what is still usually called *the* Reformation. As I edit his correspondence, I find again and again that he fits comfortably into none of the Reformation's established territories, real or metaphorical. Pole's name usually arises in the anglophone universe as 'Bloody' Mary's hatchetman in a botched attempt to roll back the English Reformation. Nonetheless, even his partisans regularly refuse to admit him to the ranks of the Counter-Reformation

---

* An earlier version of this talk was given to the School of Religion at the University of Iowa. I am grateful for many helpful questions there, and to David Loades for the suggestion that I give an expanded version to the Carranza symposium.

1 One of the best surveys of ideas of reform(ation) is Jürgen Miethke, 'Reform, Reformation (reformare, reformacio)', in *Lexikon des Mittelalters*, ed. Robert Auty *et al.*, 10 vols (Munich: Lexma, 1977–99), VII. 543–50, which concludes by underlining the eschatological dimension of this complex of ideas. Eike Wolgast, 'Reform, Reformation', in *Geschichtliche Grundbegriffe: Historisches Lexikon zur politisch-sozialen Sprache in Deutschland*, ed. Otto Brunner, Werner Conze, and Reinhart Koselleck, 8 vols in 9 (Stuttgart: E. Klett, 1972–97), VI. 313–60, is also useful. Konrad Repgen, 'Reform als Leitidee kirchlicher Vergangenheit und Zukunft', *Römische Quartalschrift für christliche Altertumskunde und Kirchengeschichte*, 84 (1989), pp. 5–30, primarily treats the continued utility of the concept of *perennis reformatio*.

(although one such champion recently assigned him a 'reformation' *tout court*.[2] In Continental scholarship of the last generation, Pole has become one of the principal figures in a previously unsuspected Italian Reformation. As was the case already in his day, he has therefore been identified as at least a crypto-Protestant, a doomed participant in a 'failed' or 'missing' Reformation. Thus there would appear to be no easy links between Pole and either *the* Reformation or its opposite. How can one man have been those two things, reformer in Italy, and *ecclesiae Anglicanae carnifex ac flagellum* ('butcher and scourge of the English Church') in Matthew Parker's inimitable phrase?[3]

In my recent biography, I tried to answer this question by treating Pole's career as a whole and placing it in the international nexus within which we are beginning to see that the English Reformation took place. Putting the two chief phases—English and Italian—of Pole's career together produced a (to me) surprisingly coherent figure, certainly not the showcase *inglese italianato, diavolo incarnato* ('Englishman Italianate, devil incarnate'), a tag Parker also adapted to characterize his shifty immediate predecessor as Archbishop of Canterbury. It remains inescapable that Pole was always a man in the middle. Studying a figure in the interstices of at least two Reformations provides a means to develop an extra-confessional view of 'reformation' as process, susceptible of, and indeed demanding, a dialectical interpretation. (And I would add, it makes Reformation a long-term process, with deep Patristic and medieval roots, as has been grudgingly recognized of late, but without allowing much of the sheen to be taken off the *real* Reformation in the sixteenth century.[4]) Paradoxically, then, a unified Pole reveals multiple reformations.[5]

On at least one score, Pole's thinking changed rather dramatically, over time, his views of *reformatio*. They are at all well-known only in the case of the decrees of the London Synod of 1555–6. These have been studied several times during the last thirty years, but the question of their place in Pole's

---

2   Marcus Holden, '"As cunning as a serpent and as harmless as a dove": A tribute to Cardinal Reginald Pole, 1500–2000', *The Venerabile*, 32 (2000), pp. 10–22 (p. 17).

3   Matthew Parker, *De antiquitate britannicae ecclesiae & privilegiis ecclesiæ Cantuariensis, cum archiepiscopis eiusdem 70* (Lambeth: John Day, 1572), p. 414. For discussion of Parker's image of Pole, see Thomas F. Mayer, *Reginald Pole: Prince and prophet* (Cambridge: Cambridge University Press, 2000), pp. 363–5.

4   Even John O'Malley, who has done as much as anyone to open a long-range perspective on the term, sees only two real reformations, the eleventh-century Gregorian reform and Luther's: O'Malley, 'Developments, reforms, and two great reformations: Towards a historical assessment of Vatican II', *Theological Studies*, 44 (1983), pp. 373–406 (p. 378); id., *Trent and all that: Renaming Catholicism in the early modern era* (Cambridge MA: Harvard University Press, 2000), esp. pp. 130–34.

5   Christopher Haigh, *English Reformations: Religion, politics, and society under the Tudors* (Oxford: Clarendon Press, 1993). His three-phase English reformation takes a major step in the right direction, towards a dialectical interpretation.

thinking about Reform has never been directly addressed. By 1555, Pole surely held that the English Church needed *reformatio*, but for almost twenty years before that he had thought the same of the Church Universal. As soon as he was made a cardinal, it was reported that he and his allies were talking *de reformatione ecclesiae*, and a few months later his patron, Cardinal Contarini, wrote to Pole about the *reformationis negotium* in the context of an overhaul of the Datary, one of the central papal bureaucratic organs.[6] In the wake of his first legation against Henry, Pole helped to foster the 'reformation' undertaken by one of his hosts in Flanders, Érard de la Marck, Cardinal of Liège. In a letter that may already have been known in England in the sixteenth century, Pole told De la Marck that his efforts at reformation would set 'the best example to nearby provinces'. At the same time, he wrote to two of De la Marck's collaborators to say that they were like 'angels of God' sent for 'the reformation of the flock'. All three were principally concerned at that moment with De la Marck's powers over exempt monasteries. Five years later, Pole wrote to Marcello Cervini, thanking him in like terms for his help in a similar case, the reform of the nuns of Santa Rosa in Viterbo, a town to which Pole was then legate.[7] Regulation of monastic communities was one standard medieval meaning of the term *reformatio*.[8]

In the early 1540s, while waiting for the Council of Trent to assemble (there he eventually met Bartolomé Carranza), Pole regularly connected the Council with *reformatio*—for example, in a draft of a Brief to Charles V, probably dated in 1544.[9] In his opening oration to the assembled Fathers, he cited one of the Bulls of indiction, in which the Council's aims were stated as being 'haeresum extirpatio, disciplinae ecclesiasticae et morum reformatio, ac tandem pax externa totius ecclesiae' ('the extirpation of heresy, the reformation of ecclesiastical discipline and customs, and also the external peace of the whole Church').[10] This Bull, however, gave the agenda as 'quae ad integritatem

6   Biblioteca Palatina, Parma, MS Pal. 1026/1, unfol., Carlo Gualteruzzi to Cosmo Gheri, 30 January 1537. The others named were Marcello Cervini, the future Marcellus II, and Jacopo Sadoleto. Contarini's letter is in Thomas F. Mayer, *The correspondence of Reginald Pole*, 2 vols (to date) (Aldershot: Ashgate, 2002–), I. 159–60, n° 179, 12 May 1537.

7   Mayer, *Correspondence*, I. 187, n° 217, 28 January 1538; I. 187–8, n° 218, 28 January 1538; I. 289, n° 366, 25 June 1542.

8   Wolgast, 'Reform', p. 317.

9   Mayer, *Correspondence*, I, 316–21, n° 414 (p. 320): 'Hac una denique ratione pax et iustitia Germaniae reddetur, Dissidia religionis recto modo, legitimoque et firmo conciliabuntur, christiana reformatio instituetur, Sacrum, oecumenicum, liberum, christianum, pacificum, & fructuosum concilium celebrabitur cum tua summa singularique gloria, tuique nominis fama sempiterna. Tunc vere dici poterit non cedere spiritum carni, a terrenis celestia non superari, nec divinis humana praeferri.'

10 *Concilii Tridentini diariorum, actorum, epistularum, tractatuum nova collectio*, 23 vols (to date) (Freiburg: Herder, 1901–), IV. 548–53; the Bull is n° 184, cited from p. 230.

et veritatem Christianae religionis, quae ad bonorum morum reductionem emendationemque malorum, quae ad Christianorum inter se tam principum quam populorum pacem, unitatem concordiamque pertineant, et quae ad repellendos impetus barbarorum et infidelium... sint necessaria' ('whatever pertains to the integrity and truth of the Christian religion, to the promotion of good customs and the emendation of bad ones, to peace, unity, and concord among Christians, whether princes or peoples, and to repelling the attacks of barbarians and infidels'), though failing to mention explicitly the *reformatio* of anything.[11] Thus Pole skipped the second item on this agenda, thinking the third more pressing. He did emphasize the degree to which the Church had nearly collapsed, but instead of proposing *reformatio*, he used the allied terms *instauratio* ('restoration') and *instaurare*.[12] In his peroration, Pole summed up the Council's task as being to address itself to 'omnibus autem, quae ad reformationem ecclesiae pertinent', and urged its members to imitate Christ in so doing. This suggests that there may not be all that much significance in his choice of *instauratio* over *reformatio*, although such a conclusion makes me a little nervous. By contrast, the other Bull of indiction, *Laetare Hierusalem*, which Pole is not known to have helped to draft, gave the Council's remit in words more like his own, including 'those things which stand in need of reformation among the Christian people' and which were 'to be reformed and restored to a better form' (*ea, quae in populo Christiano reformatione indigent, reformentur et in meliorem formam restituantur*).[13]

According to Pole and the other two legates, the Council had principally to deal *de reformatione*.[14] They objected to a draft Bull on that subject because it did not offer the reformation universally demanded. As they wrote to the Pope, the prelates at Trent at least wished to be granted the free and full care, or cure, of their subjects' souls. This care included attention to the essential points: collation to benefices with cure of souls; ordinations without licences; punishment of those, whether corporate bodies or individuals, who acquired exemptions from duty and did not take care of preaching, confession, and the cure of souls; indulgences for the completion of the Basilica of Saint Peter;

---

11   ibid., p. 230 (= n° 184: 'Indictio concilii Tridenti celebrandi ad cal. Novembris). According to Wolgast, 'Reform' p. 319, *reformare pacem* was the most frequently medieval formulation. Pole did not employ it in his *Discorso di pace*.

12   *Concilii Tridentini diarorum... nova collectio*, IV. 551. For Augustine's use of *instaurare* (to re-establish or restore) in the context of his notion of individual reform, see Gerhart B. Ladner, *The idea of reform: Its impact on Christian thought and action in the age of the Fathers* (Cambridge MA: Harvard University Press, 1959), pp. 277–8.

13   *Concilii Tridentini diarorum... nova collectio*, IV. 553, 548 n 4. The editor of vol. IV, Stephan Ehses, thinks that Pole must have been referring here to *Initio nostri* because this initiative alone spoke of peace.

14   Mayer, *Correspondence*, I. 344, n° 465, 7 March 1546.

and crusades. The Council Fathers were especially scandalized by two things in the Court of Rome, its avarice and pomp, which demanded reform of the Penitentiary, the Chancellery, and the Rota, this matter being 'the chief head of the whole reformation'. These changes would mean that churches were served by persons who took proper care of them. Nearly everyone, wrote the legates, complained of tithes and 'expectations', the giving of benefices in advance, especially recent grants, which made them despair of reformation. They thought that if the Pope were to begin reformation with those things that pertained to him, all would be content and the Papacy would lose no authority or obedience. Shortly after Pole left the Council, in early 1546, he wrote to Giovanni Morone, a close friend and fellow legate, that he still wanted a decree *de reformatione*, without which any statement about Justification would be defective.[15] Here he had in mind the Protestants, who would refuse to heed a doctrinal statement until they saw concrete institutional changes.[16] Following the Imperial line, Pole had consistently argued that Trent should deal wth reform first and only then with doctrine.[17]

Pole returned to *reformatio* during the conclave that elected Julius III, when, rather than capitalize on his status as the leading contender, he spent his time writing a dialogue on the papal office.[18] It exists in several versions, including a separate text, written 'outside conclave', which was also several times translated into Latin.[19] We might infer from these writings that reform was the principal topic of discussion in the conclave, although the massive documentation that I have unearthed says very little on this topic, aside from the election capitulation in which the cardinals promised to accept all of Trent's reforms and to appoint cardinal deputies for reform '*subito*'.[20] Pole was certainly identified as the 'reform' candidate. The Imperial ambassador at one point emphasized that backing him would mean 'strict' reform of both Church and Curia.[21] Pole's dialogue presents him in the same light. It opens

15 ibid., I. 357, n° 489, 28 August 1546.

16 Enough has already been said to show that Pole thought *reformatio* was partly a matter of institutions. The title of a document he issued at the end of 1546 reinforces the point: 'Reformatio seu correctio statutorum quae pro temporis ratione observari non poterunt prout ab initio' for the English hospice in Rome, of which he had been protector since 1538 (ibid., I. 365–6, n° 509, late 1546).

17 See, for example, *Concilium Tridentinum: Epistolarum pars prima*, ed. C. Gottfried W. Buschbell (Freiburg: Herder, 1916), p. 330.

18 Paul Brassell quite accurately, if probably accidentally, catalogued it as 'Dialogus ad reformationem spectans' in his *Praeformatio reformationis tridentinae de seminariis clericorum* (London: Manresa Press, 1938), pp. 11–12.

19 Mayer, *Reginald Pole*, p. 79.

20 Archivio di Stato, Florence, Carte Strozziane, ser. I, 225.

21 A. von Druffel, *Beiträge zur Reichsgeschichte 1546–1551*, 4 vols (Munich: Rieger, 1873–96), I. 319–24; Buschbell, *Concilium Tridentinum: Epistolae*, p. 973; for the conclave, Thomas

by saying that if the Pope were to take care of his entire flock, spreading the light of Christ throughout the world, 'this would be the most glorious reform that could be desired'.[22] Man had been formed in God's image, but had disobeyed Him (fol. 135v). Simply returning to obedience to Him would produce all the reform necessary (136r). The Pope held the 'office' of reform, and had to begin with himself (136v). 'The true and perfect reform' depended on rulers leading the *populus* by both word and example (139r–v). 'Reform' meant literally restoring the Church to its original form, first the spiritual 'rectors', then the secular, and finally the people. One of the interlocutors agreed with Pole that 'all reform' depended on the rulers' realizing that they had to lead an active life in order to gain salvation for themselves and others (141r).[23] As the other speaker summed all this up a few folios later, inducing 'the nobility to work' was 'the sum of reform' (145r).

Pole agreed with this view up to a point. The opposite of reformation was naturally 'deformation', which arose from concern with private good (143r).[24] The Pope could overcome 'deformation' by following Christ's example. Thus 'he will discover the true foundation of all works that pertain to the reformation of the Church, which consists in faith, in hope, and in love' (144r–v). 'His proper office' is the Church's 'spiritual architecture' (145r). When Pole restated the point, he wrote that 'the principal office' of the Pope was 'reform and to plant the kingdom of God and Christ on earth [and], in the souls of men, true faith, true hope, and true love' (146r). Although the Pope held the keys that allowed him 'to wipe out and plant kingdoms, wishing to reform the Church', the first applied to kingdoms of men, the second to the kingdom of God: 'the true reform of each in particular and of the whole of human society in general will be when man, having renounced the kingdom he has usurped… of God', instead gives all honour and power of command (*imperium*) to God (147r). This was the Pope's task (148r). He had to see to it that all were governed by right reason (151r), which demanded that appetites were held in check (153v). This, too, was reform. It began with Moses, who instituted reform through good laws forbidding concupiscence (155v–56v), a point made here at great length. The same kind of reform was needed to control the exces-

---

F. Mayer, 'The war of the two saints: The conclave of Julius III and Cardinal Pole', in his *Cardinal Pole in European context: A* via media *in the Reformation*, Variorum Collected Studies 686 (Aldershot: Ashgate Publishing), pp. 1–21.

22 BAV, Vat. lat. 5966, fol. 135r. See O'Malley, *Trent*, p. 62, for this as the understanding of reform held by 'influential Catholic leaders of the sixteenth century' (also pp. 131–3).

23 Pole had made a similar point in an early intervention at Trent (*Concilii Tridentini diarorum… nova collectio*, IV. 570–71).

24 Friedrich Nausea, sometime client of Pole, used the same pair of opposites in describing the Council's task; see Hubert Jedin, 'Das konziliare Reformprogramm Friedrich Nauseas', *Historisches Jahrbuch*, 77 (1958), pp. 229–53 (p. 238).

sive appetite for knowledge (163r). Secular learning could still be allowed, but only under the Church's guidance (168v–73r). The discussion of this point goes on for a long stretch, Pole defending the general view that the intellect has to be subordinated to faith (e.g. 174r). It concludes with a statement of the Pope's first reforming task, which is to show the people their only true resting place, which is in Christ (178r).[25]

The rest of the dialogue offers more detailed discussion of these general points, most of it concerning discipline and education. Pole asserts that 'the disorder of domestic discipline' has ruined the whole Church (181v); parents have therefore to be forced to 'circumcise' their children spiritually, in order to control their excessive appetites (182r). The Pope, the *Pater patrum*, had to see to it that each carnal father had a spiritual father to govern him and help him 'circumcise' concupiscence (182v). At this point Pole's argument takes a crucial new direction. Now, instead of laws being seen as the backbone of reform, education became the key consideration. Faulty education lets cupidity run riot and leads to a failure to obey the law and one's superiors (185r). It is up to parents to instil fear of God (185v). Pole spends eight folios discussing proper education, which had to be suited to one's station, but all once more depended on the Pope's setting an example for the cardinals of performing one's own role properly (192r). Unsurprisingly, Pole places the principal burden of reform on the latter, each of whom is to take personal responsibility for his titular church in Rome, and ensure that all his clergy's shortcomings are immediately reformed (200r).

In a sequel to this dialogue, Pole returned to reform and the role of the Pope. Now he declared forthrightly that the Pope had charge of reform because he was superior to all other prophets, this probably being a highly significant re-interpretation of his office in charismatic rather than institutional terms.[26] Pole admitted that this 'manner of speaking of reform may be a little obscure' (3v), but explained that he was only interested in general principles, above all that the Pope's task was to teach rulers that they could learn how to rule only through Christ (4r, 6r). This is very similar to the burden of the published dialogue, but when Pole later returned to his emphasis on order, and on staying in one's proper place, he introduced the concept of *vocatio*. This meant above all that the Pope had to stay within the limits of his office and act only rarely to restrain bishops. Reform meant putting everyone back into his or her proper *vocatio* (17v).[27] Again, in order to

---

25 Pole here made some interestingly sabbatarian remarks about the necessity of rest on, and observance of, the Sabbath (fols 193v–95r; see also fol. 199r).

26 ACDF, Sanctum Officium, St. E 6–a, fasc. 4, fol. 2v.

27 There is a related discussion of *reformatio* and *vocatio* in Pole's 'De educandis pueris', which may date from the time of the London Synod (BAV, Vat. lat. 5966, fols 27r–

begin the reform, the Pope had to start with himself, which meant following Paul's injunction to imitate him as he had imitated Christ (18r). One of the other interlocutors brought Pole to agree that all would be well if the Pope simply saw to the enforcement of the ancient canons, but Pole would not stop there. The Pope also had to put 'into execution all that which pertains to the reform of himself and of his private state (*stato*), which he can do without holding a Council... because in so doing he can hope for greater results in using his authority in the Council in order to reform and confirm the other bishops' (19v). This reformation depended first of all on episcopal residence (20v). Then once more came education, treated in a fashion similar to that in the first dialogue. Pole assured his listeners that such a reform would bring the heretics back. The conclusion was simple: whoever wants the 'consolation that consists in a true and perfect reform must give himself completely to prayer, asking God to make him first well understand his own deformities, and then attend to reforming himself according to his power in that regard, about which he will receive inner guidance from the spirit of Christ, so as to make his prayer more pleasing and acceptable to God.'[28]

Pole's emphasis on the Pope makes it impossible to doubt his allegiance to the Church of Rome, but at the same time a good deal of his notion of reform depends on almost distinctively Lutheran notions, including concupiscence and *vocatio*, and is not a matter of institutions and law; or, at least, those institutions now have a mainly if not exclusively spiritual function.[29] And despite his personal disappointments at Trent, for him the Council remained—at least for much of the time—the principal vehicle of reformation. In the printed text of *De summo pontifice*, Pole called a *reformatio* by the Council 'the most efficacious remedy' (*praesentissimum remedium*).[30] This is also how his most explicit treatment of reform, the unpublished 'De reformatione ecclesiae', originally begins. Given the monumental textual problems with this work, I shall simply refer the reader to the introductory treatment in my biography of Pole.[31]

31v; see Mayer, *Reginald Pole*, pp. 239–40); also fol. 37v, another fragment stressing the need for bishops to use preaching as a means to reform.

28 So, he who seeks 'la consolatione che consiste in una vera et perfetta riforma deve convertirsi tutto all'oratione con pregare Dio che gli faccia prima ben discernere le sue deformita, et attendere poi a riformarsi da se secondo lo poter suo in quella parte, della quale eli sara advertito interiormente dallo spirito di Christo per fare la oratione piu grata et accetta a Dio' (ibid., fol. 29r–v).

29 O'Malley, *Trent*, p. 33, operates with a similar dichotomy between 'ecclesiastical' and 'religious' meanings of reform.

30 Reginald Pole, *De summo pontifice in terris vicario, eiusque officio et potestate* (Louvain: John Fowler, 1569), fol. 116v. The fact that this is about the only mention of *reformatio* in this version may suggest that it was expurgated, or at least heavily edited, after Pole wrote it.

31 Mayer, *Reginald Pole*, pp. 181–5.

Instead, I will recall one of Pole's most extraordinary reflections on the subject, a letter written to his Spanish ally, the Bishop of Badajoz, Francisco de Navarra, in the wake of the suspension of Trent in 1552. Pole reassured the bishop that he should not fear that the interruption of the Council meant the death of all 'hope of reform of the Church'. All persons of piety wanted it to be recalled to its 'pristine state'.[32] 'The fabric of reform' had been taken up to heaven, where it would be better woven and returned with 'all consolation'. 'You see the example of the people of old', whose complaints God heard. Our tears are a sign that God is coming. They will become a fructifying rain and lead to hope of reform. Bishop Francisco should not be sad that the Council had been dismissed after so many years of work. If its fruits fail to appear, it must be thought that God will bring them forth in the fullness of His time. Pole offered two examples as admonitions, one old, one new. Firstly, Moses and the Hebrews, who, when liberated from Egypt, at first found only worse slavery, but did not despair. Secondly, God's new people, whom he has kept waiting for centuries, likewise will not see their hope fulfilled before experiencing the worst desperation. Both are similar to Christ's coming among the Jews, which led to his crucifixion. As Isaiah said, 'Exspectavimus lucem, & ecce tenebrae...' (Isa. 59:9). Navarra could expect no greater consolation. Why not hope for the same results in the reform of the Church as in its original formation? Pole took heart from the fact that the Pope's decision to suspend the Council fell on Good Friday. As soon as he heard this, he thought he saw Christ's dead body, like the Council, 'representing the whole Church'. The suspension grieved him terribly, but then he thought of Christ's resurrection. 'This is the kind of reformation which can have no better beginning than from the bishops' tears.' ('This is like the form of the Church which first pleased Christ, and to which He hastens to console it, the new Jerusalem.')[33] The bishops' tears will complete the reformation already begun, just as they were the foundation of the Church.[34] This is a dense passage, encapsulating a curiously 'hybrid' notion of reform, consisting in part of what John O'Malley says was the standard, institutional meaning of reform of discipline according to the ancient canons—signalled by Pole's term 'pristine state'—together with the mystical and apocalyptic side of reform, which O'Malley earlier emphasized in his studies of Giles of Viterbo.[35] Since expectation of the Apocalypse would by definition make institutional reforms nugatory, these would seem to have

32 See Wolgast, 'Reform', p. 319.
33 See also Pole, *De summo pontifice*, for further references to both Jerusalem and the bishops.
34 Mayer, *Correspondence*, II. 97–9, nº 595.
35 O'Malley, *Trent*, pp. 131–3; id., 'Historical thought and the reform crisis of the early six-teenth century', *Theological Studies*, 28 (1967), pp. 531–48 (pp. 544–6). Wolgast, 'Reform', p. 321, claims that an apocalyptic meaning of reform was found only in popular religion in the fifteenth century.

been a low priority for Pole. They would return to prominence in the future, but without undermining Pole's certainty that the end was near.[36] Pole's ideas stand at the intersection of institution and belief, the more so because his notion of reform did not undergo the narrowing into strictly institutional terms that Gerald Strauss has argued to be typical of Catholic apologists. At least he did not do this before he returned to England.[37]

Things at first look dramatically different thereafter, especially in the case of the decrees of the London Synod.[38] It is just one more irony in Pole's *Nachleben* that these decrees should recently have been edited in a volume entitled *The Anglican canons*.[39] The term *reformatio*, as used in the title of this document, carries the word's narrowest legal meaning. That 'discipline' was what *reformatio* meant in the text is abundantly clear from the conclusion of the printed version, enjoining 'prelates of the church' to exercise their *officium correctionis et reformationis*, a coupling repeated in the last line of the text.[40] Otherwise, the term *reformatio* appears only a handful of times, beginning with the pairing of *deformata* and *reformaretur* in the prefatory letter (only the first being repeated in the first decree), and a reference to the *reformationis causa* to which the Pope had exhorted Pole and the Synod. The only moment at which the word bears a sense recognizable from Pole's earlier thought is at the

36 This was a not uncommon blend; see O'Malley, 'Historical thought', pp. 544–6.
37 See Gerald Strauss, 'Ideas of *reformatio* and *renovatio* from the Middle Ages to the Reformation', in *Handbook of European history, 1400–1600: Late Middle Ages, Renaissance, and Reformation*, ed. Thomas A. Brady JR, Heiko A. Oberman, and James D. Tracy, 2 vols (Leiden: Brill, 1994–5), II. 1–30 (p. 20). By contrast, Konrad Repgen, 'Reform', in *The Oxford encyclopaedia of the Reformation*, ed. Hans J. Hillerbrand, 4 vols (Oxford: Oxford University Press, 1996), pp. 392–5, does not discuss 'Catholic' uses of the term in the sixteenth century at all, although he does demonstrate that its basic meanings had not yet narrowed into the modern sense of *the* Reformation.
38 These exist in three MSS and were published in Rome shortly after Pole's death as *Reformatio Angliae*. The precise status of the printed text remains obscure. As for the MSS, it is certain only that they are all drafts, although the one in the ASV runs close to the printed text; see Thomas F. Mayer, *A reluctant author: Cardinal Pole and his manuscripts*, Transactions of the American Philosophical Society 89/iv (Philadelphia: APS, 1999). The printed text appeared in 1562 from the press of Paolo Manuzio in Rome. The three manuscript copies of the Westminster canons are: Corpus Christi College, Cambridge, MS 121, n° 11, pp. 7–31; BL, Cotton Cleop. F. 2, fols. 72r–90r (both drafts in unidentified hands); and ASV, Arm. 32:34, fols 480r–509v.
39 Gerald L. Bray (ed.), *The Anglican canons 1529–1947*, Church of England Record Society 6 (Woodbridge: The Boydell Press and Church of England Record Society, 1998), pp. 68–161, contains both shorter and longer recensions. Bray's commentary and discussion of the texts (pp. xliv–xlvii) are to be used with caution, and his editing of the text is also confusing. I cite it here for convenience.
40 Repgen, 'Reform', p. 394; Wolgast, 'Reform', p. 324; Bray, *Anglican canons*, p. 136 (the phrasing is identical in the short and long recensions).

beginning of the third decree on clerical residence, in which it is observed that 'the beginning of the reformation of the Church should be made by them [the clergy]'.[41] To be fair to Pole, the decrees probably reflect only very imperfectly his hopes for the Synod. In various of his writings contemporary with it we find many more continuities with his earlier thought, for example on the necessity of education in relation to *vocatio*, while other key elements of his earlier ideas of reformation (for example, the importance of spiritual fathers) figured importantly at other moments in Pole's governance of the English Church. It remains notorious that the content of the *Reformatio Angliae* is disciplinary, leaving out even a survey of what was to be taught in the new seminaries.[42] The variation between these usages and Pole's earlier ideas should raise an alarm signal or two, and also bring us to his friend Carranza.

Professor Tellechea has made a compelling if necessarily hypothetical case for Carranza's involvement in the Synod and, similarly hedged around with caution, his impact on Pole's thinking about the necessity of episcopal visitation. Drawing on Carranza's *Forma visitandi diocesim toletanam*, Tellechea summarizes the author's view of reformation as virtually synonymous with visitation.[43] In this brief memorial, Carranza used *reformare/reformatio* in an identical sense to the *Reformatio Angliae*, that is, as *corrigere et reformare* or *[cum] correctione et reformatione*, but first (unlike Pole) in the context of preaching.[44] Preaching and visitation were none the less centrally important to Pole. He conducted many more visitations of English dioceses than has been thought, whatever the precise nature of the ties between him and Carranza on this point, and may have written as many as twenty sermons.[45] Although his hypothesis must remain undocumented, as is nearly all the Synod's business, Tellechea must be correct in believing that Carranza took a large hand both in its proceedings and, in all likelihood, in the preparation of the decrees, drawn up in some form in February 1556 but never promulgated, probably because the Synod was never officially brought to an end.[46] One might just note that Pole (or his

---

41 Bray, *Anglican canons*, pp. 70, 72, 74, 94, 136.

42 Mayer, *Reginald Pole*, pp. 237–42. On spiritual fathers, see Pole's instructions for dealing with heretics in BAV, Vat. lat. 5968, fols 227r ff.

43 José Ignacio Tellechea Idígoras, *Fray Bartolomé Carranza y el cardenal Pole: Un navarro en la restauración católica de Inglaterra (1554–1558)* (Pamplona: Diputación Foral de Navarra, Institución Príncipe de Viana, and CSIC, 1977), pp. 313–51 (esp. pp. 310, 321–36); the *Forma* is given on pp. 341–50.

44 ibid., pp. 348–9. Carranza here discussed the visitation of episcopal courts: 'Item: Curiae episcoporum visitandae et reformandae tollendo abusus, si qui sint.'

45 Mayer, *Reginald Pole*, pp. 288–90, 246–51; id., *Reluctant author*, pp. 68–74, on Pole's preaching.

46 Tellechea, *Carranza y Pole*, pp. 59–65. For the failure to promulgate the decrees, see Mayer, *Reginald Pole*, p. 244. The other figure who must also have been involved, though again there is no direct documentation, is Pole's datary, Niccolò Ormanetto (ibid., p. 240).

officials) used *reformatio* in one final context, the temporary injunctions issued for both universities in the wake of their visitations. In neither case does the word have a sense of *reformatio in melius*, of reform as innovation, which it often did in Continental usage in this context.[47]

In summary, Pole deployed *reformatio* in virtually every sense known, institutional, monastic, legal, looking both backwards and forwards. His invention of a charismatic view of the Papal office and reform is easily the most important example of the latter. It is probably no accident that Pole developed this view in the context of the rending of Christendom by competing concepts of reform; nor, I suggest, is it accidental that this notion of Pole's, dating from around 1550 (with key elements being preserved much later) had a good deal in common with Luther. A similar point has often (and almost as often without careful argument) been made on the score of Justification, but *sola fide* as a solidly Pauline concept is anything but distinctively Lutheran and was well known in what were to become Pole's Italian and English circles, long before Luther became prominent.[48] Instead, I would highlight the centrality to both Pole and Luther of concupiscence and *vocatio*, although, despite these areas of overlap, Pole's notion of reform, unlike Luther's, was still mimetic, in Karl Morrison's sense of the term.[49] The 'Protestant' content of Pole's beliefs, fenced in by his absolute adherence to the Papal Church, yields the *tertium quid* of what I have called 'the reform tendency'.[50] Its history of fission along personal and political rather than theological lines suggests that the reformations were not so much about doctrine but more about ecclesiology, less about the proper interpretation of Scripture than about who had authority to undertake it.[51] Pole's most striking idea of *reformatio* transcended institutions and solved the problem of authority by deriving it straight from Christ; not, however, simply giving it to the Pope, and in the process dramatically changing his concepts of the Papal and episcopal offices.

47 Wolgast, 'Reform', pp. 324–5.
48 For John Colet's soteriology, see Thomas F. Mayer, *Thomas Starkey and the commonweal: Humanist politics and religion in the reign of Henry VIII*, Cambridge Studies in Early Modern British History (Cambridge: Cambridge University Press, 1989), p. 33. For Pole's Italian circles, see: ibid., pp. 193–4; Barry Collett, *Italian Benedictine scholars and the Reformation: The Congregation of Santa Giustina of Padua*, Oxford Historical Monographs (Oxford: Clarendon Press, 1985); and Roberto Cessi, 'Paolinismo preluterano', *Atti della Accademia Nazionale dei Lincei*, 8th s. 12 (1957), pp. 3–30.
49 Karl F. Morrison, *The mimetic tradition of reform in the West* (Princeton NJ: Princeton University Press, 1982), p. 230.
50 Mayer, *Reginald Pole*, pp. 8, 9, etc.
51 Heinz Scheible was one of the first to make a similar argument: 'Reform, Reformation, Revolution: Grundsätze zu Beurteilung der Flugschriften', *Archiv für Reformationsgeschichte*, 65 (1974), pp. 108–33 (pp. 115–19). It is no coincidence that Scheible is a leading scholar in the field of Melanchthon studies.

This paper once ended with the sentence: 'That is, until he returned to England and largely let slip the opportunity to implement his views.' I may never succeed in fulfilling the rather hackneyed authorial goal of writing one true sentence, but I at least try to avoid putting out egregiously false ones, and this last, I now know, falls into this category. It must be replaced with the blunt assertion that Pole's final legation succeeded. I do not have time to make the case fully now, but let me sketch one of its key components, this being a nearly completed effort to document the impact of Pole's legation on the ecclesiastical courts in England. The other central element of my argument rests on a project designed to identify all English persons, especially clergy and women, who approached Pole for absolution and dispensation (this being part of a fourth volume of my edition of his correspondence).[52] One of the main arguments for Pole's supposed failure has been that only a very small number of cases were appealed to him, and that only slowly. Both contentions are false. Added to the statistics derived from Pole's legatine register, now in Douai, a close study of diocesan and many other lower court records demonstrates that an impressive number of people thought it worth asking for Pole's help in sorting out their religious lives, coming to him in his capacities both as legate and as archbishop, that they did so with despatch, and that they continued to do so right down to the end of the reign, despite the supposed end of his legation in mid-1557. I shall omit technical discussion of the sources and their problems, as well as of the judicial structure both of the English Church and of Pole's legatine machinery, and instead go straight to the statistics. I note that instead of forty-three cases brought before him,[53] the new total is 292. In terms of raw numbers, the appeals are divided in the proportion of almost two to one as between the legatine Court of Audience and the Court of Arches, which heard appeals in the Province of Canterbury. In terms of chronology, the amount of business in both courts increases rapidly as early as 1555, with twenty-six cases in Arches and thirty-eight in legatine Audience. The sharp initial rise suggests that word got out quite quickly, and that while there may have been no reservoir of unfulfilled religious vocations, there was pent-up demand for Papal justice, as there may also have been for the Arches variety. There were three cases just in advance of Pole's return, but I confess that I did not think to look at the rest of the reign to this point, except in London, where the annual total, seven, is identical for 1554 and 1555. It is hardly surprising that there should have been demand, given the highly evolved systems in both courts, but the fact that any

52 For the whole argument, see Thomas F. Mayer, 'The success of Cardinal Pole's final legation', in *The Church of Mary Tudor*, ed. Eamon Duffy and David Loades (Aldershot: Ashgate, 2005), pp. 149–75.

53 Rex Pogson, 'Cardinal Pole: Papal legate to England in Mary Tudor's reign', unpubl. doctoral dissertation, University of Cambridge (1972), p. 230.

appeals went to either place as early as this is impressive testimony to the depth of the desire for ecclesiastical justice at the highest level. A suspensive appeal to the Pope from York shows just how much was known about the state of play at the end of 1554.[54] The fact that in this case, and several others, the York lawyers had to invent a style for Pole, apparently borrowing from that used in addressing the Archbishop of York, in his capacity as permanent and *ex officio* Papal legate (*legatus natus*), further suggests that here at least appellants were not content to wait for word from the centre before approaching the legate.[55]

After the first dramatic increase, the numbers were fairly steady right through 1555, up to the usual December lull. Appeals to the legate in the next year increased by two-thirds to fifty-nine, while declining slightly in the Court of Arches to nineteen. Both sets of appeals hit their peak in 1557. The growth is steeper in Arches, where the number almost doubles from the previous year to thirty-four. In the Legatine Court, the number rises by almost another third to seventy-two, all but six of these occurring before the end of July of that year. Both series decline precipitously in 1558, down to eleven appeals to the Legate and fourteen to the Court of Arches, the final two being in November of that year. That business in both courts falls off well before the end of the regime, and that there were still seventeen appeals to the Pope in 1558, a dozen of them from the Prerogative Court of Canterbury, suggests that lack of time was not the problem that it has been made out to be. But what is to be made of those appeals to the Legate in the second half of 1557 and in 1558, especially two in October 1557 from York, which had previously been exceptionally *au courant* of events? Obviously, there was a period of adjustment at the end of the period of Pole's Legation as at its beginning, with eagerness to get started and reluctance to stop again: from the last appeal to Pole to the first to Pope Paul IV took from 30 October 1557 to 22 January 1558.[56] Still, why should there have been *any* appeals to the by then powerless 'Legate'? The answer seems plain: some lawyers, including some on Pole's legatine staff, and perhaps more importantly some litigants, were no more persuaded than I am that the revocation of Pole's Legation was ever formally promulgated. After all, no less a person than Cardinal Alessandro Farnese, in May 1557, confidently reported to his agent in Philip's Court in Brussels that the English Cardinal's Legation

---

54 BI, Cons. AB 20, fol. 208r.

55 On 1 February 1555, Pole was addressed both as 'sanctissimum in Christo patrem et dominum nostrum papam eius nominis tertius [*sic*] eiusque audienciam apostolicam vel legatum suum in hoc regno Anglie directe' (BI, Cons. AB 20, fol. 241v) and as the Pope's 'delegate' in England. For the form of an appeal to the Archbishop of York, see, for example, BI, Cons. AB 21, fol. 87r. Since there were apparently no appeals from York to the Court of Arches, there may have been no other model ready to hand.

56 BI, Cons. AB 21, fols 291r–323r; business in York was much reduced in the summer of 1557, since it had all been sent to the Legate.

would be restored.[57] The most substantial evidence for this proposition comes from nine documents (*significavits*) filed in the English Chancery, on behalf of Pole as Legate a latere, between 1 June 1557 and the end of Mary's reign.[58] One of the acts in December, for the restoration of the Knights Hospitaller, bears Pole's legatine seal, while at least one dispensation dated in 1558 must, according to its wording, have been issued by him as Legate *a latere*.[59] The Vicar-General's register in London diocese contains another dispensation, probably dating from July 1557, and certainly registered on the fifth of that month.[60] These documents, combined with all those appeals made after April 1557, appear to make a compelling case. Yet there are several difficulties. First, five other *significavits* from the same period treat Pole just as Archbishop and *legatus natus*.[61] Secondly, only one more appeal to the Legate was lodged after June 1557 in the Prerogative Court of Canterbury, which one might expect to have the best-informed staff.[62] Then again, this may not be all that significant, given the steady stream of appeals to the Pope from that same court, twenty-four in total, even when Pole certainly still had legatine powers. Pole himself scrupulously ceased to use, or at least to claim, his powers. If he did actually retain them, the decline in business becomes that much harder to explain, although it certainly reinforces my reservations concerning one of the two principal explanations for Pole's 'failure': insufficient time.

The concern with law and discipline demonstrated by these numbers squares pretty well with the standard interpretation of Pole's Legation, but it must immediately be observed that this is typical of the whole of the second generation of reformers all over Europe, of John Calvin's and Ignatius of Loyola's successors as much as of Pole. It also fits neatly with one of the central strands of Pole's concept of *reformatio*, producing another case of impressive consistency. Whether or not I am right about the continuation of his legatine powers right to the end, his use of the full range of his archiepiscopal and legatine powers, without the compulsive reference to Rome of which he has been accused, reinforces the evidence for his collegial (or oligarchical) notion of the constitution of the Catholic Church. Yet at the same time, and as

---

57 Annibale Caro, *Delle lettere del commendatore Annibal Caro scritte a nome del cardinale Alessandro Farnese*, 8 vols (Milan: Società Tipografica de'Classici Italiani, 1807), III. 167.

58 NA, C85/207 and 27; the PRO catalogue says that C85/207 came from York ecclesiastical province, and n° 27 is supposed to come from Canterbury province, but I see no difference in provenance. The first document from Pole in C85/207 concerns a case in Exeter diocese. Eight of the nine documents filed on Pole's behalf are from C85/207 (n°s 15–22), while the last is C85/27, n° 16.

59 Mayer, *Correspondence*, n°s 2130 and 2152a.

60 LMA, DL/C/331, fol. 2656r–v.

61 NA, C85/27, n°s 15 and 19–22.

62 NA, PROB 29/9, fol. 289r.

always with Pole, this stress on law and proper procedure shows no trace of the apocalyptic, even defeatist, strain to be found in that same concept. Thus we are further ahead on the score of practice, but not as much as we might hope on that of theory. Pole may not have been Archbishop Parker's hypo-critical *diavolo incarnato*, but he still remains what Cardinal Contarini's most recent biographer once called him: 'a slippery eel'.

CHAPTER 5

Pole, Carranza, and the pulpit

Dermot Fenlon

For St John Chrysostom it was a question whether bishops could be saved. Dante had no hesitation about envisaging a Pope in hell. By the fifteenth century things were becoming more circumspect, A window in the chapel of Hengrave Hall in Suffolk depicts a bishop suffering in the flames of purgatory. A century later, this kind of reflection was discouraged in the Catholic world. Protestant rhetoric drove it off the market. The idea of a Church under judgement was taken out of public circulation: the Spanish Inquisition made sure it was taken out of university theology. This happened as a result of the Carranza case.

Carranza was chosen by Philip II to be the shaping influence on the Catholic Reform in England. It was Carranza who sent his fellow Dominican Pedro de Soto to meet Pole at Dillingen in 1554, there to work out plans for, and a theology of, a seminary clergy. These plans were then translated into the National Synod of 1555–6: the *Reformatio Angliae* which was in turn to be taken up as normative for the whole Church in the closing phases of the Council of Trent. It was Carranza who secured Pole's entry to England in 1554, smoothing his path at Court, and overcoming the reluctance of Charles V. It was Carranza who, in 1555, arranged the Blessed Sacrament procession at Kingston upon Thames, in a striking reaffirmation of the Eucharistic Lordship of Christ over England (see Chapter 8, below). It was Carranza who played a guiding role in the renewal of Catholic theology at Oxford. It was he who wrote a Catechism for the Church, revised by Pole's secretary Priuli. Through Pole's bishops, Carranza's reform was designed to establish England as the prototype, among the King's dominions, of a reforming local Church, theologically in the tradition of the school of Salamanca, the inspiration and exemplar of a Universal Church reformed in the light of the best Catholic theology. Yet at the heart of this project there was a tension which it is the purpose of this chapter to explore. It was Carranza who advised Bishop Bonner of London, and was prominent among those who urged the trial of Cranmer. In this more vigorous pursuit of heretics he was not at one with Pole. At the close of his mission in the summer of 1558, on his way back to

Spain to take up the Primatial See of Toledo, he wrote from Flanders, accusing Pole of failing in his duty of preaching.[1] The seriousness of the accusation was not lost on Pole.

Properly to appreciate the perspective from within which Carranza wrote, it may be well to consider his own homiletic practice. On 29 June 1555, Carranza preached at Court, in the presence of Philip and Mary. It was the Feast of St Peter. Carranza's text, *Tu es Petrus*, offered him the opportunity of remarking on the duty of those who held office to answer *both* of Christ's questions: 'Who do men say that the Son of Man is?', and 'But who do you say that I am?' (Matt. 16: 13, 15). The first, explained Carranza, was directed to the state of public opinion concerning Christ. The second was a personal question to those who held office. For these were answerable for the souls entrusted to them; all the more so if the office were *'espiritual'*. The duty of clergy and rulers alike was to declare the truth with frankness, with unfeigned candour, and without flattery, thereby following the example of Christ's disciples.[2] The communication of truth, frankly spoken and joined to prayer was the answer to, and the duty arising from Christ's personal question to them. Christ did not merely ask for faith. He asked for an open profession of faith: 'Vos autem quem me esse dicitis?' (Matt. 16:15). Thus, those who held office, whether temporal or spiritual, would be called to account before God for those in their care. The *señor* must give an account of his *familia*, the *gobernador* of his *tierra*, the *rey* of his *reino*, the *padre* of his *hijos*, the *cura* of his *parroquia*, the *obispo* of his *diócesis*, the *papa* of his *Iglesia*.

1   Carranza wrote more than once, apparently to Queen Mary, and was answered, significantly, by Pole. Carranza's letters of 1558 have to be reconstructed from Pole's reply, printed in José Ignacio Tellechea Idígoras, *Fray Bartolomé Carranza y el cardenal Pole: Un navarro en la restauración católica de Inglaterra (1554–1558)* (Pamplona: Diputación Foral de Navarra, Institución Príncipe de Viana, and CSIC, 1977), pp. 191–6 (for Priuli's place in revising Carranza's *Catechism*, see pp. 138–9). Michael Williams, building on the fundamental researches of Tellechea, identifies Carranza as 'the most important' of the theologians 'specially selected by Philip', and sees him as 'one of the guiding spirits' influencing the National Synod of 1555–6, a major influence at Court, chosen by the Queen to be her confessor, and determined to bring Cranmer to trial. Williams considers that the 'role of Spanish theology' has been 'overlooked by English historians', probably because Spaniards did not hold ecclesiastical office: Michael Williams, 'William Allen: The sixteenth-century Spanish connection', *Recusant History*, 22 (1994), pp. 123–36 (p. 125). Edward Booth, in an unpublished paper on Pole's seminary legislation, draws a similar conclusion from Pole's meeting with Pedro de Soto at Dillingen in 1554, where the existing seminary, and Soto's theology of priesthood, stood as prelude to the English National Synod of the following year.

2   Tellechea, *Carranza y Pole*, p. 380: 'Porque Cristo preguntó a los suyos, que eran buenos y respondían con simplicidad y candor de ánimo; no sabían mentir, fingir ni adular, sino decir la verdad con llaneza.'

Carranza then referred to the probable objection from his audience. To speak thus frankly would surely be self-destructive in a world where each pursued his own interest and aggrandizement? In the world there is no truth spoken frankly. Everything is deception, pretence, or adulation. Thus Carranza imagines his congregation's response.[3] And he agrees: that is the reality, the truth of things. The truth of things is that there is no truth at Court. Only by residing among the faithful will good prelates come to know the truth. The bad, on the other hand, hold the judgement of the people in no account. They make no enquiry of the people, unless to intimidate and to dominate. They do not desire the truth. Therefore, Carranza concluded, those who hold office must first examine and accuse themselves, before they undertake to teach and to convert those in their charge.[4]

Here was a concept of ministry at once residential, mediatorial, and consultative. It turned on a doctrine of true and false Lordship (*dominium*). It was in the tradition of the School of Salamanca, of Juan de Ávila, of the Spanish bishops and theologians of the Council of Trent. It was a tradition which sought to protect entry to Holy Orders from what Domingo de Soto called the *perversio ordinis* whereby a clergy without vocation came to possess the lands and revenues originally provided for the sustenance and cure of souls.[5] It was a tradition rooted in a profound sense of justice and obligation to the people. God, declared Carranza, was the head of every *res publica*. The administration of justice revealed God's presence in the world. Whatever corrupted justice was of the devil. Private interest, privileges, and 'requests', he declared, were demonic influences bringing condemnation on corrupt rulers.[6]

Carranza's peroration turned on the service of Peter to the Lordship of Christ. The Church, he declared, is not of Peter, but only of Christ. Christ's

3 p. 380: 'Pero agora si yo que tengo oficio público me tengo de gobernar por lo que dijeren de mí preguntados de mí, será destruirme, porque unos tienen delante de sus ojos su interesse, su acrecentamiento, otros sus pretensiones. No hay verdad con llaneza en el mundo; todo es mentir, fingir o adular; y no con disimulación, sino devergonzadamente.'

4 p. 380: 'Esto es así verdad y así hay pocos con quien los reyes y perlados pueden hacer este oficio. No hallando en su corte de quién tomar información, se disimulaban con otros vestidos y buscaban gente simple y llana, donde, sin ser conoscidos, sabían la verdad de las cosas. Y destos exemplos tenemos las Escripturas llenas. Esto es de buenos perlados. Y que los malos tienen en poco el juicio de las otras gentes, no quieren sino ser temidos y mandar, y así no hallan quien quiera ni ose dezir la verdad. Y estos no oyen sino mentiras y lisonjas; que tantas veces se yerra por defecto suyo, como por defecto de los súbditos.'

5 José Ignacio Tellechea Idígoras, *El obispo ideal en el siglo de la Reforma*, Publicaciones del Instituto Español de Historia Eclesiástica: Monografías 9 (Rome: Iglesia Nacional Española), p. 187, etc.

6 Tellechea, *Carranza y Pole*, p. 382.

ministers were Peter and the other bishops. Theirs was the Divine command-
ment to feed the flock, not to lord over it: 'non ut dominantes in cleris, sed
forma facti gregis ex animo'.[7] Then came a sentence which was to feature in
Carranza's later interrogation before the Spanish Inquisition:

> Those who make prelates lords of the Church and give them dominion, when in
> reality they exercise only ministry, have with this error caused as much damage to
> the Church as has any of the greatest errors of Luther.[8]

Here was an account of Catholic responsibility for the divisions of
Christendom, and a critique of the system of *'dominium'*, accompanied by a
corresponding concern for a cure of souls imposed on everybody in the
Church from the Pope to private householders. It was a concern which would
define the Church's mission throughout the *ancien régime* and after. It was
entirely at one with Pole's conception of the Church and the civil order, and
of the spirit of penitence which should inform them. But Carranza's understanding of the 'truth of things' as found at the courts of kings and prelates
does not seem to be at one with Pole's.

Pole was an habitué of the Courts of Europe, first at the Court of Henry
VIII, where he had pursued the course of acquiring 'honour and utility' for his
Prince. Then, in the 1530s, following a crisis arising from a conflict between
conscience and the 'honour' of his king, he had learned in the service of the
Church to form his own Court on the model of that of Gian Matteo Giberti,
bishop of Verona, as a spiritual centre from which to engage the public world.
And when the time came, Pole defended his policy at the Court of Queen
Mary against Carranza's objection that he should return to his diocese and
spend his time preaching to the people.

In what follows, I wish to suggest that the point at issue between Carranza
and Pole was the Court itself, and the struggle for the formation of religious
policy. Carranza had depicted the Court as the scene of ultimate corruption.
He had theologized a *topos*, he had identified the Court as the habitat of
demons, the locus of disinformation. But for those actually employed at Court,
he had raised, without answering it, the question: how am I to profess the 'truth
of things'? 'It will be to destroy myself' (*'será destruirme'*). The implication was
that inside the Court there was no salvation. In reality, Carranza seems to

---

7   ibid., p. 384: 'La Iglesia no es de Pedro, sino de Cristo. Pedro no es señor de la Iglesia,
     sino Cristo. El señor deste ganado es Cristo; los ministros y pastores son Pedro y los
     otros obispos. Y así dice S[an] Pedro hablando con ellos: "Pascite gregem Dei quae in
     vobis est, non ut dominantes in cleris, sed forma facti gregis ex animo".'
8   ibid., p. 384 (see I Peter 5:2–3): 'Quien hace señores a los perlados de las Iglesias y les
     da dominio, no teniendo sino solo ministerio, ha hecho con este error tanto daño a la
     Iglesia como uno de los mayores errores de Lutero. Solo Cristo tiene este dominio, es
     una pieza de su mayorazgo, no la puede heredar otro.'

have intended his strictures to apply only to bishops resident at Court. But who were they? At the time, the most prominent bishop resident at Court was Pole.

That was in 1555. By 1558 Carranza had developed what looks like a pointed observation about absenteeism into a formal complaint about Pole's preaching policy in England. How are we to explain this? I think we should posit the existence in Carranza's case of the ambassador behind the pulpit. In 1546 the Spanish ambassador at the Council of Trent had noted Pole's difficulties with the decree on Justification. These difficulties were presumably linked, in the Inquisitorial memory, with the the completion of a Catechism written in England by Carranza and revised by Pole's secretary Priuli. Philip II's confessor, Fray Bernardo de Fresneda, now 'reminded' the Emperor of Pole's 'unreliability'.[9] We may wonder whether there followed a move to enlist Carranza, as the newly appointed Primate of Spain, to question Pole. That would have the advantage of underlining the case against Pole at Rome, Brussels, and Madrid. It would also serve to open a case against Carranza himself, henceforward under suspicion as a collaborator with Pole, and already noted, since 1555, as a severe critic of the Church's system of appointment to bishoprics. In Spain, that meant a criticism of the Crown. While himself still at the Court of Flanders, where kings could find few to guide them in 'the truth of things' and where the appointment of bishops was shortly to become the stimulus rather than the answer to political disaffection in the Netherlands, the new Primate had his enemies at home in Spain. Their best way of undermining him may well have been to renew 'questions' about Pole, who was now the uncontested guide and counsellor of the English Queen. 'Doubts' were being formulated about Pole, about his preaching policy and by implication about his bishops; doubts which, we may suppose, only an 'enquiry' from Carranza could 'dispel'. Such seems to be the likely explanation of Carranza's challenge to Pole in his letters of 1558, and such the supposition informing Pole's reply.

That Carranza should admonish him, on the strength of other people's 'judgements'—this, for Pole, was a blow which he did nothing to conceal. Others he could abide: 'Sed qui tu, R[everendissi]me Domine, mihique in Christo conjunctissime, judicas?'[10] This reply from Pole to Carranza in June 1558 is, I think, best understood as a carefully constructed exercise in Christian diplomacy. We should be correspondingly careful in the way we read it. Pole began by going straight to the point. Carranza's 'conscientious' commitment to fulfilling his duties to the Queen had won the appreciation of both the Queen and himself. The Queen had read Carranza's letters excusing his inability personally to attend her presence, and she accepted his explanation

9   Tellechea, *Carranza y Pole*, pp. 121–97.
10 ibid., p. 192.

'in optimam partem'. She fully recognized Carranza's loving dedication to her service.[11] The implication is clear. Pole, not Carranza, is the Queen's counsellor in residence.

Was there at stake here a potential clash of primacies—Toledo asserting his influence, if not jurisdiction, over Canterbury and the Queen? Whatever the case, Pole was making no concessions. Necessity, he wrote, kept him at Court: not merely civic necessity but ecclesiastical—the good of the Church depended on it. Carranza, observed Pole, 'well understood' the reason for his remaining at Court. The issue, then, was one they had discussed. Its resolution now hung upon the question, who was to advise the Queen at Court, where rulers found few to help them discern 'the truth of things'? To Carranza, Pole insisted that Canterbury was well provided for. London was the heart of the Kingdom 'ex quo magna pars disciplinae Ecclesiae pendet'. To those who accused him of neglecting the thirteen London parishes in his care, Pole replied that every day he accused himself and groaned. But why, when he might visit them whenever he wanted? Would that I were able, he continued, 'utinam possem'. For here, in this city, was the greatest need for that medicine which many considered to be the remedy of its ills—more frequent preaching of the Word of God. Yet every day, Pole declared, personal experience convinced him of the opposite. In London, where the body [of the Church] was most infected, the remedy of words wrought no effect: 'hoc reperio: ubi major est verbi copia, ibi minus homines proficere'. Pole was in no doubt about the need for preaching, but first, he declared, or simultaneously, there must be instituted an *ecclesiastica disciplina*; otherwise, the Word preached would be prejudicial rather than beneficial.[12]

Why so? Because—here Pole quotes the God of Israel speaking to Ezekiel—'they sit before you as my people, and they hear what you say but they will not do it; for... their heart is set on gain'.[13] What that indicated, continued Pole, was that *after* the preaching of the Word, unless the fear of law impelled them ('terrore legum'), the people, whose hearts were carnally inclined, would neglect both the Church's divine service and her discipline. Therefore the energies of the Church would be more usefully applied, for the moment, in those things pertaining to discipline. For Pole, we may take it, that meant a discipline of temporary, and relative, silence. It would serve as a propaideia, an habituation to liturgical customs long neglected: candles, crosses, holy water, palms. It meant a *lex orandi* as the matrix of a *lex credendi*.[14]

---

11   ibid., p. 191.
12   ibid., pp. 193–4.
13   ibid., p. 194: 'Sedent, inquit, coram te, populus meus; et audiunt sermones tuos et non faciunt eos, quia in canticum oris sui vertunt illos et avaritiam sequitur cor eorum et est eis quasi carmen musicum, quod suavi dulcique sono canitur' (see Ezek. 33: 31–2).
14   'And of the observation of ceremonyes, begynnythe the very educatyon of the

But it also meant preaching—in due course. For the discipline of the Church, Pole insisted, could not be rightly accomplished without the Word. In this, he added, the City of London was not lacking, thanks to its good bishop.[15]

In that last sentence I think we have a clue to Pole's understanding of 'necessity' and 'discipline', and the clue to his presence in London rather than in Canterbury. Bonner had burned 113 people for heresy in London alone. That was between a third and a half of the estimated total of at least 273 people burned for heresy between 1555 and 1558. His zeal, an interpretation of *'terrore legum'* unacceptable to Pole, was not that of a uniquely bloodthirsty persecutor. It was government policy, government law, executed under the order and clear supervision of the Queen's Council.[16] The presence of Bonner, and the struggle for influence at Court, was, I think, the 'necessity' which kept Pole in London: Bonner, the Council which directed him, initially under Carranza's guidance, and finally, the Queen, whose support was the prize for which Pole, Carranza, and the Council waged a silent struggle. Bonner's preaching, no less than his discipline, had failed to convince Pole. It had also failed to convince London. In 1557 Ralph Allerton, examined by Bishop Bonner himself, declared that 'there are in England three religions'. Bonner asked him, 'Which be those three?', and Allerton replied, 'The first is that which you hold; the second is clean contrary to the same; and the third is a neuter, being indifferent—that is to say, observing all things that are commanded outwardly, as though he were of your part, his heart being yet wholly against the same.'[17] Allerton here confirmed Pole's 'experience', declared as such to Carranza, that the fires of Smithfield were daily creating a population outwardly conforming and inwardly dissenting. There was a party at Court which was not afraid to

chylderne of God; as the old law doythe shewe, that was full of ceremonyes, which St Paule callythe *pedagogiam in Christum.*' Pole applied the Pauline doctrine to 'holy water, holy breade, candells, ashes, and palme'. See his address to the citizens of London, 30 November 1557, in John Strype, *Ecclesiastical memorials relating chiefly to religion, and the reformation of it, shewing the various emergencies of the Church of England,* 3 vols (6 parts) (Oxford: Clarendon Press, 1822), III. 482–510; also Eamon Duffy, *The stripping of the altars: Traditional religion in England, c. 1400–c. 1580* (New Haven CT and London: Yale University Press, 1992).

15 Tellechea, *Carranza y Pole,* 1977, p. 194: 'quamquam hoc sine verbo recte fieri non potest; quod sane boni hujus Episcopi Londinensis studio ac diligentia huic civitati non deest'.

16 Gina Alexander, 'Bonner and the Marian persecutions', in *The English Reformation revised,* ed. Christopher Haigh (Cambridge: Cambridge University Press, 1987), pp. 157–75; also Thomas F. Mayer, *Reginald Pole: Prince and prophet* (Cambridge: Cambridge University Press, 2000), pp. 252–301. Mayer's treatment of this is unsurpassed.

17 Alexander, 'Bonner', p. 167, quoting John Foxe, *Acts and monuments of these late and perilous days,* ed. J. Pratt and J. Stoughton, 8 vols (London: Religious Tract Society, 1877), VII. 407.

say this. It included the Franciscan, Alonso de Castro, who had preached at
Court against the burning of heretics, and it included Pole. It probably included
Philip II, but it did not include Carranza. It is important to emphasize that
Bonner's 'discipline' was, from 1555, worked out in daily conversation with
Carranza. Carranza, moreover, was recognized as notably influential with the
Queen.[18] Pole's reason for remaining at Court would seem to need no further
explanation. Mary lived in the middle of a tug of war. A Spanish observer,
Luis Venegas, remarked that Carranza was critical of Pole's leniency. He
reported 'that the said archbishop of Toledo was discontented with the
Legate, considering him to be more easygoing' (*más blando*') in the pursuit of
heresy.[19] Then at last, in the summer of 1557, Carranza was gone. What was in
question by then was a matter of high policy affecting not simply the future
direction of the realm, but the thrust of Spanish policy itself, not only in
England, but also in the Netherlands, in Naples, and in Milan—wherever the
repression of heretical activity might threaten to turn public opinion against
the government. England was the testing ground on which Habsburg policy
was to be decided; Pole and his policy in England was the crux.

What inspired Pole's policy? In part, the 'daily experience' of Pole that
discipline like Bonner's would not do. Only the discipline of the Church
would do; the Church, and not the government. Discipline, as Pole understood it, meant a legally imposed *compelle entrare* to the Church, lightly interpreted, and followed by a policy of liturgical implantation, promoting a slow
rediscovery of rituals long repudiated. It meant preaching—the '*vox pastoris*' in
which Pole, as he insisted to Carranza, had preached, in the outlying dioceses
and twice in London, by God's grace not without fruit.[20] Just twice? But
perhaps Pole had, after all, a realistic appreciation of the unpopularity of a Papal
Legate in London. Now, as he assured Carranza, he was in control. He was
promoting a printing programme of homilies by Bishop Watson of Lincoln
and John Boxall (described as 'the Queen's good servant'), and Carranza's
Catechism was in the course of translation into English. Its 'sound and salutary
doctrine' would supply what the people lacked. Pole concluded by emphasizing that Spain, by divine privilege, had been protected from heretical infection.
The case of England, by contrast, was without precedent. On a final note of
gentle irony, he remarked that Carranza well understood that there was no
substitute for personal pastoral experience. If I am right in my reading of
Pole's reply, his vindication of his pastoral strategy was a commentary on the
absence of good preachers, the presence of bad ones, and the new oppor-

18 Tellechea, *Carranza y Pole*, p. 49.
19 ibid., pp. 51–2: 'cree que el dicho arzobispo de Toledo andaba descontento del Legado,
    por verle más blando de lo que él quisiera en el castigo de los herejes'.
20 ibid., p. 194.

tunities opened by Carranza's *Catechism* and his departure from England. Pole's reply would seem to signal his ascendancy after a long discussion between hawks and doves at Court. It seems likely to have been written with an eye to the Inquisitors of Rome, Brussels, and Madrid. It was informed both by a lifelong conviction about the treatment of heresy by persuasion rather than coercion, and by long experience of finding the most effective way of saying the unsayable, and of accomplishing it in silence.

That was what Renaissance courtiers understood by the virtue of *prudentia*. From his first years in diplomatic negotiations, it was the virtue most assiduously cultivated by Pole. He discovered it in Paris, under the pressure of necessity, during the years in which he promoted the interest of King Henry, as he came to believe, over the interest of his soul;[21] then after 1535, when he committed himself to a prudence rooted in what St Paul had called the 'foolishness of God' (I Cor. 1:25); in the years immediately before the Council of Trent, when he regarded the Lutheran schism as soluble by compromise; after the Council, when he had increasingly to defend his orthodoxy against Cardinal Carafa and the Roman Inquisition; and finally, when he sought to promote in England a policy of domestically based reconciliation, without giving leverage to his critics and opponents on Mary's Council, and at the Courts of Rome and Flanders. What I think informed Pole's outlook was, first, a realistic understanding of human weakness—the memory of his personal experience of involvement in the royal Divorce Proceedings of the 1520s and 1530s; his understanding of the 'temptation', as he was to call it in his sermon at St Paul's Cross in 1557, to accept the break with Rome; his realization that the witness unto death of More, Fisher, and the London Carthusians in 1535 was testimony to a higher 'prudence' of divine grace, a spiritual discernment of Christ's will for the unity of His Church.[22] Pole himself had been moved by More's death to decide in favour of the truth of More's testimony. His life thereafter had been dedicated to building bridges across which the traffic, as he realized, might travel in both directions. The bad, including, in Carranza's terms, bad prelates, might become good. The good might become bad. The judgement would be God's. What counted, what he sought to promote, what

21 Mayer, *Reginald Pole*, p. 195.
22 Pole described More's temptation to 'leave the unitye of the churche, as greater tentatyon coulde not be come to a man', and More's death, together with that of Fisher, as 'the provysyon that God made to staye the multytude, that they should not so deeply fawle, which was the example of thes ij great and notable servants of God, that rather suffered theyr heddes to be stryken off, than to consent that the realme shoulde be cut off from the obedience to the hedde, that Chryste did appoynte yn earthe' (Strype, *Ecclesiastical memorials*, II. 492, 496). The relevance of all this to Pole's personal experience and his decision in 1535 to commit himself to the divine institution of the Papacy should be underlined.

he lived by, was a spirit of clemency and persuasive utterance directed to a humble submission of mind and spirit to the divinely protected doctrine of the Church. Such a perspective owed much to personal experience. Pole had successfully adopted it at Viterbo after 1541, and its roots were in the first Catholic responses to the Reformation. To understand Pole's experience and policy we must go back to the Italian cities in the 1530s and to the ideal of the Bishop formulated at Verona by Gian Matteo Giberti and his collaborator Niccolò Ormanetto, who subsequently advised Pole in England. It was an ideal which found an eloquent spokesman in Erasmus. The final reflections of Erasmus on the episcopal office, his *Ecclesiastes* of 1535, had a preface voicing sorrow over the deaths of old friends, among them More and Fisher.[23]

It is now forty years since Professor Tellechea, in a pioneering essay, disclosed an Erasmus who, in the years following the outbreak of the Reformation, directed attention to the ideal of the Bishop in the Early Church.[24] The best recent scholarship has followed him in disclosing an ageing Erasmus—one might say, the final Erasmus—who, at the request of the European bishops, among them Fisher of Rochester, developed an ideal of preaching capable of addressing the weaknesses of the Church, its wounds— as Erasmus described them—opened to full view by the Reformation, and calling not for denial but redress. The appeal to penance, the *Agite poenitentiam* of the Gospel, was to be reformulated for the conditions of the age. The call of Erasmus was for prophecy and prudence.[25]

In 1533 there appeared an English translation of Erasmus's sermon on the 'Immense Mercy of God'. The translation, by Gentian Hervet, points to a decision to deploy in England the method of preaching recommended by Erasmus. It was followed in 1537 by *Xenophons treatise of householde*, translated 'at the desyre of mayster Geffrey Pole', Pole's brother.[26] Thus the mercy of

---

23 Desiderius Erasmus, *Opera omnia*, 10 vols (Leiden: Petrus Vander Aa, 1703–6), V, cols 769–70.

24 Tellechea, *Obispo ideal*, pp. 19–44.

25 Erasmus, *Opera omnia*, V, col. 772B (*Ecclesiastes... sive de ratione concionandi*): 'Haec ita dicta sint ad ostendandam Ecclesiastici muneris sublimitatem, ut tamen meminerimus quo discrimine nobis et Christo tribuatur filii Deique cognomen... Sunt item et alia permulta honoris cognomina, quibus Scriptura dignatur homines Divinae voluntatis interpretes, *Caelos* illos appelans, qui enarrant gloriam Dei. Dicuntur *Prophetae*, de quo postea dicemus'. And again, 'Nunc, si reputemus, in eodem populo quanta sit varietas, sexuum, aetatum, conditionis, ingeniorum, opinionum, vitae institutionis, consuetudinis, quanta oportet esse praeditum prudentia Ecclesiasten, cui sic temperanda est oratio, ne, dum aliquorum medetur erroribus, aliis errandi praebeat ansam, et dum vitia persequitur, vitia doceat, aut dum scelera fortiter coarguit, seditionem excitet' (col. 782A).

26 Henry S. Bennett, *English books and readers, 1475 to 1557, being a study in the history of the book trade from Caxton to the incorporation of the Stationers' Company* (Cambridge: Cambridge University Press, 1969), pp. 45–6, 57.

God registered in works of charity was to find its first expression in the reformation of the household. The most distinctive feature of this mode of
exegesis was the insistence of Erasmus on the Old Testament as a Testament
of Mercy, pointing forward to the New. Erasmus identified the prophetic
mission as a recall to God in the midst of a history of repeated apostasies. The
call of the prophets Isaiah, Nathan, and Ezekiel was issued to the kings of
Israel and its people. It was a call answered definitively in the person of King
David, and it found exemplary expression in Psalm 50(51), *Miserere mei Deus*.
The penitential idiom of the Bible, prophetically communicated, was the
aspiration of the age; but Erasmus redirected this aspiration to its Patristic
context, away from the tone of predictive apocalyptic promoted by Savona-
rola and severely discouraged by the fifth Lateran Council. What the preacher
must demand, according to Erasmus, was faith, hope, and charity—above all
the works of mercy.[27] The sacramental and liturgical dimensions of this
Patristic pastoral strategy were further developed by the subsequent Latin
translations of works of the Greek Fathers by Gentian Hervet.[28]

Pole's rhetorical theology was consciously exercised in the manner of
Gregory Nazianzen's *Five theological orations*, a rhetoric of the Holy Spirit
liturgically operative in the Christian faithful; capable of recalling to orthodoxy a
ruler such as Henry VIII, in the manner of the Church recalling Julian the
Apostate; in the manner of a Basil, expressing the doctrine of the Holy Spirit
in the doxological formularies of the Christian tradition, and willing to
exercise a 'reserve' or 'economy' of the Word, gradually dispensed according
to the capacity of the listeners; a 'prudent' dispensation, in the sense of truly
discerning the nature of the spiritual malady and its remedy. The Christian
vocation of the preacher must take all this into account. In Pole's case this
meant the vocation, as a Cardinal, to bear witness against the self-images of
the age.[29] It seems to me highly likely that when Pole addressed King Henry
VIII in his *De unitate* of 1536, the Pope in the *De emendanda ecclesia* of 1537, and
the Fathers of the Council of Trent in 1545, he was attempting to develop a
homiletic style, a voice, and a prophetic vision—first, in 1536, as a member of
the high nobility, and then as a Cardinal of the Church in the opening address
to the Council of Trent, recalling kings and prelates, popes and rulers to their
sins, to their responsibility for the sins of their subjects, and to their duty to
acknowledge and correct them, in a manner realistically attuned to meet the

---

27 Erasmus, *Opera omnia*, V. cols 557–8.
28 Nicolaus Cabalisas, *De divino altaris sacrificio. Maximi de mystagogia; hoc est de introductione ad
Sacra Ecclesiae Mysteria, seu Sacramenta. Diui Chrisostomi et Diui Basilii Sacrificii, seu missae
ritus, ex Sacerdotali graeco, Gentiano Herveto Aurelio interprete* (Venice: Alexander Brucioli,
1548). The dedication is to Marcello Cervini.
29 See Alasdair C. Macintyre, *Against the self-images of the age: Essays on ideology and philosophy*
(London: Duckworth, 1971).

conscience of the age. It was in the manner of Gregory Nazianzen's *Five theological orations* and St Basil's theology of the Holy Spirit that Pole had sought in Italy to address the religious divisions of the sixteenth century and to formulate Christian teaching in accordance with the new emphasis on spiritual experience found in the little book, the *Beneficio di Cristo*, while redirecting that emphasis into liturgical and sacramental channels. The liturgical character of this undertaking, which requires its due emphasis, found its central point of reference in the Latin translation of St Basil's works published in 1540 under the auspices of Giberti, with a preface dedicated to the primate of the German Church ('principem inter omnes Germaniae episcopos') Albert of Brandenburg.[30] A second preface was addressed to Vittoria Colonna, the acknowledged patroness of those devout groups in Rome and the Italian cities who looked for a renewal of spiritual theology. Thus, through the works of St Basil, England, Rome, and Germany were together to rediscover the pastoral norms capable of rekindling the unity of the Church. Just as Basil in the fourth century had published his *De spiritu sancto*, emphasizing sacramental regeneration as the work of the Holy Spirit, so now Pole and his circle in the sixteenth century sought to establish a liturgical *lex orandi* which would enable separated Christians to regroup within the communal *lex credendi* of the Church. We should take it that the sobriquet *'spirituali'* applied to Pole and his followers (in the wake of the failure of the reunion conversations of 1541 in Germany), denoted this strategy of agreed sacramental praxis, preparing the ground for a gradual communication from the pulpit and through the catechism of the fullness of the Word of God. What Pole believed was that, if people could be persuaded to find Christ in the sacraments, then they would find Him in the doctrine of the Church.

Yet the term 'spirituali' as applied by Giberti after the flight of Bernardino Ochino to Switzerland in 1542 carries, I think, a charge of wryness. It implies a rejection of the 'two-tier' doctrine of justification recommended by Contarini—one for the initiated, another for the many.[31] It was a strategy henceforward exploding across the religious spectrum. The strategy of conciliation was not one that appealed to everybody. It did not appeal to Carranza, or to his enemies in the Spanish Inquisition, or to their friends at the Courts of London, Brussels, and Madrid. It was the target of Carranza's sermon of 1555. But Priuli's assistance in the production of Carranza's Catechism looks like the final acceptance of the Tridentine doctrine of

30 *Omnia D. Basilii Magni . . . Opera* (Venice, 1548). Barry Collett remarks on the dedication to Vittoria Colonna in his *A long and troubled pilgrimage: The correspondence of Marguerite d'Angoulême and Vittoria Colonna*, Studies in Reformed Theology and History, ns 6 (Princeton NJ: Princeton Theological Seminary, 2000), esp. pp. 27–8.

31 See Elisabeth G. Gleason, *Gasparo Contarini: Venice, Rome, and Reform* (Berkeley, Los Angeles CA and London: University of California Press, 1993), pp. 269 ff.

justification by the least well disposed member of Pole's circle, and a sign that Pole's religious strategy achieved a greater depth of prophetic force and pastoral discretion than his critics allowed. His homiletic style developed impressively from the initially histrionic explosion of his *De unitate* in 1536 to the quietly stable, mature mode of his address to the citizens of London in 1557. In between, there came the crisis of preaching in the Italian cities.

This was a crisis in which Pole and his associates had fully participated. From it they learned, and matured in an understanding of, the need for a new *ars praedicandi*, responding to the realities opened up by the Reformation, and by the gaps in belief which it disclosed. Theirs was an art of preaching faith, hope, and charity which shared the imperatives recognized by the Legates of the Council of Trent for preachers to meet the pressing social demands of the Italian cities. That meant better hospitals and a more equitable relief of debt. It meant provision of dowries for the poor. It meant building up households. It meant exactly what Pole preached in 1557 when he told the citizens of London 'that in Italye in two cytes onelye, there is more almes gyven to monastyres and poore folkes in one monthe, than yn this realme in a hole yeare.' As the prophet Isaiah had told the Jews, 'to doe deedes of mercye' would be to secure the mercy of God. For 'the cause thereof ys, that the doctryne of the churche ys the doctryne of mercye and almes of God'.[32] That was the spirit which, we may imagine, Pole considered to be lacking in Bonner's 'discipline'. It entailed a spirit of discretion. It meant that Pole would inform the 'possessioners' of ecclesiastical lands that they had eaten of an apple that had made them ill; and that the remedy was fasting, prayer, and penance. He did not minimize his message; neither did he confront public persons with their sins. He spoke, instead, to the privacy of their conscience. When, in 1557, Pole recalled to the City of London the country's historical 'temptation' to separate itself from the unity of the Church, he remarked on it as a temptation personally experienced by More but, by Divine Grace, over-come.[33] We may suppose that Pole was here talking also about himself, in the years 1529–35. He spoke of the subsequent spoliation of the Church's lands; of the Church's permission to the 'possessioners' who acquired them to retain them; of the need, none the less, for voluntary surrender to the Church of at least a part of the property in reparation. As 'appetite', together with the 'apple', had been the cause of England's illness, so now reparation through works of mercy must be her cure. Now was the time to rebuild the parish churches and to extend the care of the poor, constructing hospitals on the model of the Italian cities—Venice, Milan, Florence, Bologna, Rome.[34] If

---

32 Strype, *Ecclesiastical memorials*, II. 484.
33 ibid., II. 490 ff.
34 ibid., II. 507.

'temptation' and 'appetite' had led England into schism, then temptation and appetite were non-denominational. Pole spoke of his 'compassion' for the young who had been brought up outside the Church, and of the duty of parents, who had not been, to work together to convert their children.[35] From this we can see that Pole's problem was not hostility to preaching but lack of adequately trained preachers.

Why, then, did he not invite the Jesuits? No doubt he wanted a seminary-trained clergy preaching in the parishes, as in Giberti's Verona; but would not the Jesuits have offered help towards that end? In 1554, St Ignatius wrote, offering such help, but received no answer from Pole. Father Edward Booth, in an unpublished paper, suggests that Pole may not have considered Loyola's vision of the Church adequately sensitive to the episcopal and Legatine character of the *Reformatio Angliae*. He cites a letter of Loyola to Canisius in 1554, setting out the Jesuit strategy for the conversion of Germany.[36] My own belief is that Loyola's emphasis on working through the Court would not have appealed to Pole, precisely because it was Pole's own strategy. The last thing he wanted was competition at Court. Loyola's plans for Germany, translated, would have cut across Pole's strategy for England. For Pole as for Carranza, for Giberti as for St Ignatius and St Charles Borromeo, the reformation of the Church meant, first, the reformation of the household. For Pole, there was no other way; least of all, in England. There, as he put it to the citizens of London in 1557, the Church was 'famished'. It was devoid of powers of 'constraint'.[37] Its one constraint was the preaching of God's word. That was not to be confused, as Bonner did confuse it, with the government's words. It was, as Pole insisted, a matter of domestic conversion, of families encouraging each other, and of clergy encouraging the families, to take responsibility for the souls in their care, for their parish church, and for the hungry and neglected in their midst. For all of these, the responsibility began at the top, in the households of cardinals and kings, at Court. Here, Pole's views rejoined those of Carranza's homily of 1555; but he withheld himself from demonizing his environment. As a pastor, Pole was at once paternal and patrician. He believed in the 'fear of law', leniently applied, as a means of persuading people to come to church. In this, as in Carranza's case, his vision of reform was at one with the leading spirits of his age. It was a conception which appealed to 'fathers and masters' whose 'good example' was 'one of the best remedyes' for the corruption of the age.[38] It was also a consultative understanding of office. Each parish priest, each bishop, was expected to refer back, up the chain of

35 ibid., II. 497.
36 Loyola's letter is discussed in James Brodrick, *St Peter Canisius* (London: Geoffrey Chapman, 1935), pp. 211 ff.
37 Strype, *Ecclesiastical memorials*, II. 483.
38 ibid., II. 497–8.

command, the petitions and grievances of his flock, so that 'the truth of things' was heard either in Church courts or at Court, and there adjudicated. Thus, at Viterbo after 1541, Pole had successfully mediated to protect his flock from penal taxation.[39] That was what a Legate was for.

By the close of the sixteenth century, Pole's household was recalled by Cardinal Valier as an example for those who held office, or were about to hold it.[40] Valier saw Pole's household, and the Oratory of St Philip Neri as its successor, as advancing a manner of response to religiously divided people; a manner protective of the vulnerable young and hospitable to the wavering. Just as it was to be through the influence of the Roman Oratory that Henry IV and France were reconciled to the Roman Church in 1595, so, in an earlier generation, souls such as Marc'Antonio Flaminio and Pietro Carnesecchi found both a welcome at Viterbo and an invitation to relate their personal religious experience (as shaped by the doctrines of Juan de Valdés) to the eucharistic life and doctrines of the Church. Here they were introduced to an atmosphere of prayer, understanding, and spiritual conversation. They were assured of mutual assistance towards conversion of heart. Pole's household at Viterbo was remembered as a spiritual centre from within which the world of the Court, and the compromises it proposed, might be effectively engaged with a spiritually uncompromising yet politically informed approach to 'the truth of things'.

This was how Pole was remembered in Rome, outside the files of the Roman Inquisition. His posthumous reputation was not a 'myth of sanctity' generated by his biographers. His sanctity was remembered as the real thing. Had there been a hint of scandal, of the kind supposed by Professor Mayer, the Inquisition would certainly have acted on it. Instead, the suspicions of the Roman Inquisition were directed against Pole's idea of Justification and his leniency to heretics, never to questions of morals. Carafa himself was reported to have described Pole as 'a saint and an angel in his life'.[41] Pole was a courtier by conviction. Carranza was not: his denunciation of the Court was fatal. As Bonner's preceptor he helped to shape a policy of religious intolerance; and he was to become its victim. At all times he spoke with conviction and sincerity. But his sincerity was untempered by discretion; and discretion was

---

39 Mayer, *Reginald Pole*, p. 115.
40 Agostino Valier, *Il dialogo della gioia cristiana*, ed. Antonio Cistellini, Testi i Studi Oratoriana 1 (Brescia: La Scuola, 1975), pp. 44–6: 'Et in cardinalium familiis quibusdam, quae monasteriorum bene institutorum instar habere possunt, licet admirabilem laetitiam capere ex aspectu patris, sermonibus eiusdem, hoc est illius qui familiae praeest et exercitationibus variis ingenii et pietatis. Domum Reginaldi cardinalis Poli officinam fuisse virtutum audivimus; fuisse quosdam qui apud illum cardinalem vixerunt, qui maximam se dicerent percipere solitos voluptatem, cardinalem patronum audientes loquentem intuentes etiam solum.'
41 Mayer, *Reginald Pole*, pp. 214, 332.

the *sine qua non* of real effectiveness. The proceedings against Carranza reveal that what the Inquisitors objected to in his sermon of 1555 was his declaration that no good Catholic could be scandalized by public reprehension of bad bishops. The Inquisitors disagreed: such preaching, they considered, could incite open rebellion.[42] The year was 1564, and the context of their accusations was the Netherlands. The censure of Archbishop Carranza was intended to be exemplary. For, as the panel of examining theologians wrote, Carranza's view represented a broad spectrum of opinion among preachers. Such opinions, in their verdict, must be excluded from the pulpit. The censure of Carranza was intended, therefore, to send a message to the preachers and theologians of the Spanish Church. In fact, it sent a message to the Universal Church, and its implications were not lost in Italy. The Spanish Crown had arrested the Primate of Spain for talking about the system of appointment to bishoprics: heresy charges were of course 'supplied'. The vision of the episcopal reformers at the Council of Trent was now subjected to an intervention of the Spanish Crown imposing a universal silence concerning the acknowledgement of Catholic responsibility for the divisions of Christendom. Pole's opening address to the Council of Trent had underlined that responsibility.

There was a coda. In 1571–2 a Spanish priest named Alfonso de Lobo, Italianized as Lupo, infuriated the Spanish colony in Rome by preaching against the *limpieza de sangre* ('purity of blood') laws which excluded those of Muslim and Jewish descent from ordination. Lupo himself was of Jewish convert (*converso*) descent. In Rome, such *conversos* were freely ordained to the Catholic priesthood, and at the Roman Oratory, where Lupo went to discuss the questions of the day, Jewish converts were particularly welcome as expositors of the Hebrew Bible. Lupo was summoned before the Roman Inquisition—I think we should suppose as a purely formal gesture. He was briefly imprisoned and brought to trial in November 1572. He dutifully affirmed that the Spanish laws were entirely reasonable and his case was dismissed.[43] He publicly acknowledged his 'error' in the Spanish church at Rome and was instructed, apparently by Gregory XIII, to become a Capuchin. The Capuchins refused him, but the Pope was Pope, and Lupo became a Capuchin.[44]

Redeployed on circuit by St Charles Borromeo and St Philip Neri, Lupo became one of the greatest preachers of the age. His case, which was in reality

---

42 Tellechea, *Carranza y Pole*, p. 388.
43 ACDF, Sanctum Officium, Decreta 1571–1574, fols 66, 68, 70–72, 73, 75, 76, 78, 79–80. See Fedele Merelli, 'P. Alfonso Lupo, Cappucino, e San Carlo Borromeo', *L'Italia Francescana*, 64/ii–iii (1989), pp. 139–78, 322–31.
44 ibid., pp. 175–7. On p. 179, he expresses uncertainty about the date of Lupo's entry to the Capuchins. The decree for 7 November 1572 (fol. 80r) describes him as 'Alphonsus Lupum scappucinum hispanum'.

a continuation of Carranza's, reveals two things: firstly, the determination of the Spanish Inquisition to control, through the Spanish Crown, access to holy orders and the pulpit; and secondly, that a policy of circumventing and renegotiating Imperial directives was not beyond the wit of Italian Catholics. Something of the sort seems to have been identified by Lupo's principal accuser in Rome, Diego de Simancas, the Bishop of Badajoz. He complained that in Rome the authorities looked askance at the *limpieza* laws, and it is significant that he was present there to argue the Spanish view on the Carranza case. His insistence that Lupo should be allowed to preach only under Papal licence tells us a lot about the tacit accommodations worked out, around the pulpit, between the Spanish Crown and the Papacy.[45] This was a problem which would continue throughout the seventeenth century. The Curial department of *Propaganda Fide* was established to counter, among other things, the Spanish policy of excluding a native clergy from Mexico to the Philippines. Such hidden continuities of memory, privately communicated, ensured the enduring influence of Pole and Carranza in ways which went beyond the best efforts of the Inquisitors. The voice of Carranza spoke posthumously in the Roman Catechism of 1566 for centuries to come, while Pole's *Reformatio Angliae* became, in the closing stages of the Council of Trent, the point of departure for the world-wide provision of a vocationally motivated clergy.

45 ibid., p. 177.

CHAPTER 6

Carranza and Catharinus
in the controversy over the bishops'
obligation of residence, 1546–52

Patrick Preston

This chapter discusses a major problem at the Council of Trent: the bishops' obligation to reside in their dioceses. I shall consider this question mainly with regard to the period 1546–52 and I shall do so by focusing on the contributions made to the debate by two great Dominicans, the second of whom, Ambrosius Catharinus, is certainly less well known than the first, though he was the most formidable Italian anti-Lutheran polemicist of his day and the author of a large number of writings which encompassed most of the topics that preoccupied theologians in the first half of the sixteenth century. In 1546, while at Trent, he was elevated to the Bishopric of Minori, and though he was not called to the Council when it again met in 1551–2, he was promoted to the Archbishopric of Conza in 1552. He died on 8 November 1553, while on a journey to Rome to be created cardinal in the consistory of 22 December. The honour would have been in recognition of his conspicuous services in the struggle against Protestantism.[1]

The contexts in which the debate on the residence obligation took place are important for bringing out the significance of what Carranza and Catharinus were arguing about. One context was the preoccupation of the Council with the problem of residence. The other was the way in which the literary debate developed. I shall say a few words on each.

The problem was an ancient one. 'From the Council of Basle to that of Trent the demand that the bishops comply with the duty of residence runs through every memorial dealing with reform and every attempt to bring it about.' The problem had to be tackled at the root, but how? One suggestion was that of Cardinal Cajetan (Tommaso de Vio), whose teaching (in his commentary on Aquinas's *Summa*) was that the episcopal duty of residence

---

1   See Giacinto Bosco, 'Intorno a un carteggio inedito di Ambrogio Caterino', *Memorie Domenicane*, 67 (1950), pp. 103–20, 137–66, 233–66.

rested on a direct Divine ordinance.[2] This suggestion had little effect on the behaviour of bishops. The meeting of the Council at Trent was an obvious opportunity to have the whole matter thrashed out. But the legates, and in particular Cardinal del Monte, were reluctant: if the residence obligation were declared to be by the Divine Law, Papal dispensation would be ruled out, and they therefore rightly feared infringement of the Papal prerogative. But more was involved than the authority of the Pope. The immediate consequence of the rigid enforcement of the residence obligation, that is to say without dispensation, would have been the abolition of pluralism. A further consequence would have been the disruption of papal administration. Bureaucrats and diplomats regularly held episcopal office, the demands of which they could not satisfy in person because of their other commitments. Cardinals were likewise provided for. This system might be dismantled very slowly, and in fact eventually was, but the job could not be done overnight. Nevertheless, twenty canons of an enlarged reform proposal were promulgated on 22 February 1547 and confirmed between the 24th and 27th, but in spite of the fact that the legates had given some ground, the point of principle on which they had insisted remained intact: there was no declaration to the effect that the obligation to reside fell within the scope of the *ius divinum*.[3]

What about the literary debate engendered by the debate in the Council? The opening exchanges were between Carranza and Catharinus. Both had been writing about the residence obligation at the same time—Catharinus at the instigation of the Council legates—but Carranza was the first to publish.[4] His *Controversia de necessaria residentia personali episcoporum et aliorum inferiorum pastorum* appeared at Venice in 1547, and at Salamanca in 1550.[5] Carranza seems to have been well aware of his opponent's main argument.[6] No doubt he had

2   Hubert Jedin, *A history of the Council of Trent*, tr. Ernest Graf, 2 vols (London: Nelson, 1957–61), II. 321, n. 1–2.
3   ibid., II. 360–66.
4   For details of the way in which the controversy between Carranza, Catharinus, and also Domingo de Soto, developed, see Josef Schweizer, *Ambrosius Catharinus Politus (1484–1553), ein Theologe des Reformationszeitalters: Sein Leben und seine Schriften*, Reformationsgeschichtliche Studien und Texte 11–12 (Munster:Aschendorff, 1910), pp. 185–98; also *Dictionnaire de théologie catholique*, ed. J.M. Alfred Vacant, 15 vols (Paris: 1903–50), XII/ii, cols 2418–34; XIV/ii, cols 2430–31.
5   Bartolomé Carranza de Miranda, *Controversia de necessaria residentia personali episcoporum et aliorum inferiorum pastorum* (Venice: Ad Signum Spei, 1547). Subsequent editions were published at Salamanca (1550), Medina del Campo (1550), Lyon (1550), Antwerp (1554), and Venice (1562). See now the 1547 Latin text in facsimile, with Spanish translation, edited by Tellechea (Madrid: Fundación Universitaria Española, 1994).
6   See, for example, Carranza, *Controversia*, fols 3r–v and 16r: 'Exoriuntur enim (ut audio) nonnulli, qui nunc tandem in dubium revocant, unde Episcopi originem ducant, iure divino an humano fuerint constituti. Tum etiam an teneantur praesentes Episcopi suas

been able to pick up the general idea from informal conversations and from what was said in the Tridentine Congregations at which the residence question was discussed. Although Carranza had not written directly against Catharinus, the latter took some of his remarks personally and added a *Censura in libellum quendam inscriptum Controversia de necessaria residentia personali episcoporum* to his *Tractatio quaestionis quo iure episcoporum residentia debeatur*, in which he lamented that his 'friend' Carranza had permitted himself to adopt a position at variance with the thinking of the Council and the interests of peace between the participants.[7] Though issues of protocol were involved, Catharinus's main objection was to the way in which Carranza had managed his argument: he had missed the crucial point and confused the issue, and was really relying only on what Cajetan had said in his commentary on the *Summa* without realizing that, later, Cajetan had changed his opinion.

While all this was going on, Catharinus had also become involved in a dispute with a third fellow-Dominican, the Thomist Domingo de Soto, over the doctrine of the certainty of inherent grace, an aspect of the doctrine of Justification that had concerned both Catholic and Protestant theologians.[8] Catharinus intended to deal with this topic in his *Interpretatio noni capituli synodalis decreti de iustificatione*, a work that he had in fact finished, when he found once again that an opponent had forestalled him.[9] De Soto's *De natura et gratia libri tres* appeared first (again, at Venice in 1547); and in Book III of that work Soto dealt with the question of the certainty of grace. Catharinus interpreted Soto's remarks as a personal attack. In irritation, he thereupon wrote his *Defensio catholicorum, qui pro possibili certitudine praesentis gratiae disseruerunt*, a polemic against Soto, and published it along with the *Interpretatio* about three months after the appearance of the *De natura et gratia*.[10] De Soto was not the man to take this lying down. He replied with his *Apologia... qua R.P. Ambrosio Catharino de certitudine gratiae respondet*, published at Venice in that same

oves pascere: an vero satis sit mercenarium pastorem gregi praeficere, ut ipsi a cura soluti, alias res agant... Quidam voluit infirmare argumentum acceptum ab hoc loco, dicens verba huius capitis pertinere ad solum Christum, nec ad alium pastorem posse accommodari: ac proinde aiebat, quae in eo capite dicuntur, non esse requirenda ab alio pastore ecclesiastico, nec ex his sumendum argumentum, ut probareter residentia ex iure divino' (Tellechea, *Controversia*, pp. 180, 202).

7 Ambrosius Catharinus Politus, *Tractatio quaestionis, quo iure episcoporum residentia debeatur* (Venice: Gabriel Giolito de'Ferrari, 1547); id., *Censura in libellum quendam inscriptum Controversia de necessaria residentia personali episcoporum* (Venice: Gabriel Giolito de'Ferrari, 1547); Schweizer, *Ambrosius Catharinus Politus*, p. 187.

8 Schweizer, *Ambrosius Catharinus Politus*, p. 188.

9 Ambrosius Catharinus Politus, *Interpretatio noni cap[ituli] synodalis decreti de iustificatione* (Venice: Gabriel Giolito de'Ferrari, 1547).

10 id., *Defensio catholicorum, qui pro possibili certitudine praesentis gratiae disseruerunt* (Venice: Gabriel Giolito de'Ferrari, 1547).

year of 1547. I here ignore his bitter personal attack on Catharinus, and his remarks on his opponent's theories concerning the certainty of inherent grace; but in his own and Carranza's name he also proceeded against Catharinus's view, as set out in the *Tractatio*, that the foundation of the bishops' residence obligation lay in ecclesiastical law, not in the Divine Law. Catharinus, in turn, defended these views against Soto's onslaught in his *De resolutione obiectorum adversus tractationem, quo iure episcoporum residentia debeatur*. He had been called upon to defend them once again—in the *Confirmatio doctrinae de personali residentia episcoporum contra quendam novitium oppugnatorem*—when in 1551 Francisco Torres's *De residentia pastorum iure divino scripto sancita* was published in Florence.[11] I shall later say something more about the bone that Catharinus picked with Torres, but all this started with Carranza and it is therefore to Carranza's work that I now turn.

What exactly was he saying in the *Controversia*, and how did he say it? I begin with the 'how?' The answer is, with evident sincerity and great passion, fuelled by a sense of the urgency and importance of the problem that he was addressing, which was nothing less than the origin of the schism in the Church:

> O [unhappy] times, in which a good number of the bishops do not think that it is their task either to reside in their churches or to answer in person for any part of the[ir] pastoral function. When the bishops have degenerated to that extent, they have given a licence to the other prelates to do the same; and hence one has arrived at the present calamities and tribulations of the Church.[12]

> What ruined almost all of Germany but the idleness of the pastors? Wishing to be secular princes, they gave up being shepherds of their flock. The wolves came into the sheepfold. The shepherds not being found, they seized the sheep, so that [the sheep] now wander wretchedly through various heresies and sects.[13]

---

11 Ambrosius Catharinus Politus, *De resolutione obiectorum adversus tractationem, quo iure episcoporum residentia debeatur* (Bologna: Anselmo Giaccarelli, 1548); id., '*Confirmatio doctrinae eiusdem autoris de personali residentia episcoporum contra quendam novitium oppugnatorem*', in his *Enarrationes in quinque priora capita libri Geneseos* (Rome: Antonio Blado, 1552); Francisco Torres, *De residentia pastorum iure divino scripto sancita* (Florence: Lorenzo Torrentino, 1551).

12 'O tempora, in quibus iam bona pars episcoporum non putet sui esse muneris, vel residere apud ecclesias suas, vel ullam pastoralis functionis partem per se illis praestare, cumque episcopi eo degenerarint caeteris praelatis, ut idem facerent licentiam dederunt: et hinc ventum est ad praesentes Ecclesiae calamitates et aerumnas' (fol. 15r; Tellechea, *Controversia*, pp. 200–201).

13 'Quid perdidit totam fere Germaniam, nisi ocium et absentia pastorum? Volentes esse principes seculares, desierunt esse pastores. Venerunt lupi in stabulum ovium, non inventis pastoribus rapuerunt, et aberrare fecerunt oves, sicut nunc misere per varias haereses et sectas aberrant' (fol. 15v; Tellechea, *Controversia*, p. 201).

What has alienated England from the whole Church, except that there was scarcely one shepherd to be found who would lay down his life for his sheep?[14]

The residence of pastors is indeed a great thing, and it ought to be pleasing to everyone and certainly joyful to a Christian people, seeing that on it depends the whole process of renewing the Church and restoring religion, its laws, institutions and customs, and the possibility of bringing back the old, authentic Christian discipline. Since this is so and of such great moment, it is not permissible to keep silent in so great a crisis of our religion, and so great a common danger for souls, nor to have more regard for anything than for what pertains to the office of bishops and to the public well-being.[15]

After the 'how?' I turn to the 'what?'. The first chapter discusses the kind of arguments that are relevant to the matter in hand. Chapter Two provides what is called here an 'axiomatic foundation' for the whole work, and here it is important to notice that Carranza distinguishes between Divine and Natural Law. He does not provide us with a formal definition of Natural Law, but it seems, from the examples given, that he is referring to the presuppositions underlying the indispensable social and cultural institutions and practices of all societies. Carranza claims that the bishops' residence obligation derives from both Divine and Natural law, and that these laws require all ministers of the Church, especially bishops and parish priests, to perform their office not by means of paid substitutes ('mercenaries') but personally. The final chapter, the twelfth, considers excuses for absence and refutes arguments seeking to justify it.

All the remaining chapters present the case for the view that the residence obligation falls within the Divine Law, and rehearse a series of 'proofs' that are arranged in order of importance. They start, therefore, with proofs from the Old and New Testaments (four chapters) and continue with the acts of Provincial and General Councils; Papal decrees and episcopal teaching; the Early Fathers and Doctors of the Church; Cardinal Cajetan; and human reason. Chapters One and Two are vital for understanding Carranza's way of proceeding. His first move is the claim that 'in the sacred disciplines the grounds of proof are of many kinds'. One is by the evidence of the Scriptures, and this is the strongest ground of proof. Another is derived from the tradition of the

---

14   'Quid abalienavit a tota Ecclesia Angliam, nisi quod vix unus pastor inventus est, qui poneret animam suam pro ovibus suis?' (fol. 15v; Tellechea, *Controversia*, pp. 201–02).

15   'Magna quidem res est residentia pastoralis et grata omnibus esse debet et iocunda certe populo Christiano, quandoquidem ex ea omnis instaurandae Ecclesiae ratio, omnis restituendae religionis modus, leges, instituta, mores, veterem Christianam, veramque disciplinam revocandi facultas pendeat atque proficiscatur: quae cum ita sint, et tanti referant, silere non licet, neque in tanto religionis nostrae discrimine tantoque animarum communi periculo cuiquam consulere potius, quam officio nostro, et publicae utilitati' (fol. 5v; Tellechea, *Controversia*, pp. 183–4).

sacred General and Provincial Councils. A third is from the opinion of the saints and the Early Fathers:

> All these are strictly theological grounds of proof, and I shall strive to show by appeal to all of them that all ecclesiastical ministers are by Natural and Divine Law held to personal residence in the churches from which they receive their stipends. Last of all, we add human reasoning, a ground of proof that is not alien from this discipline.[16]

What is the evidence of the Scriptures? Of the four chapters devoted to this question, the first takes examples from the Old Testament, and the second and third from the New Testament. The treatment of the New Testament requires two chapters because Carranza distinguishes the Gospels and the Acts of the Apostles from the Epistles. The texts that he selects to support his case are, firstly, Numbers 18 and 27, Proverbs 27, Ezekiel 34, Zechariah 11, and Isaiah 40; secondly, Matthew 10, John 10 and 21, and Acts 20; and, finally, I Corinthians 9, I Thessalonians 5, I Timothy 3, II Timothy 4, and I Peter 5. The fourth chapter considers the terms applied to bishops 'as found in the Divine Scriptures, for these terms evidently function in such a manner that, being bestowed by the Spirit of Wisdom, they always correspond to the nature of things in themselves.'[17] The central idea of this chapter, which I shall not otherwise discuss, seems to be that the personal residence of bishops is requisite by virtue of the meaning of the term 'bishop', and of the epithets normally attached in the Scriptures to the bishop or his Old Testament forebears. Hence Carranza says:

> The bishop is said to be one who carefully observes and examines what is being done. For where we have in I Peter 5 *'providentes'* the Greek is *'episkopountes'* ... They are called 'angels' in Luke, Mark, Isaiah, and Malachi. Why so? Because they are sent as messengers to preach the word of God.[18]

---

16 'In Sacris Disciplinis multiplex est locus arguendi. Unus est ex sacrarum scripturarum testimonio, et hic est firmissimus locus argumentandi. Alter est ex sacrorum conciliorum generalium vel provincialium traditione. Tertius est ex sanctorum , et veterum patrum Ecclesiae sententia. Isti omnes sunt proprie loci theologici, quibus omnibus contendam demonstrare, universos ministros ecclesiasticos ex iure naturali, et divino teneri ad residentiam personalem in ecclesiis, a quibus temporalia stipendia desumunt. Postremo addemus et rationes humanas, qui locus arguendi non est alienus ab hac disciplina' (fol. 5r; Tellechea, *Controversia*, p. 183).

17 'Explicantur nomina episcoporum secundum usum divinarum litterarum. Nam et haec scripturae divinae partem esse videntur, quae, ut a spiritu sapientiae indita, semper consonare debent rebus ipsis' (fol. 4r–v; Tellechea, *Controversia*, pp. 181–2).

18 'Episcopus is dicitur qui speculatur, et attente rimatur, quid geratur. Nam ubi habemus I Petri cap. 5 Providentes, Graece est episkopountes... Dicuntur Angeli, cum apud Lucam et Marcum, cum apud Esi. et Malach. Cur ita? quia mittuntur ut nuncii praedicaturi verbum Dei' (fol. 27v; Tellechea, *Controversia*, p. 222).

How does the argument that the residence obligation is by Divine Law actually work?

After first distinguishing in Chapter Two between Divine and Natural Law, Carranza claims that 'the Divine Laws establish that there should be bishops and other lower pastors in the Church, and the Apostles handed these down'.[19] From this claim, he immediately deduces two conclusions that he calls axioms:

> *First Conclusion*: All ministers of the Church, especially bishops and parish priests (*parochi*), are required by Natural and Divine Law to perform their office not by means of paid substitutes but personally.

From this follows a second conclusion, which is equally certain:

> *Second Conclusion*: Bishops and parish priests are required by both kinds of Law to reside regularly and ordinarily; that is, to be physically present in their churches and dioceses.'[20]

He inclines to the view that these are merely two different ways of saying the same thing, but he provides a demonstration in case one is needed. It is to the effect that no one is held to personal residence except on account of performing the duties of his office. It is then very easy for Carranza to show that Christ's charge to Peter signified entrusting him with a task. 'He did not say to him "Be the chief priest", but "Feed, govern and rule my flock".'[21] There then follows a short list of Scriptural and Patristic texts which emphasize that episcopacy is the name of an office and task and not of an honour.

Carranza's chosen Scriptural texts, taken as a whole, yield the following set of propositions that are the foundation of the Imperial, Spanish, and French case, at Trent, for the view that the obligation to reside derives from Divine Law. They 'flesh out', so to speak, the two axioms stated in Chapter Two.

(*i*) The bishop is a worker, and workers get paid. 'Paul, I Timothy, 5:17 confirms this. "Let the elders who rule well be considered worthy of double honour, especially those who labour in preaching and in teaching." For Scripture says, "The labourer deserves his wages," and "you shall not muzzle an ox when it is treading out the grain".'[22]

---

19 'Futuros esse in Ecclesia Episcopos, et pastores alios inferiores iura divina instituunt, et Apostoli tradiderunt' (fol. 6r; Tellechea, *Controversia*, p. 185).
20 'Ex utroque iure tenentur Episcopi et parochi ad regularem et ordinariam residentiam, sive praesentiam corporalem in suis ecclesiis et dioecesibus' (fol. 6v; Tellechea, *Controversia*, p. 185).
21 '...non dixit ei: esto Pontifex, sed: pasce, guberna, rege oves meas, gregem meum' (fol. 7r; Tellechea, *Controversia*, p. 186).
22 'confirmatur hoc ex eodem Paulo I. Tim. 5 [17–18]: Qui bene praesunt praesbyteri, duplici honore digni habeantur, maxime qui laborant in verbo et doctrina. Dicit enim scriptura: Dignus est operarius mercede sua, et non alligabis os bovi trituranti' (fols 13v–14r; Tellechea, *Controversia*, p. 198).

(*ii*) One cannot obey the Biblical injunctions *in absentia* (this is supported by Ezek. 34:1, as expounded by Gregory the Great in the *Liber pastoralis*).[23]

(*iii*) With a few exceptions, to be mentioned later, there is no admissible excuse for absenteeism. 'Some offer a pretext for this [i.e. for absence from their diocese], and allege as a reason that they are justifiably occupied in business and public offices whose proper discharge is particularly necessary to the Church and so are to be exercised by learned men of undoubted probity. I think that their sin is made more serious by this excuse, since they undertake secular offices with ecclesiastical stipends.'[24] The objection here is to using the Church's money to finance secular business.

(*iv*) But those who do not work should not get paid. 'Observe the words of Paul [1 Timothy 5: 17–18]. He teaches that priests are worthy of a double reward, but only those who govern well, and those who in word and doctrine, and this he proves by Scripture, which orders that a treading ox shall not be muzzled. And so the *lazy* ox can be muzzled. Thus an idle and absent minister can be muzzled, lest he feed off the fruits of the Church. Therefore, if such wish to eat, and enjoy the fruits of their labours, they are required to work by treading Christ's harvest, and this absentees cannot do. Thus, in so far as they are required to work and to perform the duties of their office, they are also required to maintain regular presence in their churches.'[25]

(*v*) The reason why the bishop cannot discharge his responsibilities by sending in a locum is that 'I am the good shepherd. The good shepherd lays down his life for the sheep. He who is a hireling and not a shepherd, whose own the sheep are not, sees the wolf coming and leaves the sheep and flees; and the wolf snatches them and scatters them. The hireling flees because he is a hireling and cares nothing for the sheep [John 10: 11–13].'[26]

---

23 'Si haec requirenda sunt a pastoribus, si ea cura, ea solicitudo, ut quod aegrotum est in animabus fidelium contendant sanare, quod confractum est, alligare, quod abiectum est, reducere, et quod perierit ex numero fidelium revocare, viderint illi, si haec absentes et ignorantes ovium suarum quas absentes cognoscere minime potuerunt, praestare poterunt', and 'quo loco audi Grego[rium] in Pastora[libus], parte I. cap. 6' (fol. 10r–v; Tellechea, *Controversia*, p. 192).

24 'Huic veritati praetexunt aliqui, et causantur, quod sint iusto occupati in negotiis et officiis publicis, quorum recta et bona administratio est Ecclesiae maxime necessaria, et ideo per viros probos et doctos exercenda. Hac excusatione puto gravari magis peccatum eorum, quoniam stipendiis ecclesiasticis obeunt prophana munera' (fol. 11r; Tellechea, *Controversia*, p. 193).

25 Paul's injunction is even more severe: 'If anyone will not work, let him not eat' (II Thess. 3: 10). 'Observa verba Pauli, docet duplici stipendio dignos presbyteros, sed eos tantum, qui bene praesunt, et eos qui laborant in verbo et doctrina, quod probat per scripturam, quae iubet: ne infraenetur bos triturans. Unde ociosus bos poterat infraenari. Ergo et minister ociosus et absens potest infraenari, ne pascatur ex fructibus Ecclesiae. Igitur si velint pasci, et fructus desumere, tenentur labore triturando messem Christi, quod absentes facere non possunt. Ergo quatenus tenentur ad actionem ministerii et laborem, eatenus tenentur ad praesentiam regularem in ecclesiis suis' (fol. 14r; Tellechea, *Controversia*, p. 198).

26 'Ego sum pastor bonus. Bonus pastor animam suam dat pro ovibus suis: mercenarius autem, cuius non sunt oves propriae, videt lupum venientem, et dimittit oves et fugit,

Neither the material nor the arguments that Carranza uses are, of course, new. If they were, he could scarcely find support for them, as he does, in the Fathers, Popes, Doctors, and Canons of the Church, to which his next three chapters are devoted. Cardinal Cajetan, the subject of the tenth chapter, might almost be included among the Doctors. Perhaps the reason for giving him a chapter of his own was that he does introduce an element of novelty into a tradition of long duration. Carranza restricts himself to citing what he describes as Cajetan's better reasons for arguing that continuous residence in his diocese is required of a bishop by Divine Law. There are three of these.

(*i*) The bishop is required by Divine Law to look after the souls of his subjects, but, to exercise that cure of souls, the continuous personal residence of bishops is necessary. Therefore, that same law requires the latter as well as the former, as the necessary means for achieving the required end.[27]

(*ii*) The bishop, and any other ecclesiastical pastor, is required by Divine Law not to be the lord of the flock committed to him, but its true pastor. Therefore he is required by the same law to behave as a pastor and not as a lord, and accordingly to feed the flock himself, and to attend to the care of his sheep. That proposition is proved firstly from the words of Christ to Peter: 'Feed my sheep' [John 21: 17]; secondly, by the words of Paul: 'This is how one should regard us, as servants of Christ and stewards of the mysteries of God' [I Cor. 4:1]; thirdly, by the words of Peter: 'Tend the flock of God, that is your charge...not as domineering over those in your charge...but being examples to the flock' [I Pet. 5: 2, 3]. Hence in all the testimonies cited here you see that the pastoral ministry is commended and commanded, whereas dominion and lordship of the secular kind are rejected.'[28]

(*iii*) It is proved from the form of the bishop's consecration, in which it is said to a bishop about to be ordained, 'Go and preach the gospel to the people committed to your charge'. Observe those words, 'Go and preach'. It is not said, 'Send men who can feed and preach for you', but, 'Go yourself and preach to the people committed to your charge'. In conformity with this, Paul, writing to Titus and to Timothy, most

et lupus rapit, et dispergit oves. Mercenarius fugit quia mercenarius est, et non pertinet ad eum de ovibus' (fols 14v–15r; Tellechea, *Controversia*, p. 200).

27 'Primum, episcopus de iure divino tenetur ad curandas animas subditorum suorum, sed ad eam curam animarum exercendam est necessaria continua residentia personalis episcoporum; ergo eodem iure tenetur ad hanc, quo ad illud. Quoniam qua lege praecipitur aliquis finis, praecipiuntur omnia necessaria ad comparandum illum finem' (fol. 64r–v; Tellechea, *Controversia*, p. 286).

28 'Secundo, episcopus et quivis alius ecclesiasticus pastor ex iure divino debet esse non dominus gregis sibi commissi, sed verus pastor: ergo eodem iure tenetur agere pastorem, non dominum, ac proinde per se pascere et attendere curae ovium suarum. Assumptum illud probatur. Primo ex verbis Christi ad Petrum: Pasce oves meas. Secundo, verbis Pauli. Sic nos existimet homo, ut ministros Christi et dispensatores. Tertio, verbis Petri: Pascite, qui in vobis est, gregem Dei, non dominantes in cleris, etc. Ubi vides in universis citatis testimoniis, commendari et mandari ministerium pastorale, negari verum imperium et dominium seculare' (fols 64v–65r; Tellechea, *Controversia*, pp. 287–8).

rightly remarked, among many other things, that it was requisite for a bishop to be an apt teacher. Alas, how preposterous it is for the name, the honour and the wealth of a bishop to be held in person, but the work of a bishop to be done by another, for all of the former are granted to him only on account of the pastoral office, in accordance with the dictum that the benefice is bestowed on account of the office.[29]

Carranza continues:

> It has seemed appropriate to refer specifically to the opinion of Cardinal Cajetan because, in these tempestuous times, he first asserted this truth, which the contrary custom of many prelates had almost extinguished; and further because some now strive to refute his arguments and openly dare to say that the conclusions which we set out in Chapter Two of this work were not of a kind to be attached to those arguments of his—conclusions which, nevertheless, I judge to be most certain, and think that all readers will judge the same.[30]

One of those who said that Carranza's arguments in Chapter Two were inconclusive was Catharinus, a long-standing critic of Cajetan. Carranza obviously wished if possible to scotch his arguments before they appeared in print.

Yet even the addition of the material derived from Cajetan, plus the rather humdrum truths of human argument to which the final chapter is devoted, do nothing to blur the impression that what we have here is a reminder, very timely of course, of what had already been known for a very long time. But Carranza rejoices in this. Faced with inventors of novelties like Catharinus, he has combined Scripture with Tradition, and so can say triumphantly: 'Therefore, when we have so great a cloud of witnesses for the aforementioned truth, who dares doubt this opinion?'[31] There is one well-known snag, which is that the Fathers do not explicitly assert the alleged truth for which he is arguing. Carranza admits this.

---

29 'Tertio, arguitur ex forma consecrationis pastoralis, in qua ordinando episcopo dicitur: Vade, et praedica evangelium populo tibi commisso; observa verba illa, vade et praedica; non dixit, mitte qui pascant et qui praedicent, sed ipse vade, et praedica populo tibi commisso. Unde rectissime cum aliis multis annotavit Paulus scribens ad Titum et ad Timotheum, oportet episcopum doctorem esse. Heu quam preposterum est, nomen, honorem, et divitias episcopi tenere in propria persona, officium autem episcopi in aliena; cum priora omnia sint illi concessa tantum propter officium pastorale, iuxta illud: Datur beneficium propter officium' (fol. 65r; Tellechea, *Controversia*, p. 288).

30 'Visum est seorsim annotare sententiam Cardinalis Caetani: tum quia primus hac tempestate asseruit hanc veritatem, quam pene extinxerat multorum praelatorum contraria consuetudo: tum quia nonnulli nunc contendunt infirmare illius argumenta: et palam audent dicere eis argumentis non fuisse astruendas conclusiones, quas nos in 2. cap. huius controversiae posuimus, quas tamen ego arbitror certissimas, et universos lectores idipsum iudicaturos...' (fol. 66r; Tellechea, *Controversia*, pp. 289–90).

31 'Igitur cum tantam habeamus testium nubem impositam veritatis praepositae, quis audet vel dubitare hanc sententiam?' (fol. 61v; Tellechea, *Controversia*, p. 282).

Someone will say that the Fathers do not state in these terms that a bishop has the obligation of continuous residence in his diocese. If you seek a precise form of words, perhaps I shall not convince with the opinion of the Fathers. But if you inquire into the thing itself (as is just) you will find no example or word supporting your opinion in the Fathers of the Early Church. On the contrary, all without exception utterly shun your opinion as false and pernicious to the Catholic Church, as though it were Satan. If you ask why neither our Lord, nor the Apostles in the Scriptures, nor the Fathers in their commentaries explicitly formulated a law against absentee bishops, I will reply as Solon did on being asked why he did not make a law against patricides. It is said that he replied, 'Because I never thought that there would be anyone who would kill his own father'. I think that the Apostles and Fathers of the Church would make the same reply. Furthermore, how could the Fathers have condemned in such terms a point of view which never crossed their minds—the view that a bishop who was absent from his church, and involved in other matters, could be held to be discharging his episcopal office? They greatly doubted whether even those resident in their dioceses could adequately fulfil their duties.[32]

Obviously, if they cannot be entirely fulfilled by those who reside, they certainly cannot be fulfilled at all by those who do not.

In this *Controversia* of 1547, Carranza is, in my opinion, trying to succeed where Cajetan failed. That is to say, he is trying to restore a practice on which the well-being of the Church depends by reasserting Cajetan's view, novel at the time at which it was stated,[33] that the obligation to reside falls within the scope of the Divine Law. However, at the same time, he places this obligation not merely on the foundations for which Cajetan argues, but, much more effectively, on the great tradition of the Church—that is, on what so many great scholars had claimed in the past. Against this cloud of witnesses, who was to be so bold as to set up his own opinion? This was a very shrewd move on Carranza's part, for the appeal to Tradition in this sense had been a favourite

32 'Dicet aliquis, non dicunt patres in hac forma verborum, quod tenetur episcopus continuo residere in sua dioecesi. Si formam verborum requiris, forsan non convincam te patrum sententia. Si autem rem ipsam (quod aequum est) requiris, nullum exemplum nec verbum sententiae tuae invenies in patribus veteris Ecclesiae, sed omnes citra exceptionem aliquam aversantur, veluti Sathanam, hanc sententiam tuam, et falsam et perniciosam Ecclesiae catholicae. Si roges, cur nec Dominus, nec Apostoli in scripturis sacris, nec patres in suis commentariis sub hac forma tulerint legem contra absentes episcopos: Respondeo, quod Solon respondit rogatus cur non tulisset legem contra patricidas. Ferunt dixisse, quia nunquam putaram futurum aliquem, qui patrem proprium esset interempturus. Tantundem arbitror nunc responsuros et Apostolos et patres Ecclesiae. Deinde, quomodo patres damnassent in hisce verbis sententiam hanc, quibus nunquam venit in mentem quod episcopus absens ab ecclesia sua, aliis implicatus, posset defungi munere suo episcopali? Dubitarunt quidem illi vehementer, an praesentes possent suo officio satisfacere' (fols 61v–62r; Tellechea, *Controversia*, pp. 282–3).

33 The commentary on Aquinas's *Summa* was written between 1507 and 1522.

technique of Catharinus in his polemic against the heretics ever since his first anti-Lutheran tract of 1520.[34] Catharinus's animus against Cajetan had always been based in part on the charge that the latter was introducing novelty. How sweet it must have been to Catharinus's Spanish opponent to turn back that charge against him.

How had Catharinus come to put himself into this invidious position? Briefly, I think that the difficulty for Catharinus was that Scripture supported by Tradition, as understood by Carranza, threatened Papal power and authority. Catharinus had very good reasons for wanting to maintain Papal authority intact. It was not just a question of *'Tu es Petrus'*, but rather a matter of Catharinus's ecclesiology, of which one aspect was that the Church was not the creature of the Bible, but rather the Bible the creature of the Church. In this system, which is explained in his *Claves duae ad aperiendas intelligendasque scripturas sacras* (1543), the whole apparatus of ecclesiastical rules, particularly the rules for the interpretation of the Scriptures, depends on the undisputed authority of the Pope.[35] It is very probable that Catharinus wrote his first work on the residence problem at the instigation of the Council legates, particularly Del Monte, Catharinus's patron and old pupil at the University of Siena, whose reluctance to have the residence problem discussed at Trent has been referred to above. Because of his ecclesiological views, there is every reason to suppose that Catharinus would have written against Carranza on the residence question even if the Legates did not in fact put him up to it.

It is obviously time to tackle the problem of Catharinus directly. The text that I have chosen to discuss is the last of the four that he wrote on this topic: the *Confirmatio doctrinae de pastorali residentia episcoporum* (1552).[36] It is exactly what he says it is, a confirmation of views which he had formulated earlier, and defended against Carranza and De Soto. In the *Confirmatio*, these views are again defended, but this time against Torres.[37] Because of the polemical nature of the work, the argument is not set out in a way that makes its logical

---

34 Tommaso de Vio (Cajetan), *De divina institutione Pontificatus Romani Pontificis super totam ecclesiam a Christo in Petro* (Rome: Marcellus Silber, 1521); see David V.N. Bagchi, *Luther's earliest opponents: Catholic controversialists, 1518–1525* (Minneapolis MN: Fortress Press, 1991), pp. 21–2, 34–6, 43, 46, 49.

35 Ambrosius Catharinus Politus, *Claves duae ad aperiendas intelligendasque scripturas sacras* (Lyon: Pierre de Sainte-Lucie, 1543).

36 This work occupies fols 48v–62r of *Gravissimorum auctorum complurium opuscula de residentia pastorum ac de beneficiorum pluralitate*, the 'Tomus posterior' of *De summi pontificis auctoritate, de episcoporum residentia, et beneficiorum pluralitate complurium opuscula... omnia nunc primum... in duos tomos divisa* (Venice : Iordanus Ziletus, 1562).

37 Francisco Torres (1504/9–84) was a Spanish theologian, educated at the University of Alcalá de Henares, who between 1540 and 1553 was in the service of Cardinal Giovanni Salviati in Rome, where he studied the Greek Fathers and Byzantine theologians.

structure plain. I have here taken the liberty of presenting Catharinus's ideas in what I believe is their true logical form.

(*i*)   The weak link in the Carranza case is the claim that the hireling shepherd will always do a bad job. This assertion is open to empirical refutation, and Catharinus claims that there is in fact no empirical evidence for it.[38]

(*ii*)   Maybe a sense of this weakness is what induced Carranza to include his chapter on Cajetan.

(*iii*)   There is no talk in Cajetan, as quoted by Carranza, of the weakness of the hireling shepherd. Cajetan's argument is that Divine Law requires a particular person to discharge a particular office, and this he cannot do if he is absent. The Divine Law carries over to its immediate and necessary consequence, the obligation to reside.[39] It is this claim, that residence is by Divine Law, thus defended, that Catharinus must therefore refute.[40]

(*iv*)   The problem of refuting Cajetan is slightly complicated by Torres's intrusion into the debate. Torres insists that all bishops are divinely appointed, that whatever the Apostles wrote or commanded verbally is Divine Law, and that in the consecration oath, when the bishop is told to go and preach to the people, it is not man who is speaking, but God, through human speech.[41]

(*v*)   Catharinus irritatedly replies that his case, as already stated, deals adequately with Cajetan and is not vulnerable to interjections of the Torres kind.[42]

(*vi*)   Catharinus introduces two crucial distinctions. The first is between mediate and immediate actions. An immediate action by God is one that God performs Himself, as when Christ told Peter, 'Feed my sheep.' A mediate action by God is an action that God performs through an intermediary.[43] The second distinction seems to have been

38 Catharinus, *Confirmatio*, fol. 59v: 'Ea vero quae afferuntur, quod non potest praestari pastoralis cura sine personali et assidua residentia, non habent evidentiam.'

39 See note 27, above.

40 Catharinus, *Confirmatio*, fol. 50r: 'Sed illud vertitur in quaestionem, Utrum haec obligatio ad residendum sit iuris divini; an potius canonici et ecclesiastici.'

41 'Nititur hic homo suadere, quod quando mihi et cuilibet Episcopo dicitur: Vade et predica populo Dei, illud non homo mihi dicat, sed Deus solum hominis organo utens: et ideo perinde omnino esse ac si Deus immediate illud mihi, et non per hominem dixisset: quod est pervertere Dei ordinem et hierarchiam ecclesiasticam' (fol. 55v).

42 e.g. 'Haec ille, vere monstra et ostenta, que mihi longe quidem sunt difficiliora ad intelligendum, quam ad redarguendum... Si haec absurda non sunt et perversa, quae (rogo) erunt?' (fol. 51v).

43 'Quae ut explicentur, ergo, quid est tandem quod ipse [Torres] in me reprehendit? Nunquid sensum quem declaravi, an potius locutionem impropriam? Quum ego dico, applicari pontificatum Papae a Deo immediate, sensus meus est: Cum omnis potestas sit a Deo et applicetur ab illo, esse tamen aliquas ab illo immediate, idest, non per alias personas medias, qualis est summi Pontificis potestas, tametsi eligatur ab hominibus: quia electio non confert potestatem, sed personam solum discernit; cui a Deo potestas absque alio medio confertur. Aliquae vero sunt quidem a Deo, sed mediate, quales sunt

introduced to cover the case of actions in the New Testament Epistles. It is the distinction between what an Apostle says when acting as the mouthpiece of God and what he says *in propria persona*.[44]

(*vii*)   Carranza refers to these two distinctions as dangerous novelties.[45]

(*viii*)   For Catharinus, only what God orders immediately (including the case when He speaks through the mouth of an Apostle, for example) counts as Divine Law.[46]

(*ix*)   No case of the immediate kind can be found to cover the appointment of any bishop except the first among them. The Pope appoints all other bishops.[47]

(*x*)   Episcopacy, as an institution, is by Divine Law, but the detailed working of it is by ecclesiastical law, and the Pope can dispense in this case.[48] I take it, that in Catharinus's view, the Pope can deal adequately with the arrangements for the work of absentee bishops to be done by deputies, and that there is no difficulty in the separation of the *officium* and the *beneficium*. Catharinus, as a one-time canon lawyer,

---

potestates aliae quae a summo Pontifice, et per ipsum in alios derivant, sicut docuit S. Doctor noster Thomas in multis locis, asserens omnem potestatem spiritualem dependere a summo Pontifice, cui et illud suo modo convenire potest: De cuius plenitudine omnes accipimus' (fol. 52r).

44   'Vult ergo hic Magister [Torres] non minus dici praecepta Christi quae voce sua non praecepit ipse Christus, sed per Paulum aut alium Apostolum, quam quae ipsemet Dominus verbo suo expressit. Quod si verum est, cur ego B. Paulus dicebat: Non ego, sed Dominus? et rursum: ego, non Dominus [see I Cor. 7: 10, 12]. Poterat dicere: Dominus dicit (sicut solebant dicere Prophetae) si nihil intererat. Scio quod quae dicebat B. Paulus, ex spiritu Dei veniebant, cum ipse dixerit: Puto quod et ego Spiritum Dei habeam [see I Cor. 7: 40]. Sed non sunt eiusdem gradus in robore ac firmitate quae Dominus per Paulum aut Apostolos disponebat, ac illa quae per seipsum. Nec merentur ista nomen iuris divini, cum super his quae sancit per Ecclesiam, in qua est Spiritus Dei, possint ipsimet Ecclesiae pastores et principes dispensare' (fol. 56v).

45   Carranza, *Controversia*, fols 3r–v: 'Novae sunt doctrinae, nec dubito, quin illarum, quas Paulus daemoniorum vocat' (Tellechea, *Controversia*, p. 180).

46   Catharinus, *Confirmatio*, fol. 54r: 'Primo igitur et proprie iuxta doctrinam D. Thomae et veritatem, illud esse divinum ius intelligo quod Deus ore proprio locutus est et expressit...'

47   'Et hic est locus ubi decipiuntur adversarii. Putant enim ex hoc quod episcopatus est de iure divino, continuo sequi de singulis episcopis qui illi vel illi loco applicantur, quod sint et ipsi a iure divino, hoc est, a Deo immediate, ita ut non subiaceat episcopatus et cura illa particularis residentiae potestati et arbitrario Papae, sicut vere non subiaceret si iure divino, hoc est, a Deo esset commendata immediate. At non ita est' (fol. 59v).

48   'Quod talis residentia non sit iuris divini, hoc est, a iure divino praecepta, manifestum est, quia quae sunt a iure divino praecepta, indispensabilia sunt ab homine, nec sub eius arbitrio concluduntur. Modo, nemo negare potest quod multa episcopis imponuntur quae personalem illam et assiduam residentiam prohibent. Quomodo ergo posset mihi dicere Papa: Sta hic, aut veni huc, si Deus mihi sua voce dixisset: Vade illuc, aut: Sta ibi?' (fol. 55v).

sees no difficulty in the law of substitutes, a topic on which he had written an important treatise.[49]

(*xi*)   We are required by Divine Law to obey the Pope.[50]

(*xii*)   There are, in Catharinus's view, no disadvantages in advocating the position that he has developed. Firstly, he insists that the bishops must reside, except when the Pope, with good reason, calls them to other work.[51] The penalties for disobeying ecclesiastical law extend to hell-fire, and even a breach of the Divine Law incurs no worse. Secondly, if bishops will not reside in obedience to ecclesiastical law, they will not reside by Divine Law either.[52]

(*xiii*) But there are advantages in Catharinus's position. Firstly, it does not bind the Pope's hands. Secondly, it does not subvert the order of the Church.[53]

(*xiv*) There are two Parthian shots. Firstly, it is clear that the canons never directly required continuous personal residence by bishops.[54] Secondly, 'Who therefore will require personal residence, when the flock can equally well and even better be looked after by deputies?'[55]

We have in this debate two sets of arguments that differ greatly from each other, not only in scope and tendency but also in style and method: the rhetorical and passionate exuberance of Carranza on the one hand, and the clinical, forensic, and destructive vigour of Catharinus on the other. Fortunately I do not have to adjudicate between them here.

49 'Non enim evidens est quod munera episcopalia Episcopus non posset essercere per alium; cum nullum suapte natura sit indelegabile, ut patet... ' (fol. 59v). Ambrosius Catharinus Politus, *Tractatus substitutionum domini Lancelloti Politi Senensis* (Siena : Simeone di Niccolò dei Nardi, 1513).

50 '...simili modo dicimus deberi curam et residentiam ab Episcopo, non quia divini sit iuris in hoc loco, vel tali modo illum curare gregem, sed quia iuris est divini eum obedire Pontifici' (fol. 55r).

51 'Clara ergo voce testificamur Episcopos ad residentiam teneri, et gravissime peccare qui aliter faciunt. Manus tantum summo Praesuli non ligamus, si quando ad maiorem totius Ecclesiae utilitatem aliquibus viris insignibus uti opportunum iudicaret: qui tamen non sunt levi de causa a suis ovibus evocandi' (fol. 51r).

52 'Qui enim praeceptum Ecclesiae non curat, nec verbum Dei expressum curabit' (fol. 50v).

53 See above, note 41.

54 'Manifestum est enim quod personalem et assiduam residentiam simpliciter nunquam nec ipsi Canones exegerunt' (fol. 61v).

55 'Quis ergo tunc requirat personalem residentiam, cum aeque aut etiam melius possit per Vicarios curari grex?' (fol. 62r).

CHAPTER 7

The Pope, the saints, and the dead:
Uniformity of doctrine in Carranza's *Catechismo* and the printed works of the Marian theologians*

William Wizeman SJ

'Just as men have been corrupted here even more by books than by the spoken word, so they should be recalled to health through the written word'.[1] In expressing this view in his 1558 letter to his friend, Bartolomé Carranza, Cardinal Reginald Pole was describing part of the strategy that he and his fellow churchmen were employing in the renewal of early modern Catholicism in England during the reign of Mary Tudor. From 1553 to 1558, numerous books were printed that explained England's traditional religion once again, after twenty years of religious tumult. I will attempt to delineate Marian Catholicism as found in these books of doctrine, devotion, apologetics, and sermons regarding two of the most disputed issues of the English Reformation: the Papacy, and what Ronald Hutton has described, I think inaccurately, as the 'abiding casualties of the previous Reformations': prayer to the Saints and purgatory. I will also compare these elements of Marian ecclesiology and eschatology to similar material in other texts, especially the Catechism written by Carranza and intended for England, *Comentarios sobre el catechismo christiano*, which provided the basis for the Tridentine Catechism and was being translated into English in the summer of 1558.[2] Comparing this work of Carranza,

---

* I am much indebted to Dermot Fenlon CONG. ORAT., Peter Marshall, Alec Ryrie, and Larissa Taylor, for their advice during the preparation of this chapter, and to Clarence Gallagher SJ, for his help with the translation of the Latin texts.

1 Reginald Pole, *Epistolae Reginaldi Poli et aliorum ad ipsum*, ed. Angelo M. Quirini, 5 vols (Brescia: Rizzardi, 1744–57, repr. Farnborough: Gregg Press, 1967), V. 74: 'quemadmodum scriptis magis etiam quam verbis hic homines corrupti fuerunt, ita scriptis ad sanitatem revocari oportet'.

2 Ronald Hutton, 'The local impact of the Tudor Reformations', in *The English Reformation revised*, ed. Christopher Haigh (Cambridge: Cambridge University Press, 1987), pp. 114–38 (p. 131); Pole, *Epistolae*, V. 74: 'ac te quoque Dei providentia voluit, in hoc Anglicanam nostram Ecclesiam adjuvare tuo illo docto et pio Catechismo, quem dum hic esses, Hispanice scripsisti, qui nunc in nostram linguam vertitur'; see José Ignacio Tellechea

who was one of the leading proponents of Catholic Reform, with that of the religious writers whose works were published during Mary's reign is invaluable in any attempt to delineate the theology, spirituality, and strategies for reform of the Marian Church. Was it, as Geoffrey Dickens wrote, a benighted Church that 'failed to discover the Counter-Reformation', or was it a Church that was intimately connected to currents of renewal in what John O'Malley has described as early modern Catholicism in Europe, and which anticipated, as Eamon Duffy has argued, Tridentine reforms?[3]

England's reconciliation with Rome, after two decades of intense vilification, commences with the publication of numerous declamations regarding the role of the Pope in the Church. Bishops Edmund Bonner of London and Thomas Watson of Lincoln, as well as other writers, presented unequivocal discussions of the Papacy. Two sermons in Bonner's frequently reprinted collection of homilies, sermons by Archdeacon John Harpsfield and Leonard Pollard, and John Standish's book, *The triall of the supremacy*, treated the Papacy at length. But most authors, including Carranza, chose to relate discussions of the Pope's authority to other points of doctrine in their texts. For example, in his *Catholyke doctryne*, a collection of sermons on the Sacraments, Watson, the most erudite Marian Catholic theologian, referred to the role of the Pope with ardour. And the 1521 sermon by John Fisher, in which he had defended Papal Primacy at length, was reprinted twice during Mary's reign, the first edition appearing within a month of England's reunion with Rome, on 30 November 1554. As for Carranza, he treated the Papacy while discussing the Sacrament of Order and Christ's resurrection as well as in the more obvious context of the article on the Church in the Apostles' Creed. Moreover, besides the above-mentioned authors, writers who also discussed the Papacy in positive terms included Richard Smyth, John White, James Brooks, Roger Edgeworth, Miles Hogarde (Huggarde), Thomas Martin, George Marshall, and the anonymous author of *A plaine and godlye treatise concernynge the Masse*. The leading authors of the Marian Church, many of whom were also important members of its hierarchy, underlined the role of the Papacy in the face of the past twenty years of official condemnation.

Idígoras, *Fray Bartolomé Carranza y el cardenal Pole: Un navarro en la restauración católica de Inglaterra (1554–1558)* (Pamplona: Diputación Foral de Navarra, Institución Príncipe de Viana, and CSIC, 1977), p. 193. Carranza looked forward to the publication of a Latin version of his *Catechism*, remarking that it was particularly needed in England; see Bartolomé Carranza de Miranda, *Comentarios sobre el Catechismo christiano*, ed. José Ignacio Tellechea Idígoras, 2 vols, BAC 1 (Madrid: Editorial Católico, 1972), I. 107.

3   Arthur G. Dickens, *The English Reformation*, 2nd edn (London: Batsford, 1989), p. 384; John O'Malley, *Trent and all that: Renaming Catholicism in the early modern era* (Cambridge MA: Harvard University Press, 2000), pp. 19–43; Eamon Duffy, *The stripping of the altars: Traditional religion in England, c. 1400–c. 1580* (New Haven CT and London: Yale University Press, 1992), pp. 524–37, 563–4.

Marian theologians presented the Pope as the essential source of the Church's unity through his power to govern, to determine Christian belief, and to act as a bulwark against heresy. They explicated Papal prerogatives in a way that, although lacking the fine distinctions of scholastic theology and the exaggerated claims of Papalist apologists, was nevertheless doctrinally uncompromising. These authors concentrated on the Pope as the chief means for Christian unity through his power to govern the Church, an authority inherited from Peter the Apostle, first bishop of Rome. Readers and listeners were given gushing expositions of Papal power, as found in Bonner's frequently printed *Profitable doctryne*:

> And forasmuch this catholike militaunte church… hath for the preseruation of the vnitie thereof, by the ordinaunce, and appoyntment of our sauiour Christ, one pryncipal head, or chief gouernour, here vpon earth, which beynge the chief vycar, and substitute of Christe in his sayde churche, doth, and ought, with other ministers vnder hym, attende, and geue he[e]de to the good order, and rule of the sayde militant church, (S. Peter the Apostle beynge the fyrst generall vycar and gouernoure therein), and [Christ] hauyng to hym, and to al his lawful successours in the Apostolique see, the gouernaunce, rule and charge therof, chiefelye, committed and geuen… by the continuall helpe, and assistaunce of the holye spirite of GOD…[4]

According to Standish, prebendary of St Paul's Cathedral, Peter was 'the heade shepeherd' and Christ commanded him to 'alone fede and gouerne' his people in Rome and throughout 'the whole worlde'. Harpsfield continued the same theme in his 1556 sermon marking the second anniversary of England's reunion with Rome: 'Peter fyrst was placed in the chief gouernment vnder Christ, and after Peter his successours continue in the same, and haue the rule of the whole church.' Pollard, chaplain to Pole's friend, Bishop Richard Pate of Worcester, and Thomas Martin, Chancellor of the diocese of Winchester, concurred with Harpsfield's view, and the former referred to Peter's successors as 'the byshops and popes of Rome'.[5] Watson told readers and listeners in the first of his thirty sermons on the Sacraments that Christ had appointed

---

4   Edmund Bonner, *A profytable and necessarye doctryne with certayne homilies adioyned thereunto* (London: John Cawood, 1555), sig. I4v.

5   John Standish, *The triall of the supremacy wherein is set fourth ye vnitie of Christes Church militant* (London: Thomas Marshe, 1556), sigs D4v, C6v–8v; John Harpsfield, *A notable and learned sermon or homilie, made vpon saint Andrewes daye last past 1556, in the cathedral churche of S. Paule in London* (London: Robert Caly, 1556), sig. B1r–2v; Leonard Pollard, *Fyve homilies of late made by a ryght good and vertuous clerke called Master Leonarde Pollarde Prebendary of the Cathedrall Churche of Woster, directed and dedicated to the Ryght Reverende Father in God Rychard by the permissyon of God Byshoppe of Woster his specyall good lord* (London: Wyllyam Gryffyth, 1554), sig. F1v; Thomas Martin, *A traictise declaring… the pretensed marriage of priests and professed persons is no marriage* (London: Robert Caly, 1554), sigs F2r, G1r–v. Martin's work was probably greatly influenced by Stephen Gardiner: see James A. Muller, *Stephen Gardiner and the Tudor reaction* (London: Macmillan, 1926), p. 317.

'one chief lieuetenaunt of the holle army which was S. Peter, and now is his lawfull successour in the chayre of Christ, gouerning the holle army of Christ's church'. He stated that Mass was offered for members of Christ's Body, among whom were 'the Popes holynesse the Successour of Saynt Peter, to whom Christe dydde commytte the care and charge of hys uniuersall churche through oute the world'. God also gave His Church a hierarchical structure with 'one heade' to end 'discorde', according to Pollard's clear treatment of the Papacy. The eleventh-century Pope and Church reformer, Gregory VII, exemplified such a head, Martin wrote, since he had tried to end the discord resulting from Emperor Henry III's 'open markette of benefices'. In retribution, Henry had 'abolished the Popes auctoritee'. Martin also took successive Papal condemnations of clerical marriage, from the first to the ninth centuries, as strong evidence for the novelty of married priests.[6] It appears that, for these authors, Papal rule was a constitutive element of Christian unity.

Marian theologians reiterated Fisher's stance, found in the Marian editions of his 1521 sermon, that the Pope possessed authority to determine Christian doctrine. For Fisher, Christ gave Peter's successors the authority to confirm the orthodoxy of other bishops in order to 'teache the people'. Patristic sources agreed that Peter was 'the grounde' of orthodox belief, and separation from Christ's 'Vicare' meant separation from the Gospel truth.[7] Standish echoed Fisher in his book, *Whether the Scripture should be in English*, where he remarked that, according to Irenaeus and Augustine, the 'trewe meaning of scripture is to be hadde by the triall of the succession of the holye bishoppes and fathers since Peters time in the see of Rome'. He made the same point in his other Marian work, accompanied by an oblique rebuttal of those who decried Papal sins, when he stated that the Fathers of the Church:

> declare the preeminence of sainte Peter and his successours, how the establyshement of our hole fayth doeth depende thereupon, and all heresies do springe of the contrarie: but also all and euery one of Peter his successours in that seate haue confirmed and established the hyghe Authoritie: which thinge they would neuer haue done being so holy men (many of them euen martirs of Christ) without anye spotte of ambition, no nor could haue ben suffred to haue done, if they had not had that verye preeminence by Christe hym selfe.[8]

Watson stated that the doctrine of Transubstantiation had been established 'by the greatest aucthoritie that euer Christe lefte in his Churche

---

6   Thomas Watson, *Holsome and catholyke doctrine concerninge the seven sacramentes of Chrystes church* (London: Robert Caly, 1558), fols. 3v, 77r; Pollard, *Fyve homilies*, sigs G4r–H1r; Martin, *Traictise*, sigs Kk1r, I2r–I4v.

7   John Fisher, *A sermon very notable, fruitfull and godlie, made at Paules Crosse 1521* (London: Robert Caly, 1554), sigs B1r–v, A9r–B8r.

8   John Standish, *A discourse wherin is debated whether it be expedient that the scripture should be in English* (London: Robert Caly, 1554), sig. I5v, and id., *Triall*, sig. C2r.

... by the judgement of the successour of saynct Peter in the chayre of Christe, and of the Byshops and pastours of Christes flocke called from all partes of the world in a general counsell'. It would be difficult to attribute Conciliarism to Watson, however, given his views cited earlier; rather, he envisaged a Pope teaching *ex cathedra* united with a General Council as the clearest sign of the Church's infallibility. Martin, too, coupled the decisions of General Councils with the 'ordinaunces of suche as succeded in the Apostolicalle Sea'.[9] In *A plaine and godlye treatise, concernynge the Masse*, the anonymous author described numerous General Councils as having been summoned by various Popes. In his *Diacosio-Martyrion*, which offered more than two hundred witnesses to Christ's corporeal presence in the Eucharist, John White, Bishop of Winchester, also referred to the General Councils of Lateran IV and Basle as 'under' [*sub*] the authority of Innocent III and Eugenius IV, respectively. Writing during Edward's reign, White nevertheless cited Innocent and his *De officio Missae*, as well as numerous popes who had succeeded Peter in Rome ['*a Petro sedit*'].[10] George Marshall reminded readers in his poem on the Sacrifice of the Mass that England had not been fully converted to Christianity until Pope Gregory the Great's efforts, and so asked: 'Why should we at Rome now haue despyte | That chaunged our darkenesse agayne to light?'. From such emphasis on Papal teaching authority, it is not surprising that Bonner submitted the *Profitable doctryne* 'vnto the judgement of the catholyke churche, and the see Apostolycke, in all poyntes'.[11]

Marian theologians, emulating the views of Fisher, consistently underscored the traditional doctrine of the Pope's authority to govern and teach the Universal Church. In these emphases, they also concurred with Carranza's *Catechism*. According to him, Christ had entrusted to Peter the dual authority to govern and teach the entire Church. Peter was also Christ's first Vicar, standing in his place on earth in order to exercise that two-fold commission. Peter's authority to order and instruct all people, including bishops, in the Church had been handed on to his successors in the See of Rome. Carranza was unique in adding explicitly that the Petrine succession and its ministry would continue until the end of time.[12]

9 Watson, *Holsome doctrine*, fol. 47r; Martin, *Traictise*, sig. F1r.

10 Anon., *A plaine and godlye treatise, concernynge the Mass* (London: John Wayland, 1557?), sig. C2r–v; John White, *Diacosio-martyrioni id est ducentorum virorum testimonium, de veritate Corporis, et Sanguinis Christi, in Eucharistia* (London: Robert Caly, 1553), fols 3r–4v, 11r–v, 12r–v, 15v–16r, 62v, 63v, 70r–v.

11 George Marshall, *A compendious treatise in metre declaring the firste originalle of sacrifice, and of the buylding of aultares and churches, and of the firste receauinge of the Christen fayth here in Englande* (London: John Cawood, 1554), sig. C1r; Bonner, *Profytable doctryne*, sig. Ccc 1r–v.

12 Carranza, *Comentarios*, I.278: 'Aquí escribe S. Juan [John 21:15–17] que, acabada esta comida, encomendó nuestro Señor a S. Pedro tres veces la gobernación de la Iglesia';

To English writers, obedience to the Papacy ensured freedom from heresy; a point which Carranza chose not to discuss expressly. James Brooks, Bishop of Gloucester, quoted Augustine as saying: 'I am holden in [the Church] by the succession of Priestes, from Peters own sea, continuallye stylle euen to this present bishoprike'. In contrast to heretics who claimed an ancient pedigree for married clergy, Martin stated that 'the Apostolical see and Latin church had historically admitted virgins and those promising celibacy to the priesthood. Since Rome, Pollard wrote, 'hath alwayes byn most free and pure of heresie' and remained the only diocese in which Apostles had continuously resided (the others being in Turkish hands), it thus stood 'aboue all the other sees, and therfore eyther we must confess it to be chiefe, or else deny our beliefe'.[13] In Bonner's view, anyone who denied Papal authority could no longer claim membership in the Universal Church; outside the Pope there was no salvation. Moreover, noting the 'miseries fallen vppon us' in the Evangelical revolution, it was evident to Pollard that 'we ought to haue a heade, and stande as much [in] need of a heade as ever dyd [the Primitive Church]'.[14] Marshall noted that England had not been in such religious darkness since before King Lucius of the British had sent for missionaries from Pope Eleutherius in the second century.[15]

It was an 'inwarde ghostely relyfe', Harpsfield proclaimed, to be free from the 'tumult, fear and tyrannye' of heresy and reunited with Peter's successor. The providentially ordained fate of those who denied the Pope's prerogatives contained evidence enough for his authority, in the view of both Martin and Harpsfield. The Greek Churches had been overrun by Turks, and Evangelical Germans had been constantly at war with peasants, with the Emperor, and with each other ever since Luther's repudiation of the Papacy.[16]

In confirming Rome as the 'chiefe' See, these writers emphasized what they took to be numerous Scriptural and Patristic proofs of Peter's authority

and II.304: 'El quinto y supremo grado [of the priestly order] tiene el patriarca de Roma, el cual preside sobre todos los otros grados y órdenes y personas de la Iglesia', and I.389: '[la Iglesia] es una y católica; toda ella tiene una cabeza en el cielo, que es Christo, y un vicario en la tierra. El primero fue San Pedro, y después los sucesores suyos en la Iglesia de Roma; y así lo es agora, y lo será hasta la fin del mundo el obispo que por tiempo fuere de Roma.'

13 Edmund Bonner et al., *Homelies sette forthe by the Righte Reuerende Father in God, Edmunde Byshop of London* (London: John Cawood, 1555), fol. 43v; James Brooks, *A sermon very notable, fruictefull and godlie, made at Paules Crosse... with certain additions* (London: Robert Caly, 1554), sig. C3v–4r; Martin, *Traictise*, sig. A2r; Pollard, *Fyve homilies*, sig. H1v–2r.

14 Bonner, *Profytable doctryne*, sigs I4v–K1r; Pollard, *Fyve homilies*, sig. H1r.

15 Marshall, *Compendius treatise*, sig. B3r. John N.D. Kelly, *The Oxford dictionary of popes* (Oxford and New York: Oxford University Press), p. 11, points out the confusion behind this story.

16 Harpsfield, *Sermon*, sig. B6v–7v; Martin *Traictise*, fol. 4r–v; Bonner et al., *Homelies*, fol. 52r.

over the other Apostles, and how the bishops of Rome inherited the same prerogatives. The 'Popes authoritie, whiche from the beginnyng was the cheife of the Church here vpon yearth,' Miles Hogarde wrote in *The displaying of the Protestantes*, 'was sufficiently recorded, as well in the volumes of aunctient doctours, as in al cronicles written from the begynning'.[17] Marian theologians interpreted such traditional Biblical evidence as Matt. 16: 18–19, Luke 22: 32 and John 21: 17 very much as Erasmus, Pole, Cajetan, and Carranza had done.[18] Moreover, Marian authors could be discerning about the texts they used to support the Papacy. In his *Sermons very fruitfull*, Roger Edgeworth, Chancellor of the diocese of Bath and Wells, rebuked those who took John 1: 42 as a proof of Peter's 'successors the popes of Rome to be head of all the churche of all countreys, whiche thoughe it be very true, yet this text proueth not so much'. He further remarked that 'ther be as well holye Scriptures as aunciente wryters, whiche proueth abundauntly the sayd primacy of the pope'.[19]

For all these writers, the Pope possessed powers of governance over the Church and authority in determining doctrine, all in order to maintain ecclesial unity. But their discussion of the Papacy was not without ambiguity. Standish remarked that while

> Christes vicar the pope as a priuate person and as an infirme man may erre both in lyuynge and beleuinge (and then neither heade nor member of Christes churche being cut of[f]) but as pope and head he can not decide nor determine anye thinge amisse [because] quicklye by the authoritie of the see and the holy ghoste the matter hath been reformed againe, so that the faith hath not bene counted there to faile, nor more then the righteous man fallinge vii. times in the day is counted to lose the name of a righteous man.[20]

He did not explain how 'the authoritie of the see and the holy ghoste' actually 'reformed' individual 'infirme' popes. Standish and his peers were not systematic in their discussions of Papal primacy, and this was only part of their reluctance or inability to present a more precise ecclesiology.[21] But careful systematization of doctrine was not a strength of Humanist scholarship, and

---

17 Bonner *et al.*, *Homelies*, fols 42v–54v (fol. 53v); Standish, *Triall*, sigs B4v–7r, F5r–H7v; Fisher, *Sermon*, sig. B1r–6v; Miles Hogarde (Huggarde), *The displaying of the Protestantes, and sondry their practices, with a description of diuers their abuses of late frequented* (London: Robert Caly, 1556), fol. 104r.

18 Jaroslav Pelikan, *The Christian tradition: A history of the development of doctrine*, 5 vols (Chicago IL and London: University of Chicago Press, 1971–89), IV. 269–72; Carranza, *Comentarios*, I. 278, II. 304.

19 See Janet Wilson (ed.), *Sermons very fruitfull, godly and learned by Roger Edgeworth: Preaching in the Reformation, c. 1535–c. 1553* (Cambridge: Derek Brewer, 1993), pp. 193–4; Roger Edgeworth, *Sermons very fruitfull, godly and learned* (London: Robert Caly, 1557).

20 Standish, *Triall*, sig. H2v–3r.

21 For contemporary views on heretical popes, see Pelikan, *Christian tradition*, IV. 270.

Marian writers were very much in that mould. In this point, as in so many others, they followed Fisher. Richard Rex has noted the 'absence of fine distinctions' in the latter's writings on the Church, in particular over the issue that Standish failed to address clearly. But this was not merely a problem for Marian theologians. The Council of Trent nearly collapsed over questions of Papal authority in the early 1560s.[22]

But Marian theologians also appear equivocal regarding the name of Peter's successor. The word 'Pope' cannot be found in the *Profitable doctryne* and *Homilies*, except in the three collects 'for our mooste holye father the Pope' at the end of the former. In his *Triall of the supremacy*, Standish employed 'pope' more often in describing corrupt ones than otherwise. Yet he also spoke of 'the Popes holynes' in positive terms.[23] Richard Smyth implored Evangelicals to return to 'Saincte Peter's shippe' and allegiance to 'the general heade of it', but he also referred to praiseworthy bishops of Rome as 'Pope' throughout *The seconde parte of a Bucklar of the Catholyke fayeth*.[24]

Why was there such apparent uncertainty about the Pope's title? Rex has carefully traced the progression of Henrician papal nomenclature in the early 1530s, culminating in 'pope' having been turned into a word of derision, and the neutral title, 'bishop of Rome', transmuted into a denial of his universal authority.[25] Under Edward VI both terms denoted Antichrist. By 1554, 'Pope' and 'Bishop of Rome' had been lightning rods for a generation, and the reappearance of the Pope in the liturgy of Mary's reign no doubt jolted English worshippers. In their last moments, Evangelical martyrs were 'raylynge at the stake and fyre agaynste the Popes holynesse', according to the author of *A plaine and goodlye treatise*.[26] Given their vigorous convictions concerning the Pope's power, cited above, it seems that Marian writers were subtly working to reclaim these and other Papal titles, and simultaneously restore the doctrine of Papal authority in England, from the legacy of Henrician and Edwardian

---

22 Richard Rex, *The theology of John Fisher* (Cambridge: Cambridge University Press, 1991), p. 107; Hubert Jedin, *Crisis and closure of the Council of Trent: A retrospective view from the Second Vatican Council* (London: Sheed and Ward, 1967), pp. 80–98.

23 Standish, *Triall*, sigs H2v–4r, C8r; id., *Discourse*, sigs D7v, E3r.

24 Richard Smyth (Smith), *A bouclier of the Catholyke fayth of Christes Church, conteynyng diuers matiers now of late called into controuersy, by the newe gospellers* (London: R. Tottell, 1554), sig. CC1r–2v; id., *The seconde parte of the booke called a Bucklar of the Catholyke fayeth* (London: Robert Caly, 1555), sigs B7v, H1v, I3r–v; all this *pace* Paul O'Grady, *Henry VIII and the conforming Catholics* (Collegeville MN: Liturgical Press, 1990), who described Smyth as a 'lukewarm Papist' (p. 133).

25 Richard Rex, 'The crisis of obedience: God's Word and Henry's Reformation', *Historical Journal*, 39 (1996), pp. 863–94; see also Geoffrey R. Elton, *Policy and police: The enforcement of the Reformation in the age of Thomas Cromwell* (Cambridge: Cambridge University Press, 1972), p. 228.

26 Anon., *Plaine and godyle treatise*, sig. G6r.

propaganda. And so they intermingled their use of 'pope' and 'bishop of Rome' with expressions like 'chief vycar' and 'heade shepherde' in an attempt to re-educate the people as to what 'pope' and 'bishop of Rome' actually meant. Perhaps for similar reasons, Carranza, who was minded to serve the needs of English as well as Spanish parish priests, defended in his *Catechism* the word 'pope' as an ancient title, found in Patristic sources.[27]

It would appear that Carranza and the Marian theologians were united in their views of the Papacy. Carranza's treatment, however, is also noteworthy for its brevity, and in this respect, as well as in content, the Tridentine Catechism followed suit.[28] Some historians have noted that Marian writers did not give as extensive attention to the Papacy as they would expect, but Papal authority was hardly 'passed over in silence'.[29] Like Marian English theologians, Carranza, and the compilers of the Tridentine Catechism, others also refrained from expansive discussion of the Pope. François le Picart, of the University of Paris, the popular preacher to whom Calvin ascribed the resilience of Parisian Catholicism from the 1530s to the 1550s, spoke of the Pope infrequently in his many sermons, though when he did, he stressed the need for obedience to Rome.[30] There are many possible reasons for the relative reticence of these writers, English, Spanish, and French: deteriorating relations between the Papacy and England and Spain from 1555, Gallicanism in France, and the fact that the doctrines regarding Papal teaching authority would not receive 'form and clarity' until the next century, according to Jaroslav Pelikan.[31] But one cause may have been a subtle yet insistent strategy of defending the Pope, similar to the advice Ignatius gave to Jesuits on their way to Ingolstadt in 1549: 'Let them [these Jesuits] defend the Apostolic See and its authority and draw people to authentic obedience to it in such a way that they not make themselves, like Papists [*tamquam papiste*], unworthy of credence by exaggerated defences'.[32] Theologians of traditional religion during Mary's reign presented

27 Carranza, *Comentarios*, II. 304: 'Llámase por especial nombre papa, que en griego quiere decir padre, porque, dado que los otros obispos sean padres espirituales, el romano lo es por excelencia.'
28 John McHugh and Charles Callan (trs), *Catechism of the Council of Trent for parish priests, issued by order of Pope Pius V* (New York: Joseph Wagner, 1934), pp. 102–4, 333.
29 Lucy E.C. Wooding, *Rethinking Catholicism in Marian England*, Oxford Historical Monographs (Oxford: Clarendon Press, 2000), p. 130.
30 Larissa Taylor, *Heresy and orthodoxy in sixteenth-century Paris: François le Picart and the beginnings of the Catholic Reformation*, Studies in Medieval and Reformation Thought 77 (Leiden: Brill, 1999), pp. 165–6.
31 Pelikan, *Christian tradition*, IV. 341.
32 *Monumenta historica Societatis Iesu, Monumenta Ignatiana*, 1st s: *Epistolae et instructiones*, ed. Mariano Lecina SJ and Vicenç Agustí SJ, 12 vols (Madrid: Gabriel López del Horno, 1903–11), XII. 244, quoted in John O'Malley, *The first Jesuits* (Cambridge MA: Harvard University Press, 1993), p. 296.

the authority of the Papacy firmly and unequivocally, but without the inflated claims of 'Papists', as they would continue to do upon the accession of Elizabeth. Archbishop Heath and Bishop Scot in their speeches to the 1559 Parliament, and Heath and Bishops Bonner, Bourne, Turverville, and Poole in a letter to the new Queen, denounced the alteration of religion, and advocated the 'supremacy of the church of Rome' in no uncertain terms.[33]

As well as advocating union with the Eternal City, both Marian English churchmen and Carranza desired reunion of the English Church with the Heavenly City. The Englishmen, and Carranza at some length, underlined the communion of saints as intercessors, as patterns of virtue and as friends within the fellowship of God, whose aid was to be sought through the veneration of public images and through private prayer. Due to their holiness, and hence their proximity to God, saints served as powerful intercessors. Watson described the saints as beings who are 'careful for us', and who 'cease not to communicate with us in prayer'. In his *Spirituall exercyses*, a book modelled on that great source of Counter-Reformation spirituality, Ignatius Loyola's *Spiritual exercises*, the English Dominican Superior, William Peryn, offered a prayer into which readers could insert the names of their patron saints, and thus ask for their intercession. White described how Christ had heard the intercessions of such holy women as the Virgin Mary, Mary Magdalen, and others, and remarked that 'to none does he [Christ] close his generous heart' (or 'to no one of generous devotion does he close his heart'), and added: '[o]f pious women, whom has he turned away?'.[34] Moreover, Christians received such care and communication through the merits as well as the prayers of saints. Bishop Cuthbert Tunstall of Durham prayed:

> O king and gouernor of the world direct vs, kepe vs, throughe the faith of thy patriarches, the merytes of thy prophetes, the predication of thy Apostles, the victories of th[y] martyres, the charitie of thy confessoures, the contynence of thy virgynes and through the intercession of all thy Sayntes, the whych haue pleased the[e] from the beginning of the world.

In another prayer, addressed to the Virgin Mary, who was holy 'euen from the wombe' of the 'mooste holy' St Anne, Tunstall asked for her intercession with the Trinity for the forgiveness of the sins of Christians, so that they might exult with her and acclaim her in heaven. But Smyth reminded Marian readers and listeners of the origin of these merits, while discussing lights before sacred images. By lighting candles, Christians

---

33 John Strype, *Annals of the Reformation and establishment of religion, and other various occurrences in the Church of England, during Queen Elizabeth's happy reign* (Oxford: Clarendon Press, 1824), I/i. 217, I/ii. 399–400, 403–5, 409–11, 414–15.

34 Watson, *Holsome doctrine*, fol. 77v; William Peryn, *Spirituall exercyses and goostly meditacions, and a neare waye to come to Perfection and lyfe contemplatyve* (London: J. Waley, 1557), sig. D2v–3r; White, *Diacosio-martyrioni*, fols 61v–62v: 'quam reppulit ille piarum [?]'.

remembre the holy Saynctes faythe and their vertuous lyfe, whiche did shine in thys worlde lyke lampes and candelles as also in sygne and token that they are now in the glory eternal. Wherfore such lightes are not set vp principally to the saynctes Images but to the Saynctes, and fynally to god, which made holy these saynctes, and endued there soules, with the glori and brightnes of heauen.[35]

Carranza too discussed the intercessory role of the saints and their merits in a very traditional way. In language reminiscent of that employed concerning indulgences, he explained that the saints added the merits of their good works to that of Christ, in the great treasury of grace which the Church possessed. However, like Smyth, Carranza underlined the point that the merits of the saints were due to God; they could not confer grace themselves. Following Thomas Aquinas, Carranza stated that Christ was the only 'perfect mediator' in that He alone reconciles humankind to God.[36]

The saints were not only intercessors, they also manifested a closer union with God and so stood as patterns of Christian living, a conviction that possessed strong medieval antecedents, according to André Vauchez.[37] In his sermon at Paul's Cross, Hugh Glasier, chaplain to Mary Tudor, remarked how the saints possessed the divine gifts of humility, charity, and dependence upon God. Bishop John Christopherson of Chichester, in *An exhortation agaynst rebellion*, encouraged people to read 'the godly ecclesiastical story of Saycnte Bede', where they would find 'how many vertuous and holy men haue bene within this realme, and howe God dyd in all thinges prosper vs'. And the author of *A plaine and godlye treatise* reminded readers and listeners that the writings of such 'holy sainctes' as Bede and Anselm and the witness of martyrs exemplified right belief. Bonner wrote that all must pray for 'grace to followe theyr goodnes and holy lyuing', in order to join them in heaven, where one receives

> the true reward of all godlines, God hym selfe, the sight and fruition of whom is the ende and reward of all beleife, and of all our good workes, and of all those thinges which were purchased for vs by Chryste. He shalbe our sacietie, our fulnesse, and desyre, he shalbe our lyfe, our helth, our glory, our honour, our peace, our euerlasting rest and ioye.

Bonner praised the Virgin Mary as a special example of devotion to God. Because 'she beleued, and humbly consented' to the designs of the Trinity and the Incarnation of Christ, she was above all angels, and it is for her faith and humility that she received 'laudes, prayse and thankes for her excellent and singular vertues' when Christians prayed the *Ave Maria*. Carranza, too, expli-

35 Cuthbert Tunstall, *Certaine godly and deuout prayers*, tr. John Paynell (London: John Cawood, 1558), sigs C6v–7r, D2r–3r; Smyth, *Bouclier*, fols 42v–43v.
36 Carranza, *Comentarios*, I. 387, 460–64.
37 André Vauchez, *Sainthood in the later Middle Ages*, tr. Jean Birrell (Cambridge: Cambridge University Press, 1997), pp. 388–90, 538.

cated the role of the saints as standards of holiness: people celebrated the holy lives and deaths of the saints, such as Mary, in order to imitate those lives and deaths.[38]

In Marian texts, the saints revealed diverse paths to companionship with God, a late medieval view noted by John Bossy. John Angel quoted Cyprian as saying that they were humanity's 'familiare neighbours'.[39] For Carranza the saints were the siblings and co-heirs with Christians on earth, and he described eternal life as an ecstasy of living and conversing with angels, saints, the Virgin Mary, and Christ.[40] If Christians lost the friendship of Christ through grave sin, Pollard wrote, they necessarily lost 'the loue and frendshyp of al his blessed sayntes our frendes, yea our brethren, yf we were his chyldren'.[41]

The Virgin Mary was the saint who especially exemplified this friendship with the divine. The frequently printed primers of Mary's reign included the 'Little Office of the Virgin' and the 'Euensonge of the Compassion of Oure Ladye', in which readers prayed for the compassion of Mary and the mercy of Jesus on Calvary.[42] All the primers contained a series of prayers devoted to the Virgin.[43] In Peryn's *Exercyses*, Mary was the model of intimacy with God in Christ, especially in contemplating His Passion. Readers sought her aid because

38 Henry Glasier, *A notable and very fruictefull sermon made at Paules Crosse* (London: Robert Caly, 1555), sig. A6r; John Christopherson, *An exhortation to alle menne to take hede agaynst rebellion* (London: John Cawood, 1554), sig. X6v–7v; Anon., *A plaine and godlye treatise*, sigs C3r–D6v, G2r; Bonner, *Profytable doctryne*, sigs Kk2r–v, L2v, Aaa3r–Bbb2r; Carranza, *Comentarios*, I. 460–61: 'celebramos su memoria por la imitación de su vida y de sus costumbres, que es una de las mayores honras que ellos quieren recebir de nosotros; que los sigamos y imitemos en la vida, como ellos siguieron a Jesucristo, y conformemos la vida con la profesión que hacemos'.

39 John Bossy, *Christianity in the West, 1400–1700*, OPUS (Oxford: Oxford University Press, 1985), pp. 11–12; John Angel (Aungell), *The agrement of the holye Fathers and Doctores of the Churche vpon the cheifest articles of Christian religion…very necessary for all curates* (London: William Harford for William Seres, 1555?), fol. 90r.

40 Carranza, *Comentarios*, I. 460: '[Christians venerate the saints] para celebrar la fe de los santos, con la cual vencieron los reinos del mundo y del infierno y su potencia, y después conquistaron el reino de los cielos. Hacemos también esto para tener en admiración su fe y honrarlos a ellos como a perpetuos hijos de Dios y hermanos y herederos con Cristo'; and I. 419: '¡Qué gloria es conversar con tantos santos mártires y con tantos confesores; hallarse entre coros de sagradas vírgines; y lo que más se debe estimar, nunca apartarse de la compañía de Jesucristo N[uestro] S[eñor] y de la sacratísima Virgen María, su madre y señora nuestra!'

41 Pollard, *Fyve homilies*, sig. H4r.

42 Anon., *Primer in Englysh after Salysburie use, sette out at length with manye godlie prayer* (London: John Wayland, 1558), sig. K4r.

43 See Anon., *Primer in Englysh*, sig. L2r–3v; Anon., *The primer in Latin and Englishe (after the use of Sarum) with many godlye and deuoute prayer* (London: John Wayland, 1555), sigs A1r–P7v.

of the 'most bitter compassion' that she endured 'for him and me' in witnessing the Crucifixion. For one who sought intimate union with Christ, Peryn valued reflection on 'the excedynge grate and moost ardent burning loue' between Jesus and Mary.[44] Moreover, his stress on the sorrowful Virgin probably reflected the harsh times of Marian England, which were marked not only by crop failure, famine, and a devastating influenza epidemic, but also by the reduction of parochial images of the Virgin to the one standing under the Rood, due to the slow recovery from Evangelical iconoclasm.[45] In discussing the Creed, Carranza also offered an extended prayer to Mary at Calvary, one of the relatively few times that he interrupted his text with a devotional prayer of his own composition.[46]

The accentuation of the cult of the Virgin Mary, the Handmaid of the Lord and Queen of Heaven, in Marian England found expression in the praise of Mary Tudor herself. The authors concerned described her in language other-wise used exclusively for the Mother of God, to denote the importance of Queen Mary's role in the re-Catholicization of England; as one Mary possessed an essential role in human salvation, the other possessed an essential role in England's participation in that salvation. John Proctor marvelled that tradi-tional religion had been 'newlye recouered and set furthe by oure heauenly and vertuous maiden Quene'. To Christopherson she was 'the humble hande-mayde of God, elected and chosen by him to rule and reforme this realme'. It was not by chance that God had triumphed through a woman named Mary, wrote John Gwynneth, for 'nothynge escapethe his infinite prouidence'.[47] Such comparisons inspired Court musicians such as Gwynneth to compose some of the finest English polyphony in the sixteenth century. According to Daniel Bennett Page, much of the religious music of Christopher Tye, Thomas Tallis, John Sheppard, and others probably alluded to Mary Tudor in both hagiographic and political terms.[48] In contrast, Carranza did not indulge in such comparisons, yet nevertheless wrote that the English 'nation owes the life and health of its bodies and souls to Mary'.[49] But Marian authors relished

---

44 Peryn, *Exercyses*, sigs D2v, K7r–v, F7v–8r, I8r–v.

45 Duffy, *Stripping of the altars*, p. 563. On the impact of famine and epidemic in Marian England, see Clifford S.L. Davies, 'England and the French War, 1557–9', in *The mid-Tudor polity, c.1540–1560*, ed. Jennifer Loach and Robert Tittler, Problems in Focus (London: Macmillan, 1980), pp. 159–85 (pp. 161–2, 180).

46 Carranza, *Comentarios*, I. 255–7.

47 John Proctor, *The waie home to Christ and truth... by that famous and great clearke Vincent* (London: Robert Proctor, 1556), sig. D1v (see also sig. A3r); Christopherson, *Exhortation*, sig. M1v (also sig. I5v–6r); John Gwynneth, *A brief declaration of the notable victory geuen of God to oure soueraygne ladye Quene Marye* (London: John Cawood, 1553), sigs C6v–D4r.

48 Daniel B. Page, 'Uniform and Catholic: Church music in the reign of Mary Tudor (1553–1558)', unpubl. doctoral dissertation, Brandeis University (1996), pp. 153–208.

49 Carranza, *Comentarios*, I. 107: 'la Serenísima Reina nuestra señora, a quien debe aquella nación la vida y salud de sus cuerpos y de sus almas'.

portraying the Queen as most like the Virgin, by whose intercession God had redeemed England from heresy. The exaltation of the Virgin Queen Elizabeth, therefore, was hardly original, but the Virgin Mary was under no threat of near 'deletion' under Mary Tudor, as she would be under the Queen's half-sister, according to Helen Hackett.[50]

Other holy advocates and friends may be found in the nascent public cults of the martyrs of the Henrician Reformation. Miles Hogarde compared John Fisher and Thomas More to that other, posthumous, victim of Henry, Thomas Becket, who had died 'for the zeale he had to gods churche', and whose shrine Henry VIII would order to be destroyed.[51] William Rastell told Mary that More

(beynge with almightie GOD, and lyuynge in heauen with hym) with much greater zeale and deuotion towardes your maiestie, than he had whyle he liued here on earth, ceaseth not to praye to God ... for your hyghnesse, your subiectes... and the catholyke religion of the same.[52]

White and Gwynneth also praised Fisher and More. But Hogarde acclaimed many other Henrician martyrs 'to whom death was nothing ferefull for the quarell of God and his churche', and whose 'memory shall be magnified tyll the ende of the worlde'.[53] But the silence of most of the Marian clergy regarding these martyrs is noteworthy. One cause may be the 'crisis of canonization': the Western Church's 'failure of nerve' in not canonizing saints, in the face of Evangelical attacks, before 1588.[54] But a more likely, and more specific, cause was the Marian churchmen's failure of nerve: many of them had capitulated to Henry, unlike those venerated by Hogarde, Rastell, White, and Gwynneth.

While hesitant about modern martyrs, Marian writers were not tentative about venerating images. The anonymous ballad, *An exclamation upon the sprite of heresy*, defended them as '[t]he lay mans booke, theron to look, to folowe their lyues [there]by'. Bonner oddly used the Evangelical enumeration of the Decalogue to discuss images. This form had Augustine's approval, but Bonner's striking shift from the traditional reckoning was not emulated by his peers. Did he think he was aligning England with the Eastern Churches' enumeration of the Decalogue and devotion to icons, as Gardiner had done in his *Detection*

---

50 Helen Hackett, *Virgin mother, maiden Queen: Elizabeth 1 and the cult of the Virgin Mary* (Basingstoke: Macmillan, 1995), pp. 34–7, 237.

51 Hogarde, *Displaying*, fol. 68v.

52 In *The workes of Sir Thomas More Knyght, sometime Lorde Chancellour of England, wrytten by him in the Englysh tonge* (London: John Cawood, John Waley, and Richard Tottell, 1557), sig. C2v.

53 White, *Diacosio-martyrioni*, fols 84r, 87r–v; John Gwynneth, *A manifest detection of the notable falshed of that part of John Frithes boke which he calleth his foundation* (London: T. Berthelet, 1554), fol. 45r; Hogarde, *Displaying*, fol. 68v.

54 Peter Burke, 'How to become a Counter-Reformation saint', in *The Counter-Reformation: The essential readings*, ed. David M. Luebke, Blackwell Essential Readings in History (Oxford: Blackwell, 1999), pp. 129–42 (pp. 131–2, 139).

of the Devils sophistrie?[55] In any event, by employing this typical Evangelical weapon against images, he underscored their value. For Bonner, images were not idols, but reflections of true beings, and in 'beholdyng the pictures or images, [we] might be brought thereby in remembraunce of them, thyr lyves, doinges, and deathes'.[56] Carranza also discussed veneration of the saints in the context of the Decalogue, but at greater length. Christian veneration of images possessed an ancient pedigree—the incarnation of Christ himself— but bishops were to correct any abuses and instruct the ignorant so as to prevent excesses; yet, unlike Evangelicals, he refused to equate inordinate veneration with idolatry. His stance was very traditional, except that he was extremely cautious about images of the incorporeal angels and God the Father: images without the approbation of Scripture and the Church could lead to erroneous belief.[57] What Carranza said regarding images of the incorporeal Holy Spirit, however, the Tridentine Catechism stated about images of the Trinity: they could be depicted according to 'certain forms under which they appeared in the Old and New Testaments'. The Catechism did not make Carranza's reservations explicit, nor did Marian authors reiterate his misgivings.[58]

But, like Carranza, some authors extolled the veneration of relics. James Brooks lamented 'the burninge of tried holy reliques'. Hogarde found it '[a] pityfull case and wyth teares too be lamented, that the innumerable relyques of Christes true martirs were so wyckedlye neglected, as they haue bene in the late malicious tyme'.[59] The 1555 and 1558 editions of the Wayland Primer included a collect 'Of the saintes, whose relikes remayne in the holy Churche'. John Angel quoted a work attributed to Augustine in defence of praying before relics and of going on pilgrimage, but he was the only Marian writer to mention the merit of going to holy places.[60] It is true that Mary restored the royal cult of St George; Abbot John Feckenham rebuilt the shrine of Edward the Confessor at Westminster Abbey; Bishop Thomas Goldwell, a Theatine

55 Anon., *An exclamation upon the erronious and fantasticall sprite of heresy, troubling the vnitie of the Church* (London: Richard Lant, 1553?); Bonner, *Profytable doctryne*, sig. Gg3r–v; Stephen Gardiner, *A detection of the Deuils sophistrie, wherwith he robbeth the vnlearned people of the true byleef in the most Blessed Sacrament of the Aulter* (London: John Harford for Robert Toye, 1546), fols 31r–32r.

56 Bonner, *Profytable doctryne*, sigs Hh4r–Ii3v (see also sig. Kk1r–3r).

57 Carranza, *Comentarios*, I. 459–72: 'Estas cosas espirituales [the Holy Trinity and angels], que no se pueden ver con los ojos ni alcanzar con otro sentido, no las podemos pintar sino con muchas impropiedades, que provocan al pueblo a risa y no a devoción, y da ocasión a algunos errores' (p. 471).

58 McHugh and Callan, *Catechism*, p. 375.

59 Carranza, *Comentarios*, I. 473–5; Brooks, *Sermon*, sig. I3r; Hogarde, *Displaying*, fol. 63v.

60 Anon., *Primer in Latin and Englishe*, sig. F4r–v; Angel, *Agrement*, fols 91v–92r.

and friend of Pole, renewed the shrine and indulgences of St Winifred's Well, in Holywell (Flintshire); Pole himself called upon the Dean of Christ Church Cathedral in Oxford to restore the relics of St Frideswide to a place of honour; the shrine of Our Lady of Worcester was restored in that city's cathedral; Sheriff Robert Broddis of York, in his 1553 will, expressed the desire to be buried at the foot of St William's tomb; and bequests were made to St William of Chichester. But it would have taken longer than Mary's reign to renew the pilgrimage quest for saintly and holy places.[61] Nevertheless, the continuance of pilgrimages to Winifred's Well during Elizabeth's reign testifies to the successful resuscitation of devotion to saints' wonder-working power, which Duffy believed to have been their primary role in the late Middle Ages.[62]

Despite the many continuities with medieval devotion, the role of the saints in the Marian Church nevertheless appears to have been altered. The lack of the renewal of guilds and the reduced number of images in parish churches denote not only the need to spend limited resources on more essential parochial demands, in hard times, but also 'the narrower devotional range of Marian Catholicism'.[63] Helen White noted the reduction in the number and 'colourful' quality of prayers to the saints in contrast to primers printed before the break with Rome; it seems that by such reductions the editors of the Marian primers intended not only to respond to accusations of idolatry but also to underscore the centrality of Christ in the Church's worship. This stance united them with the Christocentric imperative of other Marian authors, whose discussions of saints were also in harmony with Carranza's *Catechism* and the sermons of Le Picart.[64] Moreover, their writings illustrate what H. O. Evennett regarded as characteristic of Counter Reformation spirituality, and Eamon Duffy has described as

---

61 Page, 'Uniform', pp. 148–50; David Knowles, *The religious orders in England*, 3 vols, (Cambridge: Cambridge University Press, 1948–59), III. 433; Thomas E. Bridgett and Thomas F. Knox, *The true story of the Catholic hierarchy deposed by Queen Elizabeth* (London: Burns and Oates, 1889), p. 225; Margaret Aston, *England's iconoclasts*, I: *Laws against images* (Oxford: Clarendon Press, 1988), p. 292; Diarmaid MacCulloch, 'Worcester: A cathedral city in the Reformation', in *The Reformation in the English towns, 1500–1640*, ed. Patrick Collinson and John Craig, Themes in Focus (Basingstoke: Macmillan, 1998), pp. 94–112 (p. 110); Christopher Wilson, *The shrines of St William of York: An account written to commemorate the 750th anniversary of the canonisation of Saint William* (York: Yorkshire Museum, 1977), p. 10; David Loades, 'The piety of the Catholic restoration in England, 1553–8', in his *Politics, censorship, and the English Reformation* (London: Pinter, 1991), pp. 200–21 (p. 206).

62 Ronald C. Finucane, *Miracles and pilgrims: Popular beliefs in medieval England* (New York: St Martin's Press, 1975), pp. 215–16; Duffy, *Stripping of the altars*, pp. 169–70.

63 Duffy, *Stripping of the altars*, p. 563.

64 Helen C. White, *Tudor books of private devotion* (Madison WI: University of Wisconsin Press, 1951), p. 122; Taylor, *Heresy*, pp. 104–5, 135, 174–5.

the Counter-Reformation's deliberate redirection of the exuberant but sometimes unfocused piety of the pre-Reformation laity towards a more evangelical emphasis on Christ and his redemptive suffering, a feature of other parts of sixteenth- and seventeenth-century Catholic Europe as well as Marian England.[65]

In fact, the Marian Church's particular emphasis on the role of Christ and the Virgin underscores the continuity of what Ronald Finucane described as the efforts by the official Church since the fourteenth century to redirect devotion. Nevertheless, the primers possessed collects for fifteen of the most popular medieval saints, and litanies full of English saints.[66] The frequently printed primers, along with the works of Marian theologians, bear witness to the prominent place of the saints in the Church's public worship and attest to their enduring popularity in private prayer.

Like the Pope and the saints, purgatory made significant appearances in the works of Marian writers, after a long hiatus. The second edition of Thomas Paynell's translation of a selection of Augustine's sermons included 'Of the fyre of Purgatory and howe it purgyth not mortall, but veniall synnes'. In the *Profitable doctryne*, Bonner wrote that the temple of Christ's mystical body was not only built of the spiritual stones of faithful Christians but also of 'tymber, hey and stubble'. These last were those who had not made satisfaction for their sins in this life and would be purged of their sinful inclinations after death. Watson explained succinctly that the Church offered Mass for the living and 'the perfection of them that be deade, that they being for atyme deteyned in the temporall afflictions and purgacions, might the sooner by the vertue of thys blessed sacrifice be deliuered and brought to light and eternall peace, where nothing entreth that is spotted and unperfite'.[67] Notably, Bonner and Watson described purgatory and prayer for the dead in the context of the Eucharist, the greatest Sacrament and the one of chief concern to Marian authors. These bishops therefore treated purgatory in pivotal sections of their texts, in contrast to the *Bishops' book* and the *King's book* of Henry's reign, where it had been relegated to the end.

But most writers chose to elucidate the means to aid the dead rather than discuss the nature of purgatory. Through good works and prayer, and especially in the celebration of the Eucharist, Christians could assist the entry of the dead into eternal life. Release from purgatory was an 'vnspeakeable

---

65 Duffy, *Stripping of the altars*, p. 364; H. Outram Evennett, *The spirit of the Counter-Reformation: The Birkbeck lectures in ecclesiastical history given in the University of Cambridge in May 1951*, postscript John Bossy (Cambridge: Cambridge University Press, 1968), p. 41.

66 Finucane, *Miracles*, pp. 195–202; Anon., *Primer in Latin and Englishe*, sigs π2v–4r, c2v–d1v, o4v–p7v, E3v–G1v, R1r–2v; Anon., *Primer in Englysh*, 1558, sig. π2r–7v.

67 Thomas Paynell (tr.), *Certaine sermons of sainte Augustines translated out of Latyn* (London: John Cawood, 1557), sigs I5r–K7r; Bonner, *Profytable doctryne*, sigs Z3v–&3v; Watson, *Holsome doctrine*, fol. 77r–v.

fruyte' of the Mass, and Bonner and other Marian theologians underlined this point. Smyth believed that St Paul and Augustine held that 'praying for the dead, geuing of almes to the pore, and saying of masses for the soules departed' all aided those in purgatory. Only the extent of John Angel's treatment of the Eucharist and the saints exceeded that of prayer for the dead in his book of sources that supported traditional religion; and the topic of such prayer was placed second only to the Eucharist in the book.[68] Bernard of Clairvaux's *The golden epystell*, found in William Peto's two 1556 editions of Richard Whitford's translation of the *Imitation of Christ*, offered an extensive list of the dead for whom Christians should pray. They were to intercede for the dead whom they had harmed in this life, for deceased relatives, benefactors, enemies, those who 'haue greatest paines in purgatory', and for all the dead. Peryn reminded readers that forgetting to pray for souls in purgatory was a sin to be confessed.[69] In such ways, concern for assisting the dead marked the writings of most Marian theologians.

This concern can also be seen in numerous examples of prayers for the deceased to be found in Marian primers. To the youth of London the catechetical work, *An honest instruction for children*, offered prayers for the dead in the possibly frequently prayed graces for meals, and presented an abbreviated Office for the departed. Similar prayers appeared near the beginning and at the end of the Children's Primer. The 1558 Wayland Primer contained the Office and two other prayers for the dead. The 1555 edition had included the same prayers, followed by five collects and the commendations of the departed.[70] Readers interceded for the deceased in three other places in the primer. In his book of prayers, Tunstall included the faithful departed as part of the 'tripartite churche' who prayed to God 'in heuen, on earth, and in purgatory'. At the end of the book, he explicated the doctrine of purgatory and prayer for the dead in the form of a collect:

> Haue mercy, we beseche the[e] O Lorde god... of those soules, that which haue no intercessors that remember them, or that doth put the[e] in remembraunce of them, nor no consolation, nor no hope in [their] torments, but onelye that they are created and made lyke vnto thy similtude and Image, and markyd with the [sign]

68 Watson, *Holsome doctrine*, sigs K6v, K8v, fols 77r–v, 79v [*sic*]; Bonner, *Profytable doctryne*, sigs Z3v–&3v; Smyth, *Bouclier*, fols 22r–24v, 29r–32r; Angel, *Agrement*, fols 83v–87v.

69 Thomas à Kempis, *The folowinge of Chryste translated out of Latyn into Englysh, wheruunto is added the golden Epystell of Saynte Barnarde*, tr. Richard Whitford (London: William Peto, 1556), sig. E4v–5r; Peryn, *Exercyses*, sig. D1r.

70 Edmund Bonner, *An honest godlye instruction, and information for the tradynge and bringinge vp of children* (London: Robert Caly, 1556), sig. B1r–4v; Anon., *The primer in English for children after the vse of Sar[um]* (London: John Wayland, 1556?), sigs. B1v–2v, K8r; Anon., *Primer in Englysh*, sigs O6v–T6v, L3v–4v, O4r, O5r; Anon., *Primer in Latin and Englishe*, sigs d3r, e2r, p2v–3r, p3v–s4v, *1v, y1v, &4r.

of thy faith... Spare them O lord, and defende thy workmaneship in them... and beynge deliuered from the tormente of paynes, brynge them through thy great mercies... to the felowshyp of the heuenly citizens, which liuest and reigneste God, thorowe all worldes.[71]

Christ, the only source of redemption, delivered His faithful people from the purgation they must undergo in preparation for His Kingdom. Prayers for the dead were thus manifestly present in all the Marian prayer books.

It appears that these theologians wanted purgatory and prayer for the dead to have a significant place in the Marian Church, though it will probably remain uncertain whether their emphasis on purgatory influenced the increase in bequests of Masses for the dead in Marian England.[72] Still, the manner in which these doctrines and collects were presented reveals some ambiguity. For example, the editors of the primers, while restoring prayers for the dead, left out the indulgences. Neither the wonderful, apocryphal promises, sometimes attributed to indulgenced prayers, nor the more sober indulgences themselves, reappeared.[73] Interestingly, Carranza, the editors of the Tridentine Catechism, and Le Picart were as silent as the compilers of the Marian prayer books in referring to indulgences by name. And while Marian theologians stressed the value of prayer for the dead, the place of purgation was not evoked. Gone were the times when purgatory stood as 'the focus of Christian fear', and the purging fires were described in graphic detail.[74] Both Bonner and Watson described purgatory tersely. This seems surprising, especially in the *Profitable doctryne*, a work given to explaining controversial matter. Yet, in his *Catechism*, Carranza treated purgatory with equal brevity, limiting himself to giving a clear, succinct definition and remarking that the Mass and prophets of the Old Testament had been purified of their sins in purgatory. Carranza also defined purgatory in the fifth article of the Creed, referring to Christ's descent into Hell, with the implication that it was an essential part of Christian belief.[75] The Tridentine Catechism imitated Carranza's description in the same context, adding, like Bonner and Watson, that souls undergo such punishment so as to enter Paradise without the stain of sin. Like these Marian bishops, Carranza

---

71 Tunstall, *Certaine prayers*, sigs B6v, D3v–4v.
72 Peter Marshall, *Beliefs and the dead in Reformation England* (Oxford: Oxford University Press, 2002), pp. 114–23.
73 For the significance of indulgences in primers, see Duffy, *Stripping of the altars*, pp. 287–98.
74 Taylor, *Heresy*, pp. 167–8; Duffy, *Stripping of the altars*, p. 341.
75 Carranza, *Comentarios*, I. 261–2: [In the descent into Hell, Christ visited places like] 'el lugar que llaman purgatorio, donde temporalmente son castigados algunos por sus pecados'; also II. 213: '...la consagración del pan y del vino, que es la sustancia del sacramento, y la oblación que se hace a Dios de ello después de consagrado por los que son vivos en la Iglesia y por los difuntos que murieron con fe y gracia de Dios en unión de la Iglesia: y éste es el sacrificio que se hace en la Misa'.

and the Catechism described how the sacrifice of the Mass aided the dead in the context of the Eucharist. The Conciliar decree of Trent was equally laconic: 'there is a Purgatory, and... the souls there detained are aided by the suffrages of the faithful and chiefly by the... sacrifice of the altar'.[76] All these texts were similar in their minimal approach to purgatory.

A further curiosity remains. The word 'purgatory' is not to be found in the Wayland Primer, or in the works of Bonner, Watson, and Angel. Why present the traditional teaching yet not use its traditional name? Most Marian authors, such as Christopherson, Martin, Peryn, Tunstall, Smith, Edgeworth, and Paynell, had no such inhibitions. Like 'Pope', the word 'purgatory' was a victim of the Evangelical propaganda wars, and both became 'verba non grata' in Henry's reign. Edgeworth described purgatory as necessary for salvation, but discreetly called it by the letter 'A', as a code, during Henry's reign. Yet 'Purgatory the vocable' appeared in the 1557 edition of his sermons. Henry Joliffe and Robert Jonson, canons of Worcester Cathedral, wisely expressed indifference regarding the name of purgatory during Edward's reign, but still told Bishop Hooper that 'Augustine... makes open mention of purgatory'.[77]

Why this seeming caution regarding the nature and name of purgatory? There appears to have been a development in the presentation of the doctrine over the first half of the sixteenth century. In the late medieval period, 'the horrible vividness' of the pains of purgatory had been evoked, according to Eamon Duffy, 'to stir the Christian to action on his own behalf while still in health... to live a mortified life, [and] be generous in charity'. But such graphic depictions of purgatory, as well as indulgences which promised marvels, exuded 'a heady mix of fear, hope, self-interest, altruism, punishment, purgation and salvation', that 'rendered [purgatory], of all the centrepieces of medieval theology, perhaps the most vulnerable to deconstruction and vilification', thus leading to its rigorous denunciation by Latimer and other Evangelicals.[78]

---

76 McHugh and Callan, *Catechism*, pp. 63, 259; Henry J. Schroeder (tr.), *The Canons and Decrees of the Council of Trent* (Rockford IL: Tan Books, 1978), p. 214 (this closely restated the decrees of the Councils of Florence and Lyon II). See also Germain Marc'hadour (ed.), *The Yale edition of the complete works of St Thomas More*, VII: *The supplication of souls* (New Haven CT and London: Yale University Press, 1990), pp. xci–xcvi.

77 Christopherson, *Exhortation*, sig. Y6v–7r; Martin, *Institution*, sig. R3v; Anon., *The institution of a Christen man* (London: T. Berthelet, 1537), fol. 97r; Anon., *A necessary doctrine and erudition for any Christen man, set furthe by the kynges maiestie of Englande* (London: J. Mayler, 1543), sig. πe6r–v; Wilson, *Sermons*, pp. 109, 128–30; Stephen Gardiner *et al.*, *Responsio venerabilium sacerdotum, Henrici Ioliffi et Roberti Ionson, sub protestatione facta ad illos articulos Ioanis Hoperi* (Antwerp: Christopher Plantin, 1564), fol. 90r: 'De nomine Purgatorii nullum nobis negocium, quanquam Augustinus contra Manichaeum de Genesi ad literam, apertam facit mentionem Purgatorii.'

78 Duffy, *Stripping of the altars*, p. 342; Peter Marshall, 'Fear, purgatory and polemic in Reformation England', in *Fear in early modern society*, ed. William G. Naphy and Penny

Theologians of traditional religion responded by rejecting this assault, and insisted on the value of Masses and prayers for the dead, but they chose not to return to defining the fearful flames. Thus Stephen Gardiner wrote in Edward's reign: 'regarding Pugatory, what is its nature, God knows; but that purgatory exists, the holy fathers of the church have been convinced by the scriptures themselves'.[79] Peter Marshall has described the 'reverential agnosticism' among Catholic writers in the later sixteenth century regarding the location of purgatory.[80] Such uncertainty seems to have been growing as regards the nature of purgatory itself. John Fisher, for example, was cautious in portraying purgatory in his popular exposition of the Penitential Psalms, which were reprinted in Mary's reign. Furthermore, English theologians were not unique in their uncertainty. Their Continental counterparts, such as the former Lutheran Georg Witzel, were also 'hard put to provide "a definition or even description"' of purgatory.[81]

But the Marian approach to purgatory may have been a device to draw people back into traditional religion. By, on the one hand, insisting on the necessity of the doctrine, and, on the other, de-emphasizing the long-vilified name, along with flames and indulgences, these theologians hoped to offer purgation of sins after death as a solace for the fearful and a goad to those capable of greater holiness. For example, after listing deceased family, friends, and others for whom to pray in purgatory, *The golden epystell* encouraged Christians to use their time well in this life, so as to avoid both Hell and purgatory. More, Fisher, and Edgeworth had promoted this stance in their sermons and books in the 1520s and 1530s, and this position continued to be upheld through their works which were printed or reprinted during Mary's reign. If Marian authors were employing this strategy, then their efforts foreshadowed the 1563 decree of the Council of Trent:

Roberts, Studies in Early Modern European History (Manchester: Manchester University Press, 1997), pp. 150–66 (p. 161); Dickens, *English Reformation*, pp. 20–21, 29–30; Duffy, *Stripping of the altars*, pp. 375–6, 391.

79 Gardiner *et al.*, *Responsio*, fol. 100r: 'de ipso quidem Purgatorio quale sit, Deus nouit: sed esse Purgatorium, piis ecclesiae patribus ex ipsis scripturis est persuasum'.

80 Peter Marshall, '"The map of God's Word": Geographies of the afterlife in Tudor and early Stuart England' in *The place of the dead: Death and remembrance in late medieval and early modern Europe*, ed. Bruce Gordon and Peter Marshall (Cambridge: Cambridge University Press, 2000), pp. 110–30 (pp. 120–21).

81 John Fisher, *The treatise concernyng the fruytfull saynge of Dauyd the Kynge and Prophete in the Seuen Penytencyall Psalme* (London: T. Marshe, 1555), sigs A7r, B3v–4r, C2r, E6r–v; *pace* Marc'hadour, who remarked that Fisher's view of Purgatory 'seems closer to Hell than Gerson's or More's' (*Yale edition*, VII. cxvii); Georg Witzel, *On the question of the fire of Purgatory* (Cologne: P. Quentel, 1545), sigs B8r, C4v, quoted in Pelikan, *Christian tradition*, IV. 251.

The Holy Council commands... that the sound doctrine of Purgatory... be everywhere taught and preached. The more difficult and subtle questions, however, and those that do not make for edification and from which there is for the most part no increase in piety, are to be excluded from popular instructions to uneducated people.[82]

If underlining the doctrine of purgatory, while underplaying its late medieval exaggerations, was the course that Marian theologians took, it was very similar to that taken by Carranza and Le Picart. Although a keen advocate of the poor, Carranza nevertheless stated that the spiritual works of mercy, including praying for the dead, were of a higher order than the corporal works.[83] Yet he was somewhat suspicious of chantries. Alms should be given in this life, although perpetual foundations did benefit the souls of those who, for the lack of faith or charity, were not generous to the needy while they lived.[84] Larissa Taylor has noted that while affirming purgatory, Le Picart spoke little of it, and while insisting that those in purgatory lived in hope, he remarked that he would rather be a woman in labour for a hundred years in this life than suffer one hour there.[85]

The Pope, the saints, and the dead were not fatal casualties of the reformations of Henry VIII and Edward VI. Rather they reappeared in the numerous published works of theology and spirituality of Mary Tudor's Church, which were grounded in late medieval religion and the Humanist writings of John Fisher. Their views, however, had also been tempered by twenty years of religious revolution, and Marian theologians presented the Papacy, as well as prayers to saints and for the dead, strategically. Attempts to address Evangelical concerns and careful reticence about some controversial points accompanied uncompromising discussion of the core of these doctrines and uncompromising adherence to the core religious practice associated with these doctrines, in early modern English, as well as some

82 Kempis, *Folowinge of Chryst*, p. 154; Schroeder, *Canons and Decrees*, p. 214.
83 Carranza, 1972, II. 472–5: 'De estas dos órdenes de obras de misericordia, las obras de la primera orden son de mayor dignidad. Lo primero, porque lo que se da y lo que se recibe es más excelente, porque son cosas espirituales. Y lo segundo, porque el sujeto que se remedia por las limosnas espirituales, que es el alma, es más excelente que el cuerpo' (p. 474).
84 ibid., II. 496–8: 'La mejor y la más fructuosa limosna es la que se hace en vida, cuando el hombre da de lo que puede gozar. Pero si por flaqueza de fe o por malicia no lo has hecho en la vida, hazlo en la muerte, que te será provechoso. Aunque muchas veces estas limosnas que se hacen para después de la muerte son sospechosas: porque, como no pudieron llevar la hacienda consigo y en vida no se quisieron deshacer de ella, quieren también en la muerte gozar de ella como pueden y celebrar sus nombres en la tierra . . . Y aunque hacer fundaciones perpetuas donde se haga limosna perpetua es cosa loable y pía y religiosa, pero son menester algunas circunstancias de tiempo y lugar' (p. 496).
85 Taylor, *Heresy*, pp. 167–8.

Spanish, Catholicism. And by comparing the works of Marian authors with Carranza's *Catechism*, as well as with the canons, decrees, and Catechism of Trent and the sermons of Le Picart, we see that Mary Tudor's Church had found, and sometimes foreshadowed, the spirit of the Counter-Reformation.

CHAPTER 8

Corpus Christi at Kingston upon Thames:
Bartolomé Carranza and the Eucharist in Marian England

John Edwards

The Sacrament of the Lord's Supper was not by Christ's ordinance reserved, carried about, lifted up, or worshipped.' (Part of n° 28 of the Thirty-Nine Articles of Religion)

On the Thursday after Trinity Sunday 1555, the Feast of Corpus Christi, a public procession of the Blessed Sacrament, the consecrated bread of the Eucharist, took place at Kingston upon Thames. During his subsequent trial by the Inquisition, Fray Bartolomé Carranza gave his own account of the events of that day.

> The Lutheran heretics having removed in England the processions which were customarily made for reverence and veneration of the Most Holy Sacrament, the aforesaid Most Reverend [Archbishop] of Toledo managed to have them restored and made once again, for this purpose asking His Majesty for wax, ornaments, the Chapel [Royal, of Philip] and all its music. And thus he organized, in Kingston in the aforesaid year [15]55, a procession with all solemnity, having altars placed in the street, and preaching against what the heretics had done, by preventing the practice of such processions. In which procession, apart from members of the Royal Household, there were many other people. And in this way notable service was done to the Christian religion.[1]

From the evidence later given by Carranza's compatriots to the Inquisition, it appears that the main participants in the liturgical procession at Kingston were Spanish. Fray Bartolomé himself preached a sermon, which was later much praised by witnesses for its devotional inspiration, though, as none of them specify the language in which it was preached, it is impossible to know what

---

1 José Ignacio Tellechea Idígoras (ed.), *Fray Bartolomé Carranza: Documentos históricos*, 7 vols, Archivo Documental Español 18 etc. (Madrid: 1962–94), III. 23–4, repr. in id., 'Bartolomé Carranza y la restauración católica inglesa (1554–1558)', *Anthologica Annua*, 12 (1964), pp. 159–282, and again in id., *Fray Bartolomé Carranza y el cardenal Pole: Un navarro en la restauración católica de Inglaterra (1554–1558)* (Pamplona: Diputación Foral de Navarra, Institución Príncipe de Viana, and CSIC, 1977), pp. 15–118 (p. 55).

effect, if any, it had on those of Queen Mary's English subjects who were present.

Carranza's reference to Philip's *Capilla* is crucial to a proper understanding of what happened in the Kingston Corpus Christi procession of 1555. Just a year later, when Charles V abdicated from the Spanish throne, Mary's husband was to inherit what Bernardette Nelson has recently described as 'the most important and prestigious court chapel in Europe'. Although it is still uncertain exactly what musical and liturgical establishment Philip brought with him to England, a good guide is provided by the newly-discovered *Orden que se tiene en los Officios en la Capilla de su Magestad* ('Order which is maintained in the Offices in the Chapel of His Majesty'), which appears to have been first compiled in 1550, was revised probably in 1559, and has now been edited and studied by Nelson (2000). The document was compiled by one 'Aguirre', who was *'capellán de Su Magestad y receptor de su Capilla'* ('Chaplain to His Majesty and Receiver-General of his Chapel'). Even if the surviving version of the *Orden* dates from after Philip's return to Spain, and very probably from the ill-fated year in which the Seville and Valladolid 'Protestants' were repressed by the Inquisition and Carranza himself was arrested, it is hard to imagine that the future archbishop was not able to call on at least some of these resources (*'toda su música'*, as he later said of Philip) when he organized the Kingston procession. According to Aguirre's *Orden*, the whole Octave of Corpus Christi, from the vigil on the Wednesday after Trinity Sunday to the Thursday after Corpus Christi day itself, was celebrated with well co-ordinated liturgy and music. On the day of Vigil, a sung Mass (*Missa cantata*) would be celebrated, during which a Host would be consecrated, and subsequently placed in a monstrance, for use in the following day's procession and Benediction. Both when the consecrated Body of Christ was taken to its place of repose on the Vigil, and on Corpus Christi day itself when the procession took place, the priest who bore the Blessed Sacrament in a monstrance would be followed by the King and members of the Court, carrying white candles. Benediction would then take place, the priest blessing the kneeling people with the Sacrament, while the last two verses of St Thomas Aquinas's Eucharistic hymn *Pange lingua* (*Tantum ergo sacramentum* and *Genitum genitoque*) were sung.[2]

Accounts subsequently given to the Inquisition by compatriots who were with Carranza in England, though tantalizingly silent on the subject of the music, suggest that a similar order was followed by the Spanish courtiers and members of the King's Chapel who processed through Kingston in 1555. Neither Philip nor his Queen seem to have put in an appearance, but large white candles (*hachas*) were apparently carried in procession by one of the

---

2   Bernardette Nelson, 'Ritual and ceremony in the Spanish Royal Chapel, c.1559–c.1561', *Early Music History*, 10 (2000), pp. 105–200 (pp. 141–2).

King's secretaries, Pedro de Hoyos, and other noblemen and knights. Among those present, as participants or possibly onlookers, were Philip's favourite Ruy Gómez de Silva (later Prince of Eboli), the Cordoban magnate Don Alonso de Aguilar, the royal quartermaster-general (*aposentador mayor*) Luis Venegas, the prior of the Military Orders Don Antonio de Toledo, and the Dominican prior of Alcañiz (Teruel) Fray Alonso Hazaña. The Eucharistic Host was carried by a chaplain of the Royal Chapel (Capilla de los Reyes) in Toledo, Cristóbal Becerra. It appears that the occasion passed off without any untoward incident. Indeed, later Spanish witnesses, who were admittedly attempting to defend Carranza against inquisitors' accusations of 'Lutheran' heresy, supported the friar's own testimony by stating that many English people viewed and followed the procession devoutly. In Canterbury, the archbishop, Cardinal Reginald Pole, organized a similar Corpus procession.[3]

The procession at Kingston in 1555 was not the first attempt to revive the full Corpus Christi liturgy in Mary's England. In the previous year, before Philip's arrival to become her husband, and when the only legal religious services in the kingdom were those of Archbishop Cranmer's reformed Church, the ceremonies of Corpus Christi Day had been observed in London. On that occasion, Protestant opposition was strong, and a priest was stabbed. It appeared that objections to this public embodiment and exposition of Catholic Eucharistic teaching were combined with protests against the forthcoming Spanish marriage, which threatened to subordinate England to Habsburg hegemony. With this background, and despite the fact that Roman Catholic worship was now legal once again, it must have appeared to be a brave, or even foolhardy act, when Carranza organized the Kingston procession. All subsequent Spanish testimony suggested that the event was very much the friar's personal initiative. This seems at least likely, given that, on the first Tuesday in Lent in 1555, Carranza preached a sermon in the Chapel Royal, to King Philip and his courtiers, on the proper reception of the newly restored Mass. As a result of this sermon, Carranza was asked by Juan de la Cerda, Duke of Medinaceli, to compose a short treatise on the subject, which still survives.[4] The fact that the Kingston procession passed off without violence appears to have inspired further efforts in the following year, when two processions took place in the less controllable environment of London. According to Carranza's own later testimony, during his trial by the Inquisition, on Corpus Christi day 1556, the Sacrament was carried by the Bishop of London, that hammer of heretics, 'bloody' Edmund Bonner himself. Again, the event

3   Tellechea, *Documentos históricos*, III. 55-6; Thomas F. Mayer, *Reginald Pole: Prince and prophet* (Cambridge University Press, Cambridge, 2000), p. 299
4   José Ignacio Tellechea Idígoras, 'Un tratadito de Bartolomé Carranza sobre la Misa', *Archivio Italiano per la Storia della Pietà*, 11 (1988), pp. 145-79.

took place in the relatively secure precincts of the Bishop's Palace at Fulham. On the Sunday of the Octave, however, a further procession was held in the highly exposed and highly symbolic setting of Whitehall. On both occasions, Carranza was called upon, or else volunteered, to provide the necessary liturgical ornaments and to organize the music. In the Sunday procession in Whitehall, Fray Bartolomé himself had the honour of carrying the Blessed Sacrament. The Toledan royal chaplain, Cristóbal Becerra, who had performed this office at Kingston in the previous year, later described to the inquisitors the reaction of the English public to the Whitehall procession:

> In the second procession which was held in London, the expenditure of the aforesaid procession was at the charge of the Most Reverend [Archbishop] of Toledo [Carranza] and of this witness [Becerra]. And he saw many English people who with great haste and excitement came to see the aforesaid procession. And when the aforesaid Most Reverend [Archbishop Carranza] raised the Most Holy Sacrament in his hands, [this witness] saw many English people kneeling on their knees, weeping, and giving thanks to God because they were seeing such a good thing, and calling down blessings on those who had been the cause of it.[5]

In an editorial published on 20 January 1899 and reprinted exactly one hundred years later, the High Church Anglican weekly the *Church Times* attacked the building of the Roman Catholic Cathedral at Westminster. The writer criticized its architectural style as a 'symbol of its foreign spirit and purpose'. His particular bile, though, was directed against the proposed importation from Spain of the Blessed Sacrament for reservation in Cardinal Vaughan's new Cathedral church:

> Spain is to have the honour of transferring a share of her merits to the foundation of the Cardinal's new church. We do not pretend to know how this is to be done; it is enough to point out the anti-national character of such a proposal. And Spain of all countries! The memory of the Great Armada, which united every Englishman, Catholic and Romanist [i.e. Anglo- or Roman Catholic] alike, 'to hang those dogs of Seville', makes this new Spanish invasion appear like a national insult. And Spain too, with her hideous tale of the Inquisition, her living barbarities of the arena, her present national decrepitude, and her second defeat by the English-speaking race [the American victory in Cuba in the previous year]! England, dull and unspiritual though she be, needs no infusion of the Spanish spirit at all events.[6]

Leaving aside the ambiguities of nineteenth-century Anglo-Catholicism, which appear all too clearly in this extract from its 'party' newspaper, the question that needs to be addressed is whether Carranza's liturgical activity for Corpus Christi in Mary's reign was indeed an exotic and 'anti-national' import.

5   Tellechea, *Carranza y Pole*, p. 67.
6   *Church Times*, 20 January 1899, repr. in *Church Times*, 20 January 1999.

The work of numerous scholars has effectively demonstrated the hold that was gained over the population of large parts of late medieval England by the Feast of Corpus Christi. Having been declared mandatory by the Council of Vienne, in 1311–12, an order reaffirmed by Pope John XXII in 1317, the celebration of the Eucharistic festival had become, by 1500, an essential part of the English year.[7] Inevitably, the best records of Corpus Christi liturgies and other associated activities come from the larger towns, but the feast was kept in the countryside as well. Writing retrospectively, Roger Martin, a gentleman farmer at Long Melford in Suffolk, where he became church-warden in Mary's reign, referred to the Corpus celebrations of earlier years:

> On Corpus Christi day [the clergy] went likewise [as on Palm Sunday] with the Blessed Sacrament in procession about the Church green in copes.[8]

The Corpus Christi Festival was placed, in the liturgical calendar, after the great commemorative cycle of Jesus's Passion, Crucifixion, and Resurrection, from Ash Wednesday to Pentecost. Its position, in the week after Trinity Sunday, also made it a part of the Midsummer celebrations, which were mainly focused on the Feast of the Nativity of St John the Baptist (24 June), when there was as good a chance as any that the English weather would be tolerable.[9] By the time of Henry VIII, the liturgical processions, which took much of their form and content from the older ceremonies of Palm Sunday, had been greatly elaborated. In England, as elsewhere, the Host was carried, under a canopy, either in a monstrance, such as was used within church precincts for the exposition of the Sacrament and Benediction, or else in a processional shrine or tabernacle (in Spanish a *custodia*). The York example was made of silver and gold, and was valued at the colossal sum of £211 when it was confiscated in 1548, after the royal order of the previous year for the abolition of processions, including those of Corpus Christi. In earlier years, this Feast was for many, both clerical and lay, the apparent highpoint of the liturgical year. In Sherborne (Dorset), as in Long Melford, the Sacrament was carried in procession in an elaborate *custodia*, and a special play was performed in a tent in the churchyard (for fear of the weather?). In the London parish of St-Mary-at-Hill, in the 1520s as in previous decades, the churchwardens purchased, for the annual Corpus Christi procession, five dozen garlands of flowers, to be worn by the clergy and choir, and also to be used to adorn the

---

7 Robert N. Swanson, *Religion and devotion in Europe, c.1215–c.1515*, Cambridge Medieval Textbooks (Cambridge: Cambridge University Press, 1995), p. 142.

8 Quoted by Eamon Duffy, 'Cranmer and popular religion', in *Thomas Cranmer: Churchman and scholar*, ed. Paul Ayris and David Selwyn (Woodbridge: The Boydell Press, 1993), pp. 199–215 (p. 208).

9 Ronald Hutton, *The rise and fall of Merry England: The ritual year, 1400–1700* (Oxford: Oxford University Press, 1996), p. 40.

processional crosses, while the parishioners carried lights. The rector and wardens would provide bread, ale, and wine for the choristers. In many English cities and towns, the canopy over the Sacrament would be carried by distinguished laymen, past houses decorated with cloths and tapestries, and along streets strewn with flowers and herbs. In smaller towns, such as Sherborne in Dorset and Ashburton in Devon, for which churchwardens' accounts survive up to the end of Henry VIII's reign, church bells were rung for Corpus Christi, processions were held, and plays were performed. In cities, such as York and Coventry, the regular and secular clergy were commonly accompanied in procession by civic authorities and craft guilds. In many towns, guilds and confraternities put on pageants or performed miracle plays, recounting the Christian story, for which they kept props, and probably scripts, from year to year, often bickering over the expense in times of economic hardship.[10]

On the surface, the abolition of Corpus Christi ceremonies and entertainments, once King Henry's death had freed Archbishop Thomas Cranmer to proceed more rapidly towards a Reformed Church of England, brutally ended a comfortable, and comforting, example of Ronald Hutton's 'Merry England' or Eamon Duffy's 'traditional religion'. The violence of the government assault on the religious and social feelings and values of Edward VI's subjects, in the destruction of the Corpus Christi celebration, is perhaps most vividly illustrated by events in Durham. There, at the city parish church of St Nicholas (perhaps in anticipation of later ecclesiological developments there, which included a drastic re-ordering by Archbishop George Carey), Christians were, in Professor MacCulloch's words, treated to 'the remarkable spectacle of a royal commissioner jumping up and down on the city's giant Corpus Christi processional monstrance in order to smash it up more effectively'.[11] Yet this conception of the destruction by the Crown of a uniformly loved manifestation of traditional Catholic religion and social cohesion may not be entirely accurate. Even before the changes that were introduced in the reigns of Henry VIII and Edward VI, annual Corpus Christi processions had already largely become exclusive and well-policed occasions. In England, as elsewhere,

10 Eamon Duffy, *The stripping of the altars: Traditional religion in England, c. 1400–c. 1580* (New Haven CT and London: Yale University Press, 1992), pp. 43–4; id., 'Cranmer', p. 207; Hutton, *Rise and fall*, p. 41; Christopher Haigh, *English Reformations: Religion, politics, and society under the Tudors* (Oxford: Clarendon Press, 1993), pp. 32–3, 158, 210; Heather Swanson, *Medieval artisans: An urban class in late medieval England* (Oxford: Blackwell, 1989), pp. 16–17, 22, 37, 67, 91, 94, 119–20; Miri Rubin, *Corpus Christi: The Eucharist in late medieval culture* (Cambridge: Cambridge University Press, 1991), pp. 233–71; Charles Phythian-Adams, *Desolation of a city: Coventry and the urban crisis of the late Middle Ages*, Past and Present Publications (Cambridge: Cambridge University Press, 1979), pp. 44–5, 111–12.

11 Diarmaid MacCulloch, *Tudor Church Militant: Edward VI and the Protestant Reformation* (London: Allen Lane, 1999), p. 73.

a primary function of authorities, guilds, and confraternities was to *protect* the Sacrament. Indeed, studies of equivalent celebrations in pre-Reformation France and Spain have highlighted the 'risk' that Christ took in exposing His own risen and ascended body to His body on earth, the Church.[12] By 1500, in England as elsewhere in Catholic Europe, the 'great and the good', who included for this purpose those who would in subsequent centuries become known as 'the aristocracy of labour', marched, somewhat smugly perhaps, behind the cosmic symbol and substance of the crucified and risen Prince of Peace. Policing was necessary partly because so many were excluded from active participation in the liturgical proceedings—all women, most male workers, and most children.[13] Thus even without the addition of theological and ecclesiological conflict between those groups of Western Christians who were just beginning to be distinguished as 'Catholics' and 'Protestants', Fray Bartolomé Carranza's attempted restoration of the Corpus Christi liturgy, in a country where it had been until very recently traditional, may well have been seen by many as a 'sign of contradiction'. In the context of the friar's inter-vention during Mary's reign, perhaps the most interesting case, which has been fully studied and may serve as a precedent for the 1555 Kingston experiment, is that of the port of Bristol. There, it seems that the municipal authorities did not, as in other towns, attend the Corpus procession formally. Instead, the ceremonies were entrusted entirely to the town's clergy, and in particular to the Dominican and Franciscan ('Black' and 'Grey') friars. The Mendicants apparently used the occasion both to attempt to mend fences with the parish clergy, who were so often their rivals, and also to appeal evangelistically to the bulk of the lay population, as it were over the heads of the secular hierarchy.[14]

Carranza and his Spanish companions arrived, of course, from a country in which the tradition of Corpus Christi liturgy and celebration was equally well established. Between 1264, when Pope Urban IV declared the Feast to be a universal observance in the Roman Church, and the Council of Vienne (1311–12), when it was made obligatory, Corpus processions had already begun to be held in Spain, for example in Toledo in 1280 and Seville in 1282. In Seville, the Hermandad del Cuerpo de Dios (Brotherhood of the Body of God) was established well before 1300, while in about 1380, a Cofradía del Santísimo Sacramento (Confraternity of the Most Holy Sacrament) was set up in the Seville suburb of Triana, on the south side of the river Guadalquivir.[15] *Arcas,*

---

12 See, for example, Antoinette Molinié Fioravanti (ed.), *Le corps de Dieu en fêtes*, Sciences Humaines et Religions (Paris: Les Éditions du Cerf, 1996), pp. 7–12 (editor's intro-duction).

13 Rubin, *Corpus Christi*, pp. 265–7; Molinié, *Corps de Dieu*, pp. 7–12.

14 Martha C. Skeeters, *Community and clergy: Bristol and the Reformation, c.1530–c.1570* (Oxford: Clarendon Press, 1993), pp. 28–30, 212–13, 218.

15 Molinié, *Corps de Dieu*, p. 13.

or processional monstrances modelled, as in England, on the Ark of the Jewish Covenant, are recorded in Spain by the mid-fourteenth century, for example in Seville in 1363.[16] In the Mezquita-Catedral ('Mosque-Cathedral') of Córdoba, a chapel of Corpus Christi was founded in 1393 by a local nobleman, Diego Gutiérrez de los Ríos, lord of Fernán Núñez, and remained in that form until rebuilding took place in the Cathedral in 1547. Still employed in Córdoba at Corpus Christi is a massive processional monstrance (*custodia procesional*), in the form of a tower, which became the customary style in Spain by the end of the fifteenth century. The example in Córdoba was made, between 1514 and 1518, by Heinrich von Harff (known in Spain as Enrique de Arfe) and Bernabé García de los Reyes.[17] In the case of Toledo Cathedral, Carranza's future see, Queen Isabella had left provision in her will for a new processional monstrance (*ostensorio*), which was duly acquired, in 1508, by her confessor and Toledo's Cardinal Archbishop, Francisco Jiménez de Cisneros. Ten years later, Cisneros, perhaps having seen the subordinate see of Córdoba's new acquisition, apparently decided that something more splendid was required for his own cathedral. A competition was held, and it was won by Von Harff, who duly provided a *custodia*, similar to that in the Mezquita, which again is still processed, in the particularly elaborate Corpus ceremonies which are held each year in Toledo.[18] Thus the work of many hands demonstrated that, when Fray Bartolomé and his companions arrived in England from Spain, he and they were moving from one piece of fertile Eucharistic ground to another.

By the time Carranza arranged the Kingston procession in 1555, despite Martin Luther's (and Henry VIII's) determined defence of the 'real presence' of Christ's Body and Blood in the consecrated elements of the Eucharist, the nature of this sacrament had been very differently interpreted, by native Swiss reformers, by John Calvin, and by Archbishop Cranmer himself. In article 29 of his 1537 Catechism, entitled 'The Supper of the Lord', Calvin stated that, in this sacrament, 'the signs are the bread and the wine, under which the Lord presents to us the true yet spiritual communication of his body and his blood.' He adds that 'this communication is content with the bond of His spirit, and does not require at all a presence of the flesh enclosed under the bread, or of the blood under the wine'.[19]

16 María Jesús Sanz Serrano, *La custodia procesional Enrique de Arfe y su escuela* (Cordoba: Cajasur Publicaciones, 2000), p. 12.

17 Manuel Nieto Cumplido, *La catedral de Córdoba* (Cordoba: Cajasur Publicaciones, 1998), pp. 472, 649; Sanz, *Custodia*, pp. 12–13, 32–3.

18 Juan Estanislao López Gómez, *La procesión del Corpus Christi en Toledo* (Toledo: Diputación Provincial de Toledo, 1993), pp. 84–92.

19 John Calvin, *Instruction in faith (1537)*, ed. and tr. Paul T. Fuhrmann (Louisville KY: John Knox Press, 1992), p. 68.

Such was evidently the basis of Cranmer's successful attempt to have his 'King Josiah' order the abolition of the Eucharistic festival of Corpus Christi, with its attendant liturgical processions and plays. In 1551, during the controversy, some of it violent, which followed the orders of 1547, Cranmer wrote the following in answer to the criticisms of Bishop Stephen Gardiner:

> When I say and repeat many times in my book [*Of the Sacrament of the Body and Blood of our Saviour Christ*], that the body of Christ is present in them that worthily receive the sacrament, but any man should mistake my words and think that I mean, that although Christ be not corporally in the outward and visible signs, yet he is corporally in the persons that duly receive them, this is to advertize the reader that I mean no such thing, but my meaning is that the force, the grace, the virtue and benefit of Christ's body that was crucified for us, and of His blood that was shed for us, be really and effectively present with all them that duly receive the sacrament…[thus] wheresoever in the Scripture it is said that Christ, God, or the Holy Ghost is in any man, the same is understood spiritually by grace.[20]

For Cranmer, one natural consequence of this understanding of the Eucharist was evidently the formulation of the twenty-eighth Article of Religion, including its apparent condemnation of all the liturgical practices associated with the Feast of Corpus Christi.

In stark contrast, or so it appeared, the commitment of Carranza to the Catholic doctrine of the Eucharist had been evident in his interventions at the Council of Trent. In his *Comentarios* of 1558, he reaffirmed this teaching, no doubt in the light of his English experience. In his treatment of what he there calls the 'Sacrament of Communion', he affirms Christ's real presence in the consecrated bread and wine, as being 'the same in substance which was born of the Virgin Mary His Mother, and the same that suffered for our redemption on the Cross, and rose again on the third day, and after forty days ascended to the heavens, and is now at the right hand of God the Father.' More specifically, he affirmed the doctrine of Transubstantiation, stating, concerning this Sacrament, that 'before the consecration it was the substance of bread and wine, after the consecration it is the substantial flesh and blood of Jesus Christ.' Despite these dogmatic statements, Carranza stresses the mystery involved in the Sacrament of the Altar, using expressions highly reminiscent of the mighty theologian of his Dominican order, the 'Angelic Doctor' Thomas Aquinas:

> The tongue of man may speak this truth, which Faith teaches by means of this ineffable Sacrament, and may adore with humility, because to presume to speak of,

---

20 Henry Jankyns, *The remains of Thomas Cranmer, D.D., Archbishop of Canterbury* (Oxford: Oxford University Press, 1882), repr. in Henry Wace (ed.), *Archbishop Cranmer on the true and Catholic doctrine and use of the sacrament of the Lord's Supper* (London: Charles J. Thynne and Jarvis, 1928), pp. xiv–xv.

or to understand, the mysteries which God encloses there, would be a mad presumption. It is enough to know that God wished to declare Himself in this mystery.

Fray Bartolomé goes on to state that the Holy Communion was instituted for three reasons, as food, as a sacrifice, and in order to redeem humankind. He then lists the names by which this Sacrament is commonly known—Holy Communion, Eucharist, Viaticum, Sacrifice, Memorial, the Lord's Supper, and (as in Cranmer's 1549 Prayer Book) last of all, the Mass. Carranza, in an evidently heartfelt passage, also refers specifically to the observance of the Feast of Corpus Christi, to which he had devoted so much time and energy during his stay in England:

> After tyrants and heretics began shamelessly to abuse this Most Holy Sacrament, the Church became more determined in venerating it. For this reason it was ordained, three hundred years ago, that on the first Thursday after Trinity should be celebrated, with much solemnity, the festival of this Most Holy Sacrament, with its Octave. This is done generally among Catholics, and in the greater part of the Church it is customary to make solemn processions, with celebrations [*fiestas*] and honest rejoicings, carrying the Most Holy Sacrament, with much reverence, publicly through the streets. This custom is very holy and religious, and should be observed much more in the present time than in the past, because the shamelessness of the heretics against reverencing this Sacrament is greater than ever. Thus it is proper that Catholics should insist more on the public veneration of this Sacrament, the prelates and secular justices always ensuring that, in these public acts, no indecency occurs.[21]

Carranza's contemporary, Maestro Juan de Ávila, developed in his preaching a similar concept of the nature and meaning of the Eucharist. In a sermon delivered on the Vigil of Corpus Christi, in 1551 or soon afterwards, Juan discoursed on the Blessed Sacrament as the Ark of the New Covenant, an image which seems to be well represented in the processional monstrance illustrated in Luke Shepherd's 1548 anti-Catholic dialogue between the Evangelical John Bon and the traditionalist Master Parson. For Juan de Ávila, the Corpus Christi procession was both a focus of penitence before the Lord, when personal as well as social sins might be put away, and also an occasion to rejoice in the faith of Christ, untrammelled by the shadow of Gethsemane and Golgotha which inevitably looms over the commemoration of the Institution of the Lord's Supper, on Holy [Maundy] Thursday.[22]

21 Bartolomé Carranza de Miranda, *Comentarios sobre el Catechismo christiano*, ed. José Ignacio Tellechea Idígoras, 2 vols, BAC 1 (Madrid: Editorial Católico, 1972), II. 202–11, 223–4.
22 Juan de Ávila, *Obras completas del Beato Juan de Ávila*, 2 vols, ed. Luis Sala Balust, BAC (Madrid: Editorial Católico, 1952–3), II. 502–05, 566–9; Duffy, *Stripping of the altars*, p. 460; MacCulloch, *Tudor Church*, pp. 74–5.

This concept of a living and passionate devotion to the Body and Blood of Christ, which was evidently in the minds and hearts of Carranza and his Spanish companions, raises important questions, not only about the nature of Catholicism in Spain at the time, but also about the character of the so-called 'Restoration' of Catholicism in Mary's England. Spanish currents of Church reform, in which Carranza had been actively involved during the period preceding his arrival in England, might appear, like their Protestant equivalents, to adopt a 'top-down' approach. In this scheme of things, which had been traditional in late medieval discussion of reform and had been actively pursued, for example, by Ferdinand and Isabella, the prevailing assumptions were, firstly that a clergy free of ignorance and secular compromises would lead a better and purer Christian life, and secondly that this evangelical discipleship would 'trickle down' to the laity. Reform in the 'head', to use the contemporary jargon, would inevitably reach the 'members' too. Yet, while demonstrating strong enthusiasm for the reform of clerical abuses, the writings of Carranza and some of his Spanish contemporaries, including Juan de Ávila, were also, in Lu Ann Homza's words, 'full of concern for the laity's physical well-being'.[23] The leadership provided by a reformed clergy was essential for the well-being of the Church, but this could not, in the view of Carranza and others, be detached from the full involvement of the entire Body of Christ, lay as well as ordained. Carranza set down his understanding of the nature of the Church in his 1558 commentary on the articles of the Apostles' Creed: 'Credo... in unam sanctam Catholicam et Apostolicam ecclesiam, sanctorum communionem.' Here he states that 'The Church of Christ has two parts. The one is called triumphant and the other militant.' The Church Triumphant is 'that fortunate assembly of souls who reign in heaven with Christ, who, having departed this life, triumph over the world, the flesh, and the devil, and reign secure with Christ, without fear of losing the state that they possess.' The Church Militant, on the other hand, consists, in Carranza's words, of 'all the assembly of the faithful who are on earth'. 'It is called militant because they [the faithful] struggle here with the enemies we have spoken of, and with all the power of hell.' The Church militant, though, is divided into two parts. One of them is 'the assembly of good Christians, who are not only united in one profession of faith and sacraments, but are also united in one Spirit, and in a union of grace and charity'. He stresses, though, that this 'better part' of the Church is known only to God [compare II Tim. 2: 19, 'The Lord is He who knows His own']. In reality, though, the Church 'always had, and will have until the end of the world, mixed with the good, many wicked people, and all are parts and members of the mystical body, although in

---

23 Lu Ann Homza, *Religious authority in the Spanish Renaissance*, Johns Hopkins University Studies in Historical and Political Science, 118th s. 1 (Baltimore MD and London: The Johns Hopkins Press, 2000), p. 131.

different ways'. The message seems clear. The notion of a 'gathered Church', as held by some Protestant reformers, on the grounds that the elect can be known on earth, and that those excluded from it are not in reality Christians, is firmly rejected by Carranza as a means of governing the 'Church Militant'. There is indeed a 'Church of the elect', but God alone knows who is in it, and the only certainty of election lies with the saints in heaven, from whose eyes the Lord has wiped away every tear. For Carranza, to believe otherwise is to share in that Donatism which Augustine condemned.[24] Thus it may be argued that the Corpus Christi processions which Fray Bartolomé and others revived in Mary's England, not only rejected Reformed notions of Eucharistic doctrine, including Cranmer's, but also challenged views of Justification which went back to Luther. How, though, did Carranza's ideas and practices relate to their English equivalents, and what effect, if any, did they have?

The indigenous English Catholic tradition, which Lucy Wooding has studied, unsurprisingly contains much contemporary devotional and doctrinal writing connected with the Eucharist.[25] Indeed, it has been suggested, by Thomas Mayer, that Carranza's activity to restore the Corpus Christi celebration was partly inspired by urging from Bishop Edmund Bonner, who also wrote an important Catechism and indeed, as has been seen, took an active part in the revival of Corpus processions. Certainly, religious processions, including those of the Feast of the Body and Blood of Christ, had been revived before Carranza came to England.[26] The questions, though, of what exactly was revived in these ceremonies, how widespread and effective the revivals were, and to what extent they represented lay or conservative clerical tradition rather than the ideas and schemes of reforming clergy, whether Spanish or English, are not easy to answer. Firstly, there has been much dispute among historians (often reflecting, it must be said, their own respective doctrinal and ecclesiological predilections) over the reasons for the limited response in the parishes to the liturgical instructions of Mary's government. Those with Protestant sympathies prefer to see a rapid rooting of the 'evangelical' Reformed faith, while those of a Catholic turn of mind talk more (and not without documentary basis) of economic and social crisis and the depredations which had been suffered by the Church (and which undoubtedly obsessed Reginald Pole and his friends) during the reigns of Henry and Edward.[27] It should also be borne in mind not only that approximately half of England's population in 1555 was too young ever to have experienced a

24 Carranza, *Comentarios*, I. 371–2.
25 Lucy E.C. Wooding, *Rethinking Catholicism in Marian England*, Oxford Historical Monographs (Oxford: Clarendon Press, 2000), pp. 166–76.
26 Mayer, *Reginald Pole*, p. 299; Duffy, *Stripping of the altars*, pp. 534–5.
27 On the mid-Tudor economy, see Clifford S.L. Davies, *Peace, print and Protestantism, 1450–1558*, Paladin History of England (St Alban's: Paladin, 1977), pp. 243–62.

Corpus procession, but that a violent repression of Protestantism was in progress at the time, particularly in London and the south-east of England, where Carranza and his compatriots were especially active.[28] What is clear is that much of the equipment for Corpus liturgies and plays, in towns and villages all over the kingdom, had been lost, in and after 1548. Monstrances had been melted down, vestments turned into curtains, play props and scripts dispersed. These factors undoubtedly limited the revival, and the death of the Queen of course brought it to a rapid end, though attempts were made, in places, to continue at least the plays into the first year of Elizabeth's reign.[29] There seems to be little doubt that parish clergy, local authorities, and guilds, who restored processions after 1554, intended to carry on, as far as possible, where they had been forced to leave off a few years before.[30] It is noticeable, though, that, to judge from the available accounts of the processions organized by Carranza, no reference is made to non-liturgical trappings, such as were popular in Spain at the time (giants, mumming, and Moors), just as they had quite recently been in England. The suggestion here is that Carranza had in his mind, not a revival of 'Merry England', let alone 'Reconquest Spain', but a reformed understanding of Eucharist and Church to which he held with a fervour at least equal to that of Cranmer.

---

28 David Loades, *The reign of Mary Tudor: Politics, government, and religion in England, 1553–58*, 2nd edn (London and New York: Longman, 1991), pp. 272–7; John Edwards, 'A Spanish Inquisition?: The repression of Protestantism under Mary Tudor', *Reformation and Renaissance Review*, 4 (2000), pp. 62–74.
29 Haigh, *English Reformations*, pp. 214–15.
30 For a well-documented case of the revival of 'traditional' religion in a Devon village, see Eamon Duffy, *The voices of Morebath: Reformation and rebellion in an English village* (New Haven CT and London: Yale University Press, 2001), pp. 153–68.

CHAPTER 9

Carranza and the English universities

Andrew Hegarty

This paper seeks to examine Bartolomé Carranza's relations with, and influence on, the English universities, and it may be wise at the outset to dampen expectations. For whether or not there is a subject here at all rather depends on the national provenances and languages of the surviving documentary evidence. Italian sources, whether ecclesiastical or diplomatic, seem notably silent about Carranza's relations with the universities. More surprisingly, there is no reference to Bartolomé Carranza in the records of the University of Cambridge, and no less an industrious digger than Anthony Wood, having written of other Spanish friars who made an impact on the Marian University of Oxford, declares that, despite what 'some are pleased to averr' as to an involvement, there is no trace of him in the registers here either. Elsewhere he declares that, unlike the other friars of whom he has written, Carranza was neither incorporated in, nor a university teacher at, Oxford, but that he had seemingly abided there some time as a 'stranger'.[1] Nicholas Sanders, whom Carranza had known well, failed to mention him as a university reformer in his history of the Anglican schism, and even the expanded version of that work produced by Ribadeneira ignored any intervention by him.[2] Given what happened to Carranza afterwards, this silence is perhaps understandable. For direct contemporary or near-contemporary evidence of his active involvement, therefore, we must rely on Spanish sources and above all on Carranza's own, usually rather general, assertions. This makes for a necessarily tentative and patchy narrative, and indeed one that will focus largely on one of the two English universities, that of Oxford.

It would, of course, have been surprising if a man of Carranza's academic and institutional antecedents had not taken an interest in the universities while

---

1 Wood, Anthony (à), *The history and antiquities of the University of Oxford*, ed. J. Gutch, 2 vols in 3 (Oxford: printed for the author, 1792–6), II. 127; id., *Fasti oxonienses*, ed. Philip Bliss, 2 parts (London: F.C. and J. Rivington, 1815-20), I. col. 148.

2 Nicholas Sanders, *De origine ac progressu schismatis anglicani libri tres, aucti prius per E. Rishtonum, nunca vero addita R. P. Petri Ribadeneirae Soc. Iesu, iterum in Germania locupletius & castigatius editi* (Cologne: Peter Henning, 1610).

assisting Queen Mary and Cardinal Pole to restore England to the Catholic fold. In his youth he had been sent to Cardinal Cisneros's new University of Alcalá de Henares where, under the wing of an uncle who held a chair there, he was placed for three years in the Colegio de San Eugenio, which specialized in grammar and humanistic studies, and then for some two years in the Colegio de Santa Balbina, where philosophy was taught. These were secular colleges. After entering the Dominican Order in 1520 and completing his noviciate, it is likely that he studied theology, for a time, in the great Dominican convent-college of San Esteban in Salamanca. In 1525 he was nominated to membership of the Dominican convent-college of San Gregorio in Valladolid, with which he was to have a long association. In due course he went on to teach arts there from 1530 and then theology from 1533, quite possibly to audiences which included students other than Dominicans. He attained its senior internal teaching position in theology in 1536, and was rewarded by his Order with the title of Master of Theology in 1539. He continued at San Gregorio until 1545 when he was summoned to attend the Council of Trent.[3] Although, unlike other leading contemporary Dominicans, he never attained a university chair in open competition outside the convent, Carranza was none the less acquainted with each of the three great imperial universities of early modern Spain— Salamanca, Valladolid, and Alcalá de Henares. The convent-colleges of San Esteban and San Gregorio sought to form an élite for the Dominican Order, and Carranza was active as a scholar and teacher in the early years of what amounted to a golden age in their theological teaching and production. Spanish Dominican theologians had, moreover, been much concerned with the great public and moral issues of the day, both in the relative tranquillity of the convent or university and at Court or at Trent. Carranza, as was common for theologians of his Order, had experience also of working as a *consultor* to the Spanish Inquisition, in his case for the Valladolid tribunal which had within its jurisdiction the universities of Salamanca and Valladolid.[4] He was, therefore, by academic training and experience of ecclesiastical and public affairs, by no means unqualified to work for university restoration and reform in England.

In the final analysis it will never be easy to assess fairly the achievements of the short Marian regime in Oxford and Cambridge, for the seedlings it

3   José Ignacio Tellechea Idígoras, *Fray Bartolomé Carranza: Documentos históricos*, 7 vols, Archivo Documental Español 18 etc. (Madrid: Real Academia de la Historia, 1962–94), III. 7–9 ; Pedro Salazar de Mendoza, *Vida y sucesos prósperos y adversos de Don Fr. Bartolomé Carranza y Miranda...por el Doctor Salazar de Mendoza, Canónigo Penitencial de la Santa Iglesia de Toledo. Dada a luz por D. Antonio Valladares de Sotomayor. Con Privilegio Real y las licencias necesarias* (Madrid: Joseph Doblado, 1788), pp. 1–11 ; Gonzalo de Arriaga, *Historia del Colegio de San Gregorio de Valladolid*, ed. Manuel M. Hoyos, 3 vols (Valladolid: Imp. Cuesta, 1928–40), I. 344–9.

4   Tellechea, *Documentos*, III. 12 ('Preguntas del interrogatorio de abonos', 18–20).

planted were uprooted long before they had come to ripeness and harvesting. The fields it inherited had, moreover, given its predecessor a less than easy time. During Edward VI's reign Peter Martyr Vermigli, Regius Professor of Theology in Oxford, had found his auditors very recalcitrant. He had not enjoyed the public disputations of the University and of Christ Church in which he had had no choice but to participate and to preside. 'I have,' he wrote to Bullinger on 1 June 1550, 'a continual struggle with my adversaries, who are indeed most obstinate.' It was these latter that John Burcher had in mind when he wrote to Bullinger on 10 August 1551 after Bucer's death intimating that 'the Cambridge men [will not be found] so perversely learned as Master Peter found those at Oxford', and suggesting that 'their studies have always been of a purer character than those at Oxford'.[5] Two decades ago G.D. Duncan found that the Edwardian regime had utterly failed to effect significant changes in Oxford. Even at Cambridge, where Bucer had had a warmer welcome from the younger scholars in his lecture hall, 'the ancient members, learned and unlearned', Burcher admitted, had suspected them of heresy.[6]

Shortly after her accession Queen Mary wrote to the universities, on 20 August 1553, requiring them to observe and live by their ancient statutes, such as had been in force before her brother's reign. She made her expectations clear in expressing a desire that university men should 'by there preachyng instruct and confirm the rest of our subiects'.[7] The text of the letter she actually sent out, a gentler and far less threatening version of the surviving first draft, appeared to take the universities' good will for granted and sought rather to encourage than to compel. The approach appears to have been welcomed by an overwhelming majority of Oxford men and by at least a sizeable minority in Cambridge. It squares well with Elizabeth Russell's suggestion that Mary 'was bent... on revitalizing English Catholicism as it had been for centuries', rather than on a precocious 'Counter-Reformation' project.[8] Oxford's

5 Hastings Robinson (ed. and tr.), *Original letters relative to the English Reformation, written during the reigns of King Henry VIII, King Edward VI, and Queen Mary: Chiefly from the Archives of Zurich*, 2 vols, Publications of the Parker Society 37–8 (Cambridge: Cambridge University Press, 1846–7), II. 481, 680.

6 G. D. Duncan, 'The Heads of Houses and religious change in Tudor Oxford 1547–1558', *Oxoniensia*, 45 (1980), pp. 226–34; Robinson, *Original letters*, II. 680.

7 John Lamb (ed.), *A collection of letters, statutes, and other documents from the MS Library of Corp[us] Christ[i] Coll[ege], illustrative of the history of the University of Cambridge* (London: John W. Parker, 1838), pp. 165–6: Queen Mary to Bishop Stephen Gardiner of Winchester, Chancellor of Cambridge University, 20 August 1553. See also Rex H. Pogson, 'Cardinal Pole: Papal legate to England in Mary Tudor's reign', unpubl. doctoral dissertation, University of Cambridge (1972), p. 345.

8 Elizabeth Russell, 'Marian Oxford and the Counter-Reformation', in *The Church in pre-Reformation society: Essays in honour of F. R. H. Du Boulay*, ed. Caroline M. Barron and Christopher Harper-Bill (Woodbridge: The Boydell Press, 1985), pp. 212–27 (pp. 212–13).

existing Chancellor, Sir John Mason, appeared ready enough to collaborate with the new order and even insisted in a letter to the University on 15 April 1554 that an adequate appointment be made to the apparently moribund Lady Margaret Professorship of Theology.[9] Bishop Stephen Gardiner, rapidly restored to the chancellorship of Cambridge, actively promoted a return to Catholic practice there, as well as in the several important colleges of Oxford of which he was Visitor. In Oxford he found New College and Corpus Christi College mainly Catholic in sentiment and only at Magdalen College, where Protestantism had apparently gone far deeper than elsewhere, did he have to resort to wholesale expulsions in late 1553 and in 1554. In both Oxford and Cambridge many Protestants departed of their own accord as soon as the Queen's intentions became clear. Only three heads of house were deprived initially in Oxford. In Cambridge most heads had to be replaced, but afterwards, as in Oxford, restoration and revival on the ground was left by the government for some time in the hands of the chancellors, vice-chancellors, college visitors, and heads of house.[10] Gardiner, it is true, decided to require an oath of religious conformity from Cambridge men in March 1554 and obtained subscription to fifteen articles of religious belief by all regents and non-regents the following year, but he was dealing with a university where Protestantism was better established and where colleges often lacked episcopal Visitors, and no such demand seems to have been regarded as necessary in Oxford.[11] The often rather unsympathetic treatment of the universities by the Henrician and Edwardian regimes probably made for a spirit of co-operation with the Queen's expressed good intentions towards them. The Queen and her advisers evidently believed she would win co-operation more by the carrot than by the stick, and in May 1554 she granted the University of Oxford three ex-monastic rectories which trebled its income. The impact of such a gesture can be too easily underestimated in the aftermath of two reigns noted for spoliation. The University's letter and address to her dated 28 June 1554 was warmly appreciative of what she had done to date to restore ancient discipline. Her general abstention from interference in the choice of college heads and fellows throughout the reign must have been equally welcome.[12] The generosity of the Queen towards the universities extended, incidentally, beyond the grave, for she left by will to both of them the sum of £500 to relieve poor scholars.[13] Her Spanish husband, the Cardinal Legate, and Carranza appeared

---

9   OUA, NEP/supra/Reg. I, fol. 143v (copy).

10 Russell, 'Marian Oxford', pp. 215–16.

11 Lamb, *Letters*, pp. 170–76.

12 Wood, *History*, II. 118; *CSPD*, I. 62; Russell, 'Marian Oxford', p. 214.

13 J. Bass Mullinger, *The University of Cambridge*, 3 vols (Cambridge: Cambridge University Press, 1873–1911), II. 165.

on the scene in England only after a certain style of handling the universities was already in place.

Cardinal Pole's first priority after his arrival in November 1554 was reconciliation and in Oxford University's Archives there is a general dispensation and faculty for reconciling heretics issued by him in March 1555.[14] Pope Julius III's Bull of 8 March 1554 granting Pole powers to reunite England to the Holy See had explicitly mentioned persons in colleges and universities.[15] The Legate's powers, as his register covering the period up to 16 July 1557 shows, enabled him to extend the Catholic regime's benevolence towards scholars by means of dispensations for beneficed students to reside at the universities and for those he deemed learned to be ordained despite canonical impediments.[16]

No trace of direct Spanish influence on the University of Cambridge during the reign survives, but in Oxford there was a very different state of affairs. Two Spanish Dominicans appeared there in the latter stages of the processes against Cranmer, Latimer, and Ridley in which both were involved.[17] The senior of the two was Fray Pedro de Soto who arrived in the country around the beginning of May 1555 at the direct bidding of the Cardinal Legate. He had been confessor to the Emperor Charles V and had latterly been a close ally of the Cardinal Bishop of Augsburg in establishing a Catholic redoubt at the University of Dillingen, where he had held the senior chair of Theology for six years and had engaged in controversy with leading Protestants. The Venetian ambassador in London noted that Pole deferred a great deal to his judgement.[18] Observing while in Oxford that what the University most needed was scholastic theology through a course on the Sentences of Peter Lombard, he had volunteered to undertake the task. Pole discussed the matter with the Lord Chancellor, Bishop Gardiner, and, on his advice, requested the Queen to convert the Regius Professorship of Hebrew, which had few or no auditors, to this purpose. The interests of the incumbent Professor, Richard Bruerne,

---

14 OUA, WPβ/M/22. See also Bodleian Library, MS Twyne 7, fol. 147v (p. 88).

15 David Wilkins (ed.), *Concilia Magnae Britanniae et Hiberniae, a synodo Verolamiensi, AD 446 ad Londinensem, AD 1717*, 4 vols (London: R. Gosling *et al.*, 1737), IV. 91–3.

16 Lambeth Palace Library, microfilm copy of Pole's Legatine Register (Bibliothèque Municipale de Douai MS 922); Christina H. Garrett, 'The Legatine Register of Cardinal Pole 1554–57', *Journal of Modern History*, 13 (1941), pp. 189–94 ; Thomas F. Mayer, *Reginald Pole: Prince and prophet* (Cambridge: Cambridge University Press, 2000), p. 255 (Professor Mayer, in the passage cited, and in a private communication, has corrected the dating of the final Register entry given by Garrett from September to July); Pogson, 'Cardinal Pole', pp. 347–8.

17 Wood, *History*, II. 125–6; Richard Monckton Milnes and James Gairdner (eds), 'Bishop Cranmer's recantacyons', *Miscellanies of the Philobiblon Society*, 15/iv (1877–84), pp. 51 ff.

18 *CSPV*, VI/i. 8–9, Pole to Cardinal of Augsburg, 19 January 1555; pp. 60–63, Giovanni Michiel to the Doge and Senate, 6 May 1555.

were to be considered.[19] Soto is duly listed in the Dean's Register of Christ Church as if Professor of Hebrew from October 1555 to August 1556,[20] and Bruerne, who seems in fact to have continued formally to hold the chair, was consoled in 1557 with a canonry of Windsor.[21] Soto was a very distinguished theologian, a doctor of theology who had, like Carranza, received the accolade of Mastership from his own Order. He was incorporated Doctor of Divinity at Oxford on 14 November 1555 and was rumoured shortly afterwards, with Pole's enthusiastic support, to be on the point of becoming a Cardinal.[22] He set about undoing the harm perceived as having been done by Peter Martyr during the previous reign and, except when working for the Legate at the national church Synod, devoted himself to this task until summoned away from the country by the Emperor in August 1556. Carranza had been, since the middle of 1555, Soto's religious superior in England, and will certainly have been consulted on his undertaking in Oxford, even if the surviving evidence suggests that Soto was very much the Cardinal Legate's man.[23]

The second Spanish Dominican to play a significant role in Oxford was Juan de Villagarcía. A Valladolid pupil and protégé of Carranza, he came to England with his master in mid-1554 and spent the next year working with him around the Court, and acting as confessor to the Queen.[24] By his own account he went to Oxford in October 1555, in time to be involved in the last days of Bishops Latimer and Ridley and to tackle Archbishop Cranmer—with more success than Pedro de Soto. He may have been for a time Carranza's confessor, as otherwise it is hard to explain the older man's signing off as 'filius tuus' or 'tuus filius' in letters to him. Carranza later declared that he had taken Villagarcía with him to England specifically with a view to his engaging in university teaching.[25] The Dominican incorporated as Bachelor of Divinity

19 ibid., pp. 225–7, Pole to King Philip, 26 October 1555; portion of Latin text cited in Venancio D. Carro, *El Maestro Fray Pedro de Soto OP (confesor de Carlos V) y las controversias político-teológicas en el siglo XVI*, 2 vols, Biblioteca de Teólogos Españoles 15 (Salamanca: Convento de San Esteban, 1931–50), I. 246–7, from *Epistolarum Reginaldi Poli et aliorum ad ipsum pars quinta*, ed. Angelo M. Quirini, 5 vols (Brescia: Rizzardi, 1744–57).
20 Information communicated by Mrs J. Curthoys, Archivist of Christ Church, Oxford.
21 *DNB*, *s.v.* 'Bruerne, Richard 1519?–1565'.
22 *CSPV*, VI/i. 284–5, Pole to Bernardino Scotti, ?17 December 1555.
23 Justo Cuervo (ed.), *Historiadores del Convento de San Esteban de Salamanca*, 3 vols (Salamanca: Imprenta Católica Salmanticense, 1914–15), III. 597; OUA, NEP/supra/Reg., I, fol. 155v; *CSPV*, VI/i. 346, Pole to King Philip, 17 February 1556; Carro, *Soto*, I. 51; *CSPV*, VI/i. 588–9, Giovanni Michiel to the Doge and Senate, 2 September 1556.
24 Tellechea, *Documentos*, II/i. 487; Arriaga, *Historia*, II. 135, 138. He is sometimes called 'Garcina' or 'Joannes Fraterculus' in English sources.
25 Monckton Milnes and Gairdner, 'Cranmer's recantacyons', pp. 43, 51–2; Tellechea, *Carranza y Pole*, pp. 257–73; id., *Documentos*, V. 200.

in the University on 14 November.[26] A few days later he was elected to the Readership in Theology of Magdalen College, the Cardinal's own *alma mater*, a position which he held until a successor was appointed on 7 July 1557, although he resided at Lincoln College.[27] His lectures, by the foundational statutes, were open to all members of the University.[28] In 1556, perhaps to reinforce his position and to raise the Dominican profile in Oxford on the departure of Soto, Villagarcía was also appointed Regius Professor of Theology when the incumbent, Dr Richard Smith, resigned, probably with official encouragement.[29] This post he held until the end of the reign, just before which, on 11 July 1558, he took the degree of Doctor of Divinity. According to Anthony Wood's account Miles Windsor had praised his extraordinary range of philosophical and theological learning and had called him 'scientissimus'.[30]

While these two distinguished Dominican theologians probably found most Oxford men ready enough to welcome their teaching, there can be little doubt that this intravenous injection of Spanish theology did much to eradicate such traces of Protestant thinking as survived and to reinforce Catholic sentiment. Nicholas Sanders was full of praise for Soto and Villagarcía in the oration he made to welcome the legatine visitors to Oxford.[31] On the other side of the confessional divide, in a letter of 20 March 1559 John Jewel told Peter Martyr, the former Regius Professor of Theology, that 'two famous virtues, namely, ignorance and obstinacy, have wonderfully increased at Oxford since you left it: religion, and all hope of good learning and talent is altogether abandoned'. A little later, on 22 May, he informed Henry Bullinger:

26 OUA, NEP/supra/Reg. I, fol. 155r.

27 Magdalen College Archives, MS 730(a), Vice-President's Register I. 25, 29 (fols. 13v, 15v); William D. Macray, *A register of the members of St Mary Magdalen College, Oxford, from the foundation of the College*, ns, 8 vols (London: Henry Frowde, 1894-1915), II. 31, 90. For his statement before the Spanish Inquisition about his having resided at Lincoln College, see Tellechea, *Documentos*, II/ii. 513. He has left no trace in the records of Lincoln College.

28 'Statutes of Magdalen College, Oxford', in *Statutes of the colleges of Oxford, with royal patents of foundation, injunctions of visitors, and catalogues of documents relating to the University, preserved in the Public Record Office*, 3 vols (Oxford: J. H. Parker, 1853), II. 47; Henry A. Wilson, *Magdalen College*, University of Oxford College Histories (London : F. E. Robinson, 1899), p. 39.

29 G. D. Duncan, 'Public lectures and professorial chairs', in *The collegiate University*, ed. James McConica, History of the University of Oxford 3 (Oxford: Clarendon Press, 1986), pp. 335–61 (p. 353).

30 OUA, NEP/supra/Reg. I, fol. 176r; Wood, *History*, II. 842–3.

31 John Strype, *Ecclesiastical memorials relating chiefly to religion, and the reformation of it, shewing the various emergencies of the Church of England*, 3 vols (6 parts) (London: John Wyat, 1721), III. 230.

Our universities are so depressed and ruined, that at Oxford there are scarcely two individuals who think with us, and even they are so dejected and broken in spirit, that they can do nothing. That despicable friar Soto and another Spanish monk, I know not who, have so torn up by the roots all that Peter Martyr had so prosperously planted, that they have reduced the vineyard of the Lord into a wilderness. You would scarcely believe so much desolation could have been effected in so short a time.

On the previous day John Parkhurst had written to Henry Bullinger complaining that Oxford was 'as yet a den of thieves, and of those that hate the light. There are but few gospellers there, and many papists'.[32]

When, therefore, the Legate's national Church Synod opened at Westminster, much of the theological teaching publicly imparted in Oxford was already entrusted to two Spanish friars. At the Synod, Pole, as he told King Philip by letter, employed both Carranza and Soto.[33] This council was prorogued in February 1556, intendedly until November but, in fact, never to meet again. The bishops were to return to their dioceses for Lent and to perform visitations before the next synodal session, and the universities, too, were to be visited. Carranza had been party to these decisions.[34] The initial context, therefore, of the visitations carried out in Oxford and Cambridge over the next year or so was that of the Synod, and the objective was explicitly ecclesiastical and religious. Formal commissions were issued by Cardinal Pole as *Legatus a latere*, and the records, such as they are, of both universities leave no room for doubt in this respect. The visitations were legatine. When, eight decades later, the Anglican Archbishop William Laud sought to vindicate a metropolitical right of visitation in the universities, the legatine/papal nature of Pole's intervention was generally deemed to invalidate it as a precedent.[35] It is curious, therefore, that Carranza alone, writing a few years later during his travails with the Inquisition in Spain, should have suggested that these visitations had been performed by royal as well as legatine authority.[36] This probably reflects his prior experience in Spanish universities where royal visitations since the time of the Reyes Católicos had been controversial, due in good measure to a perceived secular intromission into what had been regarded for a

---

32 Hastings Robinson (ed. and tr.), *The Zurich letters, comprising the correspondence of several English bishops and others, with some of the Helvetian Reformers, during the early part of the reign of Queen Elizabeth*, 2 vols, Publications of the Parker Society 50–51 (Cambridge : Cambridge University Press, 1842), pp. 11, 33, 29.

33 *CSPV*, VI/i. 346, Pole to King Philip, 17 February 1556.

34 Tellechea, *Documentos*, III. 25.

35 John Rushworth (ed.), *Historical collections*, 4 parts in 7 vols (London: T. Newcomb for G. Thomason, 1659–1701), II. 331. Laud argued that Pole's acting as *Legatus a latere* did not invalidate his capacity to act as metropolitan archbishop.

36 Tellechea, *Documentos*, III. 25; id., *Carranza y Pole*, p. 96.

long time before as an essentially papal jurisdiction.[37] At the same time the university he knew best, that of Valladolid, had thrown off the unpopular papal constitutions of Salamanca imposed on it by ecclesiastical authority and had received in 1545 new Statutes from Charles, King Philip's father.[38] In any event, Carranza's Spanish academic background will certainly have imbued him with a special sensitivity to such matters and made him keen to avoid juris-dictional conflict if possible. In the English context, as he must have well known, Letters Patent of Philip and Mary had cleared the way in 1554 for Cardinal Pole to enter the country 'with his said authority of jurisdiction, and to use and exercise his authority legatine by himself, or by his officers and ministers under him, of whatsoever nation, country, state, or condition soever they be, denizens or not denizens, and that his said repair with his said authority is unto us most acceptable'. On 2 November 1555 further Letters Patent in the names of Philip and Mary had been issued with the imminent Synod in view:

> We to avoid all daungers, dowte, and ambiguitie, which might arise in that case by reason of any lawes, statutes, customes, or prerogatives of us, or of this our realme of England; and for the more ample declaration of our said lettres patents, have graunted, declarid and signified, and by thes presents do graunte, declare, and signifie, that our will, pleasure, and consent is; that as well the said most reverend father cardinal Pole, legate de latere of the popes hollyness and the see apostolike, may freely without lett of us, or danger of any of our said lawes, statutes, customes, or prerogatives, caule and celebrate the said synode, or any other synode hereafter, at his will and pleasure; and in the same synode ordeyne and decree any holsom canons for the good lief and ordour of the clergye of this our realme of England, or of any other of our realmes and dominions, and do any other thing for the better executing of their office and duetie.[39]

These orders alone might have warranted Carranza's claiming of royal authority for the university visitations, but there had been yet another. For the Queen had sent a memorandum in her own hand to Pole during the Synod with five suggestions with regard to religious affairs. The third of these proposed a

---

37 For a later overview of this process, written from the perspective of a university deter-mined to assert a papally guaranteed jurisdictional independence of the Crown, see Salamanca, 1625, with a twelve-page dedication to the University by delegates who had produced the compilation.

38 For the abrogation of the Salamancan Constitutions and the new Statutes see *Estatutos de la insigne Universidad Real de Valladolid: Con sus dos visitas, y algunos de sus reales privilegios, y bullas apostolicas* (Valladolid: Bartolomé Pórtoles, 1651); also Isidoro González Gallego, 'La Universidad de Valladolid y los poderes institucionales', in *Historia de la Universidad de Valladolid*, ed. Jesús M. Palomares Ibáñez and Luis A. Ribot García, 2 vols (Valladolid: Universidad de Valladolid, 1989), I. 299–333. It should be noted that this Spanish King (Charles I) had uniquely enjoyed a pseudo-universal imperial jurisdiction (as the Emperor Charles V) which alone could rival that of the Pope.

39 Wilkins, *Concilia*, IV. 109–10, 130–31.

visitation of the dioceses and universities by persons approved by herself and the Cardinal.[40] It is far from inconceivable that Carranza, ever shuttling between Queen and Legate, had played a part in preparing this document, and thereby in moving visitations by a twofold authority which, to the Spanish mind at least, might obviate potential objections.

Carranza's direct personal role in visiting is far from clear. No contemporary source suggests that he was ever in Cambridge, and we must conclude that, whatever his influence from Lambeth and the Court, he played no part *in situ* there. Although even Nicholas Sanders, who was to become a good friend, failed to mention him when naming the five official commissioners for Oxford in his speech of welcome, Anthony Wood certainly suspected that other commissioners had accompanied the Visitors known to him by name.[41] Carranza stated a few years later that King Philip, leaving for Flanders in 1555 but aware of the need to settle religious affairs in England, for which it would be necessary to call a Synod and visit the universities, had singled him out to stay behind in order to advise in these matters. Pole frequently consulted Carranza on religious affairs, including these visitations, and the friar had often been sent by the Queen to the Legate to discuss such affairs. Villagarcía later explicitly affirmed that Carranza had once spent fifteen days in Oxford. We have, moreover, Carranza's own word for his actual participation in the visiting of Oxford University and its thirteen colleges.[42]

The Visitors began their work in Oxford about 20 July 1556, and among Carranza's papers is a copy of the oration of welcome made by Nicholas Sanders which he said he had heard *viva voce*.[43] It was perhaps politic for a Spaniard whose essential role was as representative of King Philip to keep his head down, but the utter lack of official notice taken of his presence in both university and college records is surprising. The Visitor closest to Pole was Niccolò Ormanetto, Datary and friend to the Legate. Ormanetto had graduated Doctor of Laws of Padua at the height of that university's international prestige, and had had plenty of administrative experience on difficult visitations in the diocese of Verona under his early patron, Bishop Gian Matteo Giberti. He was later to serve as Bishop of Padua from 1570 to his death in January 1577.[44]

40 *CSPV*, VI/iii. 1647–8 : 'Opinion of the Most Serene Queen of England which she wrote with her own hand and gave to his Right Reverend Lordship the Legate [Cardinal Pole] at the time when the Synod was held [translated from the English tongue]', para. 3.
41 Strype, *Memorials* (1721), III. 229–31; Wood, *History*, II. 131 : 'with some others, whose names I cannot yet learn'.
42 Tellechea, *Documentos*, I. 347, II/ii. 502, 514, III. 26.
43 Wood, *History*, II. 131; Tellechea, *Documentos*, V. 230.
44 Cuthbert Robinson, *Nicolo Ormaneto : A papal envoy in the sixteenth century* (London : Catholic Repository, 1920), pp. 7–10; Pius B. Gams, *Series episcoporum Ecclesiae Catholicae* (Graz: Akademische Druck und Verlagsanstalt, 1957), p. 798.

If the reader were to take at face value the assertions made by Ormanetto's fellow-Italian, Priuli, in a letter to the Archbishop of Ragusa dated 15 December 1556, he might receive the impression that the Datary alone had carried out the visitation.[45] There can be no doubt of his competence, or of the Legate's confidence in him, but he was by no means sole Visitor. The formally senior Visitor, accepted as such by the English sources, in keeping with his ecclesiastical rank and the intra-synodal nature of the act, was Bishop James Brooks of Gloucester, an Oxford Doctor of Divinity, formerly Master of Balliol and Vice-Chancellor, who had been almoner and chaplain to Bishop Gardiner.[46] The third named Visitor was Walter Wright, Archdeacon of Oxford, a Doctor of Civil Law of the University who had served as Principal of Peckwater Inn and as Vice-Chancellor from 1547 to 1550. He had been one of Bishop Gardiner's commissioners for visiting colleges in Oxford in late 1553.[47] The Visitors' most venerable figure in terms of years was Robert Morwen, President of Corpus Christi College since 1537.[48] But the most active of them, at least rivalling Ormanetto in the role he played, was Henry Cole. He had been a Fellow of New College from 1521 to 1540, during which time he had travelled abroad, certainly to Padua and Paris, in pursuit of juridical learning. In the latter year he received his Doctorate in Civil Law at Oxford, and went on to serve as Warden of New College from 1542 to 1551. He had been active, with Brooks, in handling the Protestant bishops in Oxford and had become a Canon of Westminster and Provost of Eton in 1554. Trusted by Pole, he was to be appointed by the Archbishop Vicar-General and Dean of the Arches in 1557.[49] That the key working Visitors were Ormanetto and Cole is attested also by the fact that they were the only two of the five to be included also in the commission to visit Cambridge months later, and that they alone are recorded as having continued to treat with the University after the formal first stage of the commissioners' work was completed (see below, p. 171). As was noted by Sanders in his oration, the named visitatorial body of five had, perhaps surprisingly, a clear majority of jurists, and it may be that Carranza was present specifically to add theological expertise.[50]

45 Mark A. Tierney, *Dodd's Church history of England*, 5 vols (Westmead : Gregg International Publishers, 1971), II, Appendix, item XXXI, Aloysio Priuli to Lodovico Beccatello, Archbishop of Ragusa, 15 December 1556 (Pole, *Epistolarum*, V. 345).

46 Alfred B. Emden, *A biographical register of the University of Oxford AD 1501 to 1540* (Oxford: Clarendon Press, 1974), pp. 73–4 (as 'Brokes'); *DNB*, as 'Brooks, James 1512–1560'.

47 Emden, *Biographical register*, p. 641 (as 'Wryght'); Wood, *History*, II. 120.

48 Emden, *Biographical register*, p. 404; *DNB*, under 'Morwen, Morwent, or Morwyn, Robert 1486?–1558'.

49 Emden, *Biographical register*, pp. 128–9; *DNB*, under 'Cole, Henry 1500?–1580'.

50 Lamb, *Letters*, pp. 181–3, etc.; Strype, *Memorials* (1721), III. 231.

There has always been confusion about the length and stages of the visitation, due to the deficiencies of documentary sources and, indirectly, to Wood's
handling of what does appear in them. A reconstruction of what happened,
necessarily conjectural in part, will help to elucidate Carranza's role.

It is unclear how long the first stage of actual visitation by commissioners
on the ground in Oxford lasted, but it may well have been the fortnight
('quinze días') that Carranza is said by Villagarcía to have spent in the University. The visitation of the colleges has left little trace in the records. At Merton
College, for example, the Register mentions only the handing over of a sealed
inventory requested by the Visitors on 1 August.[51] To assist their work, the
commissioners had received from Pole thirty articles of enquiry, some of
which made explicit reference to the Synod. The expressed concerns related
to religious orthodoxy and practice, the behaviour of those in authority, the
administration of property, heretical or scandalous persons and books, and,
only marginally, academic exercises.[52] They by no means suggest a coherent or
thorough programme of reform, but rather a determination that the University should be orthodox, on an even disciplinary keel, and properly run. Given
the nature of the London Synod, of which the visitation was in some measure
a part, this is unsurprising. If Carranza is to be believed as regards Pole's
consulting him in such matters, he was almost certainly involved in drawing
the articles up. At the departure of the non-resident commissioners, the
visitation appears to have been formally continued, as in Cambridge a little
later, at the Cardinal's pleasure.[53] Wood writes of a closure in April of the
following year, but the passage in the University Register to which he refers
does not support such an inference.[54] As far as can be judged from the
documentary evidence, there was never a formal winding up. While it is not
entirely clear that Pole ever formally laid down his legateship, or indeed that
Pope Paul IV properly completed its revocation, it may be that the visitation
effectively lapsed with the Cardinal cautiously ceasing active exercise of this
function from around July 1557.[55] Because, however, Sir John Mason had

51 Tellechea, *Documentos*, II/ii. 514; John M. Fletcher (ed.), *Registrum Annalium Collegii Merto-
    nensis 1521–1567*, Oxford Historical Society ns 23 (Oxford: Clarendon Press for the OHS,
    1974), p. 156. The Register lists only the same five Visitors as Wood and Sanders.
52 Bodleian Library, MS Twyne 7, pp. 155–7.
53 Lamb, *Letters*, p. 223.
54 Wood, *History*, II. 135; OUA, NEP/supra/Reg. I, fol. 166v.
55 Garrett, 'Legatine Register', p. 189, but see also Mayer, *Reginald Pole*, pp. 309–17. Revo-
    cation of the Legatine authority was pronounced by the Pope in Consistory on 9 April
    1557 and confirmed in Consistory on 14 June. It continued, however, to be resisted by
    the Queen. Professor Mayer, in a private communication, has drawn attention to
    serious doubts about the effectiveness of the revocation, and indeed to some late
    references to Pole as Legate in Chancery *significavits*.

been induced to resign the University's chancellorship in October 1556, and had been replaced by Pole, there was to be no break in the Cardinal's capacity for authoritative intervention in the University.[56] This may, in part at least, explain the confusion. The timing of Pole's admission to the Chancellorship had in all probability a deeper significance. In a letter of 10 November 1556 presented to the University by Dr Cole, unaccompanied by any other Visitor, and by the new Vice-Chancellor, Dr Reynolds, the Cardinal accepted the office and, being now the University's internal head as well as Legate, provided injunctions which were to remain in force provisionally, until such time as a commission of delegates from each of the faculties, including that of the restored Canon Law, should have revised all the statutes and made new provisions where necessary. Cole and Reynolds were to make the Cardinal's mind clear to Convocation and the faculty delegates were to work closely with them.[57]

Now this manner of proceeding in what might be termed the second, or 'internal' stage of visitation, following the more specifically religious or intra-synodal intervention, mirrors the style favoured by the Spanish royal government in reforming universities over the previous half-century (namely, one or two Visitors appearing with letters and settling new statutes alongside local delegates, with an external confirmation to follow) and it may well be that Carranza's influence is to be seen here.[58] If he was indeed behind the form of the action, he was probably also party to the choice of Cole as agent. In a Convocation held on 14 November 1556 and continued the next day, the provisional injunctions brought up by Dr Cole were read and fourteen delegates were elected for work on the statutes. The injunctions were, as was doubtless anticipated, mainly concerned with doctrinal and related matters. Some good advice, however, was proffered to lecturers. It is impossible to assess Carranza's contribution to the text as a whole, but there is a distinctly Spanish flavour in one point at least. Lecturers were asked to stay behind after their lectures to resolve students' doubts. This required availability of teachers 'al poste' after lectures was an ancient tradition in some Spanish universities and, if not the direct contribution of Carranza, it may reflect a practice recently introduced in Oxford by Soto and Villagarcía. The regulation was later incorporated into the 1636 Laudian code of statutes, without attribution.[59]

---

56 OUA, NEP/supra/Reg. I, fol. 162v.

57 ibid., fol. 163v.

58 For a near-contemporary account of the Salamanca pattern, see Pedro Chacón, *Historia de la Universidad de Salamanca*, ed. Ana M. Carabias Torres (Salamanca: Ediciones Universidad de Salamanca, 1990).

59 *Statuta antiqua Universitatis Oxoniensis*, ed. Strickland Gibson (Oxford: Clarendon Press, 1931), pp. lii, 374; Agueda M. Rodríguez Cruz, *Historia de la Universidad de Salamanca*

Less than a fortnight later, on 23 November, Vice-Chancellor Reynolds wrote to Pole and claimed that progress had already been achieved in reform by the good efforts of Dr Cole. Unfortunately, no details were given, but Reynolds did request that injunctions be sent for redress of abuses noted in the recent visitation of particular colleges and houses.[60]

On 5 May 1557, the University's Convocation had read to it a letter jointly signed by Ormanetto and Cole as 'visitors of the reverend Cardinal and Chancellor of the University' and directed to heads of house, urging them to root out negligence in the studies of the students under their charge. On the same day Convocation received new statutes for halls presented by the Vice-Chancellor for its acceptance.[61] It is possible, given the Vice-Chancellor's concern, that it was on these statutes that Cole had actually worked with delegates during his visit at the end of the previous year. Perhaps because of priority given to this matter, it would seem that nothing much had yet been achieved towards ordering and reforming the University's statutes as a whole, and new delegates from each of the faculties were nominated for this purpose at the same meeting. It is a striking coincidence, although no more can be claimed, that after mid-1557, when Carranza departed, nothing more is recorded of reforming the statutes for the remainder of the reign. It must also be acknowledged, however, that by the autumn of that year Pole had accepted the lapse of his legateship, and Cole had been entrusted with absorbing new work by the Archbishop of Canterbury.

A provincial ecclesiastical Convocation of Canterbury in January 1558, called by Pole as Archbishop, produced a few decrees treating of universities and schools. Since Carranza was no longer in the country it would be difficult to claim direct influence by him. There was, none the less, perhaps a Spanish flavour to an article requiring that one professor of theology should read a part of the Bible and, scholastic discipline being declared especially necessary in the faculty, another read from the Book of Sentences *or from another scholastic theologian.*[62] Now it was the great Dominican *Catedrático de Prima* of Salamanca, Vitoria, who had openly read the *Summa theologiae* of St Thomas Aquinas instead of the Sentences, even when this practice was not permitted by the statutes,[63] and it is tempting to conjecture that the provincial order reflected a

---

(Madrid and Salamanca: Congregación de Santo Domingo, 1990), p. 189; John Griffiths, *Statutes of the University of Oxford codified in the year 1636 under the authority of Archbishop Laud Chancellor of the University* (Oxford: Clarendon Press, 1888), p. 42.

60 *CSPD*, VI. 446–7.

61 OUA, NEP/supra/Reg. I, fol. 166v.

62 Wilkins, *Concilia*, IV. 158.

63 Luis E. Rodríguez-San Pedro Bezares, *La Universidad Salmantina del Barroco, período 1598–1625*, 3 vols, Acta Salmanticensia: Historia dela Universidad 45 (Salamanca: Universidad de Salamanca, 1986), II. 519.

new practice in Oxford introduced either by Soto and those who, like Sanders, followed him in the converted Hebrew chair, or perhaps by Carranza's own disciple, Villagarcía.

Something must be said of Carranza's attitudes to, and the parts he played in, the processes held in Oxford against the three Protestant bishops, the exhumation and disposal of the remains of Peter Martyr's wife, and the burning of books in the University. Contemporary and near-contemporary accounts of Oxford in Mary's reign, both Catholic and Protestant, suggest that these were the events of greatest significance to have occurred. Theatrical they may have been, but they were not, it can safely be assumed, extrinsic to policy with regard to the universities or mere aberrations, nor would the time and energy expended on them have seemed excessive to men living through those days. All were intended to make lasting impressions on university men in a manner that official regulations, easily circumvented by the traditional academic resort to dispensations, could not.

Carranza was certainly involved in advising Queen and Cardinal on the treatment of those deemed to be heretics, by no means in a lenient direction, and specifically urged toughness with Cranmer.[64] The active role played by his protégé, Villagarcía, in Cranmer's last days points to his interest in what Wood called 'this most noted memorable'.[65] Had Cranmer been shut away somewhere for the term of his earthly life after his recantation, the effect of the performance on the academic world would surely have been far greater than it was after royal insistence on his execution had produced another turnabout on the victim's part.

Carranza claimed to have actively promoted and even initiated the exhumation and dishonourable disposal of the remains of Peter Martyr's wife.[66] This did not take place during the initial stage of visitation but was evidently considered at Lambeth and at Court afterwards. Carranza's knowledge of Spanish inquisitorial practice with the remains of deceased heretics may have suggested the procedure.[67] An order from Pole to the Dean of Christ Church to proceed with exhumation from the Cathedral was not penned until 7 November 1555 and was probably designed to awe the academic community just as the new Vice-Chancellor and Dr Cole were presenting the Legate's provisional injunctions and embarking upon the next stage of reform, which

64 Tellechea, *Carranza y Pole*, pp. 68–70.
65 Wood, *History*, II. 127.
66 Tellechea, *Documentos*, III. 26. On 27 September 1554, Carranza had written to Pole voicing the scruples of some among King Philip's suite as to whether the celebration of Mass was permitted where heretics had been buried, with resultant pollution of churches (Tellechea, *Carranza y Pole*, p. 186). Professor Mayer kindly drew this letter to my attention.
67 I owe this valuable suggestion to John Edwards.

Dr Reynolds expected to be very unpopular.[68] The succeeding regime was to pay its predecessor's sense of theatre a compliment by deliberately and formally reversing the procedure with the exonerated remains to the extent that such an operation was then possible.[69]

Carranza was deeply worried by the ready supply of heretical books in England and there is little doubt that he approved the book-burning that took place in Oxford during the visitation.[70] Wood repeated a tradition that Dr Cole was especially enthusiastic about this burning.[71] As has been noted, however, the named Visitors, including Cole, were mainly lawyers and they must have turned to theologians for an assessment of what was heretical. Here Carranza, formerly a *consultor* to the Valladolid Inquisition and one who had read with official permission many Protestant works, and his associate, Villagarcía, must have been to the fore.[72] We do not know in detail what was burned, although Wood more or less suggests, for what his late account is worth, that there was a concentration on English Bibles and commentaries for this act, and that other heretical books in libraries or private hands were dealt with separately.[73] It is likely in any event that it was the show, and the impression left on the mind of spectators, that counted. In all three of these theatrical public performances we may be seeing a peculiar form of catechesis inspired in some measure, if we are to credit his own claims, by Carranza.

From 1557 we have another important source for Carranza's thinking in respect of the universities and that is his surviving correspondence with Villagarcía, commencing before his departure from England but dating mainly from after that moment. Two points stand out here in the letters available to us.

Firstly, he showed himself very concerned to re-establish a Dominican convent in Oxford, to arrange finance, and to provide English and Spanish friars to staff it.[74] In passing we might add that he was for a while hopeful that another might be set up in Cambridge, but this was abandoned when it was decided—it must be presumed by the Queen or the Cardinal—to give the Franciscans a free run in that university. Carranza, ever a loyal son of St Thomas Aquinas, wryly declared it a mistake to set up a lecture on Scotus—

---

68 Wood, *History*, II. 133–4; *CSPD*, VI. 446–7, Reynolds to Pole, 23 Nov. 1556.

69 Conradus Hubertus (ed.), *Historia vera: De vita, obitu, sepultura, accusatione haereseos, condemnatione, exhumatione, combustione, honorificaq[ue] tanden restitutione beatorum atque doctiss[imorum] Theologorum, D. Martini Buceri & Pauli Fagii . . . Item historia Catharinae Vermiliae, D. Petri Martyris Vermilii castiss[imae] atque piissimae coniugis, exhumatae, eiusdemq[ue] ad honestam sepulturam restitutae* (Strasburg: [Hubertus], 1562), fols. 196r–204r.

70 Tellechea, *Documentos*, I. 347–8.

71 Wood, *History*, II. 132.

72 Tellechea, *Documentos*, III. 13 ('Preguntas del interrogatorio de abonos', 20).

73 Wood, *History*, II. 132.

74 Tellechea, *Carranza y Pole*, pp. 257–73, etc; id., *Documentos*, II/ii. 500.

the Franciscans' great doctor—in Cambridge. Although Carranza had been Vicar-General of his Order in England and his interest in such an establishment was natural enough, there was almost certainly more than an institutional interest at stake in the convent project.[75] For a Spanish Dominican, and especially perhaps for one who had spent long years teaching in a university city without holding a chair, it was almost impossible to conceive of a serious theology faculty in which the Order of Preachers did not play a pivotal role. The universities of Salamanca and Valladolid had been in their origins, and still were in terms of matriculations, overwhelmingly institutions for jurists, students of the Canon and Civil Laws. Spanish theology faculties were largely the preserve of religious and had, indeed, in good measure owed their practical existence to them.[76] Among the religious, the Dominicans predominated and often held the senior chairs, the *Cátedra de Prima* and the *Cátedra de Vísperas*. The pairing of Soto and Villagarcía in Oxford had for a time reproduced at least an appearance of this Spanish state of affairs in England's premier university, and Carranza will surely have wanted to institutionalize this to the degree that local circumstances might permit. He went so far in his correspondence with Villagarcía as to suggest that a Spanish Dominican could live as well in England, and specifically (as the context seems to imply) in Oxford, as in Valladolid.[77] It is interesting to note in passing that the 1558 provincial Convocation of Canterbury proposed that restored religious houses should send some of their more apt members to study in one or other of the two universities.[78]

Secondly, Carranza's letters display a constant interest in a small group of friends, almost entirely from New College, who had gathered around Villagarcía and who had kept up a correspondence with him, too. He evidently had high hopes of them, and they were not unworthy of his esteem. The eldest and most distinguished of them was Nicholas Sanders, who had entered New College in 1546 and, perhaps in part to avoid the study of theology under Edwardian conditions, had taken a Bachelor of Civil Law degree in 1551. He became a leading figure in Marian Oxford and, although relatively junior, was selected to deliver a Latin oration welcoming Pole's Visitors. He seems to have taught Canon Law for a time, and, according to Wood, he was one of Soto's successors in imparting scholastic theology through the medium of Bruerne's chair of Hebrew. In 1561 he left Oxford, attended the Council of

75 Tellechea, *Carranza y Pole*, p. 265; Carro, *Soto*, I. 51, makes mention of a letter of the Dominican Father-General dated 23 March 1555 nominating Carranza to this position.
76 Rodríguez-San Pedro, *Universidad*, I. 239–40; Rodríguez, *Historia*, pp. 223–7.
77 Tellechea, *Documentos*, II/ii. 501.
78 Wilkins, *Concilia*, IV. 167; John Venn (ed.), *Grace Book Δ: Containing the records of the University of Cambridge for the years 1542–1589* (Cambridge: Cambridge University Press, 1910), p. xix.

Trent with Cardinal Hosius, was created a Doctor of Divinity in Rome, and
became Regius Professor of Theology at Louvain. He was at one time a
serious candidate for a Cardinal's hat. Thanks to his skill in controversy and
tireless political endeavours to unseat the Queen, he became something of a
bogeyman for the Elizabethan Protestant establishment.[79] His close contemporary, John Rastell, had entered New College in 1547, and was eventually
deprived for religious beliefs in 1560. Carranza dealt with the Legate's Datary
in London on at least one occasion over a dispensation that Rastell wanted
for a scholar in his college.[80] Carranza appears, ambiguously, to speak of
another Rastell, brother to the last-mentioned, but Edward Rastell, the only
sibling known to the records, entered the College only in 1561 and absented
himself soon after.[81] It is, of course, possible that he, or another sibling, had
resided for a time with John Rastell earlier on, but we have no more
information. William Willis entered New College in 1551 and was deprived in
Elizabeth's reign for the same reason as Rastell. After pursuing theological
studies at Louvain, he was licensed at Rome to be ordained a Catholic priest
in 1563. John Fowler was admitted to New College in 1553. He resigned in
1559, and eventually became an important Catholic printer at Antwerp and at
Louvain. The identity of the remaining individual named in Carranza's correspondence, one 'Huarte' or 'Varte', is less easy to establish. It is possible,
despite the lapse of time, that he was the John Hart who entered Douai in
1570, eventually becoming a Jesuit and dying in Poland in 1586. Wood claims
that this man was of Oxford but of unknown college.[82] This cultivation of a
serious and compact group of dedicated and cultivated Catholic scholars at
one of Oxford's more important colleges was clearly a part of Villagarcía's
work in Oxford of which Carranza highly approved and in which he played an
active part. He repeatedly declared in correspondence how dear these men
had become to him.

The visitation of Cambridge must be dealt with very briefly, not because it
was unimportant or badly documented—in fact we have a day-by-day account
of it from the pen of the Esquire Bedel, John Mere—but because there is no
clear evidence that Carranza was actively involved on the ground. He says

79 *DNB*, under 'Sanders or Sander, Nicholas 1530?–1581'; Wood, *History*, II. 843.
80 *DNB*, under 'Rastell, John 1532–1577'; Tellechea, *Carranza y Pole*, p. 258.
81 I am grateful for the information kindly supplied to me by Mrs C. Dalton, Archivist of
    New College, Oxford, on Sanders, John and Edward Rastell, Willis, and Fowler.
82 Joseph Foster, *Alumni oxonienses: The members of the University of Oxford, 1500–1714*, 4
    vols (Oxford and London: Parker and Co., 1891–2), under 'Willes, William' and 'Fowler,
    John'; Godfrey Anstruther, *The seminary priests: A dictionary of the secular clergy of England
    and Wales, 1558–1850*, 4 vols (Ushaw: St Edmund's College, Ware, and Ushaw College
    [I]°; Great Wakering: Mayhew McCrimmon [II–IV], 1968–77), I. 383; *DNB*, under
    'Hart, John d. 1586'.

only that he worked hard on Queen and Cardinal for the disinterment and burning of the remains of the apostate ex-Dominican Martin Bucer during the visitation, and that this led many to abjure their errors there.[83] The business was almost certainly handled by him at Court and in Lambeth. Since, however, the heads of the colleges, according to Mere, determined to petition the Visitors for this macabre performance, with a like treatment of the equally dead Fagius thrown in for good measure, on the very morrow of the visitation's commencement, probably to make ostentatious proclamation of their own orthodoxy, he may not have had much trouble in making it happen. It should be noted that Pole had been Chancellor of Cambridge University since Bishop Gardiner's death in November 1555, and this may explain some of the differences that appear to exist between the two university visitations.[84] Visitation on the ground in Cambridge started on 11 January 1557, only after considerable experience had been gained in Oxford. Certain elements of the Oxford visitation appear to have been assiduously copied. Cole, fresh from his stay in Oxford at the end of 1556, and Ormanetto were again the key Visitors, with three Cambridge personalities including a figurehead bishop accompanying them. The Visitors stayed until 17 February, apparently far longer than in Oxford. They may, however, have wished to complete their work there in a single stage. Although we have no contemporary account for Oxford like that of John Mere for Cambridge, and it is therefore hard to make direct comparisons, it would appear that there was a greater harshness in the treatment of Cambridge. The fact that Dr Cole was an Oxford man may be significant. The remains of Bucer and Fagius were duly exhumed and burned. There was a search for heretical books followed by a ceremonial burning on Market Hill. Colleges were visited. University and college officers were questioned. By 16 February Ormanetto was able to read new regulations to the University, while the visitation was formally declared continued during the Cardinal's pleasure. By 16 May an approved set of legatine statutes, dated at Greenwich in mid-March, arrived with a letter from Pole ordering obedience. The heads of colleges accepted them two days later. The regulations relating to discipline and matters academic were more detailed than those given to Oxford the previous year, but it is hard to detect in specifics anything that points to manifest inspiration from Carranza.[85] The Spanish friar had after all no personal knowledge of the University and no Dominican brother in place to brief him.

---

83 Tellechea, *Carranza y Pole*, p. 96.
84 Lamb, *Letters*, pp. 201–2, from the account of J. Mere. See, however, Mayer, *Reginald Pole*, p. 294, pointing out that Foxe believed the initiative to have been in reality that of the Visitors. Mullinger, *University of Cambridge*, II. 155.
85 Lamb, *Letters*, pp. 200–232, 237–69.

If the advent of Queen Elizabeth unravelled Marian intentions that the two universities should be a force for the catechizing and recatholicization of England, that does not mean that what had gone before was foredoomed to collapse or to failure. In Cambridge the five years of the reign saw a noteworthy increase in the number of degrees taken over the preceding five-year period, in itself probably an indication of returning confidence and rehabilitation.[86] If a rooted Catholicism is, as it surely must be, the best test of success in the regime's own terms, there are good indications that much had been achieved. Even if we need not take the laments of Jewel and others at face value, there can be little doubt that the teaching of Soto and Villagarcía had had a significant effect on Oxford men. The number of those who left Oxford or were expelled for religious reasons at the beginning of Elizabeth's reign, considered by Elizabeth Russell to have been perhaps two or three times as large as that of Protestants departing at the start of Mary's reign, bears eloquent testimony to this. All but one of the Marian heads of house were replaced in the first two years of Elizabeth's reign.[87] It was to take Protestant authorities years to reduce Oxford resistance to change, and decades to eradicate some pockets of Catholic sentiment. The sources may not permit precision in detail, and doubtless he failed to get his own way in everything, but there is no solid reason to doubt the essentials of Carranza's own general claims for the part he played in handling the universities during the reign of Queen Mary. He had developed a real regard for the University of Oxford at least, and for a number of its sons. In June 1558, on the eve of returning to Spain from northern Europe, the Archbishop-elect of Toledo expressed in writing to Villagarcía his intention to work for the sending there of more Spanish friars, to his own mind probably the most powerful contribution he could make to the English academic world.[88]

86 Mullinger, *University of Cambridge*, II. 153.
87 Russell, 'Marian Oxford', pp. 212–13; Duncan, 'Heads of houses', p. 234.
88 Tellechea, *Documentos*, II/ii. 501.

CHAPTER 10

The ghostly after-life of Bartolomé Carranza

Anthony Wright

In the course of Catholic Reform, the name of Bartolomé Carranza was certainly not forgotten. For example, in the Catholic restoration of seventeenth-century France, the Jesuit Jacques Sirmond (1559–1651) published, in three folio volumes, texts of ancient Gallican Councils. After the original edition of 1629 (Paris), a posthumous version of 1655 (Rouen) appeared, which included a broader range still of ancient Conciliar texts, including for instance (p. 478) Canon III of the 'Summa Toletani Concilii III' of 597: 'Ut ne quis extra necessitatem rem ecclesiae alienet'. The title of this Rouen edition, while naming Sirmond as editor, was *Summa omnium Conciliorum et Pontificum collecta per F. Barth. Carranzam Miranden. Ordinis Praedicatorum.* Whatever the intervention of Sirmond or others elsewhere in the volume, the terms of one passage, contextually, certainly voice the aspirations of Carranza himself for the Council of Trent: 'legatis et apostolicae sedis vicariis praesidentibus… et Reginaldo Polo Anglo diacono Cardinali. Verum ea res quid tandem exitus habitura sit, Deus novit. Faxit Christus quam feliciter, et ex voto universorum fidelium inchoatum est, tam feliciter absolvatur'.[1]

Nearer in time and place to Carranza is evidence of his honoured memory in Spain itself, and indeed—however much, of necessity, allusively—at Toledo. The Spanish Provincial Councils of 1565–6, following the conclusion of the Tridentine Council, had not been particularly successful, for various reasons, not least the intervention of Philip II. The Chapter of Toledo had been especially concerned at the meeting of a Provincial Council in the enforced absence of the arrested Archbishop. But the King had insisted that the Council proceed, with the senior bishop of the province, the Bishop of Córdoba, presiding, whatever other claims to seniority there might be—claims such as that of Burgos, and claims, moreover, that were a factor in the original denunciations of Carranza. By 1582, Cardinal Quiroga, archbishop of Toledo

---

1   Jacques Sirmond, *Summa omnium Conciliorum et Pontificum collecta per F. Barth. Carranzam Miranden, Ordinis Praedicatorum* (Rouen: David du Petit Val, 1655), p. 898.

from 1577 until his death in 1594, had bravely decided to attempt another provincial council, aiming to achieve what had not been managed in 1565–6.

Quiroga's 1582 Council proved to have its own difficulties in the event. The then Bishop of Córdoba, as president of the Royal Council of Castile, refused any formal presentation by Quiroga of the papal Bull *In coena Domini*, in defence of ecclesiastical liberties, thus confirming the King's insistence on the need for royal representation at a provincial council. Again, as in 1565–6, such representation precluded Roman authorization to publish the Council's decrees, even after review at Rome, though, on this occasion, Papal confirmation was finally secured.[2]

Among the preparations for Quiroga's Provincial Council, a list was drawn up 'De his que tractari poterunt in concilio provintiali', complete with reference to best contemporary practice, which was that of 'El Card[ena]l Borrhomeo en el [Concilio] Mediolanense'.[3] The selection of 'Materials for the making of new decrees' also drew from some of the aspirations of the various Spanish provincial councils of 1565–6, including 'el Compostellano passado', which had been held in 1565, though in fact at Salamanca. In the case of 'el Provincial de Valencia', in 1565 it had openly discussed, in obedience to Trent, the selection of suitable bishops, in clear contradiction of the King's requirement that the provincial councils then desist from such intrusion into his royal prerogative. But while Roman refusal to authorize publication of provincial decrees from councils at which there was official royal representation continued to pose an obstacle to further provincial legislation in the case of Valencia and elsewhere, reference could still be made in the Quiroga Council list of possible issues for discussion to 'el [Concilio] Diocesano de Valencia del Arzobispo Don Martín de Ayala', evidently held before his death in 1566. It was specially stressed that 'In the five Milan provincial councils of Cardenal Borromeo there are many good things', for indeed Charles Borromeo had held five of his eventually six provincial councils by the time that the Toledan Council of 1582 was being prepared. A reference followed to 'una Synodo Diocesana de Valencia del Arçobispo Don Juan de Ribera', who had been archbishop since 1568 and in due course, and in imitation of Borromeo, held seven diocesan synods there in all. From the same area, with its particular problems until the later expulsion of the Moriscos, there appears to be a borrowing from 'la Synodo Diocesana de

---

2   Anthony D. Wright, *Catholicism and Spanish society under the reign of Philip II, 1555–1598, and Philip III, 1598–1621*, Studies in Religion and Society 27 (Lewiston NY and Lampeter: Edward Mellen Press, 1991), pp. 17, 26, 34–7, 52–5, 68, 82, 85–6, 89, 100–101, 131, 177, 184–5, 201–4, 212; Enrique García Hernán, *La acción diplomática de Francisco de Borja al servicio del pontificado 1571–1572* (Valencia: Generalitat Valenciana, 2000), pp. 47, 137–9.

3   BNM, MS 13019, fols 2r ff.

Orihuela del Ob[is]po Don Gregorio Gallo', who in the then new see (from 1564) was bishop from 1566 to 1577 and held a synod in 1569.[4]

Following this cumulative review of the best examples of the application of Tridentine reform, with that of Borromean Milan at its centre, a further reference was made: 'Michael Thomasio in his book *De Concilio* says that in provincial councils it would be desirable...'.[5] This was apparently Miguel Thomás de Taxequet (1529–78), a Spanish cleric who, after attending the Council of Trent, produced a report to the Pope, in 1563, on its conclusion. What he thought would be well in provincial councils was that 'Every third year inventories should be made—at the expense of incumbents—of the possessions of each benefice and church, and placed in the archives of the church and of the bishop, this being a proposal of Cardinal Pole'.[6] This last was a most telling additional specification, for indeed, as Professor Tellechea originally noted, in Pole's *Registrum*, under 'Articuli inquirendi in visitatione', there were the clauses 'Item, an sint qui habent et iniuste detinent bona ecclesiae. Item, exilitas beneficiorum inquirenda et causa eiusdem'. The Roman edition, of 1562, of the fruits of Pole's Legatine Council of 1555, the *Reformatio Angliae*, allowed Borromeo's first Milanese Synod, of 1565, to copy into its Chapter XXX Pole's decree on pastoral visitation.[7] Roman rehabilitation of Pole, which had followed almost immediately after his own death, and certainly after Paul IV's, allowed Pole's name to appear in the honourable sequence of Iberian, Italian, and other names cited as examples of Catholic reform.[8]

It was, once again, Professor Tellechea who drew attention to the fact that Carranza preceded Pole to England and worked for the Legate's admission to the kingdom, no least as regards the matter of the resolution of the disputed fate of the ex-ecclesiastical lands held by laymen. Tellechea has further argued, on the basis of a close study of the evidence, for the strong possibility that Carranza had a prominent part in the drawing up of the London Synod's decrees, subsequently published at Rome in the *Reformatio Angliae*.[9] More

4 ibid., fols 5r–6v, 8r–v.
5 ibid., fol 8v ff.
6 'Cada tercer año se hagan inventarios de los bienes de cada beneficio y iglesia a costa de los beneficiados, y se pongan en el Archivo de la yglesia y del Ob[is]po y que este fue advertimiento del Cardenal Pole.'
7 José Ignacio Tellechea Idígoras, *Fray Bartolomé Carranza y el cardenal Pole: Un navarro en la restauración católica de Inglaterra (1554–1558)* (Pamplona: Diputación Foral de Navarra, Institución Príncipe de Viana, and CSIC, 1977), p. 307.
8 ibid., pp. 350–51. See also Paolo Simoncelli, *Il caso Reginald Pole: Eresia e santità nelle polemiche religiose del Cinquecento*, Uomini e Dottrine 23 (Rome: Edizioni di Storia e Letteratura, 1977), pp. 192–241.
9 Tellechea, *Carranza y Pole*, p. 332 (and n. 68), 321, 334. See also above, pp. 23, 75.

recently Professor Mayer has stressed the importance of Canon X of the *Reformatio*, applicable to all without special dispensations. This laid down that, in order to prevent if possible the alienation of ecclesiastical property, all administrators and holders of benefices were obliged to inventory their possessions and send a copy to a central record, irrespective of the 1554 suspension by Julius III, for England, of the rules from the time of Paul II on Church property. Thus in this same canon, 'De rebus Ecclesiae non alienandis, et bonorum inventario conficiendo…', of the *Reformatio Angliae ex decretis Reginaldi Poli Cardinalis Sedis Apostolicae Legati anno MDLVI*, published with his *De Concilio*, we read: 'quod quidem inventarium tertio quoque anno, et quoties in eadem Ecclesia seu pio loco alius quis succedit, renovetur: huius autem inventarii duo fiant publica instrumenta'.[10] It follows that:

> Metropolitani vero, et alii locorum Ordinarii in provinciam, et dioecesium suarum visitationibus, sive qui alii eorum vice visitabunt, dicta inventaria apud se habeant, et diligenter inquirant, an eorum, qui in inventario descripta sunt, aliquid desit… exceptis tamen semper iis, quae circa bona ecclesiastica, ante ab Ecclesia ablata, iam auctoritate apostolica statuta sunt, quibus per hoc nullo modo derogari volumus.[11]

Thus, in the context of the attempt in Quiroga's Toledo, despite the obstacles that presented themselves in Philip II's Spain, to resume and continue the interrupted work of Catholic reform prepared at the Council of Trent—but also, crucially, by Pole in Marian England—the reference to the restoration and conservation of ecclesiastical property enabled a local allusion to be implicitly made to the archbishop whose name could not be openly mentioned, but whose figure honourably appeared, like a shadow, behind that of Cardinal Pole.

10 Reginald Pole, *De Concilio liber Reginaldi Poli Cardinalis. Reformatio Angliae ex decretis Reginaldi Poli Cardinalis Sedis Apostolicae Legati anno MDLVI* (Rome: Paulus Manutius, 1562).
11 Thomas F. Mayer, *Reginald Pole: Prince and prophet* (Cambridge: Cambridge University Press, 2000), p. 242.

CHAPTER 11

Pedro Salazar de Mendoza and the first biography of Carranza

Ronald Truman

Carranza was nominated for the archiepiscopal see of Toledo by Philip II in the Low Countries in 1557, and on 27 February 1558 was consecrated at Brussels by Antoine Perrenot de Granvelle, Bishop of Arras and member of Philip's Council of State for the Netherlands. Shortly afterwards, at Antwerp, there came off the presses of the firm of Martin Nuyts (Martín Nucio) the work that was to have such fateful consequences for the rest of his life: his *Commentaries on the Christian Catechism*. Having arrived at Laredo on the north coast of Spain at the start of August, after a voyage of five weeks, he set out for Burgos and then moved on to Valladolid, and from there to Yuste, in Extremadura, just in time to assist at the death of Charles V. He entered Toledo on Thursday 13 October. He was arrested by agents of the Inquisitor General, Fernando de Valdés, in the early hours of Tuesday 22 August 1559. He would remain a prisoner for the next sixteen years and seven months and twenty-four days, as Salazar de Mendoza carefully informs us, at Valladolid and then in Rome. On Saturday 14 April 1576, this long captivity was brought to a conclusion when Pope Gregory XIII pronounced sentence on him. The next day, which was Palm Sunday, Carranza celebrated Mass for the first time since his arrest (he had not even heard Mass in all those years). On Easter Sunday, he said Mass in the chapel of St Thomas Aquinas in the Dominican church of Santa Maria sopra Minerva.[1] The following day, in the course of visiting the seven pilgrim Basilicas of Rome (an obligation laid upon him), he suffered the first sign of urinal obstruction.[2] A week later he was seriously ill: he died on Wednesday 2 May, at three in the morning.

---

1   In 1576 this chapel, also known by the family name of Carafa, already contained the remains of Pope Paul IV; see Isnardo Grossi OP, *The Basilica of Santa Maria sopra Minerva, Roma* (Rome: Padri Domenicani, 2001), pp. 14, 16–18.
2   The seven Roman Basilicas visited by Carranza are San Pietro in Vaticano, San Paulo fuori le Mura, San Giovanni in Laterano, Santa Maria Maggiore, San Lorenzo fuori le Mura, San Sebastiano, and Santa Croce in Gerusalemme.

Carranza's was a life-story that cried out to be recorded in detail and reflected upon: his career as a Dominican theologian, his zeal for the Faith, especially as displayed in England, his elevation to Spain's Primatial See, his mere ten months of activity in that office, his long imprisonment brought about principally by a work composed in London (though printed in Antwerp) while zealously pursuing the heretic, and his death so soon after release. It is nevertheless striking that what appears to be the first Spanish account of Carranza's misfortunes was written by Philip II's official chronicler, Ambrosio de Morales, on the instruction of his master. Morales states this explicitly at his conclusion: he had written it with his own hand on the orders of His Majesty for deposit in the library of El Escorial.[3] This is all the more intriguing in that Carranza's arrest had been carried out with Philip's as well as with Papal authority. On the other hand, it was in the name of Philip that the licence had been issued, first in London and again in Brussels, for the printing of the work that was soon to provide the chief grounds for Carranza's arrest and long imprisonment. Such was the outcome despite the fact, as he explains in his Introduction, that he had written the work—an exposition of the Apostles' Creed, the Ten Commandments, the Seven Sacraments, and the 'Three Chief Works of the Christian Life: Prayer, Fasting, and Charitable Giving', all set out at great length in terms of a discourse that is predominantly untechnical, Biblically based, and often strongly homiletic—in reaction against the many Protestant catechisms published in Germany and Geneva. He had written, he says, in order to assist the parish clergy of Spain (as in the past he had been urged to do) in teaching their people the elements of the Faith. (He repeatedly laments, here in his *Commentaries*, the failure of the bishops as pastors of the Church to instruct their people in a true understanding and practice of their religion—a failure that had left it open, as he acknowledges, to the attacks of Luther and the like.) His aim now was to bring the work out soon in Latin, so that it might be of service elsewhere, especially in England, 'where I know from experience that it is needed'. Later,

---

3   See his 'Prisión de el Arzobispo de Toledo D. Fray Bartolomé de Carranza…sucedida en 22 de agosto, año de 1559', Appendix 1 of Ambrosio de Morales, '*Noticia sobre la vida de D. Fr. Bartolomé Carranza de Miranda…y sobre el proceso que le formó la Inquisición (acompañada de documentos)*', in *Colección de documentos inéditos para la historia de España*, ed. Martín Fernández Navarrete, Miguel Salvá, and Pedro Sainz de Baranda, 113 vols (Madrid: Real Academia de la Historia, 1842–95), V.389–584 (p.584). Morales, who held the Prime Chair (*Cátedra de Prima*) of Rhetoric at Alcalá de Henares for many years, was appointed Chronicler of the Kingdom of Castile in 1563 by the Cortes of that year, and became 'Chronicler to His Majesty' in 1570. In the latter post he appears to have earned much regard from Philip, in part through his contributions to the work of building up the holdings of the Escorial library. See Enrique Redel, *Ambrosio de Morales: Estudio biográfico* (Córdoba: Imprenta del 'Diario', 1908), pp. 124–5, 161–4, 187 n.61, 197–9.

in a written submission of June 1562 to the Spanish Inquisition, he asserted that he had composed his *Catechism* on the instructions of the 1555–6 Synod of London.[4]

Morales, of course, accepts—formally, at least—the sentence finally passed on Carranza by Gregory XIII in 1576 as 'without doubt most just'. However, he at once adds that Carranza was deserving of 'pity and compassion', on the grounds that, having been raised up from the status of a 'poor friar' to the highest ecclesiastical post in Spain by virtue of his great learning and abilities, he had been struck down from the peak of felicity and cast into the ravine of greatest misfortune. These words are much more in tune with his narrative as a whole than is his assent to Pope Gregory's final resolution of the matter. Morales recalls Carranza's zeal in the cause of the Faith in London, where he 'converted more than two hundred heretics', adding that 'it would be an extraordinary and incredible thing were one who drew these souls out of the darkness [of error] to envelop his own soul in shadow'. As to Carranza's response at the moment of his arrest, in his bedroom at night, when the Inquisitor General's writ and Paul IV's Brief extending the reach of the

---

4 See Bartolomé Carranza de Miranda, *Comentarios sobre el Catechismo christiano*, ed. José Ignacio Tellechea Idígoras, 2 vols, BAC 1 (Madrid: Editorial Católico, 1972), I. 49–52, 107, 109, 110, 120; Jose Ignacio Tellechea Idígoras (ed.), *Fray Bartolomé Carranza: Documentos históricos*, 7 vols, Archivo Documental Español 18 etc. (Madrid: Real Academia de la Historia, 1962–94), III. 301–2. Carranza adds here that he had first submitted his *Commentaries* to Cardinal Pole so that he could have the work examined; it then went to 'His Majesty's Council', where it was again approved and its printing was now authorized—specifically for Philip's 'Kingdoms of Castile'. Already before his arrest, in a somewhat imprecise letter of November 1558 to the Inquisition, Carranza had said that he had written his *Commentaries* at the invitation (or with the encouragement) of Pole ('por parecer del Legado del Papa') and of 'all the members of the Council concerned with religion'. He had, he says, been writing a longer version in Latin, but had been too busy to complete it. It is not altogether clear how the writing of this Latin version (which has not so far been found) relates chronologically to the composition of the Spanish text. The latter, he suggests here, was itself completed in the Low Countries. At the same time, Carranza wrote personally to Fernando de Valdés in largely similar terms. In both cases he presents the religious needs of England as the primary reason for the writing of his book (see Tellechea, *Documentos*, i. 346–55). This is clearly at variance with the priorities expressed in the work's 'Dedication' to Philip, but fits with Pole's words to Carranza in a letter sent in June 1558 as he, Carranza, was setting out for Spain: 'ac te quoque Dei providentia voluit, in hoc Anglicanam nostram ecclesiam adjuvare tuo illo docto et pio Catechismo, quem, dum hic esses, Hispanice scripsisti, qui nunc in nostram linguam vertitur': José Ignacio Tellechea Idígoras, 'Pole, Carranza y Fresneda: Cruz y cara de una amistad y de una enemistad', in id., *Fray Bartolomé Carranza y el cardenal Pole: Un navarro en la restauración católica de Inglaterra (1554–1558)* (Pamplona: Diputación Foral de Navarra, Institución Príncipe de Viana, and CSIC, 1977), pp. 119–97 (p. 195).

Inquisition's powers to the episcopate had been read out to him, Morales sides with those who held that he had maintained a composure of spirit that was due 'either to his nature or the intrinsic valour of his sacred character, or his innocence, or all these things together, which is the most likely'. Morales repeatedly stresses the hostility and obstructiveness displayed towards Carranza by the Inquisition and by Valdés in particular. As regards Carranza's death, so soon after his sentence and release from confinement, Morales comments that 'he died like a saint with the greatest show of sorrow and contrition. May our Lord God have granted him His glory'.[5]

This same point is made, though with much more emphasis, by the Dominican Fray Juan López in the *Fourth part of the general history of Saint Dominic and his Order of Preachers*, of 1615.[6] Dominican support for Carranza and his *Catechism* would remain consistently strong through the seventeenth and eighteenth centuries, as we shall see, and, it appears, was so from the outset. Carranza himself claimed, in his 1562 paper submitted to the Inquisition, to have sent the text of the work both to his old college of San Gregorio at Valladolid and to the Dominican college of San Esteban at Salamanca, so that anything in need of revision before printing could be pointed out to him. In the event, 'no error against our Holy Catholic Faith' was found by either.[7] Fray Juan López's account of Carranza, however, is marked not by a concern with theology but by the employment of long-established hagiographical procedures to present Carranza's deathbed utterances, his departure from this life, and the remarkable outpouring of popular grief and devotion at his burial (as claimed here), as those of someone marked by exceptional sanctity. Indeed, at the very moment of his death, we are told, a friar praying in the choir of Santa Maria sopra Minerva saw Saint Antoninus, the fifteenth-century Dominican archbishop of Florence, come down from heaven, embrace Carranza, and say to him (as this friar 'clearly heard'), 'Come and rest from the afflictions you have suffered' (p. 525a). For López, Carranza was a 'servant of God' (p. 528a–b). He gives prominence to Carranza's labours and zeal in England in fighting the heretic and seeking to restore the old order: indeed, he had 'the greater part of the spiritual government of that kingdom' during his time there (p. 519a). López also makes great play of the tribute paid (as we shall see) to Carranza, after his death, by the very pope—Gregory XIII—who had so recently passed sentence on him. On the other hand, the whole story of

5   Morales, 'Prisión', pp. 493, 469, 472, 494.
6   Juan López, *Quarta parte de la historia general de Santo Domingo y de su Orden de Predicadores* (Valladolid: Francisco Fernández de Córdoba, 1615), pp. 518–28. This *Historia general* consists of five volumes, of which the first two were written by Fray Hernando de Castilla; Juan López wrote the remaining three. Volume I appeared in 1612 and volume V in 1621. López's text is given in Carranza, *Comentarios*, II. 506–15.
7   Tellechea, *Documentos*, III. 302.

Carranza's appointment to Toledo, his government of his archdiocese in the months before his arrest, his entire imprisonment and its eventual conclusion, are dealt with in just four sentences. There is no mention of how or why he came to be arrested, no mention of his *Catechism*, no mention of the Spanish Inquisition or of the role of Philip II in the matter, no mention of the theological points on which Carranza was finally declared to be 'gravely suspect of heresy'. Both these accounts of Carranza offer much of interest as regards their authors' aims, approach, and situation, in their points of resemblance as well as in their marked differences; however, the fact remains that it is Salazar de Mendoza who is entitled to be seen—and has been seen—as Carranza's first biographer.

Salazar, for his part, found encouragement to undertake the task in the fact that Carranza's story, in its main outlines, had already aroused great interest and prompted very different responses. Some, he tells us, attributed Carranza's arrest to the frustrated hopes of the Inquisitor General, who had wanted Toledo for himself; others put it down to envy of office on the part of some among Carranza's fellow-Dominicans; others explained it by the wealth of the see. Still others were not sure what to make of it. Salazar recalls meeting a learned Franciscan who told him that he looked forward to the Day of Judgement so as to know at last the truth of the matter, while a highly regarded Dominican had said to him that, if he found himself with Carranza and an Angel came and said: 'one of you is a heretic', he would think that this must be himself rather than the Archbishop.[8] Salazar would have been interested in the notable clash of opinion between Carranza's chief defending counsel, Martín de Azpilcueta ('Dr Navarro'), who, after judgement had at last been passed on the Archbishop, circulated a triumphant document claiming the outcome as substantially a vindication of Carranza's case, and an unnamed nephew of Azpilcueta's—a 'Vespers Professor' (*Catedrático de Vísperas*) at Salamanca—who responded in robust terms, claiming that sundry Commentaries by Carranza, including his *Commentaries on the Christian Catechism*, were full of borrowings from heretics: Luther, Bucer, Oecolampadius, Melanchthon, Calvin, Juan de Valdés (his *101 Considerations*). 'A fine book,' he commented, 'for the catechizing of boys and to be circulated in the vernacular so that it can be read by women and by men without education, and to be ordered to be read at your own dinner table [that is, in Rome] in front of the servants and anyone else there, when you knew very well that it contained more than 130 objectionable propositions and that the work had been banned in Spain

---

8   References to '*Vida*' follow the text of Oxford Bodleian MS Add. A.158(2), fols 81–217, which appears to occupy an early place in the MS tradition: '*Vida, causa, y sucesos prósperos y adversos del Illustrísimo y Reverendísimo Señor don Fray Bartolomé de Carranza y Miranda, Arzobispo de Toledo, de la esclarecida orden de Predicadores*'. See fols 81–2.

since 1558.'[9] Salazar had read the comments of Giovanni Antonio Gabuzio, who saw the charges against Carranza as so much calumny and attributed his long imprisonment to the obstructionism of the Spanish Inquisition.[10] He also alludes to remarks critical of Philip II's part in the matter expressed by Antonio Pérez in his *Relaciones*. However, Salazar had a more personal reason for interesting himself in the fortunes of Carranza, for he was writing as a canon of Toledo Cathedral, and his whole narrative is expressive of a sense of institutional solidarity with that cathedral's former Archbishop.

Trained in both canon and civil law, he held, at the time of writing, the office of Canon Penitentiary.[11] He was also one of a number of scholarly individuals at Toledo who, especially from the mid-sixteenth century, wrote accounts of one aspect or another of the history of the city and its cathedral. We learn from him indirectly that he had been appointed 'chronicler of the archbishops of Toledo' by Sancho Busto de Villegas, second 'Governor' of the see from 1569, in the course of Carranza's imprisonment, and a man of literary interests.[12] Over the years Salazar published 'Lives' of Cardinal Juan Pardo de Tavera, archbishop of Toledo 1534–45 and Inquisitor General 1539–45 (Toledo 1603); San Ildefonso, archbishop 657–67 (Toledo 1618); and Pedro González de Mendoza, archbishop 1482–95 (Toledo 1625). A more compendious work of a similar kind, 'A history of the archbishops of Toledo', remained in manuscript.[13] It was, however, at the urging of another archbishop of Toledo, Gaspar de Quiroga, that Salazar, as he tells us, undertook his biography of Carranza.[14] Quiroga, who had in earlier years been a canon of Toledo himself, was appointed Carranza's successor in 1577. He had also been Inquisitor General since 1573 and, according to Nicolás Antonio, had employed the young Salazar as an official and a legal adviser in his own

9 BNM, MS 1529, fols 279v–81v. The *Comentarios del Reverendísimo fray Bartholomé Carrança de Miranda, Arçobispo de Toledo, sobre el Catechismo Christiano: divididos en quatro partes* were included in the Spanish Inquisition's *Librorum prohibitorum cathalogus* of 1559.

10 See Joannes Antonius Gabutius, *De vita et rebus gestis Pii V. Pont. Max. libri sex* (Rome: Aloyse Zanetti, 1605), pp. 91–3.

11 *Vida*, fols 172–4.

12 *Vida*, fol. 214; see also Richard L. Kagan, 'La Toledo del Greco', in Jonathan Brown *et al.*, *El Greco de Toledo*, tr. Carlota Millán *et al.* (Madrid: Alianza, 1982), pp. 35–73 (pp. 49–50).

13 Nicolás Antonio, *Bibliotheca hispana nova, sive Hispanorum scriptorum qui ab anno MD. ad MDCLXXIV floruere notitia*, ed. Tomás A. Sánchez, Juan A. Pellicer, and Rafael Casalbón y Geli, 2 vols (Madrid: Joaquín Ibarra, 1783–8), II. 235–6. For some brief discussion of published works by Salazar see José Cepeda Adán, 'La historiografía', in *Historia de España, fundada por Ramón Menéndez Pidal*, ed. José María Jover Zamora, 41 vols (to date) (Madrid: Espasa-Calpe, 1947–), XXVI/i: *El siglo del Quijote (1580–1680): Religión, filosofía, ciencia*, pp. 523–643 (pp. 557–8, 586, 624–5).

14 *Vida*, fol. 82.

household.[15] To find encouragement to write a Life of Carranza coming from such a source—from a prelate, moreover, so committed to the implementation of the decrees of Trent and the instruction of the people—is clearly of interest from a number of points of view.

It was, however, many years before Salazar did so. Thanks to his habit of noting in his text the subsequent careers of former members of the Toledo Chapter and the years in which they died, one can say that his Life of Carranza dates from not earlier than 1622.[16] This places his work in the last decade of his own life (according to Nicolás Antonio he died in 1629 at the age of eighty or so) and in the first years of the reign of Philip IV.

He wrote with a high sense of the value of works of history, invoking the authority of Cornelius Celsus and Diodorus Siculus for the view that no kind of study was of more benefit to society. His method in writing—here as in other works—was strongly documentary in character. When recalling Quiroga's injunction to write this 'Life', he speaks of his own pleasure in putting to use 'the excellent documents that I possess on the matter', and frequently refers to his sources in the course of his narrative.[17] He was, moreover, clearly interested in organizing his material into a coherent narrative whole. This is evident from the pattern of the work and his numerous references relating a given chapter backwards or forwards to another one. This was not, however, a narrative exclusively restricted to the story of Carranza's life. Chapters are introduced on such things as the architectural changes made in the cloister of

15 Antonio, *Bibliotheca hispana nova*, II. 235. In the 1580s (when he was in his thirties), Salazar served as a member of the 'Consejo de Gobernación', which discharged a wide range of the Archbishop's diocesan responsibilities during his long obligatory absences in Madrid in the service of the King, both as Inquisitor General and, from 1574, as Counsellor of State (Kagan, 'La Toledo del Greco', p. 54).

16 He refers to Dr Luis de Tena, who held the canonry of Holy Scripture at Toledo and in 1616 became Bishop of Tortosa, in Catalonia, 'where he died' (*Vida*, fol. 161). His death took place on 26 September 1622: Pius B. Gams, *Series episcoporum Ecclesiae Catholicae* (Graz: Akademische Druck und Verlagsanstalt, 1957, p. 83). This appears to be the latest date that can be established on the basis of Salazar's references.

17 *Vida*, fols 214, 82. An interesting feature of the Bodleian MS is that it several times indicates uncertainty over the form of the names of individuals mentioned, even though they were persons of consequence. Thus so eminent a figure as Fray Bernardo de Fresneda, confessor to Philip II, bishop successively of Cuenca and Córdoba and archbishop of Zaragoza, is referred to as 'fray Bernardo de tremeda | u Fremeola | confesor del rey', and a few lines later as 'Flemeda', before appearing in his right form at a later point in a list of those attending the Provincial Council of Toledo in 1565 (see *Vida*, fols 117–18, 151). Since the MS appears not to be an autograph, the question arises whether these variant forms record uncertainty introduced into the copyist's mind by difficulties in the text that he was following, or initial uncertainty on the part of Salazar himself, though it would be surprising if he were uncertain of a name such as Fresneda's.

Toledo Cathedral in the second half of the sixteenth century, or on the eagerness of the Cathedral's second 'Governor', Busto de Villegas, to have Arabic
inscriptions still surviving on buildings in Toledo removed, or on the expen-
sively successful efforts of the Chapter in 1611–12 to maintain—when the
Roman Rota pronounced against it—the Cathedral's *limpieza de sangre* statute,
dating from 1547, that excluded all of Jewish origins (*conversos*) from appointment to office there. In Salazar's view, the greatest credit for this success went
to Cardinal Antonio Zapata—another former canon of Toledo, he notes—for
pressing the Chapter's case in Rome. He recalls that he himself had been one
of those who proposed that, as a mark of gratitude, a statue of Zapata be
placed on a pillar in the Cathedral Choir.[18] He had himself, he tells us, been
the first of the canons to swear a new oath of *limpieza de sangre* in June 1609.[19]
When he first joined the Chapter is not clear. What, however, his Life of
Carranza makes manifest is his deep attachment to Toledo Cathedral as an
institution, to its Chapter as a corporate body, and to its individual members,
past and present. This disposition counts for a good deal in his treatment of
Carranza's trial (*proceso*).

The outcome of that long investigation of Carranza's theological position
as expressed in his writings set limits to how any seventeenth-century Spaniard
could treat the subject. At the ceremony in which judgement on him was
delivered, Carranza was required to abjure sixteen propositions which it was
claimed he had advanced in his works and which rendered him '*vehementer
suspectus* haeresi'. They include the following: 'that any works performed without
charity are sins and offend God'; 'that faith is the first and principal instrument
by which Justification is appropriated [*apprehenditur*]'; 'that faith without works
is sufficient for salvation'; 'that those living in a state of mortal sin are
incapable of understanding Holy Scripture or discerning the things of faith';
'that natural reason in matters of religion is contrary to faith'; 'that Christ our
Lord made such efficacious and full satisfaction for our sins that no other satisfaction is required from us'; 'that the present-day Church does not possess the
same illumination or authority as the Primitive Church did'; 'that the status of
Apostles and Religious does not differ from the general status of Christians'.[20]

How was Salazar going to handle this condemnation? Clearly, it would
have been impossible for him in such a work as this to dissent from the Papal
sentence, even if he had wished to do so. In fact, he voices no opinion either

18 *Vida*, fol. 191. On the Toledo '*limpieza*' statute, see Henry Kamen, *The Spanish
Inquisition: An historical revision* (London: Weidenfeld and Nicolson, 1997), pp. 236–8.
19 *Vida*, fol. 185.
20 The full text of the judgement on Carranza is in J. Sanz y Sanz, *Melchor Cano: Cuestiones
fundamentales de crítica histórica sobre su vida y sobre sus escritos* (Madrid: Monachil-Santa Rita,
1959), Apéndice documental nº 39. A Spanish translation of this document is given by
Morales, '*Noticia*', pp. 482–93.

on the judgement passed on Carranza or on his theological position more generally considered. What he does instead, in his 'Life', is to construct a portrait of Carranza whose effect is to minimize the theological import of the condemned propositions and the further punishment imposed, while conveying to the reader a sense of a man of outstanding learning and zeal for Church and Faith whose long years of confinement and suffering must inspire a solemn feeling of pity for those caught in the chances and changes of this mortal life. In Salazar's own words, it was scarcely to be judged whether Carranza was more happy (in what he achieved) or more unhappy (in what he suffered). The story of his life, taken as a whole, was of a kind to leave us astonished, whether as regards his labours for the Church or the sufferings brought upon him by his accusers. 'His calm and serenity of spirit amidst such great misfortune amazed those who had dealings with him'.[21] Other manuscript copies of Salazar's text enlarge on this: 'From now onwards he will be the very symbol of modesty and long-suffering, the Archetype and Original of the wretchedness of human kind. What Greek, Latin, or other histories can offer cases where one finds such contrasting situations, such calamities, and such prolonged and severe travails? His life has more the character of a tragedy than a history.'[22] Nevertheless, it is time to consider now in more detail the narrative account of Carranza that Salazar gives us with a view to seeing his angle of approach and the points he emphasizes.

In writing of Carranza's professional life down to the time of his arrival in England, Salazar stresses the academic and ecclesiastical standing that he enjoyed. On his first visit to Rome, in 1539, when he received the distinction of the degree of Master in Theology at a great ceremony during a General Chapter of his Order—in the convent of Santa Maria sopra Minerva, where he would die—Pope Paul III himself authorized him to read 'forbidden books'. We are clearly intended to see that no greater mark of confidence in Carranza's theological rectitude could be bestowed, and this is plainly the sense of Salazar's further references to Carranza's activities back in Spain in the early 1540s, when he spent six years lecturing on scholastic and positive theology at the Colegio de San Gregorio in Valladolid, and served regularly as a consultant of the Inquisition. He was one to whom the Inquisition committed the task of censoring 'propositions and books'. And had he not preached at the *auto de fe* during which Francisco de San Román was condemned to the flames in 1542, and at other such occasions? Thus, even before he was sent to

---

21 *Vida*, fols 82–3.
22 BNM, MS 7864, fols 29r–85v: 'Vida y sucesos prósperos y adversos de Don Fray Bartolomé de Carranza y Miranda... copiada por Don Joseph Maldonado de Saavedra en la ciudad de Sevilla en el mes de enero de 1668' (fol. 30v). This introduction corresponds closely to that found in British Library MS Egerton 460, fols 1v–3v.

Trent in 1545, he was a man of standing, in great demand professionally, and much burdened by his duties.[23]

During that first visit to Trent, Carranza published his *Summa conciliorum et pontificum* and his *Controversia de necessaria residentia personali episcoporum*. Back in Spain in 1548 and now appointed Prior of the Dominican house of San Pablo at Palencia, he lectured—Salazar tells us—to large audiences on Paul's Epistle to the Galatians. In 1552, after the conclusion of the Second Period of Trent, to which he had been sent, he stayed on for a while, taking over from his fellow-Dominican Domingo de Soto the examination, censoring, and expurgation of books, 'burning and ripping up the bad ones' and giving 'the good ones' to the library of the Dominican house in the city. (Six years later, Soto would find himself, together with his fellow-Dominican Melchor Cano, commissioned by the Inquisitor General Valdés to examine Carranza's *Catechism*—in Soto's case very much against his will.[24]) Having returned again to Spain, Carranza found himself not only preaching to the Court at Valladolid but involved in the preparation of the *Censura generalis contra errores quibus recentes haeretici Sacram Scripturam asperserunt* (1554), in which many editions of the Bible prepared by the Reformers or those of a Reformist tendency were prohibited, unless 'purged' (that is, 'chiefly on the grounds of their summaries, annotations, and indices', as the preface by Valdés stated). Carranza subsequently recalled that it was he, together with Diego de Tavera, of the Council of the Inquisition, who 'put the final touches' to this document.[25]

Although Salazar's account of Carranza's time in England is fairly brief, it lays much stress on the high regard he enjoyed with Philip and Mary and on his continuing zeal in the defence of the Faith. It was, he says, Carranza's careful contriving that made it possible for Reginald Pole to return to England as Legate, 'to the pleasure and satisfaction of all'. On the day that the kingdom returned to the Roman obedience, Philip summoned Carranza to the Palace of Whitehall to thank him for his part in bringing this about. When news that Cranmer had been burnt was brought to the Queen, she at once summoned Carranza to inform him. He worked hard to secure the return of property to churches and notably succeeded in the case of three Dominican houses. He preached many sermons concerning the restoration of the Mass; one especially celebrated sermon was that which he preached at the great Corpus Christi procession that he caused to be held on 13 June 1555 at Kingston upon Thames, his text being: 'I have prayed for you that your faith fail not'. He

23 *Vida*, fols 86–8.

24 *Vida*, fols 89a, 89c; Carranza, *Comentarios*, I. 59.

25 *Vida*, fol. 89d. See Jesús M. Bujanda, *Index de l'Inquisition espagnole 1551, 1554, 1559*, Centre d'Études de la Renaissance: Index des Livres Interdits 5 (Geneva: Droz, 1984), pp. 87–8; José Ignacio Tellechea Idígoras, 'La censura inquisitorial de Biblias de 1554', *Anthologica Annua*, 10 (1962), pp. 89–142 (p. 94).

made a visit to Oxford and had a part in the unceremonious removal from its Cathedral of the corpse of the wife of Canon Peter Martyr Vermigli, former Regius Professor of Theology, which had been buried offensively close to the remains of Frideswide (d. c. 730), who was 'regarded there as a saint' (in fact the patron saint of the City and University). Carranza made a similar visit, as Salazar believed (see Chapter 9, above), to Cambridge where, again with his involvement, the body of the one-time Dominican Martin Bucer was exhumed and burnt. During Fray Bartolomé's time in England, many other heretics were punished, 'and more than 30,000 persons from various nations were exiled'. Much attention was given to gathering in 'heretical books, especially bibles translated into English'—these being all the more harmful since they were placed in churches on chains so that they could be more conveniently read. Rigorous punishments were decreed against printers and booksellers who brought bibles into the country. 'In all this Master Carranza was involved with the bishop of London and Drs Story and Rochester.' Carranza's praise in his sermons for the Queen's zeal in extirpating heresy, and for her care for the public good, aroused intense hostility towards him, even to the point of endangering his life.[26]

Salazar's account of the ten months of Carranza's active episcopate at Toledo stresses his exemplary character as an administrator and shepherd of his flock. In no time he had more altars placed in his Cathedral so that the canons could say Mass more often; he visited all the parish churches of Toledo as well as the nunneries, preaching and giving them help in their need. He preached often in his Cathedral, especially in Advent and Lent, when he went every night to Matins, accompanied by a page who carried a lantern. He administered Confirmation almost daily and visited prisons each week, taking food to the needy. At Christmas 1558 he sang the three Masses and preached at the last of them. He was zealous in the government of his archdiocese and would not allow anyone to buy ecclesiastical posts or rights to perform spiritual ministrations. He reformed the fees charged by his ecclesiastical and secular courts. He applied much pressure to the parish clergy to make them reside in their parishes, and took the greatest care over the appointment of clergy to benefices, insisting that they be 'good theologians and of good personal repute', and asked a man of the eminence of Fray Pedro de Soto to help him find them. (This same Pedro de Soto, at the end of 1558, had taken it upon himself to write to the Inquisitor General and tell him that he had not found anything in the *Catechism* that was not sound doctrine—when it was looked at carefully. He advised Valdés not to proceed further against Carranza's teaching.)[27] Salazar's presentation here of Carranza's exemplary character as a bishop

26 *Vida*, fols 90–93; also below, note 77.
27 Carranza, *Comentarios*, I. 72–3

becomes all the more eloquent when set against the background of the latter's *De necessaria residentia episcoporum* and the passionate concern expressed there that bishops should reside and labour in their dioceses. One recalls Professor Tellechea's judgement that, with Carranza's arrest, Spain lost its San Carlo Borromeo.[28]

Some time before the event took place, as Salazar points out, it was being said publicly that the Archbishop was going to be arrested by the Inquisition. This rumour, Salazar continues, originated in the events taking place at Valladolid in 1558, when 'a great complicity of heretics' involving people of social weight and distinction was uncovered there. It was, according to Salazar's account, in the course of the interrogation of these people, during the months leading up to the great *auto de fe* held at Valladolid on Trinity Sunday, 21 May 1559, that Carranza's newly printed *Catechism* came under suspicion. As Tellechea points out, it was in the autumn of 1558 that the Inquisitor General instructed Melchor Cano and Domingo de Soto, together with others, to examine that work.[29] As to Carranza's arrest, at Torrelaguna, in the north of his archdiocese, on the night of 21–22 August 1559, Salazar gives a detailed account of each stage of the event and of his journey under escort to Valladolid. This is followed by an account of the conditions of his confinement—in a house outside the city walls, with just two rooms for him and his two servants, without any view on to the countryside, or any place for recreation: 'the silence, secrecy, and lack of communication were just as in the secret prisons of the Holy Office'. The hearings of the investigation took place in the same building and Carranza's consultations with his lawyers were held in the presence of the 'judges'.[30] Despite the deep melancholia from which, we are told, he often suffered, he found strength to undertake in these first years of imprisonment the major task of making a revised text in Latin of his *Catechism*—amplifying and reforming it with many scholarly citations, Patristic ones above all—and making a shorter version of the published Spanish text, removing dozens of passages that left him open to attack.[31] We subsequently hear of Carranza's departure from Spain for Rome, 'seven years, three months, and fourteen days after his imprisonment', of his sailing from Cartagena with the galleys of Andrea Doria and in company with the Duke of Alba on his way to the Low Countries, and of his easier conditions of confinement in the Castel Sant'Angelo, where he arrived on 28 May 1567.

The thread of Salazar's narrative from the time of Carranza's arrest consists of an account of the successive stages of the *proceso* and of the

---

28 ibid., I. 72–3.
29 *Vida*, fols 107–08; Carranza, *Comentarios*, I. 38.
30 *Vida*, fols 110–13, 123–5.
31 Tellechea discusses both versions and presents the revised Spanish text in Carranza, *Comentarios*, III (see esp. pp. xxix–xlii).

repeated and prolonged delays that it suffered for one reason and another—whether at the highest level of diplomacy between Philip II (anxious that the whole matter should be settled in Spain and not be taken to Rome) and successive Popes, or through the deaths of Pius IV (which, Salazar records, caused a delay of a year) and Pius V, or through the decision, when Carranza had been taken to Rome, to translate the entire body of documents so far accumulated from Spanish into Latin 'so that everyone could understand them'.[32] This took a year. Further delays were cause by *fiscales* acting on behalf of the Roman Inquisition, as well as the Supreme Council of the Inquisition in Spain. Salazar does not go beyond recording their demands for further enquiries to be made; the only time that he voices an opinion on the operation of the Spanish Inquisition, he does so in favourable terms, commenting that the extreme slowness of its procedures is to be seen as indicating its extreme scrupulousness.[33] Such words are what one might expect from one who, in an earlier period of his life, in the 1580s, had served as a consultant to the Toledo inquisitors.[34] Nevertheless, his treatment of that institution generally conveys a clear impression that he felt a strong resentment against it and its officers for prolonging Carranza's confinement intolerably over so many years.

By contrast, he time and again stresses (as Ambrosio de Morales had done) the untiring support of the Chapter of Toledo Cathedral for its imprisoned archbishop, its sense of solidarity with him, its energy in seeking by every legitimate means to secure with minimum delay a happy outcome to his predicament. Only two days after his arrest, the Chapter was sending two canons to Valladolid with the no doubt vain intention of offering him support 'as though he were still on his archiepiscopal throne', and also advice. The Chapter was ceaseless in its representations to the King, 'so that one can say', claims Salazar, referring to Chapter records, 'that almost monthly letters were sent, or persons of high standing'.[35] When Carranza had reached Rome, the Chapter not only wrote to Pius V and sent two canons there but, at home, ordered nine days of Masses in the *Sagrario* (Sacrament Chapel) of the Cathedral, and three general processions through the city to invoke divine assistance on Carranza's behalf. It is implied by Salazar's narrative that the Chapter was fortified in the position it thus adopted by the knowledge that Carranza's *Catechism*, which had brought him such misfortune in Spain, had been approved by the Tridentine Commission on the Index in 1562–3, and its

32 *Vida*, fol. 146.
33 *Vida*, fol. 182: 'Las cosas del Santo Oficio se tratan con tanto tiento y consideración, con tanto cuydado y acercamiento, que lo que parece alarga su resolución suele ser para mayor bien, y mejor despacho de los que en ellas son interesados.'
34 Kagan, 'La Toledo del Greco', pp. 54, 58.
35 *Vida*, fols 121, 129. Morales comments on the zealous activity of the Toledo Chapter on Carranza's behalf ('Prisión', p. 477).

printing at Rome authorized by Pope Pius IV himself in June 1563—matters officially reported to the Toledo Chapter two months later. Although Spanish representatives in Italy succeeded in preventing the printing of a Papally authorized edition of the *Catechism*, the facts of this episode thereby lost little of their importance for the Toledo Chapter, and Salazar reports them in considerable detail.[36]

Subsequently, though he records them, he refrains from comment either on the terms of Gregory XIII's final judgement passed on Carranza or on the latter's suspension for a further five years from his archbishopric, or on the requirement that he remain confined for those five years at least in the Dominican house at Orvieto, or on the Papal banning, at this late stage, of the *Catechism*. What he does focus attention on is Carranza's liberty at last to say Mass on each day of Holy Week immediately following the conclusion of the *proceso*, his visits to the Seven Pilgrim Basilicas of Rome on Easter Monday— including St John Lateran, where he celebrated Mass for the last time—and on the Pope's personal concern for him as his illness rapidly progressed. Salazar gives especial prominence to Carranza's final *apologia pro vita sua*, delivered in Latin on his deathbed in the presence, among others, of three secretaries who had been involved in his case, and whom he had summoned—clearly—to record his words.[37] These Salazar now quotes in full, but in Spanish.

Carranza, according to this account, still saw his time in England as providing particularly powerful testimony to his devotion to the Faith.

> In all the time I taught in my Order, and in what I fterwards wrote, preached, taught, and argued in disputations, in Spain, the Low Countries, and in England, my constant and principal aim was to exalt the Faith of our Lord Jesus Christ and to impugn the heretics with all my strength. His Divine Majesty was pleased to assist me in this His task, so that, fortified by His grace, I brought back many heretics in England to the Catholic Faith and, while I accompanied the King our Lord there, and by his mandate, I caused the bodies of the chief heretics there at that time to be exhumed and, with the supreme authority of the Holy Inquisition, burnt [see below, note 77]. Catholics and heretics described me as first among the defenders of the Faith, and though I should not presume to make such claims for myself, I can truly declare that I have always been one of the foremost among those who laboured in this holy task.

36 *Vida*, fols 163–4, 115–16. Details of the fortunes of the *Catechism* at Trent are given by Ronald W. Truman, 'Jean Matal and his relations with Antonio Agustín, Jerónimo Osório de Fonseca and Pedro Ximenes', in *Antonio Agustín between Renaissance and Counter-Reformation*, ed. Michael H. Crawford, Warburg Institute Surveys and Texts 24 (London: Warburg Institute, 1993), pp. 247–63 (pp. 260–61). See also Pedro Rodríguez, *El Catecismo Romano ante Felipe II y la Inquisición española: Los problemas de la introducción en España del Catecismo del Concilio de Trento* (Madrid: Ediciones Rialp, 1998).
37 *Vida*, fol. 203. For the Latin text, which I follow in the English rendering here, see the Endnote (p. 205). Salazar's Spanish version follows the Latin closely.

Having pointed out that these labours in defence of the Faith were in many cases carried out at the order of the King, 'who can bear good witness to what I am saying', he adds:

> Furthermore, never in the whole course of my life did I preach, teach, contend for, or defend any heresy or anything that was contrary to the true and authentic mind of the Roman Church, or fall into any of the errors of which I have been suspected by those who interpreted my words and statements in a sense altogether at variance with the meaning I intended in voicing them. On the contrary, I swear by these words of mine, and by the same Lord whom I shall soon have as my Judge, that no such thought ever sullied my mind, any more than did the things that have been brought against me in this *proceso*, and that I have never in any respect had any doubts or imaginings regarding this matter. Far from that, I firmly and honestly taught, wrote about, and preached this true faith which I believe and profess as now I die.[38]

He nevertheless adds that he accepted as just the sentence passed on him by His Holiness the Vicar of Christ.

He died two days later, on 2 May 1576. The letter from the Pope reporting this was read to the Toledo Chapter on 27 May. It is, however, Gaspar de Quiroga—as Archbishop of Toledo as well as Inquisitor General—rather than the Chapter that Salazar presents as particularly eager to commemorate Carranza in due fashion in his Cathedral, just as it was at Quiroga's behest that Salazar was writing this biography. Thus we read that it was Quiroga who had the portrait of Carranza painted on the panelling of the Chapter House (where it is still to be seen) according to traditional practice, and furthermore saw to it that the usual commemorative honours paid to archbishops were now paid to his predecessor. To that end, the Chapter met on 15 April 1578, a *túmulo* (or ceremonial funerary structure) was erected between the two Choirs, and 'the exequies were celebrated on 13 and 14 July of the said year with customary solemnity'.[39] Thus Salazar concludes his biography. He has already, however, included in his narrative the final testimony of Pope Gregory XIII himself, expressed in the words he now dictated—as Professor Tellechea accepts—as an epitaph for the tomb of the man on whom he had so recently pronounced sentence. 'Celebrated for his learning, preaching and works of charity', Carranza had discharged with distinction the great tasks committed to him, 'bearing himself with modesty in favourable times and, in adverse times, with patient endurance'.[40]

---

38 Salazar's version is in *Vida*, fols 203–04 (see below n. 74). It should be noted that Carranza's words here on the misinterpretation placed, he holds, on what he had written in his *Catechism* refer to the principle of interpretation imposed at the outset by Valdés on those examining the work on his behalf: that the 'propositions' contained in that work should be interpreted '*in rigore ut iacent*'; that is, without regard to context or overall meaning (see Carranza, *Comentarios*, I. 59).

39 *Vida*, fols 215–17.

40 'D[eo] O[ptimo] M[aximo]. Bartholomaeo Carranza, Navarro, Dominico, Archiepis-

Despite Salazar's general avoidance of explicit comment on the story, a number of reasons readily suggest themselves for why his Life of Carranza did not get into print in his own lifetime. However, this was certainly not because interest in the story of Carranza ceased in Spain. Striking evidence to the contrary (apart from manuscript copies of Salazar's work) is provided by a massive tome on the primatial claims of Toledo Cathedral, written by Diego de Castejón y Fonseca and published at Madrid in 1645.⁴¹ Castejón (1580–1655) was then Bishop of Tarazona, in the province of Zaragoza, but simultaneously Archdeacon of Talavera de la Reina in the archdiocese of Toledo. A decade earlier he had been a canon of Toledo and the Archbishop's Vicar General. He was briefly Bishop of Lugo, in Galicia, in the mid-1630s, before becoming 'Governor' (*Gobernador*) of the archdiocese of Toledo, acting on behalf of the Cardinal Infante Ferdinand, younger brother of Philip IV. He subsequently held the presidency of the Council of Castile. His interest as regards Carranza lies in the fact that the lengthy chapter of his book (pp. 1060–1130) devoted to him consists of a summary of Salazar's biography, though Castejón seems nowhere to acknowledge the fact. This was to remain the sole version of Salazar in print until Valladares published a much fuller text later in the eighteenth century.

While he paraphrases Salazar at many points (and simply omits chapters not directly related to Carranza), Castejón generally reproduces the earlier text without significant revision at moments of particular importance—as one sees in his rendering of Carranza's deathbed *apologia* (pp. 1123–4). Sometimes, though, at such moments, he makes changes expressing much more explicitly than Salazar his response to the story he is telling. Thus, whereas Salazar offers no overt comment after narrating the details of Carranza's death, Castejón adds that the latter, 'released from the troubles and tribulations that fashioned for him in this life a crown to enjoy in eternal life, departed [from this world] to enjoy the fruits of his heroic long-suffering and excellent virtues' (p. 1125).

---

copo Toletano, Hispaniarum Primati, Viro doctrina, contione atque elemosynis claro, magnis muneribus a Carolo V et a Philippo II Rege Catholico sibi commissis egregie functo, animo in prosperis modesto et in adversis aequo, obiit anno 1576 die secundo Maii, Athanasio et Antonino sacro, aetatis suae 73.' See Carranza, *Comentarios*, I. 46; *Vida*, fol. 208.

41 Diego de Castejón y Fonseca, *Primacía de la Santa Iglesia de Toledo: Su origen, sus medras, sus progressos, en la contínua serie de prelados que la governaron, i a vista de las mayores persecutiones de la católica religión, defendida contra las impugnaciones de Braga* (Madrid: Diego Díaz de la Carrera for Pedro Coello, 1645). The archbishops of Braga long sustained a claim to primatial status not only in Portugal but over the Spanish Church also, though this was never accepted throughout Spain; see Peter Linehan, *History and the historians of medieval Spain* (Oxford: Clarendon Press, 1993), esp. pp. 211–12. Castejón's text is given in Carranza, *Comentarios*, II. 516–47.

Castejón's account of Carranza's personal qualities and characteristics, although briefer, clearly follows Salazar's. Both stress his humility, his works of charity, and his temperance in matters of food and drink. However, there are points of significant difference. Salazar is content to note matters of fact (as he believed them to be), while not trying to turn them always and explicitly to Carranza's advantage. This cannot be said of Castejón. Thus, Salazar notes that Carranza was a man of few words, slow and careful of speech, very discreet and a good deal given to dissimulation, whereas Castejón merely tells us that Carranza's words 'edified all and offended none'.[42] Salazar, perhaps surprisingly, goes on to write of Carranza's credulity: 'he readily believed all that he was told and appeared to him to be true, and from this there followed much unpleasantness and grief'. Castejón too presents him as 'credulous' but attributes this to the 'guilelessness' (*'la candidez'*) of his character. Salazar now makes a comment on Carranza in which an interest in psychology and overt criticism come together: 'He was so strongly disposed to give pleasure that he fell into many errors through not carrying out as much as he promised. His friends and those attached to his household noted that he was very tight and niggardly in doing good towards them while being so open-handed and generous towards strangers.' Castejón rewrites this: 'everything of benefit to himself seemed to him excessive whereas, for those around him, he judged even the greatest benefit conferred to fall short.'[43] Salazar concludes here by recalling Carranza's extraordinary sufferings in relation to his capacity to endure them—a capacity which he attributes to Carranza's *complexio* (or balance of the humours) and the temperance that marked his way of life. Castejón, on the other hand, returning to a point we have already found him making, recalls those sufferings as evidence that God, 'who predestined him for eternity with Himself', willed that Carranza should endure such misfortune so that he might receive the crown of immortality with all the greater merit.[44] Salazar has here been transmuted by the same set of attitudes as Fray Juan López. All this

42 *Vida*, fols 208–10 (fol. 209): 'en el ablar, fue detenido, de pocas palabras, y muy atinadas. Guardó mucho secreto de los negocios que convenía, usando de muchas disimulaciones'; Castejón, *Primacía*, pp. 1127–8 (p. 1127): 'sus palabras edificavan a todos: a nadie ofendían'.

43 *Vida*, fol. 209: 'era tan amigo, y amante en azer placer, que cayó en muchas faltas, por no cumplir tanto como prometía. Notáronle los amigos y familiares, ser muy corto y escogido en azerles bien, siendo tan largo y liberal con los estraños'; Castejón, *Primacía*, p. 1127: 'todo para él le parecía mucho; para los próximos lo más juzgava que era corto'.

44 Castejón, *Primacía*, p. 1128: 'Ne será excesso, piedad sí, devida a tan Religiosos antecedentes, creer que nuestro Señor, que le predestinó para sus eternidades, por este camino, con mayores méritos quiso disponerle la corona por medio de la infamia, prisiones, i desprecios, que en lo temporal se originan de semejantes causas, sin atender a las inmensas disposiciones divinas, a cuyo soberano conocimiento está reservado el de esta causa.'

maintains the key established at the start of this section, where Castejón writes
of Carranza's humility. Salazar had begun with this too, but Castejón brings an
emphasis of his own to the point, observing that 'Humility is the solid foundation of all the virtues. A humble heretic is someone whom I think the
Church has never known. In the judgement of all who had dealings with the
Archbishop, he possessed this virtue in heroic measure.'[45] Castejón thus
quietly rejects the Inquisition's labours of seventeen years to have Carranza
condemned for heresy, and his view of the matter was widely noted outside
Spain.

Nevertheless, it was not until 1788—that is, in the final year of the reign of
Charles III, Spain's 'Enlightenment' king—that Salazar's account of Carranza's
life was published in something approaching its entirety, though again with
the chapters extraneous to the main theme removed. That it came out then
was due to Antonio Valladares de Sotomayor, who, apart from being a most
prolific dramatist, was a man with an intellectual agenda. Only the year before, in
1787, he had begun to bring out his *Semanario erudito*, in the prospectus of which
he reminded his readers that Spain had once been Europe's intellectual leader.
Its subsequent decline he attributed largely to the Regular clergy—especially
those of them occupying university chairs—the 'Regular clergy which,' he wrote,
'always forms within the State a state apart, governed in its own private
interest.'[46] The project was still a delicate one. The text is preceded by a note
ordered to be placed there by the Council of Castile, warning 'the public' that
this work must be accorded intellectual acceptance only so far as is justified by
the 'historical documents that it presents'.[47] Nevertheless, Valladares' publication of the work places it within a context of debate and conflict over the
position and power of the Spanish Inquisition *vis-à-vis* the bishops and Spanish
society at large—a debate and conflict that grew more intense towards the end
of the eighteenth century and continued down to the time of the suppression
of the Inquisition voted by the Cortes of Cádiz in 1813, and after. In the

---

45 ibid., p. 1127: 'La humildad es el fundamento sólido de todas las virtudes. Herege
    humilde, no sé que le aya conocido la Iglesia. En la estimación de todos los que trata-
    ron al Arçobispo, tuvo en heroico grado esta virtud.'
46 See Richard Herr, *The eighteenth-century revolution in Spain* (Princeton NJ: Princeton
    University Press, 1958), p. 191; revised as *España y la revolución del siglo XVIII*, tr. Elena
    Fernández Mel, 2nd edn (Madrid: Aguilar, 1988), pp. 158–9. Also Luis Miguel Enciso
    Recio, 'La prensa y la opinión pública', in Jover, *Historia de España*, XXXI/i: *La época de
    la Ilustración: El Estado y la cultura (1759–1808)* (Madrid: Espasa Calpe, 1987), pp. 57–
    128 (pp. 73–4).
47 Pedro Salazar de Mendoza, *Vida y sucesos prósperos y adversos de Don Fr. Bartolomé Carranza
    y Miranda… por el Doctor Salazar de Mendoza, Canónigo Penitencial de la Santa Iglesia de
    Toledo. Dada a luz por D. Antonio Valladares de Sotomayor. Con Privilegio Real y las licencias
    necesarias* (Madrid: Joseph Doblado, 1788), sig. A2v–3r.

course of those years the case of Carranza was recalled and deployed for purposes of polemic, being mostly treated as the outstandingly egregious illustration of Inquisition tyranny, but also represented—on the other side— as an illustration of the scrupulous care that characterized that institution's investigations. On both sides one finds Salazar's biography invoked as a source of authoritative evidence.[48]

It was praised by the author of the longest and most detailed account of Carranza's *cause célèbre* before Professor Tellechea's: that is, the account of the matter given by Juan Antonio Llorente (1756–1823) in his *Histoire critique de l'Inquisition d'Espagne* (1817–18). Although, in the years immediately following Valladares' publication of Salazar, Llorente had been Secretary to the Inquisition of Madrid, his attitude towards that institution underwent radical change. This is evident in his speech of 1811 before the Spanish Academy of History entitled 'A Historical Memoir on Spanish National Opinion concerning the Tribunal of the Inquisition', into which he had been vigorously pursuing his researches since 1809. The major outcome of these researches, after he had gone into exile in France with the withdrawal of the French army from the Peninsula, was his *Histoire critique*.[49]

Here he devotes three long chapters (31–33 in the first edition) to Carranza and is at pains to make it clear at the outset that the documentary evidence available to him has enabled him to give a fuller and more detailed account of the *proceso* than Salazar de Mendoza had been able to do. He, Llorente, had read his way through the twenty-four volumes (each of 1000–1200 folios) containing the record of the proceedings down to the time that Carranza was transferred to Rome. Nevertheless, he has praise for Salazar and offers an all too brief comment on Salazar's willingness to devote his personal wealth to the preparation of his biography: 'Ce respectable et véridique écrivain a fait les recherches les plus exactes, et (ce qui n'est pas commun chez les hommes à grande fortune) il n'a épargné ni soins ni dépenses pour découvrir la vérité.'[50]

---

48 Earlier, in 1744, Melchor de Macanaz, in his MS 'Breve compendio con adiciones o notas al Tomo tercero de la *Historia civil de España desde el año de 1713 [=1700] al de 1733*, por Fray Nicolás de Jesús Belando' (Madrid, 1740–44), had contrived to view the case of Carranza, and Philip II's part in it, as illustrating the legitimate prerogatives of the Spanish Crown over the Inquisition, even when this involved challenging Papal authority and the Council of Trent (perhaps over the matter of Carranza's *Catechism*): see BL MS Add. 15616, fols 50v–51r. It was essentially the position he had set out, as *fiscal general* of the Council of Castile, in his memorandum for Philip V in 1713. (My thanks to my co-editor for drawing my attention to this point.)

49 For a study of this work, see Gérard Dufour, *Juan Antonio Llorente en France (1813–1822): Contribution à l'étude du Libéralisme chrétien en France et en Espagne au début du XIXe siècle*, Travaux d'Histoire Éthico-Politique 38 (Geneva: Droz, 1982), Pt II, chapter 2.

50 Juan Antonio Llorente, *Histoire critique de l'Inquisition d'Espagne depuis l'époque de son établissement par Fedinand V, jusqu'au règne de Ferdinand VII, tirée des pièces originales des archives*

Llorente was writing shortly after the abolition of the Spanish Inquisition had been voted by the Cortes of Cádiz in January 1813. In the lead-up to this vote, three papers advocating that abolition had been submitted to the assembly, one from the commission established to consider the matter and headed by Agustín Argüelles; one by Antonio Ruiz de Padrón, and one by Joaquín Lorenzo Villanueva. All three gave prominence to the case of Carranza and to the sufferings that his imprisonment had brought him. Both Ruiz de Padrón and Villanueva were priests who had adopted the Liberal cause.

The former, born in the Canary Islands in 1757 and at first a Franciscan, later traced his hostility towards the Inquisition to the conversations on the subject in which he unexpectedly found himself involved in Philadelphia in 1784 in the houses of Benjamin Franklin and George Washington.[51] Years later, now a secular priest and a *diputado* for the Canaries, he composed the final *dictamen* read to the Cortes (supplemented by a further lengthy *viva voce* contribution from him) immediately before the vote that decreed the Inquisition's abolition. His style in both was high-pitched, and Carranza features especially prominently in his list of 'wise and learned men whom the Tribunal [of the Holy Office] has sacrificed to its fury'. The case of Carranza presents us with 'the horrible catastrophe of a Spanish prelate worthy of eternal memory'. 'This learned man composed an erudite catechism for the instruction of his diocese, which he submitted to the correction of the Church', but in vain: the mad dogs [of the Inquisition] set upon their own master and devoured him. All Europe was astounded and scandalized to see an archbishop of Toledo, Primate of Spain, a distinguished scholar greatly recommended by his eminence of office, his learning, and his virtues alike, dragged for sixteen years through the Inquisition's dungeons.[52]

Villanueva's contribution was of a more temperate and scholarly kind, as befitted him.[53] Moreover, in a work published two decades earlier, where he

---

du Conseil de la Suprême, et de celles des tribunaux subalternes du Saint-Office, tr. Alexis Pellier, 2nd edn, 4 vols (Paris: Treuttel et Würtz, 1818), III. 184. The further account of Carranza and his *proceso* published a quarter of a century later in the *Colección de documentos inéditos para la historia de España* has already been referred to (see note 3 above). This account—for which no individual author is given—acknowledges the work of Llorente and, among his predecessors, names Salazar and Diego de Castejón. It is stressed that the author or authors of this biographical narrative have gone back beyond Valladares to a MS text of Salazar, as well as to one by Ambrosio de Morales.

51 See Miguel Villalba Hervás, *Ruiz de Padrón y su tiempo: Introducción a un estudio sobre historia contemporánea de España* (Madrid: Librería de Victoriano Suárez, 1897), pp. 20–23, 220–23.

52 ibid., pp. 192–3. Ruiz de Padrón's two contributions are given at pp. 171–229, 231–69.

53 Born in the same year as Ruiz de Padrón, but at Játiva in eastern Spain, he taught theology at Salamanca, subsequently served the Holy Office as a theological examiner

argues for the translation of the Bible into the vernacular, he had already shown an interest in Carranza, reproducing extensive passages from the second preface to his *Catechism* on that same issue.[54] Villanueva's contribution at the Cádiz Cortes is of more interest here than Ruiz de Padrón's in that it leads us back to Salazar de Mendoza, as we shall see.

However, it is worth noting, first, that both Ruiz de Padrón's and Villanueva's speeches to the Cortes—very quickly published, together with the document prepared by the Ecclesiastical Commission—soon elicited an impassioned response, in which Carranza was to occupy a prominent place, from as far away as Mexico City, where, in 1814, Fray José de San Bartolomé, Prior of the Discalced Carmelites, published his *Act of mourning for the Inquisition, or Condolences offered by a philosopher of the Old School to his beloved compatriots, the true Spaniards, on the extinction of so holy and valuable a Tribunal*.[55] This makes the Cádiz document its central target, rebutting case by case the catalogue of 'victims' of the Inquisition presented by Villanueva as well as by Ruiz de Padrón. Carranza's case receives especially detailed consideration, and at every point and on every score the charges urged at Cádiz against the Inquisition are vigorously challenged and rejected. What gives San Bartolomé particular interest as regards our present discussion is the fact that—as he himself explains—having completed his *Act of mourning*, he unexpectedly found in his hands Valladares' edition of Salazar's biography, which he did not know before, and was prompted by it to compose a supplement of forty-four pages wholly devoted to the case of Carranza.[56]

('*calificador*'), and enjoyed the protection of successive Inquisitors General. He became a royal chaplain and a member of the Royal Academies of History and Language, holding the post of librarian of the latter. At the Cortes of Cádiz he represented the province of Valencia, and he was a member of the Ecclesiastical Commission. In 1823 he emigrated, as did other Spanish Liberals, to London, and died in Dublin in 1837. See the biographical article on him by I. Lasa in *Diccionario de historia eclesiástica de España*, ed. Quintín Aldea Vaquero *et al.*, 4 vols (Madrid: CSIC Instituto Enrique Flórez, 1972–75), IV. 2762–3.

54 However, Villanueva gives as his source not Carranza's *Catechism* but 'the History that he wrote of the prohibitions against the reading of the Scriptures in the vernacular': see Joaquín Lorenzo Villanueva, *De la lección de la sagrada escritura en lenguas vulgares* (Valencia: Benito Montfort, 1791), p. lxxvii. Carranza himself concludes his second preface by linking its arguments on the issue to 'the position I adopted at Trent' (Carranza, *Comentarios*, I. 115). Villanueva's immediate source for the point remains unclear.

55 José de San Bartolomé OCD, *El duelo de la Inquisición, o Pésame que un filósofo rancio da a sus amados compatriotas los verdaderos españoles por la extinción de tan santo y utilísimo Tribunal* (Mexico City: Doña María Fernández de Jáuregui, 1814).

56 José de San Bartolomé, *Apología del Santo Tribunal de la Inquisición en la memorable historia del ilustrísimo señor D. Fr. Bartolomé Carranza*. No separate date is given for the publication of this work, which one finds bound with the *Duelo*, though with separate

San Bartolomé's ideological position was at the opposite pole to that of Valladares, but he nevertheless found much to praise in Salazar's work. It presented the events of Carranza's life, now favourable, now unfavourable, with the greatest simplicity and without seeking to impose an interpretation on them. Rather, it sought to give an exact idea of the life and history of so memorable a figure, and in its impartiality bore every sign of being reliable and true.[57] San Bartolomé undertakes to address his subject with the same impartiality as he credits to Salazar, and he does indeed begin by acknowledging what Salazar had written about Carranza's virtues and talents, his reluctance to accept appointment to Toledo, his diligence as archbishop, and his zeal in England. He furthermore quotes at length the deathbed declaration in which Carranza had insisted on his innocence of heresy. Nevertheless, the hostile approach of his *Act of mourning* now reasserts itself and by the end of this *Apology* the Inquisition has, he contends, been wholly vindicated. Those who had taken Carranza's side at Cádiz, he repeatedly and disparagingly dismisses as those '*anti*-inquisicionales', that sect of '*Carrancistas*'. His maximum concession is that, even if Carranza was innocent as regards God and of right intention, he was not so in matters external and as regards men, whose judgements are not required to penetrate the secrets of the heart but to follow the principle of assessing matters 'juxta alegata et probata'.[58] As for Carranza's deathbed profession of orthodoxy, San Bartolomé dismisses it as no more than evidence that self-love had rendered him incapable of acknowledging the truth about himself (pp. 13–15).

In addressing himself to the published text of Villanueva's defence of Carranza, San Bartolomé cites (pp. 25–6) a paragraph in which Villanueva recalls writers of earlier centuries—Salazar among them—who, as he says, had taken Carranza's side. This is all the more interesting since Villanueva returned to this point at some length in his subsequent autobiography, published in London in 1825, where he incorporated material from the document that San

---

pagination. The title-page bears a quotation taken from St Jerome, Ep. 125, *Ad rusticum monachum*, and reapplied here: 'Non de maiorum sententia judices, cujus oficii est obedire'.

57 San Bartolomé, *Apología*, p. 1: 'El siempre debe hacer una gran fe, por que habiendo sido escrito en Toledo de donde su autor era canónigo, descubriendo todos los sucesos ya prósperos ya adversos con la mayor sencillez, sin calificarlos ni interpretarlos, denotando en lo anticuado del estilo mucha vecindad a ellos, y proponiéndose dar una idea exacta de la vida e historia de tan memorable personage, lleva consigo todos los signos de cierta y verdadera.'

58 ibid., p. 6: 'Por tanto: enhorabuena que el arzobispo Carranza fuese inocente para con Dios, y recto en su intención, mas no fue así en lo exterior y para con los hombres, cuyos juicios estando desobligados de penetrar el corazón, no lo están de estribar en las presunciones vehementes que tan de cerca tocan la verdad para juzgar según ellas.'

Bartolomé had before him.[59] Here Villanueva's most immediate debt is to Antonio Tavira y Almazán (1737–1807), Bishop of Salamanca from 1798, whom Villanueva calls his 'great friend and companion'.[60] Tavira was one of the most significant figures in the intellectual and religious life of late eighteenth-century Spain, and through him especially we are led back to Salazar.

Joël Saugnieux and others have drawn attention to the concern of many among the higher clergy in Spain at that time—including those most committed, as was Tavira, to bringing about the intellectual, moral, and indeed religious renewal of the Spanish Church and society—to defend the prerogatives of the episcopate in the discharge of its office and functions. They summoned frequent diocesan synods, were strongly attached to the tradition of national Councils, and adopted an attitude of reserve and even open hostility towards the Roman Curia.[61] One finds this in Tavira: still more does one find a hostility towards the Spanish Inquisition, and it underlines his interest in Carranza.

Already in the early 1790s Tavira had submitted to Charles IV a paper protesting that the Spanish Inquisition was seeking to deprive bishops of the jurisdiction that belonged to them by Divine institution. He argued this still more strongly in another paper which he submitted to Jovellanos, the Minister of Justice and a personal friend, in March 1798.[62] From this document Villanueva quotes at length. 'Ever since the Inquisition was established in Spain, the jurisdiction of bishops began to decline.' The Holy Office aimed its shots at prelates in order to intimidate them and so obtain a clear field for itself. Of this the case of Carranza was the outstanding example. Tavira recalls both Carranza's sixteen-year-long imprisonment and also the fact that his *Catechism* had been examined by the Fathers at Trent and, as he puts it, had received their entire approval. Tavira's further remarks show that he had taken a close interest in the matter and even, it seems, compiled a dossier of related documents. He had a copy of the Antwerp *Catechism* in his own library.[63] He

---

59 Joaquín Lorenzo Villanueva, *Vida literaria de Don Joaquín Lorenzo Villanueva, o Memoria de sus escritos y de sus opiniones eclesiásticas y políticas, y de algunos sucesos notables de su tiempo, con un apéndice relativo a la historia del Concilio de Trento*, 2 vols (London: n.pr.).

60 Villanueva, *Vida literaria*, I. 352. A convenient summary biographical account of Tavira is provided by F. Marcos in Aldea, *Diccionario*, IV. 2536–8.

61 See Joël Saugnieux, 'Les problèmes du pouvoir: L'épiscopalisme', in *Foi et Lumières dans l'Espagne du XVIIIe siècle*, ed. Saugnieux (Lyon: Presses Universitaires de Lyon, 1985), pp. 27–33; also Teófanes Egido, 'El regalismo y las relaciones Iglesia-Estado en el siglo XVIII', in *Historia de la Iglesia en España*, ed. Ricardo García-Villoslada, 5 vols in 6, BAC: Mayor 16–21 (Madrid: EDICA, 1979–), IV. 125–249 (pp. 188–208). Tavira receives frequent mention in Antonio Mestre Sanchis, 'Religión y cultura en el siglo XVIII', in García-Villoslada, *Historia*, IV. 583–743.

62 Tavira, 'Informe…sobre agravio a la jurisdicción ordinaria de Granada por el Tribunal de la Inquisición'.

63 Joël Saugnieux, *Le Jansénisme espagnol du XVIIIe siècle, ses composantes et ses sources*, Textos y

had a copy too, he says, of the Tridentine document approving that work, and notes that the original was kept in Toledo Cathedral. Furthermore, he had in his possession no fewer than fifteen statements approving the *Catechism* drawn up by learned Spanish prelates and theologians, one of the latter being Pedro de Soto, 'whose great learning was so much appreciated by the whole Council'. And what was the outcome of all this? Carranza was obliged to abjure *de vehementi* sixteen propositions 'among which there is not one to which a Catholic sense cannot be given if they are considered fairly and with regard to the intentions of their author'. These were, moreover, propositions that should have been examined in relation to other statements of his and with due regard for his previous irreproachable teaching and piety.[64] And who, asks Tavira, had given more proofs of innocence than Carranza in both respects? Nevertheless, neither his eminence of position, his great merits, nor his innocence preserved him from becoming the victim of a cabal whose only aim was to maintain and further its own powers and position to the detriment of the whole episcopate.[65]

It is clear, then, that while Tavira's view of Carranza's *proceso* was closely related to issues of his own day, his interest in the matter had a historical— indeed, a historian's—aspect. His biographer writes of 'Tavira, amateur comme on sait de livres rares et des manuscrits'.[66] The Bishop bases his account of Carranza on sources that he names. So we find ourselves brought back to Salazar de Mendoza and Diego de Castejón y Fonseca 'in his defence of the primacy of Toledo'.[67] However, the connection between Tavira and them was strengthened by another tradition of sympathetic interest in Carranza, that is, the Dominican one, embodied in massive histories of the Order and its members, of the kind produced, as we have seen, by Hernando de Castilla and Juan López more than a century earlier in Spain.

Estudios del Siglo XVIII 6 (Oviedo: Facultad de Filosofía y Letras, Universidad de Oviedo, 1975), p. 122.

64 Villanueva, *Vida literaria*, p. 359: 'dieziséis proposiciones, de las cuales no hay una a que no se pueda dar un sentido católico, si se miran con equidad y atendiendo al intento de su autor, que se ha de investigar por otras proposiciones suyas, y en que debe tenerse mucha consideración a la doctrina acreditada anteriormente del que las profería, y a su piedad'.

65 ibid., p. 359: 'Este suceso puede dar a S[u] M[ajestad] una idea cabal de la prepotencia, y aun me atreveré a decir astucia, con que la Inquisición ha ajado a los obispos, que vieron desde entonces en este desgraciado personage, su ilustre compañero, todo lo que podían temer, cuando ni su alta dignidad, ni sus grandes méritos, ni su inocencia le preservaron de ser víctima de una cabala, que no se propuso sino afianzar y llevar adelante su sistema con mengua y deshonor de todo el episcopado, con escándalo de la Iglesia universal, y no sin nota y aun infamia de la nación española.'

66 Joël Saugnieux, *Un prélat éclairé, Don Antonio Tavira y Almazán (1737–1807): Contribution à l'étude du Jansénisme espagnol* (Toulouse: Université de Toulouse, 1970), p. 167.

67 Villanueva, *Vida literaria*, p. 359.

Thus, the first name among his sources that Tavira mentions is that of the Dominican Antoine Touron, compiler of the six-volume *Histoire des hommes illustres de l'ordre de saint Dominique* (Paris, 1743–9). One can safely say that no more powerful an apologia for Carranza was ever written than one finds in the lengthy account of him given here.[68] Touron sets his tone at the very beginning:

> L'Histoire, que nous allons écrire, nous représente un de ces Prélats; qui, dans le seizième siècle, ont fait honneur non-seulement à l'Ordre de saint Dominique, & aux Royaumes d'Espagne, mais aussi à l'Église Universelle; & qui auroient pû tenir un Rang distingué parmi les Évêques de la Primitive Église.

He in turn indicates the sources on which he drew. These include the six-volume Quétif/Échard *Scriptores Ordinis Praedicatorum* (Paris, 1719–21), the forty-three volumes of Jean-Pierre Nicéron's *Mémoires pour servir à l'histoire des hommes illustres dans la république des lettres, avec un catalogue raisonné de leurs ouvrages* (Paris, 1727–45), Nicolás Antonio's *Bibliotheca hispana nova*—and both Salazar de Mendoza and Castejón y Fonseca.

Salazar receives from Touron more recognition than simple mention in a marginal note. In the concluding lines of his account of Carranza one reads:

> Le Cardinal Gaspard [*sic*] de Quiroga, qui fut son successeur dans ce grand Siège, après avoir fait célébrer un Service très solomnel pour le Repos de son Âme, attentif à transmettre à la postérité la connoissance de ses vertus, & de ses belles actions, pria un Auteur de réputation d'écrire avec soin l'Histoire de sa vie.[69]

This may indicate a direct familiarity with Salazar's biography. As for the lengthy Quétif/Échard account of Carranza and his writings, this is explicitly stated to be a shorter version of that of Castejón y Fonseca, who—it is explained—himself made public Salazar's 'Life'.[70] Jacques Quétif and Jacques Échard were no less concerned than their fellow Dominican Touron to present Carranza—their brother in Religion—as the victim of great wrongdoing on the part of the Spanish Inquisition, but they strike a different note, especially in their conclusion, which is expressed in terms of notable bitterness.

> When the bark of Peter is being tossed by fierce storms stirred up by heretics, it frequently happens that certain men of semi-learning, inflamed with zeal but 'not according to knowledge', rise up against the Church's most strenuous defenders and, carried along by a blind and furious spirit, confuse these with the enemies of the Faith. They bring even the most innocent before tribunals as though they were criminals, spare no effort to obtain their condemnation, drawing on whatever

68 Touron, *Histoire*, IV. 421–38 (p. 421).
69 *Vida*, pp. 437–8.
70 Jacques Quétif and Jacques Échard, *Scriptores Ordinis Praedicatorum recensiti, notisque historicis et criticis illustrati*, 6 vols (Paris: Ballard, 1719–21), II. 236a–243b, 242b.

credit they enjoy with rulers, and while they wish to be seen as defending the cause of the Church, perfidiously perform acts of deepest betrayal.[71]

The case of Carranza is linked here with two others, the first being that of Francisco de Borja, the future General of the Jesuits and Saint, whom Carranza had named in his own defence. Suspect in the eyes of the Inquisition for this and other reasons, Borja prudently took refuge in Portugal. If it had not been for this prudence—one reads here—the Inquisition would have had him in chains. The second case is that of the Benedictine Alfonso Ruiz de Virués, famous for his learning and for his eloquence, a celebrated royal preacher, zealous in the cause of Rome against Luther (though also, one may add, a devotee of Erasmus), who nevertheless 'through the calumnies of certain monks' was kept prisoner by the Inquisition for over three years in the 1530s before being appointed Bishop of the Canary Islands by Charles V.[72]

John O'Malley has written as follows about the case of Carranza:

> Registering their support or condemnation of Carranza were some of the most prestigious persons and institutions of the age. Few cases reveal so clearly the overheated religious atmosphere of Spain and Rome in the middle of the sixteenth century or illustrate so dramatically the confusing and overlapping networks of jurisdictions, loyalties, and ecclesio-political policies and antagonisms within Catholicism. Few cases reveal such patent injustice.[73]

We have seen that a sense of that injustice animated all the writers considered here (with the exception of the Carmelite Fray José de San Bartolomé).[74] It is evident already in the account of Carranza's misfortunes

---

71 ibid., II.243a: 'Nimirum cum saevis aliquando tempestatibus ex parte haereticorum Petri navicula iactatur, saepius evenit, ut homines quidam semidocti, zeloque sed non secundum scientiam ferventes, in ipsos Ecclesiae strenuissimos defensores insurgant, eos cum fidei hostibus caeco & impotenti animo confundant, ad tribunalia innocentissimos ceu reos trahant, ac damnari qua valent apud principes gratia, totis viribus satagant, cumque causam Ecclesiae tueri videri volunt, tum eam maxime prodant.' There is clearly an intentional echoing here of Romans 10:2–3, where Paul condemns those who 'aemulationem Dei habent, sed non secundum scientiam; ignorantes enim justitiam Dei, et suam quaerentes statuere, justitiae Dei non sunt subjecti' ('I bear them witness that they have a zeal for God but it is not enlightened. For, being ignorant of the righteousness that comes from God, and seeking to establish their own, they did not submit to God's righteousness').

72 ibid., II.243a.

73 John O'Malley, *The first Jesuits* (Cambridge MA: Harvard University Press, 1993), p.317.

74 A much more celebrated rejection of the charge of injustice is, of course, that of Marcelino Menéndez y Pelayo, in his *Historia de los heterodoxos españoles*, first published in 1880–82, where, at the conclusion of his chapter on Carranza, he declares the essential point of the whole matter to be that 'Carranza fue justamente perseguido y justamente sentenciado' (Bk. IV ch. 8 *ad fin.*, various editions). He allows that those judging Carranza in Spain were 'biased and envious', and that Melchor Cano was excessively severe in

given by Ambrosio de Morales, writing though he was on the orders of Philip II. Subsequent writers were strengthened in the view they shared of the matter by a powerful sense of institutional solidarity with Carranza, whether as a Dominican or as head of the Metropolitan Cathedral of Toledo. We have seen how strongly this sense of solidarity marks Salazar's biography of Carranza—a work undertaken, as Salazar tells us, at the behest of Carranza's successor as archbishop, Gaspar de Quiroga. It is by no means the least point of interest in this story that Salazar was thus encouraged by the man who, while being Carranza's immediate successor (and a former canon of Toledo), was also Inquisitor General and thus, in effect, the successor at one remove of the man —Fernando de Valdés—who was more responsible than any other for Carranza's imprisonment.[75]

We have seen that Dominican commemoration of Carranza was indebted to Salazar largely in the form in which Salazar was made known by Castejón y Fonseca, and how the two traditions of knowledge of, and reflexion on, Carranza—the Dominican one and that deriving from Salazar by way of Castejón and Valladares—were put to serve the purposes of polemic on the subject of the Spanish Inquisition in the late eighteenth and early nineteenth centuries. However, in this process, the distinctive features and colouring of Salazar's account underwent change and loss in varying degrees. That distinctiveness now has its own claim on our attention. Salazar, though he was urged to write this work by Quiroga, took many years, it seems, to settle to the task. As we have seen, he gives us textual evidence that he was engaged in writing it nearly thirty years after Quiroga's death in 1594. In those intervening years he was busy with other archiepiscopal 'Lives' and other kinds of writing. However, the long delay before he set about his Life of Carranza is clearly not to be explained by mere procrastination or any lack of a sense of its importance. The case is rather that his personal commitment to the task was at the same time a serious scholarly and intellectual commitment, the depth of which is to be seen in the strength and detail of the documentary basis on which his carefully framed narrative rests. His aim was clearly to write a

---

his treatment of the *Catechism*; furthermore, Philip II displayed an animus against Carranza that was 'unworthy of a king'. On the other hand, his remarks here on those who had condemned the fundamental approach of the Inquisition as regards Carranza are markedly similar in substance and tone to those of San Bartolomé. As for Salazar, Menéndez y Pelayo sees him as determined—like Llorente—to 'defend the archbishop through thick and thin' (*loc. cit.*, n. 1), but undertakes no examination of Salazar's biography.

75 Valdés was succeeded by Diego de Espinosa (1566–72). The latter's appointed successor, Pedro Ponce de León, died before taking up office, so that Quiroga followed Espinosa in April 1573. See Ricardo García Cárcel and Doris Moreno Martínez, *Inquisición: Historia crítica* (Madrid: Ediciones Temas de Hoy, 2000), p. 61.

comprehensive and authoritative account of Carranza's remarkable and exceptionally significant life. Biography is, of course, by its very nature, a problematic genre for writer and reader alike, but within the terms and limits of Salazar's own understanding of the task he undertook here, he may surely be said to have succeeded in his aims. The value of his biography of Carranza for the purposes of modern scholarship is beyond question, and it serves as an invitation to undertake a much fuller examination and assessment of his historical work as a whole than has been done so far.

Endnote[76]

...

juro per hunc eundem Dominum & per proximi transitus mei praesentem statum, perque rationem, quam divinae suae Majestati statim a me reddendam certe scio & expecto, me toto illo tempore, quo in Religione legi aut postmodum scripsi, praedicavi, docui, disputavi in Hispania, Germania, Anglia, ad id semper & maxime attendisse, ut fidem Domini nostri Jesu pro virili extollerem, haereticosque impugnarem. Placuit divinae suae Majestati sic me in hoc suo juvare negotio, ut sua desuper accedente gratia haereticos plurimos ad fidem catholicam revocarim in Anglia, dum nostrum regem eo sum comitatus: cujus accedente mandato praecipuorum illius temporis haereticorum cadavera exhumari, ac summa cum sanctae Inquisitionis auctoritate cremari curavi.[77] Catholici & haeretici me primum fidei defensorem dixere, licet id de me asserere vel sentire non praesumam, me tamen inter primos semper extitisse, qui sancto huic allaborarunt negotio, possum affirmare, plurimaque circa id a me peracta jussu ac nutu Domini nostri regis plurimorum quae hic refero testis optimi ... Praeterea non modo toto vitae meae decursu aliquam haeresim, vel quodlibet vero ac genuino sanctae Romanae Ecclesiae sensui contrarium nec praedicavi, nec docui, nec propugnavi, aut defendi: nec in ullum de quibus me suspectum habuerunt, dicta propositionesque meas in absonum alienumque ab eo quo a me prolata fuerant sensum interpretantes, errorem prolapsus sum. Sed juro per supra dicta, perque eundem Dominum quem mox accipiam judicem, ne vel leviori quidem hactenus cogitatione similium aut eorum quae mihi sunt in processu objecta, fuisse... me contaminatum, nec circa id ullatenus a me dubitatum aut imaginatum: sed contra legisse semper, scripsisse, docuisse praedicasseque firmiter & sincere fidem hanc veram quam modo credo, quam & moriens profiteor... [78]

---

76 See above, p. 190.
77 Carranza, in a submission of June 1562 to the Spanish Inquisition, referred to his collaboration in England with 'the Commissaries who discharged the office of inquisitors' there, naming them as the bishop of London [Bonner], 'Drs Story and Rochester' [= John Story, a Civil Lawyer and a Crown Proctor in Cranmer's trial, and Sir Robert Rochester, Controller of the Royal Household, one of the inner ring of the Queen's counsellors, and warm in his feelings for the Papacy] (see Tellechea, *Carranza y Pole*, p. 51; David Loades, *The reign of Mary Tudor: Politics, government, and religion in England, 1553–58*, 2nd edn, London and New York: Longman, 1991, *s.v.* Rochester, Sir Robert). On the Inquisition in Mary's England, see John Edwards, 'A Spanish Inquisition?: The repression of Protestantism under Mary Tudor', *Reformation and Renaissance Review*, 4 (2000), pp. 62–74.
78 Quétif and Échard, *Scriptores Ordinis Praedicatorum*, II. 240a–b.

Bibliography

Aldea Vaquero, Quintín *et al.* (eds), *Diccionario de historia eclesiástica de España*, 4 vols, Madrid: CSIC Instituto Enrique Flórez, 1972–5.

Alexander, Gina, 'Bonner and the Marian persecutions', in Haigh, *The English Reformation revised*, pp. 157–75.

Amos, N. Scott, Andrew Pettegree, and Henk van Nierop (eds), *The education of a Christian society: Humanism and the Reformation in Britain and the Netherlands: Papers delivered to the thirteenth Anglo-Dutch Historical Conference*, St Andrew's Studies in Reformation History, Aldershot: Ashgate, 1999.

Angel (Aungell), John, *The agrement of the holye Fathers and Doctores of the Churche vpon the cheifest articles of Christian religion… very necessary for all curates*, London: William Harford for William Seres, 1555?

Anon., *The institution of a Christen man*, London: T. Berthelet, 1537. Facsimile edn, The English Experience 789, Amsterdam: Walter Johnson Inc., Norwood NJ and Theatrum Orbis Terrarum Ltd, 1976.

——, *A necessary doctrine and erudition for any Christen man, set furthe by the kynges maiestie of Englande*, London: J. Mayler, 1543.

——, *An exclamation upon the erronious and fantasticall sprite of heresy, troubling the vnitie of the Church*, London: Richard Lant, 1553?

——, *Censura generalis contra errores qui[bus] recentes haeretici Sacram Scripturam asperserunt*, Valladolid: F. Fernández de Córdoba, 1554.

——, *The primer in Latin and Englishe (after the use of Sarum) with many godlye and deuoute prayer*, London: John Wayland, 1555.

——, *The primer in English for children after the vse of Sar[um]*, London: John Wayland, 1556?

——, *A plaine and godlye treatise, concernynge the Mass*, London: John Wayland, 1557?

——, *Primer in Englysh after Salysburie use, sette out at length with manye godlie prayer*, London: John Wayland, 1558.

——, [editorial], *Church Times*, 20 Jan. 1899. Repr., *Church Times*, 20 Jan. 1999.

Anstruther, Godfrey, *The seminary priests: A dictionary of the secular clergy of England and Wales, 1558–1850*, 4 vols, Ware, and Ushaw: St Edmund's College and Ushaw College [I]; Great Wakering: Mayhew McCrimmon, [II–IV], 1968–77.

Antonio, Nicolás, *Bibliotheca hispana nova, sive Hispanorum scriptorum qui ab anno MD. ad MDCLXXIV floruere notitia*, ed. Tomás A. Sánchez, Juan A. Pellicer, and Rafael Casalbón y Geli, 2 vols, Madrid: Joaquín Ibarra, 1783–8.

Apocrypha. The new Oxford annotated Apocrypha, Oxford: Oxford University Press, 1991.

Arriaga, Gonzalo de, *Historia del Colegio de San Gregorio de Valladolid*, ed. Manuel M. Hoyos, 3 vols, Valladolid: Imp. Cuesta, 1928–40.

Aston, Margaret, *England's iconoclasts*, I: *Laws against images*, Oxford: Clarendon Press, 1988.

Ávila, Juan de, *Obras completas del Beato Juan de Ávila*, 2 vols, ed. Luis Sala Balust, Biblioteca de Autores Cristianos, Madrid: Editorial Católico, 1952–3.

Avilés Fernández, Miguel, *Erasmo y la Inquisición (El libelo de Valladolid y la Apologia de Erasmo contra los frailes españoles)*, Publicaciones de la FUE: Documentos Históricos 10, Madrid: Fundación Universitaria Española, 1980.

——, 'Erasmo y los teólogos españoles', in Revuelta and Morón, *El erasmismo en España*, pp. 175–93.

Ayris, Paul and David Selwyn (eds), *Thomas Cranmer: Churchman and scholar*, Woodbridge: The Boydell Press, 1993.

Azcona, Tarsicio de, 'El hecho episcopal hispánico en tiempo de Carlos V (1516–1558)', in Revuelta and Morón, *El erasmismo en España*, pp. 265–88.

——, *Isabel la Católica: Estudio crítico de su vida y su reinado*, Biblioteca de Autores Cristianos 237, Madrid: Editorial Católico, 1993. First publ. 1964.

Bagchi, David V.N., *Luther's earliest opponents: Catholic controversialists, 1518–1525*, Minneapolis MN: Fortress Press, 1991.

Bale, John, *The image of bothe Churches*, Amsterdam: S. Mierdman?, 1548.

Barron, Caroline M. and Christopher Harper-Bill (eds), *The Church in pre-Reformation society: Essays in honour of F.R.H. Du Boulay*, Woodbridge: The Boydell Press, 1985.

Basil, St, *Omnia D. Basilii Magni . . . Opera*, Venice: 1548.

Bataillon, Marcel, *Érasme et l'Espagne: Nouvelle édition en trois volumes*, ed. Daniel Devoto and Charles Amiel, Travaux d'Humanisme et Renaissance 250, Geneva: Librairie Droz, 1991.

Bennett, Henry S., *English books and readers, 1475 to 1557, being a study in the history of the book trade from Caxton to the incorporation of the Stationers' Company*, Cambridge: Cambridge University Press, 1969.

Bernard, George, 'The making of religious policy, 1533–1546: Henry VIII and the search for the middle way', *Historical Journal*, 41 (1998), pp. 321–49.

——, 'The piety of Henry VIII', in Amos *et al.*, *The education of a Christian society*, pp. 62–88.

Biddle, Martin *et al.*, *King Arthur's Round Table: An archaeological investigation*, Woodbridge: The Boydell Press, 2001.

Bonner, Edmund, *A profytable and necessarye doctryne with certayne homilies adioyned thereunto*, London: John Cawood, 1555.

——, *An honest godlye instruction, and information for the tradynge and bringinge vp of children*, London: Robert Caly, 1556.

—— *et al.*, *Homelies sette forthe by the Righte Reuerende Father in God, Edmunde Byshop of London*, London: John Cawood, 1555.

Bosco, Giacinto, 'Intorno a un carteggio inedito di Ambrogio Caterino', *Memorie Domenicane*, 67 (1950), pp. 103–20, 137–66, 233–66.

Bossy, John, *Christianity in the West, 1400–1700*, OPUS, Oxford: Oxford University Press, 1985.

Boyden, James M., *The courtier and the king: Ruy Gómez de Silva, Philip II and the Court of Spain*, Berkeley and Los Angeles: University of California Press, 1995.

——, '"Fortune has stripped you of your splendour": Favourites and their fates in fifteenth- and sixteenth-Century Spain', in Elliott and Brockliss, *The world of the favourite*, pp. 26–37.

Brady, Thomas A. JR, Heiko A. Oberman, and James D. Tracy (eds), *Handbook of European history, 1400–1600: Late Middle Ages, Renaissance, and Reformation*, 2 vols, Leiden: Brill, 1994–5.

Brassell, Paul V. SJ, *Praeformatio reformationis tridentinae de seminariis clericorum*, London: Manresa Press, 1938. Shortened version of a doctoral dissertation presented at the Pontifical Gregorian University, Rome.

Bray, Gerald L. (ed.), *The Anglican canons 1529–1947*, Church of England Record Society 6, Woodbridge: The Boydell Press and Church of England Record Society in association with The Ecclesiastical Law Society, 1998.

Bridgett, Thomas E. and Thomas F. Knox, *The true story of the Catholic hierarchy deposed by Queen Elizabeth*, London: Burns and Oates, 1889.

Brigden, Susan, *London and the Reformation*, Oxford: Clarendon Press, 1989.

——, *New worlds, lost worlds: The rule of the Tudors, 1485–1603*, Penguin History of Britain 5, London: Allen Lane, 2000.

Brodrick, James, *St Peter Canisius*, London: Geoffrey Chapman, 1935.

Brooks, James, *A sermon very notable, fruictefull and godlie, made at Paules Crosse... with certain additions*, London: Robert Caly, 1554.

Brooks, Peter N., *Thomas Cranmer's doctrine of the Eucharist: An essay in historical development*, 2nd edn, London: Macmillan, 1992.

Brown, Jonathan *et al.*, *El Greco de Toledo*, tr. Carlota Millán *et al.*, Madrid: Alianza, 1982. Catalogue of exhibition mounted by Toledo Museum of Art, the Museo del Prado, the National Gallery of Art, Washington, and the Dallas Museum of Fine Arts.

Brunner, Otto, Werner Conze, and Reinhart Koselleck (eds), *Geschichtliche Grundbegriffe: Historisches Lexikon zur politisch-sozialen Sprache in Deutschland*, 8 vols in 9, Stuttgart: E. Klett, 1972–97.

Bujanda, Jesús M. (with René Davignon and Ela Stanek), *Index de l'Inquisition espagnole 1551, 1554, 1559*, Centre d'Études de la Renaissance: Index des Livres Interdits 5, Geneva: Droz, 1984.

Burke, Peter, 'How to become a Counter-Reformation saint', in Luebke, *The Counter-Reformation*, pp. 129–42.

Buschbell, C. Gottfried (ed.), *Concilium Tridentinum: Epistolarum pars prima*, Freiburg: Herder, 1916.

Bushe, Paul, *A brefe exhortation*, London: John Cawood, 1556.

Cabalisas, Nicolaus, *De divino altaris sacrificio. Maximi de mystagogia; hoc est de introductione ad Sacra Ecclesiae Mysteria, seu Sacramenta. Diui Chrisostomi et Diui Basilii*

Sacrificii, seu missae ritus, ex Sacerdotali graeco, Gentiano Herveto Aurelio interprete, Venice: Alexander Brucioli, 1548.

Calendar of Patent Rolls, Philip and Mary, 4 vols, London: HMSO, 1936–9.

Calendar of state papers: Domestic, 1547–1580, ed. Robert Lemon and Mary A. Green, 7 vols, London: Longman, Brown, Green, Longmans, and Roberts, 1856–71. Repr. Nendeln: Kraus Reprint, 1967.

Calendar of state papers: Spanish, ed. Royall Taylor, 13 vols in 20, London: Longman, Brown, Green, Longmans, and Roberts, 1904–54,

Calendar of state papers: Venetian, ed. Rawdon Brown *et al.,* 38 vols in 40, London: Longman, Brown, Green, Longmans, and Roberts, 1864–1947.

Calvin, John, *Instruction in faith (1537),* ed. and tr. Paul T. Fuhrmann, Louisville KY: John Knox Press, 1992. First publ. 1949.

Caro, Annibale, *Delle lettere del commendatore Annibal Caro scritte a nome del cardinale Alessandro Farnese,* 8 vols, Milan: Società Tipografica de'Classici Italiani, 1807.

Caro Baroja, Julio, *El señor Inquisidor y otras vidas por oficio,* Madrid: Alianza Editorial, 1997. First publ. 1968.

Carranza de Miranda, Bartolomé, *Summa conciliorum,* Venice: Ad Signum Spei, 1546.

——, *Controversia de necessaria residentia personali episcoporum et aliorum inferiorum pastorum,* Venice: Ad Signum Spei, 1547.

——, *Controversia de necessaria residentia personali episcoporum et aliorum inferiorum pastorum,* Salamanca: Andreas de Portonariis, 1550.

——, *Comentarios sobre el Catechismo christiano,* ed. José Ignacio Tellechea Idígoras, 2 vols, Biblioteca de Autores Cristianos 1, Madrid: Editorial Católico, 1972.

——, *Comentarios sobre el Catechismo christiano,* ed. José Ignacio Tellechea Idígoras, III: *Obra corregida y abreviada por el autor en las cárceles inquisitoriales,* Biblioteca de Autores Cristianos: Mayor 61, Madrid: Editorial Católico, 1999.

——, *Tratado sobre la virtud de la justicia (1540),* ed. and tr. Teodoro López, Ignacio Jericó Bermejo, and Rodrigo Muñoz de Juana, Pamplona: Ediciones Universidad de Navarra, 2003.

Carranza y su tiempo: Actas del Congreso Internacional V centenario del nacimiento del arzobispo Bartolomé Carranza de Miranda (Universidad de Navarra, Pamplona, 11–13 diciembre 2003), in press.

Carro, Venancio D., *El Maestro Fray Pedro de Soto OP, (confesor de Carlos V) y las controversias político-teológicas en el siglo XVI,* 2 vols, Biblioteca de Teólogos Españoles 15, Salamanca: Convento de San Esteban, 1931–50.

Castejón y Fonseca, Diego de, *Primacía de la Santa Iglesia de Toledo: Su origen, sus medras, sus progressos, en la contínua serie de prelados que la governaron, i a vista de las mayores persecutiones de la católica religión, defendida contra las impugnaciones de Braga,* Madrid: Diego Díaz de la Carrera for Pedro Coello, 1645.

Catharinus Politus, Ambrosius, *Tractatus substitutionum domini Lancelloti Politi Senensis,* Siena: Simeone di Niccolò dei Nardi, 1513.

——, *Claves duae ad aperiendas intelligendasqve scripturas sacras,* Lyon: Pierre de Sainte-Lucie, 1543.

——, *Censura in libellum quendam inscriptum. Controversia de necessaria residentia personali episcoporum*, Venice: Gabriel Giolito de'Ferrari, 1547.

——, *Tractatio quaestionis, quo iure episcoporum residentia debeatur*, Venice: Gabriel Giolito de'Ferrari, 1547.

——, *Interpretatio noni cap[ituli] synodalis decreti de iustificatione*, Venice: Gabriel Giolito de'Ferrari, 1547.

——, *Defensio catholicorum, qui pro possibili certitudine praesentis gratiae disseruerunt*, Venice: Gabriel Giolito de'Ferrari, 1547.

——, *De resolutione obiectorum adversus tractationem, quo iure episcoporum residentia debeatur*, Bologna: Anselmo Giaccarelli, 1548.

——, '*Confirmatio doctrinae eiusdem autoris de personali residentia episcoporum contra quendam novitium oppugnatorem*', in his *Enarrationes in quinque priora capita libri Geneseos*, Rome: Antonio Blado, 1552.

Cepeda Adán, José, 'La historiografía', in Jover, *Historia de España*, XXVI/i (1986): *El siglo del Quijote (1580–1680): Religión, filosofía, ciencia*, pp. 523–643.

Cessi, Roberto, 'Paolinismo preluterano', *Atti della Accademia Nazionale dei Lincei*, 8th s. 12 (1957), pp. 3–30.

Chacón, Pedro, *Historia de la Universidad de Salamanca*, ed. Ana M. Carabias Torres, Salamanca: Ediciones Universidad de Salamanca, 1990.

Christopherson, John, *An exhortation to alle menne to take hede agaynst rebellion*, London: John Cawood, 1554.

Collett, Barry, *Italian Benedictine scholars and the Reformation: The Congregation of Santa Giustina of Padua*, Oxford Historical Monographs, Oxford: Clarendon Press, 1985.

——, *A long and troubled pilgrimage: The correspondence of Marguerite d'Angoulême and Vittoria Colonna*, Studies in Reformed Theology and History, ns 6, Princeton NJ: Princeton Theological Seminary, 2000.

Collinson, Patrick, 'Windows in a woman's soul', in his *Elizabethan essays*, London: Hambledon Press, 1994, pp. 89–118.

—— and John Craig (eds), *The Reformation in the English towns, 1500–1640*, Themes in Focus, Basingstoke: Macmillan, 1998.

Constitutiones apostolicas, y estatutos de la muy insigne Universidad de Salamanca: Recopilados nuevamente por su comisión, Salamanca: Diego Cusio, 1625.

Crawford, Michael H. (ed.), *Antonio Agustín between Renaissance and Counter-Reformation*, Warburg Institute Surveys and Texts 24, London: University of London, Warburg Institute, 1993.

Cross, Frank L. and Elizabeth A. Livingstone (eds), *Oxford dictionary of the Christian Church*, 3rd edn, Oxford: Oxford University Press, 1998.

Cuervo, Justo (ed.), *Historiadores del Convento de San Esteban de Salamanca*, 3 vols, Salamanca: Imprenta Católica Salmanticense, 1914–15.

Davies, Clifford S.L., *Peace, print and Protestantism, 1450–1558*, Paladin History of England, St Alban's: Paladin, 1977. First publ. 1976.

——, 'England and the French War, 1557–9', in Loach and Tittler, *The mid-Tudor polity*, pp. 159–85.

Dickens, Arthur G., *The Counter Reformation*, London: Thames and Hudson, 1968.

——, *The English Reformation*, 2nd edn, London: Batsford, 1989. First publ. 1967.

Dictionary of national biography from the earliest times to 1900, 66 vols, London: Smith, Elder and Co., 1885–1901. Repr. in 22 vols, London: Oxford University Press, 1921–2.

Doran, Susan, 'Elizabeth's religion: The evidence of her letters', *Journal of Ecclesiastical History*, 51 (2000), pp. 699–720.

Duffy, Eamon, *The stripping of the altars: Traditional religion in England, c. 1400–c. 1580*, New Haven CT and London: Yale University Press, 1992.

——, 'Cranmer and popular religion', in Ayris and Selwyn, *Thomas Cranmer*, pp. 199–215.

——, *The voices of Morebath: Reformation and rebellion in an English village*, New Haven CT and London: Yale University Press, 2001.

—— and David Loades (eds), *The Church of Mary Tudor*, Aldershot: Ashgate, 2005.

Dufour, Gérard, *Juan Antonio Llorente en France (1813–1822): Contribution à l'étude du Libéralisme chrétien en France et en Espagne au début du XIXe siècle*, Travaux d'Histoire Éthico-Politique 38, Geneva: Droz, 1982.

Duncan, G.D., 'The Heads of Houses and religious change in Tudor Oxford 1547–1558', *Oxoniensia* 45 (1980), pp. 226–34.

——, 'Public lectures and professorial chairs', in McConica, *The collegiate University*, pp. 335–61.

Edgeworth, Roger, *Sermons very fruitfull, godly and learned*, London: Robert Caly, 1557.

Edwards, John, *The Spain of the Catholic Monarchs, 1474–1516*, History of Spain, Oxford: Blackwell, 2000.

——, 'A Spanish Inquisition?: The repression of Protestantism under Mary Tudor', *Reformation and Renaissance Review*, 4 (2000), pp. 62–74.

——, 'Carranza y la Iglesia en Inglaterra', in *Carranza y su tiempo*.

——, 'Spanish religious influence in Marian England', in Duffy and Loades, *The Church of Mary Tudor*.

Egido, Teófanes, 'El regalismo y las relaciones Iglesia-Estado en el siglo XVIII', in García-Villoslada, *Historia de la Iglesia en España*, IV (1979), 125–249.

Ehses, Stephan *et al.* (eds), *Concilii Tridentini diarorum, actorum, epistularum, tractatuum nova collectio*, 23 vols (to date), Freiburg: Herder, 1901–.

Elliott, John H. and Laurence W. Brockliss (eds), *The world of the favourite*, New Haven CT and London: Yale University Press, 1999.

Elton, Geoffrey R., *Policy and police: The enforcement of the Reformation in the age of Thomas Cromwell*, Cambridge: Cambridge University Press, 1972.

Emden, Alfred B., *A biographical register of the University of Oxford AD 1501 to 1540*, Oxford: Clarendon Press, 1974.

Enciso Recio, Luis Miguel, 'La prensa y la opinión pública', in Jover, *Historia de España*, XXXI/i (1987): *La época de la Ilustración: El Estado y la cultura (1759–1808)*, pp. 57–128.

Erasmus, Desiderius, *The paraphrase of Erasmus upon the Newe Testamente*, 2 vols, London: Edward Whitchurch, 1548–9.

——, *The epistle… unto Conradus Pelicanus*, London: John Cawood, 1554.

——, *Opera omnia*, 10 vols, Leiden: Petrus Vander Aa, 1703–6.

——, *The collected works of Erasmus*, ed. Richard J. Schoeck and Beatrice Corrigan, 84 vols (to date), Toronto: Pontifical Institute for Medieval Studies, 1979–.

Estatutos de la insigne Universidad Real de Valladolid: Con sus dos visitas, y algunos de sus reales privilegios, y bullas apostolicas, Valladolid: Bartolomé Pórtoles, 1651.

Evennett, H. Outram, *The spirit of the Counter-Reformation: The Birkbeck lectures in ecclesiastical history given in the University of Cambridge in May 1951*, postscript John Bossy, Cambridge: Cambridge University Press, 1968.

Fernández Navarrete, Martín, Miguel Salvá, and Pedro Sainz de Baranda (eds), *Colección de documentos inéditos para la historia de España*, 113 vols, Madrid: Real Academia de la Historia, 1842–95.

Finucane, Ronald C., *Miracles and pilgrims: Popular beliefs in medieval England*, New York: St Martin's Press, 1975.

The first and second Prayer Books of Edward VI, London: The Prayer Book Society, 1999. First publ. 1910.

Fisher, John, *A sermon very notable, fruitfull and godlie, made at Paules Crosse 1521*, London: Robert Caly, 1554.

——, *The treatise concernyng the fruytfull saynge of Dauyd the Kynge and Prophete in the Seuen Penytencyall Psalme*, London: T. Marshe, 1555.

Fletcher, John M. (ed.), *Registrum Annalium Collegii Mertonensis 1521–1567*, Oxford Historical Society ns 23, Oxford: Clarendon Press for the OHS, 1974.

Foster, Joseph, *Alumni oxonienses: The members of the University of Oxford, 1500–1714*, 4 vols, Oxford and London: Parker and Co., 1891–2.

Foxe, John, *Acts and monuments of these late and perilous days*, London: John Day, 1563.

——, *Acts and monuments of these late and perilous days*, London: John Day, 1570.

——, *Acts and monuments of these late and perilous days*, 2 vols, London: John Day, 1583.

——, *Acts and monuments of these late and perilous days*, ed. J. Pratt and J. Stoughton, 8 vols, London: Religious Tract Society, 1877.

Gabutius, Joannes Antonius, *De vita et rebus gestis Pii V. Pont. Max. libri sex*, Rome: Aloyse Zanetti, 1605.

Gams, Pius B., *Series episcoporum Ecclesiae Catholicae*, Graz: Akademische Druck und Verlagsanstalt, 1957. Facsimile repr. of the original in 3 pts, Ratisbon: G.J. Manz, 1873–86.

García Cárcel, Ricardo and Doris Moreno Martínez, *Inquisición: Historia crítica*, Madrid: Ediciones Temas de Hoy, 2000.

García Hernán, Enrique, *La acción diplomática de Francisco de Borja al servicio del pontificado 1571–1572*, Valencia: Generalitat Valenciana, 2000.

García-Villoslada, Ricardo (ed.), *Historia de la Iglesia en España*, 5 vols in 6, Biblioteca de Autores Cristianos: Mayor 16–21, Madrid: EDICA, 1979–80.

Gardiner, Stephen, *A detection of the Deuils sophistrie, wherwith he robbeth the vnlearned people of the true byleef in the most Blessed Sacrament of the Aulter*, London: John Harford for Robert Toye, 1546.

—— *et al.*, *Responsio venerabilium sacerdotum, Henrici Ioliffi et Roberti Ionson, sub protestatione facta ad illos articulos Ioanis Hoperi*, Antwerp: Christopher Plantin, 1564.

Garrett, Christina H., *The Marian exiles: A study in the origins of Elizabethan Puritanism*, Cambridge: Cambridge University Press, 1938.

——, 'The Legatine Register of Cardinal Pole 1554–57', *Journal of Modern History*, 13 (1941), pp. 189–94.

Gibson, Strickland (ed.), *Statuta antiqua Universitatis Oxoniensis*, Oxford: Clarendon Press, 1931.

Glasier, Henry, *A notable and very fruictefull sermon made at Paules Crosse*, London: Robert Caly, 1555.

Gleason, Elisabeth G., *Gasparo Contarini: Venice, Rome, and Reform*, Berkeley CA and London: University of California Press, 1993.

Glucklich, Ariel, *Sacred pain: Hurting the body for the sake of the soul*, Oxford: Oxford University Press, 2001.

González Gallego, Isidoro, 'La Universidad de Valladolid y los poderes institucionales', in Palomares and Ribot, *Historia de la Universidad de Valladolid*, I. 299–333.

Goodman, Christopher, *How superior powres oght to be obeyd of their subiects*, Geneva: John Crispin, 1558.

Gordon, Bruce and Peter Marshall (eds), *The place of the dead: Death and remembrance in late medieval and early modern Europe*, Cambridge: Cambridge University Press, 2000.

Gregory, Brad S., *Salvation at stake: Christian martyrdom in early modern Europe*, Harvard Historical Studies 134, Cambridge MA and London: Harvard University Press, 1999.

Griffiths, John, *Statutes of the University of Oxford codified in the year 1636 under the authority of Archbishop Laud Chancellor of the University*, Oxford: Clarendon Press, 1888.

Grossi, Isnardo P. OP, *The Basilica of Santa Maria sopra Minerva, Roma*, Rome: Padri Domenicani, 2001.

Gwynneth, John, *A brief declaration of the notable victory geuen of God to oure soueraygne ladye Quene Marye*, London: John Cawood, 1553.

——, *A manifest detection of the notable falshed of that part of John Frithes boke which he calleth his foundation*, London: T. Berthelet, 1554.

Hackett, Helen, *Virgin mother, maiden Queen: Elizabeth I and the cult of the Virgin Mary*, Basingstoke: Macmillan, 1995.

Haigh, Christopher (ed.), *The English Reformation revised*, Cambridge: Cambridge University Press, 1987.

——, *English Reformations: Religion, politics, and society under the Tudors*, Oxford: Clarendon Press, 1993.

Hall, Basil, 'Cranmer's relations with Erasmianism and Lutheranism', in Ayris and Selwyn, *Thomas Cranmer*, pp. 3–37.

Harpsfield, John, A *notable and learned sermon or homilie, made vpon saint Andrewes daye last past 1556, in the cathedral churche of S. Paule in London*, London: Robert Caly, 1556.

Heal, Felicity, *Reformation in Britain and Ireland*, Oxford History of the Christian Church, Oxford: Clarendon Press, 2003.

Herr, Richard A., *The eighteenth-century revolution in Spain*, Princeton NJ: Princeton University Press, 1958.

——, *España y la revolución del siglo XVIII*, tr. Elena Fernández Mel, 2nd edn, Madrid: Aguilar, 1988.

Hillerbrand, Hans J. (ed.), *The Oxford encyclopaedia of the Reformation*, 4 vols, Oxford: Oxford University Press, 1996.

Hogarde (Huggarde), Miles, *The assault of the Sacrament of the Altar*, London: Robert Caly, 1554.

——, *The displaying of the Protestantes, and sondry their practices, with a description of diuers their abuses of late frequented*, rev. and enlarged, London: Robert Caly, 1556.

Holden, Marcus, '"As cunning as a serpent and as harmless as a dove": A tribute to Cardinal Reginald Pole, 1500–2000', *The Venerabile*, 32 (2000), pp. 10–22.

Homza, Lu Ann, *Religious authority in the Spanish Renaissance*, Johns Hopkins University Studies in Historical and Political Science, 118th s. 1, Baltimore MD and London: The Johns Hopkins Press, 2000.

Hubertus, Conradus (ed.), *Historia vera: De vita, obitu, sepultura, accusatione haereseos, condemnatione, exhumatione, combustione, honorificaq[ue] tanden restitutione beatorum atque doctiss[imorum] Theologorum, D. Martini Buceri & Pauli Fagii, quae intra annos XII. in Angliae regno accidit. Item historia Catharinae Vermiliae, D. Petri Martyris Vermilii castiss[imae] atque piissimae coniugis, exhumatae, eiusdemq[ue] ad honestam sepulturam restitutae*, Strasburg: [Hubertus], 1562.

Hughes, James F. and Paul L. Larkin, *Tudor royal proclamations*, 3 vols, New Haven CT and London: Yale University Press, 1964–9.

Hughes, Philip, *The Reformation in England*, 3 vols, London: Hollis and Carter, 1952–4.

Hutton, Ronald, 'The local impact of the Tudor Reformations', in Haigh, *The English Reformation revised*, pp. 114–38.

——, *The rise and fall of Merry England: The ritual year, 1400–1700*, Oxford: Oxford University Press, 1996.

Jankyns, Henry, *The remains of Thomas Cranmer, D.D., Archbishop of Canterbury*, Oxford: Oxford University Press, 1882.

Jansen, Sharon L., *The monstrous regiment of women: Female rulers in early modern Europe*, Basingstoke: Palgrave Macmillan, 2002.

Jedin, Hubert, *A history of the Council of Trent*, tr. Ernest Graf, 2 vols, London: Nelson, 1957–61.

——, 'Das konziliare Reformprogramm Friedrich Nauseas', *Historisches Jahrbuch*, 77 (1958), pp. 229–53.

——, *Crisis and closure of the Council of Trent: A retrospective view from the Second Vatican Council*, London: Sheed and Ward, 1967.

Jones, Norman, *The English Reformation: Religion and cultural adaptation*, Oxford: Blackwell, 2002.

Jover Zamora, José María (ed.), *Historia de España, fundada por Ramón Menéndez Pidal*, 41 vols (to date), Madrid: Espasa-Calpe, 1947–.

Kagan, Richard L., 'La Toledo del Greco', in Brown *et al.*, *El Greco*, pp. 35–73.

Kamen, Henry, *Philip of Spain*, New Haven CT and London: Yale University Press, 1997.

——, *The Spanish Inquisition: An historical revision*, London: Weidenfeld and Nicolson, 1997.

Kelly, John N.D., *The Oxford dictionary of popes*, Oxford and New York: Oxford University Press, 1986.

Kempis, Thomas à, *The folowinge of Chryste translated out of Latyn into Englysh, wheruuto is added the golden Epystell of Saynte Barnarde*, tr. Richard Whitford, London: William Peto, 1556.

Knowles, David, *The religious Orders in England*, 3 vols, Cambridge: Cambridge University Press, 1948–59.

Ladner, Gerhart B., *The idea of reform: Its impact on Christian thought and action in the age of the Fathers*, Cambridge MA: Harvard University Press, 1959.

Lamb, John (ed.), *A collection of letters, statutes, and other documents from the MS Library of Corp[us] Christ[i] Coll[ege], illustrative of the history of the University of Cambridge*, London: John W. Parker, 1838.

Linehan, Peter, *History and the historians of medieval Spain*, Oxford: Clarendon Press, 1993.

Llorente, Juan Antonio, *Histoire critique de l'Inquisition d'Espagne depuis l'époque de son établissement par Fedinand V, jusqu'au règne de Ferdinand VII, tirée des pièces originales des archives du Conseil de la Suprême, et de celles des tribunaux subalternes du Saint-Office*, tr. Alexis Pellier, 2nd edn, 4 vols, Paris: Treuttel et Würtz, 1818.

Loach, Jennifer, 'The Marian establishment and the printing press', *English Historical Review*, 101 (1986), pp. 135–48.

——, *Parliament and Crown in the reign of Mary Tudor*, Oxford Historical Monographs, Oxford: Clarendon Press, 1986.

—— and Robert Tittler (eds), *The mid-Tudor polity, c.1540–1560*, Problems in Focus, London: Macmillan, 1980.

Loades, David M., *Mary Tudor: A life*, Oxford: Blackwell, 1989.

——, *The reign of Mary Tudor: Politics, government, and religion in England, 1553–58*, 2nd edn, London and New York: Longman, 1991.

——, *Politics, censorship, and the English Reformation*, London: Pinter, 1991.

——, 'The piety of the Catholic restoration in England, 1553–8', in Loades, *Politics, censorship, and the English Reformation*, pp. 200–12.

——, 'The spirituality of the restored Catholic Church (1553–1558) in the context of the Counter Reformation', in McCoog, *The reckoned expense*, pp. 3–20.

—— (ed.), *John Foxe and the English Reformation*, St Andrew's Studies in Reformation History, Aldershot: Scolar Press, 1997.

—— (ed.), *John Foxe: An historical perspective*, Aldershot: Ashgate, 1999.

——, *The chronicles of the Tudor Queens*, Stroud: Sutton Publishing, 2002.

López, Juan, *Quarta parte de la historia general de Santo Domingo y de su Orden de Predicadores*, Valladolid: Francisco Fernández de Córdoba, 1615.

López Gómez, Juan Estanislao, *La procesión del Corpus Christi en Toledo*, Toledo: Diputación Provincial de Toledo, 1993.

Luebke, David M. (ed.), *The Counter-Reformation: The essential readings*, Blackwell Essential Readings in History, Oxford: Blackwell, 1999.

Maccoby, Hyam, *Judaism on trial: Jewish-Christian disputations in the Middle Ages*, London and Toronto: Associated University Presses, 1982.

McConica, James (ed.), *The collegiate University*, History of the University of Oxford 3, Oxford: Clarendon Press, 1986.

McCoog, Thomas M. SJ (ed.), *The reckoned expense: Edmund Campion and the early English Jesuits: Essays in celebration of the first centenary of Campion Hall, Oxford (1896–1996)*, Woodbridge: The Boydell Press, 1996.

MacCulloch, Diarmaid (ed.), *The reign of Henry VIII: Politics, policy and piety*, Problems in Focus, Basingstoke: Macmillan, 1995.

——, *Thomas Cranmer: A life*, New Haven CT and London: Yale University Press, 1996.

——, 'Worcester: A cathedral city in the Reformation', in Collinson and Craig, *The Reformation*, pp. 94–112.

——, *Tudor Church Militant: Edward VI and the Protestant Reformation*, London: Allen Lane, 1999.

McHugh, John and Charles Callan (trs), *Catechism of the Council of Trent for parish priests, issued by order of Pope Pius V*, New York: Joseph Wagner, 1934.

Macintyre, Alasdair C., *Against the self-images of the age: Essays on ideology and philosophy*, London: Duckworth, 1971.

Macray, William D., *A register of the members of St Mary Magdalen College, Oxford, from the foundation of the College*, ns, 8 vols, London: Henry Frowde, 1894–1915.

Marc'hadour, Germain (ed.), *The Yale edition of the complete works of St Thomas More*, VII: *The supplication of souls*, New Haven CT and London: Yale University Press, 1990.

Marshall, George, *A compendious treatise in metre declaring the firste originalle of sacrifice, and of the buylding of aultares and churches, and of the firste receauinge of the Christen fayth here in Englande*, London: John Cawood, 1554.

Marshall, Peter, 'Fear, purgatory and polemic in Reformation England', in Naphy and Roberts, *Fear in early modern society*, pp. 150–66.

——, 'Papist as heretic: The burning of John Forest, 1538', *Historical Journal*, 41 (1998), pp. 351–74.

——, *Beliefs and the dead in Reformation England*, Oxford: Oxford University Press, 2002.

——, 'Evangelical conversion in the reign of Henry VIII', in Marshall and Ryrie, *The beginnings of English Protestantism*, pp. 14–37.

——, '"The map of God's Word": Geographies of the afterlife in Tudor and early Stuart England', in Gordon and Marshall, *The place of the dead*, pp. 110–30.

—— and Alec Ryrie (eds), *The beginnings of English Protestantism*, Cambridge: Cambridge University Press, 2002.

—— and ——, 'Introduction: Protestantisms and their beginnings', in Marshall and Ryrie, *The beginnings of English Protestantism*, pp. 1–13.

Martin, Thomas, *A traictise declaring… the pretensed marriage of priests and professed persons is no marriage*, London: Robert Caly, 1554.

Mayer, Thomas F., *Thomas Starkey and the commonweal: Humanist politics and religion in the reign of Henry VIII*, Cambridge Studies in Early Modern British History, Cambridge: Cambridge University Press, 1989.

——, *A reluctant author: Cardinal Pole and his manuscripts*, Transactions of the American Philosophical Society, 89/iv (Philadelphia : APS, 1999).

——, *Reginald Pole: Prince and prophet*, Cambridge: Cambridge University Press, 2000.

——, *Cardinal Pole in European context: A* via media *in the Reformation*, Variorum Collected Studies 686, Aldershot: Ashgate Publishing, 2000.

——, 'The war of the two saints: The conclave of Julius III and Cardinal Pole', in his *Cardinal Pole in European context*, pp. 1–21.

——, *The correspondence of Reginald Pole*, 2 vols (to date), Aldershot: Ashgate, 2002–.

——, 'The success of Cardinal Pole's final legation', in Duffy and Loades, *The Church of Mary Tudor*, pp. 149–75.

Menéndez y Pelayo, Marcelino, *Historia de los heterodoxos españoles*, 3 vols, Madrid: Librería Católica de San José, 1880–82.

Merelli, Fedele, 'P. Alfonso Lupo, Cappucino, e San Carlo Borromeo', *L'Italia Francescana*, 64/ii–iii (1989), pp. 139–78, 322–31.

Mestre Sanchis, Antonio, 'Religión y cultura en el siglo XVIII', in García-Villoslada, *Historia de la Iglesia en España*, IV. 583–743.

Monumenta historica Societatis Iesu, Monumenta Ignatiana, 1st s: *Epistolae et instructiones*, ed. Mariano Lecina SJ and Vicenç Agustí SJ, 12 vols, Madrid: Gabriel López del Horno, 1903–11.

Miethke, Jürgen, 'Reform, Reformation (reformare, reformacio)', in *Lexikon des Mittelalters*, ed. Robert Auty *et al.*, 10 vols, Munich: Lexma, 1977–99, VII (1995), 543–50.

Molinié Fioravanti, Antoinette (ed.), *Le corps de Dieu en fêtes*, Sciences Humaines et Religions, Paris: Les Éditions du Cerf, 1996.

Monckton Milnes, Richard (Lord Houghton) and James Gairdner (eds), 'Bishop Cranmer's recantacyons', *Miscellanies of the Philobiblon Society*, 15/iv (1877–84), pp. 51 ff.

Morales, Ambrosio de, 'Noticia sobre la vida de D. Fr. Bartolomé Carranza de Miranda… y sobre el proceso que le formó la Inquisición (acompañada de documentos)', in Fernández *et al.*, *Colección de documentos inéditos*, V (1844), 389–584.

More, Thomas, *The workes of Sir Thomas More Knyght, sometime Lorde Chancellour of England, wrytten by him in the Englysh tonge*, London: John Cawood, John Waley, and Richard Tottell, 1557.

Morrison, Karl F., *The mimetic tradition of reform in the West*, Princeton NJ: Princeton University Press, 1982.

——, *Understanding conversion*, Page-Barbour Lectures 1991, Charlottesville VA and London: University Press of Virginia, 1992.

Mozley, James F., *John Foxe and his book*, New York: Octagon, 1970. First publ. 1940.

Muller, James A., *Stephen Gardiner and the Tudor reaction*, London: Macmillan, 1926.

Mullinger, J. Bass, *The University of Cambridge*, 3 vols, Cambridge: Cambridge University Press, 1873–1911.

Murphy, Virginia, 'The literature and propaganda of Henry VIII's first divorce', in MacCulloch, *The reign of Henry VIII*, pp. 135–58.

Naphy, William G. and Penny Roberts (eds), *Fear in early modern society*, Studies in Early Modern European History, Manchester: Manchester University Press, 1997.

Nelson, Bernardette, 'Ritual and ceremony in the Spanish Royal Chapel, c.1559–c.1561', *Early Music History*, 10 (2000), pp. 105–200.

Nicéron, Jean-Pierre et al., *Mémoires pour servir à l'histoire des hommes illustres dans la république des lettres, avec un catalogue raisonné de leurs ouvrages*, 43 vols in 44, Paris: Briasson, 1727–45.

Nichols, John G. (ed.), *Diary of Henry Machyn, citizen and merchant-taylor of London, 1550 to 1563*, Camden Society, 1st s. 42, London: Printed for the Camden Society, 1848.

—— (ed.), *The chronicle of Queen Jane and of two years of Queen Mary, and especially of the rebellion of Sir Thomas Wyat, written by a resident in the Tower of London*, Camden Society, 1st s. 48, London: Printed for the Camden Society, 1850.

Nieto Cumplido, Manuel, *La catedral de Córdoba*, Cordoba: Cajasur Publicaciones, 1998.

Nieto Soria, José Manuel, *Iglesia y génesis del estado moderno en Castilla (1369–1480)*, Colección Historia, Madrid: Editorial Complutense, 1993.

Nock, Arthur D., *Conversion: The old and the new in religion from Alexander the Great to Augustine of Hippo*, Baltimore MD and London: The Johns Hopkins University Press, 1998. First publ. Oxford, 1933.

O'Grady, Paul, *Henry VIII and the conforming Catholics*, Collegeville MN: Liturgical Press, 1990.

Ogier, Darryl M., *Reformation and society in Guernsey*, Woodbridge: The Boydell Press, 1996.

Olsen, V. Norskov, *John Foxe and the Elizabethan Church*, Berkeley CA and London: University of California Press, 1973.

O'Malley, John, 'Historical thought and the reform crisis of the early sixteenth century', *Theological Studies*, 28 (1967), pp. 531–48.

———, 'Developments, reforms, and two great reformations: Towards a historical assessment of Vatican II', *Theological Studies*, 44 (1983), pp. 373–406.

———, *The first Jesuits*, Cambridge MA: Harvard University Press, 1993.

———, *Trent and all that: Renaming Catholicism in the early modern era*, Cambridge MA: Harvard University Press, 2000.

Page, Daniel B., 'Uniform and Catholic: Church music in the reign of Mary Tudor (1553–1558)', unpubl. doctoral dissertation, Brandeis University, 1996.

Palomares Ibáñez, Jesús M. and Luis A. Ribot García (eds), *Historia de la Universidad de Valladolid*, 2 vols, Valladolid: Universidad de Valladolid, 1989.

Parker, Matthew, *De antiquitate britannicae ecclesiae & privilegiis ecclesiæ Cantuariensis, cum archiepiscopis eiusdem 70*, Lambeth: John Day, 1572.

Paynell, Thomas, *The piththy and moost notable sayinges of al Scripture*, London: T. Gaultier for R. Toye, 1550.

——— (tr.), *Twelve sermons of Saynt Augustine*, London: John Cawood, 1553.

——— (tr.), *Certaine sermons of sainte Augustines translated out of Latyn*, London: John Cawood, 1557.

Pelikan, Jaroslav, *The Christian tradition: A history of the development of doctrine*, 5 vols, Chicago IL and London: University of Chicago Press, 1971–89.

Persons, Robert SJ, *A treatise of three conuersions of England from paganisme to Christian religion*, 3 vols, St-Omer: François Bellet, 1603–4.

Peryn, William, *Spirituall exercyses and goostly meditacions, and a neare waye to come to Perfection and lyfe contemplatyve*, London: J. Waley, 1557.

Pettegree, Andrew, 'A.G. Dickens and his critics: A new narrative of the English Reformation', *Historical Research*, 77 (2004), pp. 39–58.

Phythian-Adams, Charles, *Desolation of a city: Coventry and the urban crisis of the late Middle Ages*, Past and Present Publications, Cambridge: Cambridge University Press, 1979.

Pogson, Rex H., 'Cardinal Pole: Papal legate to England in Mary Tudor's reign', unpubl. doctoral dissertation, University of Cambridge, 1972.

———, 'Reginald Pole and the priorities of government in Mary Tudor's Church', *Historical Journal*, 18 (1975), pp. 3–21.

Pole, Reginald, *De Concilio liber Reginaldi Poli Cardinalis. Reformatio Angliae ex decretis Reginaldi Poli Cardinalis Sedis Apostolicae Legati anno MDLVI*, Rome: Paulus Manutius, 1562.

———, *De summo pontifice in terris vicario, eiusque officio et potestate*, Louvain: John Fowler, 1569.

———, *Epistolae Reginaldi Poli et aliorum ad ipsum*, ed. Angelo M. Quirini, 5 vols, Brescia: Rizzardi, 1744–57. Repr. Farnborough: Gregg Press, 1967.

Pollard, Leonard, *Fyve homilies of late made by a ryght good and vertuous clerke called Master Leonarde Pollarde Prebendary of the Cathedrall Churche of Woster, directed and dedicated to the Ryght Reverende Father in God Rychard by the permissyon of God Byshoppe of Woster his specyall good lorde*, London: Wyllyam Gryffyth, 1554.

Ponet, John, *A shorte treatise of politicke power and of the obedience which subiectes owe to kynges and other ciuile gouernours*, Strasburg: W. Köpfel, 1556.

Proctor, John, *The waie home to Christ and truth... by that famous and great clearke Vincent*, London: Robert Proctor, 1556.

Quétif, Jacques and Jacques Échard, *Scriptores Ordinis Praedicatorum recensiti, notisque historicis et criticis illustrati*, 6 vols, Paris: Ballard, 1719–21.

Redel, Enrique, *Ambrosio de Morales: Estudio biográfico*, Cordoba: Imprenta del 'Diario', 1908.

Redworth, Glyn, *In defence of the Church Catholic: The life of Stephen Gardiner*, Oxford: Blackwell, 1990.

Repgen, Konrad, 'Reform als Leitidee kirchlicher Vergangenheit und Zukunft', *Römische Quartalschrift für christliche Altertumskunde und Kirchengeschichte*, 84 (1989), pp. 5–30.

——, 'Reform', in Hillerbrand, *The Oxford encyclopaedia of the Reformation*, pp. 392–5.

Revuelta Sañudo, Manuel and Ciriaco Morón Arroyo (eds), *El erasmismo en España: Ponencias del coloquio celebrado en la Biblioteca de Menéndez Pelayo del 10 al 14 de junio de 1985*, Estudios de Literatura y Pensamiento Hispánicos 5, Santander: Sociedad Menéndez Pelayo, 1986.

Rex, Richard, *The theology of John Fisher*, Cambridge: Cambridge University Press, 1991.

——, *Henry VIII and the English Reformation*, British History in Perspective, Basingstoke: Macmillan, 1993.

——, 'The crisis of obedience: God's Word and Henry's Reformation', *Historical Journal*, 39 (1996), pp. 863–94.

Robinson, Cuthbert, *Nicolo Ormaneto: A papal envoy in the sixteenth century*, London: Catholic Repository, 1920.

Robinson, Hastings (ed. and tr.), *The Zurich letters, comprising the correspondence of several English bishops and others, with some of the Helvetian Reformers, during the early part of the reign of Queen Elizabeth*, 2 vols, Publications of the Parker Society 50–51, Cambridge: Cambridge University Press, 1842.

—— (ed. and tr.), *Original letters relative to the English Reformation, written during the reigns of King Henry VIII, King Edward VI, and Queen Mary: Chiefly from the Archives of Zurich*, 2 vols, Publications of the Parker Society 37–8, Cambridge: Cambridge University Press, 1846–7.

Rodríguez, Pedro, *El Catecismo Romano ante Felipe II y la Inquisición española: Los problemas de la introducción en España del Catecismo del Concilio de Trento*, Madrid: Ediciones Rialp, 1998.

Rodríguez Cruz, Agueda M., *Historia de la Universidad de Salamanca*, Madrid and Salamanca: Congregación de Santo Domingo, 1990.

Rodríguez-San Pedro Bezares, Luis E., *La Universidad Salmantina del Barroco, período 1598–1625*, 3 vols, Acta Salmanticensia: Historia de la Universidad 45, Salamanca: Universidad de Salamanca, 1986.

Rubin, Miri, *Corpus Christi: The Eucharist in late medieval culture*, Cambridge: Cambridge University Press, 1991.

Rummel, Erika, *Erasmus and his Catholic critics*, 2 vols, Biblioteca Humanistica et Reformatorica 45, Nieuwkoop: De Graaf, 1989.

Rushworth, John (ed.), *Historical collections*, 4 parts in 7 vols, London: T. Newcomb for G. Thomason, 1659–1701.

Russell, Conrad, *The crisis of Parliaments: English history 1509–1660*, Short Oxford History of the Modern World, Oxford: Oxford University Press, 1971.

Russell, Elizabeth, 'Marian Oxford and the Counter-Reformation', in Barron and Harper-Bill, *The Church in pre-Reformation society*, pp. 212–27.

——, 'Mary Tudor and Mr Jorkins', *Bulletin of the Institute of Historical Research*, 63 (1990), pp. 263–76.

Salazar de Mendoza, Pedro, '*Vida, causa, y sucesos prósperos y adversos del Illustrísimo y Reverendísimo Señor don Fray Bartolomé de Carranza y Miranda, arzobispo de Toledo, de la esclarecida orden de Predicadores*', OB MS Add. A.158(2), fols 81–217.

——, *Vida y sucesos prósperos y adversos de Don Fr. Bartolomé Carranza y Miranda [...] por el Doctor Salazar de Mendoza, Canónigo Penitencial de la Santa Iglesia de Toledo. Dada a luz por D. Antonio Valladares de Sotomayor. Con Privilegio Real y las licencias necesarias*, Madrid: Joseph Doblado, 1788.

San Bartolomé, José de OCD, *El duelo de la Inquisición, o Pésame que un filósofo rancio da a sus amados compatriotas los verdaderos españoles por la extinción de tan santo y utilísimo Tribunal*, Mexico City: Doña María Fernández de Jáuregui, 1814.

Sanders, Nicholas, *De origine ac progressu schismatis anglicani libri tres, aucti priùs per E. Rishtonum, nunca vero addita R.P. Petri Ribadeneirae Soc. Iesu, iterum in Germania locupletiùs & castigatiùs editi*, Cologne: Peter Henning, 1610.

Sanz Serrano, María Jesús, *La custodia procesional Enrique de Arfe y su escuela*, Cordoba: Cajasur Publicaciones 2000.

Sanz y Sanz, J., *Melchor Cano: Cuestiones fundamentales de crítica histórica sobre su vida y sobre sus escritos*, Madrid: Monachil-Santa Rita, 1959.

Saugnieux, Joël, *Un prélat éclairé, Don Antonio Tavira y Almazán (1737–1807): Contribution á l'étude du Jansénisme espagnol*, Toulouse: Université de Toulouse, 1970.

——, *Le Jansénisme espagnol du XVIIIe siècle, ses composantes et ses sources*, prologue José Miguel Caso González, Textos y Estudios del Siglo XVIII 6, Oviedo: Facultad de Filosofía y Letras, Universidad de Oviedo, 1975.

——, 'Les problèmes du pouvoir: L'épiscopalisme', in Saugnieux (ed.), *Foi et Lumières dans l'Espagne du XVIIIe siècle*, Lyon: Presses Universitaires de Lyon, 1985, pp. 27–33.

Scarisbrick, Jack J., *Henry VIII*, London: Eyre and Spottiswoode, 1968.

Scheible, Heinz, 'Reform, Reformation, Revolution: Grundsätze zu Beurteilung der Flugschriften', *Archiv für Reformationsgeschichte*, 65 (1974), pp. 108–33.

Schroeder, Henry J. (tr.), *The Canons and Decrees of the Council of Trent*, Rockford IL.: Tan Books, 1978.

Schweizer, Josef, *Ambrosius Catharinus Politus (1484–1553), ein Theologe des Reformationszeitalters: Sein Leben und seine Schriften*, Reformationsgeschichtliche Studien und Texte 11–12, Munster: Aschendorff, 1910.

Shagan, Ethan H., *Popular politics and the English Reformation*, Cambridge Studies in Early Modern History, Cambridge: Cambridge University Press, 2003.

Simoncelli, Paolo, *Il caso Reginald Pole: Eresia e santità nelle polemiche religiose del Cinquecento*, Uomini e Dottrine 23, Rome: Edizioni de Storia e Letteratura, 1977.

Sirmond, Jacques, *Summa omnium Conciliorum et Pontificum collecta per F. Barth. Carranzam Miranden, Ordinis Praedicatorum*, Rouen: David du Petit Val, 1655.

Skeeters, Martha C., *Community and clergy: Bristol and the Reformation, c.1530–c.1570*, Oxford: Clarendon Press, 1993.

Smith, Lacey B., *Tudor prelates and politics*, Princeton Studies in History 8, Princeton NJ: Princeton University Press, 1953.

Smyth (Smith), Richard, *A bouclier of the Catholyke fayth of Christes Church, conteynyng diuers matiers now of late called into controuersy, by the newe gospellers*, London: R. Tottell, 1554.

——, *The seconde parte of the booke called a Bucklar of the Catholyke fayeth*, London: Robert Caly, 1555.

Standish, John, *A discourse wherin is debated whether it be expedient that the scripture should be in English*, London: Robert Caly, 1554.

——, *The triall of the supremacy wherein is set fourth ye vnitie of Christes Church militant*, London: Thomas Marshe, 1556.

Starkey, David, *Elizabeth: Apprenticeship*, London: Chatto and Windus, 2000.

Statutes of the colleges of Oxford, with royal patents of foundation, injunctions of visitors, and catalogues of documents relating to the University, preserved in the Public Record Office, 3 vols, Oxford: J.H. Parker, 1853.

Statutes of the Realm, printed by command of His Majesty King George the Third, in pursuance of an address of the House of Commons of Great Britain, from original records and authentic manuscripts, London: George Eyre and Andrew Strahan, 1810–32.

Strauss, Gerald, 'Ideas of *reformatio* and *renovatio* from the Middle Ages to the Reformation', in Brady *et al.*, *Handbook of European history*, II. 1–30.

Strype, John, *Ecclesiastical memorials relating chiefly to religion, and the reformation of it, shewing the various emergencies of the Church of England*, 3 vols (6 parts), London: John Wyat, 1721.

——, *Ecclesiastical memorials relating chiefly to religion, and the reformation of it, shewing the various emergencies of the Church of England*, 3 vols (6 parts), Oxford: Clarendon Press, 1822.

——, *Annals of the Reformation and establishment of religion, and other various occurrences in the Church of England, during Queen Elizabeth's happy reign*, Oxford: Clarendon Press, 1824.

Sullivan, Ceri, '"Oppressed by the force of truth": Robert Persons edits John Foxe', in Loades, *John Foxe*, pp. 154–66.

Swanson, Heather, *Medieval artisans: An urban class in late medieval England*, Oxford: Blackwell, 1989.

Swanson, Robert N., *Religion and devotion in Europe, c.1215–c.1515*, Cambridge Medieval Textbooks, Cambridge: Cambridge University Press, 1995.

Taylor, Larissa, *Heresy and orthodoxy in sixteenth-century Paris: François le Picart and the beginnings of the Catholic Reformation*, Studies in Medieval and Reformation Thought 77, Leiden: Brill, 1999.

Tellechea Idígoras, José Ignacio, 'La censura inquisitorial de Biblias de 1554', *Anthologica Annua*, 10 (1962), pp. 89–142.

—— (ed.), *Fray Bartolomé Carranza: Documentos históricos*, 7 vols, Archivo Documental Español 18 etc., Madrid: Real Academia de la Historia, 1962–94.

——, 'La biblioteca del arzobispo Carranza', in *Miscelánea conmemorativa del Concilio de Trento (1563–1963): Estudios y documentos*, Madrid and Barcelona: CISC Instituto Enrique Flórez, 1963, pp. 458–99.

——, *El obispo ideal en el siglo de la Reforma*, Publicaciones del Instituto Español de Historia Eclesiástica: Monografías 9, Rome; Iglesia Nacional Española, 1963.

——, 'Españoles en Lovaina en 1551–1558: Primeras noticias sobre el bayanismo', *Revista Española de Teología*, 23 (1963), pp. 21–45.

——, 'Bartolomé Carranza y la restauración católica inglesa (1554–1558)', *Anthologica Annua*, 12 (1964), pp. 159–282. Repr. in Tellechea, *Fray Bartolomé Carranza y el cardenal Pole*, pp. 15–118.

——, 'Pole y Paulo IV: Un célebre "Apologia" del cardenal inglés (1557)', *Archivum Historiae Pontificiae*, 4 (1966), pp. 105–54. Repr. in Tellechea, *Fray Bartolomé Carranza y el cardenal Pole*, pp. 119–97.

——, 'Pole, Carranza y Fresneda: Cruz y cara de una amistad y de una enemistad', *Diálogo Ecuménico*, 8 (1974), pp. 287–393. Repr. in Tellechea, *Fray Bartolomé Carranza y el cardenal Pole*, pp. 119–241.

——, 'Inglaterra, Flandes y España (1557–1559) en cartas inéditas de Carranza y otros', in *Miscelánea José Zunzunegui, 1911–1974: Estudios históricos*, 5 vols, Vitoria: Seminario de Vitoria, 1975, I. 375–421. Repr. in Tellechea, *Fray Bartolomé Carranza y el cardenal Pole*, pp. 243–88.

——, *Fray Bartolomé Carranza y el cardenal Pole: Un navarro en la restauración católica de Inglaterra (1554–1558)*, Pamplona: Diputación Foral de Navarra, Institución Príncipe de Viana, and CSIC, 1977.

——, *Ignacio de Loyola: Sólo y a pié*, Reestructuradores de la Iglesia 3, Madrid: Ediciones Cristiandad, 1986.

——, 'El protestantismo castellano (1558–1559): Un *topos* (M. Bataillon) convertido en *tópico* historiográfico', in Revuelta and Morón, *El erasmismo en España*, pp. 306–21.

—— (ed.), *Controversia sobre la necesaria residencia personal de los obispos*, Madrid: Fundación Universitaria Española, 1994. Facsimile edn of Carranza's *Controversia de necessaria residentia personali episcoporum et aliorum inferiorum pastorum*.

——, 'Un tratadito de Bartolomé Carranza sobre la Misa', *Archivio Italiano per la Storia della Pietà*, 11 (1998), pp. 145–79.

——, *El papado y Felipe II: Colección de Breves pontificios*, 3 vols, Publicaciones de la FUE: Monografías 73, Madrid: Fundación Universitaria Española, 1999–2002.

——, 'Españoles en Lovaina en 1557', in Thomas and Verdonk, *Encuentros en Flandes*, pp. 133–55.

——, *Fray Bartolomé Carranza de Miranda (investigaciones históricas)*, Historia 109, Pamplona: Gobierno de Navarra, Departamento de Educación y Cultura, 2002.

Thomas, Werner and Robert A. Verdonk (eds), *Encuentros en Flandes: Relaciones e intercambios hispanoflamencos a inicios de la Edad Moderna*, Avisos de Flandes 6, Leuven: Leuven University Press and Fundación Duques de Soria, 2000.

Thompson, Stephen, 'The pastoral work of the English and Welsh bishops, 1500–1558', unpubl. doctoral dissertation, University of Oxford, 1984.

Tierney, Mark A., *Dodd's Church history of England*, introd. Antony F. Allison, 5 vols, Westmead: Gregg International Publishers, 1971. Photographic repr. of the London edn of 1839–43.

Tommaso de Vio (Cajetan), *De divina institutione Pontificatus Romani Pontificis super totam ecclesiam a Christo in Petro*, Rome: Marcellus Silber, 1521.

Torres, Francisco, *De residentia pastorum iure divino scripto sancita*, Florence: Lorenzo Torrentino, 1551. Book I of his *De summi pontificis supra concilia auctoritate*.

Touron, Antoine, *Histoire des hommes illustres de l'ordre de saint Dominique*, 6 vols, Paris: Babuty, 1743–9.

Truman, Ronald W., 'Jean Matal and his relations with Antonio Agustín, Jerónimo Osório de Fonseca and Pedro Ximenes', in Crawford, *Antonio Agustín*, pp. 247–63.

Tunstall, Cuthbert, *Certaine godly and deuout prayers*, tr. John Paynell, London: John Cawood, 1558.

Vacant, J. M. Alfred (ed.), *Dictionnaire de théologie catholique*, 15 vols, Paris, 1903–50.

Valier, Agostino, *Il dialogo della gioia cristiana*, ed. Antonio Cistellini, Testi i Studi Oratoriana 1 (Brescia : La Scuola, 1975.

Vauchez, André, *Sainthood in the Later Middle Ages*, tr. Jean Birrell, Cambridge: Cambridge University Press, 1997.

Venn, John (ed.), *Grace Book Δ: Containing the records of the University of Cambridge for the years 1542–1589*, Cambridge: Cambridge University Press, 1910.

Villalba Hervás, Miguel, *Ruiz de Padrón y su tiempo: Introducción a un estudio sobre historia contemporánea de España*, Madrid: Librería de Victoriano Suárez, 1897.

Villanueva, Joaquín Lorenzo, *De la lección de la sagrada escritura en lenguas vulgares*, Valencia: Benito Montfort, 1791.

——, *Vida literaria de Don Joaquín Lorenzo Villanueva, o Memoria de sus escritos y de sus opiniones eclesiásticas y políticas, y de algunos sucesos notables de su tiempo, con un apéndice relativo a la historia del Concilio de Trento*, 2 vols, London: n.pr., 1825.

Vincent of Lerins, St, *The waie home to Christ and truth leadinge from Antichrist and errour*, tr. John Proctor, London: Robert Caly, 1554.

Vives, Juan Luis, *The education of a Christian woman: A sixteenth-century manual*, ed. and tr. Charles Fantazzi, Other Voice in Early Modern Europe, Chicago IL and London: University of Chicago Press, 2000.

von Druffel, A., *Beiträge zur Reichsgeschichte 1546–1551*, 4 vols, Munich: Rieger, 1873–96.

Wace, Henry (ed.), *Archbishop Cranmer on the true and Catholic doctrine and use of the sacrament of the Lord's Supper*, London: Charles J. Thynne and Jarvis, 1928. First publ. 1907.

Watson, Thomas, *Twoo notable sermons made the thirde and fyfte Fridayes in Lent last past, before the quenes highnes, concernynge the reall presence of Christes body and bloude in the blessed sacrament*, London: John Cawood, 1554.

——, *Holsome and catholyke doctrine concerninge the seven sacramentes of Chrystes church*, London: Robert Caly, 1558.

White, Helen C., *Tudor books of private devotion*, Madison WI: University of Wisconsin Press, 1951.

White, John, *Diacosio-martyrioni id est ducentorum virorum testimonium, de veritate Corporis, et Sanguinis Christi, in Eucharistia*, London: Robert Caly, 1553.

Wilkins, David (ed.), *Concilia Magnae Britanniae et Hiberniae, a synodo Verolamiensi, AD 446 ad Londinensem, AD 1717*, 4 vols, London : R. Gosling *et al.*, 1737.

Williams, Michael, 'William Allen: The sixteenth-century Spanish connection', *Recusant History*, 22 (1994), pp. 123–36.

Williams, Patrick, *Philip II*, European History in Perspective, Basingstoke: Palgrave, 2001.

Wilson, Christopher, *The shrines of St William of York: An account written to commemorate the 750th anniversary of the canonisation of Saint William*, York: Yorkshire Museum, 1977.

Wilson, Henry A., *Magdalen College*, University of Oxford College Histories, London : F.E. Robinson, 1899.

Wilson, Janet (ed.), *Sermons very fruitfull, godly and learned by Roger Edgeworth: Preaching in the Reformation, c.1535–c.1553*, Cambridge : Derek Brewer, 1993.

Witzel, Georg, *On the question of the fire of Purgatory*, Cologne: P. Quentel, 1545.

Wizeman, William L. SJ, 'Recalled to life: The theology and spirituality of Mary Tudor's Church', unpubl. doctoral dissertation, University of Oxford, 2002.

Wolgast, Eike, 'Reform, Reformation', in Brunner *et al.*, *Geschichtliche Grundbegriffe*, VI. 313–60.

Wood, Anthony (à), *The history and antiquities of the University of Oxford*, ed. J. Gutch, 2 vols in 3, Oxford: printed for the author, 1792–6.

——, *Fasti oxonienses*, ed. Philip Bliss, 2 parts, London: F.C. and J. Rivington, 1815–20.

Wooding, Lucy E.C., *Rethinking Catholicism in Marian England*, Oxford Historical Monographs, Oxford: Clarendon Press, 2000.

Wright, Anthony D., *Catholicism and Spanish society under the reign of Philip II, 1555–1598, and Philip III, 1598–1621*, Studies in Religion and Society 27, Lewiston NY and Lampeter: Edward Mellen Press, 1991.

Index